IT Governance in a Networked World:
Multi-Sourcing Strategies and Social Capital for Corporate Computing

Laurence Lock Lee
Optimice Pty Ltd., Australia

INFORMATION SCIENCE REFERENCE

Hershey · New York

Director of Editorial Content: Kristin Klinger
Senior Managing Editor: Jamie Snavely
Managing Editor: Jeff Ash
Assistant Managing Editor: Carole Coulson
Typesetter: Michael Brehm
Cover Design: Lisa Tosheff
Printed at: Yurchak Printing Inc.

Published in the United States of America by
        Information Science Reference (an imprint of IGI Global)
        701 E. Chocolate Avenue, Suite 200
        Hershey PA 17033
        Tel: 717-533-8845
        Fax: 717-533-8661
        E-mail: cust@igi-global.com
        Web site: http://www.igi-global.com/reference

and in the United Kingdom by
        Information Science Reference (an imprint of IGI Global)
        3 Henrietta Street
        Covent Garden
        London WC2E 8LU
        Tel: 44 20 7240 0856
        Fax: 44 20 7379 0609
        Web site: http://www.eurospanbookstore.com

Library of Congress Cataloging-in-Publication Data

Lee, Laurence Lock, 1953-

  IT governance in a networked world : multi-sourcing strategies and social capital for corporate computing / by

Laurence Lock Lee.   p. cm.

  Includes bibliographical references and index.

  Summary: "This book takes a critical look at IT Governance challenges in a world that is becoming

ncreasingly networked. IT firms are becoming increasingly reliant on alliances and partnerships to generate new

value"--Provided by publisher. ISBN 978-1-60566-084-4 (hardcover) -- ISBN 978-1-60566-085-1 (ebook) 1.

Information technology--Management. 2. Management information systems. 3. Business--Data processing. I.

Title. HD30.2.L443 2009 004.068'4--dc22

                              2008047742

British Cataloguing in Publication Data
A Cataloguing in Publication record for this book is available from the British Library.

All work contributed to this book is new, previously-unpublished material. The views expressed in this book are those of the authors, but not necessarily of the publisher.

Table of Contents

Section IV:
Leveraging Emerging Practice

Chapter XII
Guidelines for IT Governance and Multisourcing in the Networked

Appendix:
Corporation Social Capital Links to Firm Performance:
Research Methods Used

Foreword

It does not take reading this book for long to realise that Laurence Lock Lee is on to something very important. Faced with constant change in degrees of interdependence, upgrades in technologies and what they make possible, together with developments in the IT services market, and shifts in the importance of knowledge, services and intangible assets, the network economy requires serious, and constant, rethinking when it comes to even navigating corporate pathways, let alone establishing any level of control. In such situations the subject of governance—including accountabilities, decision rights the rules of the game, and degrees of regulation—come to the fore. What kind of governance? Are command-and-control models still appropriate?

Narrowing down our questions to the world of sourcing information and communications technologies, Laurence Lock Lee provides a distinctive meditation that endeavours to go beyond merely discerning best practice for IT Governance. In order to do so he draws widely on diverse fields and topics including Intellectual Capital, Intangible Asset Management, social networks and sociology, as well as the more obvious literatures and experiences in Information Technology outsourcing. A real strength of this book is the recognition that changing contexts, and the acceleration of that change has deep implications for how, indeed whether, IT Governance can be effectively pursued. A further strength is the focus on what the author calls a firm's corporate social capital, and how to link that to the organisation's overall performance. Laurence Lock Lee also tackles head on what has been the dominant trend in IT outsourcing, namely the use of multiple suppliers and the complexity this introduces to managing and governing relationships, and achieving results from any sort of contemporary outsourcing strategy. He also explicitly deals with the crucial, but perennially problematic area of inter-organisational relationships, going beyond mere contractual obligations and compliance to point out how such relationships can be pursued and leveraged. At the same time the author brings in the distinctive attributes of specific technologies, and indeed reflects on the challenges posed by Web 2.0 and coming technologies for future IT Governance.

This book is a mine of information and ideas and provides a real thought piece for those concerned with the never-ending struggle to read themselves into technology trajectories, to invent pragmatic strategies in dynamic complex environments, and, operationally, to get the job done in a way that does not mindlessly apply instant recipes in the vain hope that this will cut through the complexities being experienced. Laurence Lock Lee makes the world seem a more complex and risk-ridden place, but this is an important positioning. Handing over valuable assets and activities to third parties is inherently risky, but to do so when technology is developing so fast, in a business world so uncertain, really does need considerable open-eyed recognition of pitfalls, and much more creativity and flexibility on plotting ways forward. This book will move the boundaries of your vision of IT Governance further; perhaps further than you thought they could go.

Leslie Willcocks
London School of Economics and Political Science, UK

Leslie P. Willcocks is professor of technology work and globalization at the London School of Economics and Political Science, head of the Information Systems and Innovation group and director of the outsourcing unit there. He is known for his work on global sourcing, information management, IT evaluation, e-business, organizational transformation as well as for his practitioner contributions to many corporations and government agencies. He holds visiting chairs at Erasmus, Melbourne and Sydney universities and is associate fellow at Templeton, University of Oxford. He has been for the last 20 years editor-in-chief of the Journal of Information Technology, and is joint series editor, with Mary Lacity, of the Palgrave book series Technology Work and Globalization. He has co-authored 31 books, including most recently Major Currents in Information Systems (Sage, London 2008, with Allen Lee), and Global Sourcing of Business and IT Services (Palgrave, London, 2006, with Mary Lacity) He has published over 180 refereed papers in journals such as Harvard Business Review, Sloan Management Review, MIS Quarterly, MISQ Executive, Journal of Management Studies, Communications Of The ACM, and Journal of Strategic Information Systems.

Preface

The Internet may be the most visible face of the change towards a networked economy; however the growth in the interdependence between firms and organisations across the globe has been evident for several decades. Several scholars have predicted the changing nature of the global economy from one reliant on manufacturing and physical assets to one reliant on knowledge, services and intangible assets (Drucker, 1992; Quinn, 1992; Stewart, 1997; Sveiby, 1997). The experience of these changes in the Information Technology (IT) industry is best exemplified through the changes experienced by industry stalwart IBM. After over a century's involvement in manufacturing IBM was forced to turn its focus to services in the early 1990s to survive. IBM is now the dominant force in outsourced IT services. In terms of IT Governance, the scope has expanded beyond the walls of the single enterprise to encompass multisourced providers and also potential business alliance partners. Whereas governance has been traditionally associated with "compliance" to a pre-determined company standard there is now a growing appreciation for a "co-operative" approach to governance, where no single authority exists and leaders are forced to operate through the influence of their peer to peer relationships. The growth in outsourced IT services is the trigger for reassessing how IT Governance and sourcing should be conducted.

The outsourcing of IT services has been with us now for well over a decade. The outsourcing phenomena was launched through a number of outsourcing "mega-deals" with significant organisations like the United Kingdom Inland Revenue, the South Australian Government, Campbell Soup, Dupont, British Steel and Lucent Technologies. Many of these deals were for periods of up to 10 years for contract amounts in the billions of dollars. The advent of multi-sourcing has virtually been with us from the start, with organisations like Dupont and British Petroleum purposefully undertaking multi-sourcing strategies from the beginning. The growth in the adoption of multi-sourcing strategies and shorter contract terms is however a direct result of the disenchantment in sole sourced outsourcing deals (Gedda, 2007). The fast pace of technology change in the IT sector, the perceived inflexibility of arrangements and lack of innovation with single vendors have combined to work against the continuance of the practice of long term single vendor outsourcing contracts. A recent global study by IBM of 765 CEOs revealed that 75% were looking to partners outside of their organisations to create innovation, yet only 50% of organisations are currently achieving this (IBM, 2006). Consequently the drive for increased innovation will also fuel the drive for increased levels of multisourcing.

It can therefore be argued that the movement toward "best of breed" multisourcing strategies has been more as a result of the failure of sole source arrangements, than a purposeful business enhancement strategy. Outsourcing researchers and commentators have been united in identifying the client / vendor relationship as being a most critical element in a successful outsourcing arrangement (Deloitte, 2005; Thomas Kern & Willcocks, 2001; Willcocks & Cullen, 2006). Willcocks & Cullen (2006) have stated that:

In our study of organisations seeking IT cost savings via outsourcing, we found that good relationship management made a 40 per cent difference in cost savings. Another study of 235 client organisations identified good relationships as one of the most important factors contributing to effective delivery and successful contract management.

The increased complexity in the required governance arrangements, together with the organisational change management aspects of the outsourcing arrangements have been identified as the two most reported problem areas for outsourcing clients (Deloitte, 2005). The movement from a single supplier situation to multiple suppliers would therefore appear to only exacerbate the relationship and governance problem. This leaves us with an interesting contradiction. Organisations are now embarking on multisourcing strategies, which in turn can only increase the risk of failure. This shift increases the complexity of the identified largest problem area coming from outsourcing experiences to date; that being the governing of the outsourcing relationship.

Coinciding with the trend towards outsourcing and now multisourcing are changes in the business landscape in general. Firstly, the increasing importance of intangibles and intangible assets is occupying an increasing proportion of firm share market valuations, much of this attributed to the growing services sectors (Hall, 1992; Lev, 2001; Lev & Zarowin, 1999; Low & Kalafut, 2002). Secondly, the growth in alliances as a business growth vehicle continues to grow inexorably at a rate of 25% a year despite a failure rate of between 60% and 70% (Hughes & Weiss, 2007). We therefore now have a situation where market place interconnectedness is accelerating at unprecedented rates as organisations race to build new alliance partnerships, develop outsourcing relationships with multiple suppliers and aim to leverage intangible assets to build shareholder value. It is no longer possible to view suppliers as independent entities. They too will be participating in their own alliance arrangements with other suppliers which can, and will, change the nature of their service offerings. Client businesses will also be changing dynamically where mergers, acquisitions and alliances will also change the nature of the business requirements for IT services provision. The above business trends along with failure rate experiences in excess of 50% for IT outsourcing and alliances are the platforms on which this book has been written.

This book is focused on governance of the business relationship. Unlike many of the excellent texts and reports that have been produced to address the client/supplier outsourcing or selective sourcing arrangements (Cullen & Willcocks, 2003; T. Kern & Willcocks, 2000; Lacity & Willcocks, 2001) or those extending such frameworks to multiple suppliers (Cohen & Young, 2006), this book focuses on the socialisation aspects of the relationship. Much of the literature on IT Governance reflects a compliance approach to governance whether it relates to sourcing decisions or information security and/or protection (Calder & Watkins, 2008), contracts and contract management, business processes, tendering and tender evaluation or life cycle management frameworks (Cullen *et al.*, 2005). The current guidance literature on IT Governance has focused on allocating decision rights to appropriate roles within an organisation with the intent of encouraging desirable behaviours (Broadbent, 2002; Weill, 2004). However, allocating accountabilities is only part of the answer. The relationships held between the identified roles will go a long way to determining the success of a governance arrangement. Many an executive charged with implementing a compliance regime for IT Governance will note that the practice is more about socialisation than policing. These texts do an excellent job of synthesising management frameworks from both management theory and analysis of case study experiences. The treatment of relationship management however is largely limited to identifying the structural elements for governance bodies and the creation of charters for developing behavioural norms or codes of conducts for the relationship. As valuable as these are for addressing a single relationship there is reasonable doubt as to whether these techniques will be sufficient to succeed in a highly networked and interdependent market place. Cohen & Young (2006) acknowledge among their four key themes for multisourcing that *"Multisourcing is built on a network of relationships – not transactions"* and proceed to extend the code of conduct approach by defining a useful "Confidence Index" for monitoring confidence in relationships. However, it falls short of appreciating the network effects identified in their key theme which can undermine a "one size fits all" use of index measures.

In order to provide a greater insight into operating successfully in a networked market place this book draws heavily from the fields of sociology, social networks, Intellectual Capital and Intangible Asset Management. Unlike the majority of texts written on IT Governance this book does not attempt to synthesise a "best practice" from numerous case study examples. Instead it looks to identify emergent practices through analysing overall changes in the business landscape that are occurring and the theoretical literature underpinning these changes. Building from a theoretical basis underpinning a social capital theory of the firm, the book will initially take the reader through a treatise of interdisciplinary research which incorporates foundations for governing in a networked business environment, theories of the firm, multisourced supply networks and a view of IT Governance from the sociological viewpoint. This will be followed by the reporting on empirical research conducted on linking a firm's Corporate Social Capital (SC) to its overall performance. From empirical research the book then moves on to identify emerging practices associated with operating in a networked business environment. These include Value Network Analysis (Allee, 2003), networked based approaches to market intelligence (Gloor & Cooper, 2007) and the whole Web 2.0 and social software phenomena. The final section looks to synthesise across the identified emergent practices to provide some early guidelines on IT Governance and multisourcing in the networked business environment. The schematic in Figure P-1 places this book in the context of current treatments of outsourcing and multisourcing and IT Governance:

Existing treatments of IT Governance, outsourcing and multisourcing have been classified above as a "business process view". Essentially these treatments have been concerned with the business process flow from developing outsourcing strategies, architecting a desired IT environment, tendering and selecting suppliers, transitioning the business and then finally installing the governance arrangements through

Figure P-1.

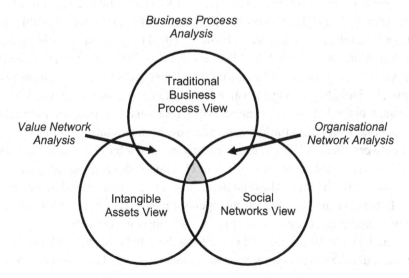

allocating decision rights. The treatment of the critical relationship aspects has been largely from a business process management viewpoint that is what instruments can be designed and installed to "manage or govern" the relationship. Treatment of IT Governance from an information protection perspective (Calder & Watkins, 2008) could be seen as an "Intangible Asset" view, with company information being the intangible asset.

This book targets IT Governance and the sourcing relationship, and amplifies its treatment through the introduction of a perspective from the discipline areas of *Intangible Asset Management* (also called Intellectual Capital Management) (Hand & Lev, 2003; Holland, 2001; Low & Kalafut, 2002; Zambon *et al.*, 2003), *Social Capital* (Lin, 2002; Lin *et al.*, 2001), and *Social Networks* (Borgatti *et al.*, 1998; Burt, 2000; Rob Cross & Parker, 2004; Inkpen & Tsang, 2005; Knoke, 1999; Tsai & Ghoshal, 1998). These discipline areas bring an additional richness to the understanding of how to work with and improve business relationships for the overall benefit of organisations. The intersections between the business process view and the intangible asset and social network views are explored through the analytical techniques of Value Network Analysis (VNA) and Organisational Network Analysis (ONA). In the three-way intersection between views sits the ever present technology platform as a key enabler for extending the reach for governance and sourcing activities.

Emergent techniques arising from these disciplines are introduced for assisting with the governance of multisourcing relationships. Firstly, the ONA technique is derived from a mature technique called Social Network Analysis (SNA), originally used by sociologists to study personal relationship patterns (R. Cross *et al.*, 2002; Scott, 2000; Wasserman & Faust, 1994). SNA applied to organisations at the personal, organisational and inter-organisational levels is often referred to as ONA. ONA can provide insight into how the network of individual actors in multisourcing arrangements relate to each other and how designed interventions can impact on the behaviour of the network. VNA (Allee, 2000, 2003, 2008) derives from the Intangible Asset Management field as a complementary technique for business process mapping by including intangible value flows into the business analysis. VNA is an important tool for designing or evaluating organisational structures around a relationship network, identifying the key roles and how both tangible and intangible value flows between them. VNA has been recently endorsed by ITIL (an acknowledged best IT practice organisation) as a leading IT strategy development practice (ITIL, 2007). Web 2.0 technologies has enabled emergent practices around social networking, collaborative market research and open source development which promises to have profound impacts on IT Governance and sourcing activities.

The audience for this book will range from the scholar or student looking to better understand the governance mechanisms in a networked business environment, through to the IT manager who is struggling with complex business relationships issues for which there is currently minimal guidance. While the issues of governance are addressed in an IT context many of the underlying theories identified and practices developed may be equally applicable to other non-IT service industries. It will draw equally from the client and supplier sides of the IT marketplace. Traditionally the literature on outsourcing is either polarised around advice for clients undertaking outsourcing activities or the shorter term market research supporting the supplier market place. By focusing on the relationship between client and supplier, between supplier and supplier and also potentially client and client, this book will be of equal value to both client and supplier firms.

Much of the terminology in this book may be new to the casual reader. Many of the terms are simply extending a traditional definition to encompass new developments in the field. To assist the reader Table P-1 is provided to identify and link a selection of new terminology with the more traditional terms.

Table P-1.

Traditional Term	Extended Terminology/Explanations
Procurement, Sourcing	**Single sourcing:** procurement from single or prime vendor **Multisourcing:** procurement from multiple vendors with no identifiable prime or managing vendor. **Outsourcing:** services sourced from entities outside the formal boundaries of the firm or organisation
Supply Chain	**Supply Network:** extends the notion of a linear chain of supply to an interdependent network of suppliers and clients i.e. allows for the possibility of reciprocal arrangements where two firm may both buy and sell to each other, or alliance to sell to a third party.
Supplier	**Vendor:** used interchangeably with supplier
Intangibles	**Intangible assets, Intellectual Capital:** these terms extend the accounting term "intangibles" beyond "goodwill" to encompass all intangible assets including competence, information, reputation, brand, client relationships etc.
Service firm	**Intelligent Enterprise:** used to emphasise knowledge over physical assets as the critical competitive resource of the firm. The intelligent enterprise therefore leverages intangible assets and Intellectual Capital.
Capital	**Social Capital, Intellectual Capital:** these terms extend the traditional notion of capital as it relates to finance, to other less tangible elements as being of equal or greater importance to financial capital.
Social Capital	**Corporate Social Capital:** Social Capital in a corporate context.
Social Network Analysis (SNA)	**Organisational Network Analysis (ONA):** SNA applied in a business setting.
WWW	**Web 2.0, Enterprise 2.0:** These terms extend the notion of the web / WWW as a place to publish (identified and Web 1.0) to a place to collaborate (Web 2.0). Enterprise 2.0 describes the corporate use of Web 2.0 tools.

The book is structured as follows:

Section I: Foundations of IT Governance in a Networked World

The introduction positions the book around IT Governance and multisourcing strategies and a firm's social capital embodied in its relationship networks in the IT market place. Data is provided to show the growth in multi-sourcing arrangements and the increased inter-connectedness of the IT services marketplace.

A review of the IT Governance literature and its current state of the art leads into governance decision making and the increasingly complex business environments in which these decisions are now being taken. The Cynefin decision making framework, which caters for complexity, is introduced to assist with untangling the different levels and types of IT Governance decisions that need to be made ,and providing some sense as to the conditions under which a particular decision making process might be adopted. The notion of a co-operative approach to IT Governance is introduced to balance the traditional compliance approach.

Multisourcing is addressed by taking a networking view of multisourcing arrangements. Business evolution is traced from the industrial era, through to supply chain management and now value networks. The traditional view of the "firm" is challenged by the growth in the multiplicity of alliance and joint venture relationships.

The final foundational element is the emergence of the "intelligent enterprise". In essence the intelligent enterprise is a services centric firm which relies more on intangible assets and Intellectual Capital than the traditional manufacturing enterprise and a reliance on physical assets. The growth in the IT services market exemplifies the rise of the intelligent enterprise.

Section II: A Sociological View of Governance

This section begins with separate examinations of the foundation literature on corporate social capital and the intelligent enterprise. The two fields are then synthesised through the author's own research into corporate social capital and its application to the IT industry. The linkage between multisourcing strategies and corporate social capital is reinforced.

The maturation of the IT industry and the growing importance of relationship skills for IT professionals are then addressed. Relationships between IT providers and their business clients, or peer relationships with alliance partners, are requiring IT professionals to move beyond the comfort of a technical discipline and into the soft skills areas of networking cultures and reciprocity.

Inside organisations the IT function is often viewed as a "support" or "staff" function providing services to the core lines of business. Business alignment or business integration of the IT function has been in the top three IT success criteria for decades. With organisational structures evolving towards a greater use of matrix and network management, how IT positions itself within the network of the other lines of business will become critical. This section closes by exploring some different models of IT/Business alignment based on the network paradigm.

Section III: Research, Applications and Future Directions

The sociological view of governance is now reinforced through the reporting of some empirical research and emerging practices. Empirical research linking a firm's Corporate SC and its overall performance is presented. A network representation of the global IT outsourcing market is provided and relevant research methods are detailed in the appendices. Hypotheses test results are presented showing how the sub-elements of Corporate SC influence firm performance measures.

The emerging practice of Value Network Analysis and its adoption by ITIL is introduced. ITIL is fast becoming the IT industry's de facto best practice guide for the provision of IT services. The latest version of ITIL has acknowledged the evolution of value chains into value networks. This chapter provides a detailed description of how value networks can be applied to IT services provision. This section will draw from the value network practitioner's own "best practice" guides.

The evolution of the global IT outsourcing market is analysed from a networks perspective. This is accompanied by commentary identifying the growth in multisourcing networks and who the main global players are in this evolution. In this chapter the innovation question is addressed from a multisourcing and network perspective, hoping to shed some light on the innovation dilemma.

The impact of emerging technologies on IT Governance is addressed to close this section. In particular, the emergence of the suite of Web 2.0 technologies will provide fuel to the networking fire by putting advanced communications tools in the hands of individuals within the business. The current suite of social software tools like blogs, Wikis and discussion lists are finding their way from the public domain to inside organisations. This section looks at the issues and opportunities afforded by Web 2.0 and the current net mining research which promises to be the next generation of business intelligence.

Section IV: Leveraging Emerging Practice

The previous sections were rich in terms of research, case studies, technologies and methods for working with business networks in the IT discipline. In this section the threads will be synthesised into a suite of guidelines as to what individuals, IT executives and business executives can do to improve their collective IT Governance performance in a networked economy where multi-sourcing has become the norm.

REFERENCES

Allee, V. (2000). The Value Evolution: Addressing larger implications of an intellectual capital and intangibles perspective. *Journal of Intellectual Capital, 1*(1), 17-32.

Allee, V. (2003). *The Future of Knowledge: Increasing Prosperity through Value Networks*: Butterworth-Heinemann.

Allee, V. (2008). Value Network Analysis for Accelerating Conversion of Intangibles. *Journal of Intellectual Capital, 9*(1), 5-24.

Borgatti, S., Jones, C., & Everett, M. G. (1998). Network Measures of Social Capital. *CONNECTIONS, 21*(2), 1-36.

Broadbent, M. (2002). *CIO Futures - Lead with Effective Governance.* Paper presented at the ICA 36th Conference, Singapore.

Burt, R. S. (2000). The Network Structure of Social Capital. In R. I. Sutton & B. M. Shaw (Eds.), *Research in Organizational Behaviour, 22*, 345-423. Greenwich: JAI Press.

Calder, A., & Watkins, S. (2008). *IT Governance: A Manager's Guide to Data Security and ISO 27001/ISO 27002.*

Cohen, L., & Young, A. (2006). *Multisourcing - Moving Beyond Outsourcing to Achieve Growth and Agility.* Harvard Business School Press.

Cross, R., Borgatti, S. P., & Parker, A. (2002). Making invisible work visible: Using social network analysis to support strategic collaboration. *California Management Review, 44*(2), 25-46.

Cross, R., & Parker, A. (2004). *The Hidden Power of Social Networks*: Harvard Business School Press, Boston, MA.

Cullen, S., Seddon, P., & Willcocks, L. (2005). Managing outsourcing: The lifecycle imperative. *MIS Quarterly Executive, 4*(1), 229-246.

Cullen, S., & Willcocks, L. (2003). *Intelligent IT Outsourcing.* Butterworth-Heinemann.

Deloitte. (2005). *Calling a Change in the Outsourcing Market*. Retrieved 20/11/2007, from http://www.deloitte.com/dtt/cda/doc/content/Outsourcing%20report.pdf

Drucker, P. (1992). The New Society of Organizations. *Harvard Business Review* (September - October).

Gedda, R. (2007). *Westpac's outsourcing architects show true colours*. Retrieved 22/11/2007, from http://www.cio.com.au/index.php?id=1398665489

Gloor, P., & Cooper, S. (2007). *Coolhunting*. New York: AMACOM.

Hall, R. (1992). The Strategic Analysis of Intangible Resources. *Strategic Management Journal, 13*, 135-144.

Hand, J., & Lev, B. (2003). *Intangible Assets: Values, Measures and Risks*. Oxford: Oxford University Press.

Holland, J. (2001). Financial institutions, intangibles and corporate governance. *Accounting, Auditing & Accountability Journal, 14*(4), 497-529.

Hughes, J., & Weiss, J. (2007). Simple Rules for Making Alliances Work. *Harvard Business Review* (November), 122-131.

IBM. (2006). CEOs are expanding the innovation horizon: implications for CIOs. Retrieved 22/11/07, from http://www-03.ibm.com/industries/retail/doc/content/bin/IBM_CEO_Study.pdf

Inkpen, A., & Tsang, E. (2005). Social Capital, Networks, and Knowledge Transfer. *Academy of Management Review, 30*(1), 146-165.

ITIL. (2007). *Service Strategy*. The Stationery Office (TSO), London.

Kern, T., & Willcocks, L. (2000). Exploring information technology outsourcing relationships: theory and practice. *Journal of Strategic Information Systems, 9*(4), 321-350.

Kern, T., & Willcocks, L. (2001). *The Relationship Advantage*: Oxford University Press.

Knoke, D. (1999). Organizational Networks and Corporate Social Capital. In R. Leenders & S. Gabbay (Eds.), *Corporate Social Capital and Liability* (pp. 17-42): Boston: Kluwer.

Lacity, M., & Willcocks, L. (2001). *Global information technology outsourcing: in search of business advantage*. Chichester; New York: Wiley.

Lev, B. (2001). *Intangibles: Management, Measurement, and Reporting*. Washington, D.C.: Brookings Institution Press.

Lev, B., & Zarowin, P. (1999). The Boundaries of Financial Reporting and How to Extend Them. *Journal of Accounting Research, 37*(2), 353-385.

Lin, N. (2002). *Social Capital: A Theory of Social Structure and Action*. Cambridge University Press.

Lin, N., Cook, K., & Burt, R. (2001). *Social Capital: Theory and Research*. Aldine Transaction.

Low, J., & Kalafut, P. C. (2002). *Invisible Advantage: How Intangibles are driving business performance*. Perseus Publishing.

Quinn, J. B. (1992). *Intelligent Enterprise: A Knowledge and Service Based Paradigm for Industry*. Free Press.

Scott, J. (2000). *Social Network Analysis* (2nd ed.). Thousand Oaks, CA: Sage.

Stewart, T. A. (1997). *Intellectual Capital: The New Wealth of Organizations*. New York: Doubleday.

Sveiby, K. E. (1997). *The New Organizational Wealth: Managing & Measuring Knowledge-Based Assets*: Berret-Koehler Publishers, Inc.

Tsai, W., & Ghoshal, S. (1998). Social Capital and Value Creation: The Role of Intrafirm Networks. *Academy of Management Journal, 41*(4), 464-476.

Wasserman, S., & Faust, K. (1994). *Social Network Analysis: Methods and Applications*. UK: Cambridge University Press.

Weill, P. (2004). Don't Just Lead, Govern: How Top-Performing Firms Govern IT. *MIS Quarterly Executive, 8*(1).

Willcocks, L., & Cullen, S. (2006). *The Outsourcing Enterprise: The Power of Relationships*. Retrieved 20/11/07, from http://www.logicacmg.com/r/8000/the+o utsourcing+enterprise%3a+the+power+of+relationships/400009147

Zambon, S., Abernethy, M., Wyatt, A., Bianhi, P., Labory, S., & Lev, B. (2003). *Study on the Measurement of Intangible Assets and Associated Reporting Practices*: Commission of the European Communities - Enterprise Directorate General.

Acknowledgment

This book draws substantially from more than a decade of research and practice on the topic and hence a multitude of influences and influencers. Unfortunately limited space and powers of recollection do not allow me to acknowledge all of them, so I apologise in advance for not doing so. Living on the cusp of research and practice is never easy and I have taken much motivation from both my "strong and weak ties" in compiling this book.

In terms of my research I had direct support from Professors James Guthrie from the University of Sydney and Natalie Gallery from Queensland University of Technology in the supervision of my PhD dissertation. Professor Les Willcocks from the London School of Economics, who kindly provided the foreword to this book, and Professor Ron Burt from the Chicago Graduate School of Business were inspirations, both through their published research and the conversations that I have been fortunate enough to have with them. From a practitioner perspective I want to acknowledge John Galloway, a true pioneer in the use of Social Network Analysis techniques and the one who introduced me to the craft over a decade ago. Since then people like Steve Borgatti, Rob Cross, Valdis Krebs, Patti Anklam, Ross Dawson, Verna Allee, Karl Erik Sveiby, David Snowden, Doug Neal, John Taylor and Peter Gloor have all influenced my thinking in one way or another though their writing and the conversations we have had. I would also like to acknowledge the folks from Computer Sciences Corporation's Leading Edge Forum, who produce some of the most thoughtful and enduring research on IT management issues in the industry and for which I was grateful to be a small part.

On the creation of the manuscript I want to acknowledge the helpful comments of the three IGI Global reviewers, as well as Matt Moore, Richard Vines and my Optimice co-founder, Cai Kjaer for taking the time to work through the whole manuscript and provide specific feedback to me. My copy editor Lyn Tong provided a valuable service in her ability to see typographical and grammatical errors that defied my detection. Last but not least my family has provided the stable home life that is important when undertaking a project like this. My wife Julie and my now adult children Erin and Gavin had learnt to live with me locked away in my office for long hours. Hopefully they will be able to see now that I was doing more than just surfing the Internet!

Section I
Foundations of IT Governance in a Networked World

Chapter I
Introduction

The information technology (IT) industry has a relatively short history in global markets but can put claim to a disproportionate number of "business innovations" that it either participated in or has been the catalyst for. Concepts such as business process re-engineering (BPR), supply chain management (SCM), IT outsourcing (ITO), business process outsourcing (BPO), off-shoring and now multisourcing are tightly associated with the IT industry. The growth in the services economy and rapid escalation in the use of alliances and joint ventures for business growth is also clearly evident in the IT sector. A characteristic of an industry being a leader in the introduction of new business concepts is that it gets to experience both the excitement of forging new paths but unfortunately also the pain of unfulfilled aspirations. Inevitably new concepts like BPR, SCM, ITO, BPO are launched with much fanfare and then fail to live up to the lofty expectations initially set. Rarely however, are such approaches completely abandoned. Having experienced the pain of what Gartner calls the "Trough of Disillusionment" in its Hype Cycle characterisation (Fenn, 2007), organisations typically learn from their mistakes and with some perseverance are able to ultimately achieve some level of improved productivity. Approaches to IT Governance in a rapidly changing business environment are also going through a maturity cycle. Presently the focus is on developing IT Governance mechanisms that draw from accepted corporate governance mechanisms as described in Chapter II. These standards are high level and therefore generically applicable, but fall short of providing detailed guidance. This is left to the more fluid professional group guidelines like COBIT, ITIL and CMM. A major challenge for all IT Governance guidelines is the changing nature of the firm brought about by the increasing use of alliances, joint ventures and IT outsourcing.

With respect to the IT outsourcing industry the "trough of disillusionment" has led to a virtual abandonment of sole source outsourcing and now a complete focus on multisourcing. Paradoxically, the evidence in support of IT outsourcing as a business beneficial activity is mixed and therefore a move to multisourcing would appear counterintuitive. The majority of studies on the success or otherwise of IT outsourcing activities has relied on self reporting by company executives (M. Lacity & Willcocks, 2000b; Mary Lacity & Willcocks, 2001), rather than through more objective empirical studies. In fact empirical studies looking to link outsourcing and company profitability have shown some positive linkages for material inputs but a negative influence for outsourced external services (Gorg & Hanley, 2004; Gorzig & Stephan, 2002), though the studies have not specifically addressed IT services.

Multisourcing has therefore emerged as the "new" way of sourcing IT services more by default than by superior business results achieved. It has however attracted the attention of many major corporations that have now made significant commitments to an IT multisourcing strategy (Annesley, 2006; Gibson, 2005, 2006; Thibodeau, 2005, 2006). Ultimately multisourcing will face its own "trough of disillusionment". This book is aimed at helping the reader minimise the potential damage from being ill-prepared in embarking on multisourcing strategies. While there exists some lessons from early adopters of multisourcing to be had (Kern & Willcocks, 2001), this book takes a more fundamental perspective of multisourcing relationships. Ultimately multisourcing strategies will require the astute management of a network of relationships both internal and external to the organisation. Experience from existing sole source IT outsourcing contracts has already identified the relationship as a most critical success factor (Kern & Willcocks, 2001). Multisourcing accentuates the relationship factor not only by the additional number of vendors involved but in many cases also the relationships between the chosen vendors.

Drawing from the fields of sociology, economics and management theory and practice, this book is looking to equip the business manager with the fundamental tools for managing multiple relationships that go beyond contract management and new business process implementations. The concept of Corporate Social Capital (SC), defined as *"the set of resources, tangible or virtual, that accrue to a corporate player through the player's social relationships, facilitating the attainment of goals"* (Leenders & Gabbay, 1999, p3), is introduced as core to successfully managing multisourcing relationships. Complementary to existing advice around contract management the structural element of IT Governance, Corporate SC brings a deeper appreciation of the fundamental elements of relationship networks and the intangible aspects of relationships. Corporate SC directly addresses the paradox regularly experienced in outsourcing relationships where "all service level agreements are successfully met but the client (and vendor) is still not happy".

The IT outsourcing industry was launched around 1994 with several high profile long term sole vendor outsourcing contracts signed by both public and private sector firms. Figure 1 provides a view of the trends in ITO since 1994. The data identifies two distinct periods. From 1994 to around 2001/2 the ITO market was in growth mode. The total number and value of contracts signed each year had been growing steadily and at the same time the average deal size was reducing. The second period since this time has been relatively stable, with average deal sizes and terms at around $US100mill. over 4 years.

Contrary to popular belief, multisourcing has been with us virtually from the beginning. A survey in 2000 found selective sourcing to be the dominant outsourcing mode (M. Lacity & Willcocks, 2000a). Selective sourcing in this case meant that the organisations had chosen to outsource only part of their IT requirements; meaning that the additional IT services source was mostly an internal one, yet still a form of multisourcing. While the overall outsourcing industry has been somewhat stable over recent years, the number of organisations that are participating in multisourcing is however on a continuing upward trend. Figure 2 shows the growth in the number of client organisations that are participating in outsourcing contracts larger than $US1 million, together with the relative growth of these client organisations that are sourcing a significant proportion of their IT services from more than one source. By the end of 2007 some 25% of organisations outsourcing IT services had signed contracts in excess of $US1 million with two or more vendors.

The compelling question for client IT managers now is whether best practices for sole source outsourcing can scale to accommodate multisourcing arrangements?

Figure 1. IT outsourcing trends (Source: Datamonitor Contracts Database)

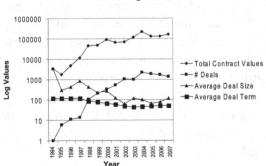

Figure 2. Multisourcing trends (Source: Datamonitor Contracts Database)

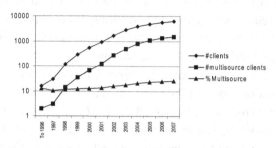

Can existing contracts be simply replicated to accommodate additional vendors? Can governance committees be simply expanded to accommodate additional vendor representatives? Can client relationship managers simply accommodate multiple vendors as part of their current responsibilities? Perhaps if each selected vendor's services were clearly independent of each other this might be the case. However, this is increasingly becoming not the case. The interdependency of tasks being undertaken by vendors and retained IT staff appears to be increasing. The Lacity and Willcocks (2000a) survey identified that "Management Overhead" was the largest risk in adopting a multisourcing strategy.

British Petroleum Exploration (BPX) was one of the earliest adopters of a multisourcing strategy involving multiple suppliers beyond their own internal IT resources. During the 1990s BPX signed five year contracts with several IT vendors that were structured with the intention of encouraging vendors to work as a strategic alliance. The result however was one of latent competition, rather than alliancing between vendors. While the relationships eventually stabilised between BPX and the alliance, the outsourcing cost savings objectives had not been met and the alliance approach was eventually abandoned in 1998 (Kern & Willcocks, 2001). One could argue that organisations embarking on a multisourcing path today are simply retracing the steps of BPX a decade ago, with potentially the same result. The BPX case study, as reported by Kern & Willcocks (2001), indicates that BPX contracts were structured on the principles of partnering concepts on which all vendors had agreed. In practice the vendors found it increasingly difficult to partner with their "competitors" as part of the alliance. The BPX case study highlights a situation where even with the best of intentions and a comprehensive contracting and alliance framework, getting market place competitors to cooperate for the benefit of the client requires more than a good contract and governance structure. While the alliance appeared to be cooperative, in the end, the critical cooperation needed to achieve the cost savings required by BPX was not present, leading to the arrangement being abandoned.

So what can be done to help multisourcing organisations avoid the same "trough of disillusionment" that BPX experienced? It could be argued that BPX was set up to fail before the contracts had been signed. BPX followed the accepted wisdom in choosing "best of breed" IT expertise in a given area. However the most critical factor of how well each vendor could work with other alliance partners to provide a seamless full service was missing from the evaluation. By attempting to force an alliance through contracting means BPX underestimated the power of the adversarial relationships that could develop and undermine the whole arrangement. The additional governance costs incurred by BPX in having to facilitate or act as "referee" between the vendor alliance partners, in the end, made the whole arrangement uneconomic. So what could BPX have done differently? Perhaps if BPX had sought visibility of how prospective vendors had collaborated in the past, either contractually or as part of pre-contract market development alliances' agreements, they could have chosen vendors who had a track record in successfully working with each other. The benefits lost by selecting some non "best of breed" vendors could be more than recouped through the effectiveness of the alliance of multi-sourced providers and lower governance costs. This book will provide examples and a means by which market place alliance networks can be explored for building multisourced outsourcing arrangements. The movement toward a more cooperative approach to IT Governance, from a compliance only approach, is central to devising a way forward.

Underpinning the successful governance of an IT multisourcing arrangement is the management of the network of relationships involved. The relationship complexity involved in multisourcing arrangements has already been shown to be beyond a pure economic rationalist approach. The introduction of the "intangible factor" in the form of an organisation's Corporate SC requires the reader to be exposed to some fundamental theories and practices in fields not commonly visited by the typical IT executive. Hence a section is devoted to some of the fundamental principles underpinning Corporate SC and empirical research linking Corporate SC to firm performance, before moving forward into how Corporate SC can be used to better govern multisourcing arrangements. The emerging practices of value network analysis (VNA), organisational network analysis (ONA), Networked based market intelligence and the Web 2.0 phenomenon are used to both identify new challenges and resolutions to today's IT Governance challenges. Many of the concepts developed in this book result from original research undertaken by the author, informed by many years of practical experience in the field. As such, the book will have equal appeal to the IT scholar, looking to make fundamental contributions to the field, as well as the business executive looking to take advantage of the undoubted benefits of a multisourcing strategy while not repeating the mistakes of the past.

HOW TO READ THIS BOOK

As noted above, the intended readership for this book ranges from the academic scholar or student through to the IT executive with a curiosity for new ways of working.

Figure 4 provides a framework for how a reader may choose to navigate this book according to their own personal context. Part I identifies the basis for why this book has been written. What is the core issue for governance and networks being addressed here and why? A review of the literature on "theories of the firm" is conducted to highlight the emergence of the above issue and the growing importance of Corporate SC and Intellectual capital (IC) to firms operating in today's more service centric economy. Part I should be relevant to the full readership. Part II takes a view of governance from the sociological perspective. Chapter V explores the research literature on Corporate SC and IC and is likely to be of more appeal to the academic scholar interested in the research foundations for these concepts. Chapters VI and VII address levels of networks ranging from one's personal networks through to networks that exist within organisations. Figure 3 illustrates how these different levels of networking relate, including inter-organisational networks and market places.

The study of social networks is seen as fundamental to understanding relationship patterns. The emerging sociologically based practices should be of interest to both the scholar and practitioner.

Figure 3. Levels of networks

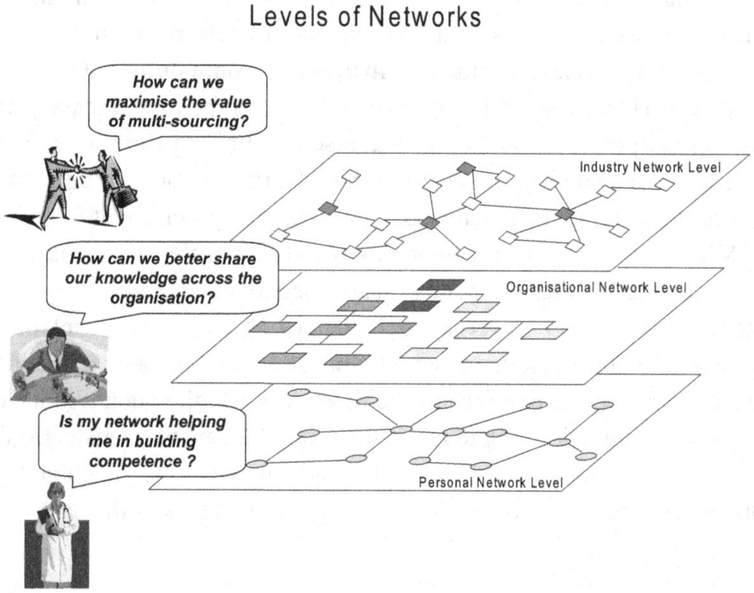

Levels of Networks

Figure 4. Reader's framework

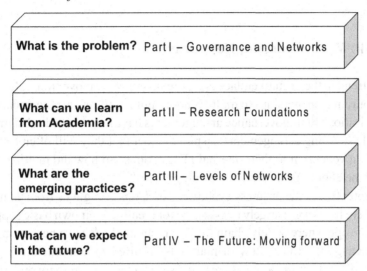

What is the problem? Part I – Governance and Networks

What can we learn from Academia? Part II – Research Foundations

What are the emerging practices? Part III – Levels of Networks

What can we expect in the future? Part IV – The Future: Moving forward

Part III provides a bridge between research and practice. Chapter VIII provides a detailed description of empirical research linking Corporate SC and IC to firm performance and should be of interest to both the scholar and practitioner. For the scholar, details of the research methods employed are included in the appendices. Chapters IX through XI describe emerging practices that are likely to impact on IT Governance. This includes the practice of Value network analysis (VNA), new methods for undertaking market intelligence and leveraging innovation, as well as identifying the impact of Web 2.0 technologies. This section is relevant to both the scholar and practitioner. Finally Part IV is aimed at the practitioner, where the concepts, themes and emergent practices described in previous chapters are synthesised to facilitate direct application in the field.

A more detailed description of the ensuing chapters is provided as follows:

Chapter II: IT Governance

In this chapter the current state-of-the-art for IT Governance is reviewed before taking a closer look at governance decision making and the different models of decision making that are available. A focus on decision making in complex environments is then introduced in response to the increasingly complex business environments within which much of the IT Governance decisions are now being taken. The Cynefin decision making framework (Snowden & Boone, 2007) is used to identify approaches to governance decision making dependent on the relative complexity of the decision making environment. The concept of a cooperative approach to IT Governance is introduced to contrast with the existing compliance based approaches.

Chapter III: Multi-Sourcing Networks

A common trend in the IT marketplace is for organisations to move from sole sourcing IT outsourcing partnerships to multi-vendor, multi-sourcing arrangements. For many organisations their governance arrangements have not changed substantially from the sole sourcing arrangements despite the fact that they will often be inviting competing vendors into their internal IT functions. So how did multisourcing networks come about? What were the driving forces?

This chapter traces the business evolution which has brought us from an industrial age; where firms were largely responsible for creating their own basic supplies, through to the age where supply chain management methods have been employed to tightly manage the linear flow of materials required to manufacture a given product; to today, where linear flows are being supplanted by value networks. These complex webs of interdependent organisations are independently collaborating to cooperatively develop and share in value creating activities. The traditional view of what constitutes a "firm" is challenged in this chapter.

Chapter IV: The Intelligent Enterprise

Building on Quinn's book: *The Intelligent Enterprise* (Quinn, 1992) this chapter initially reviews the topic of knowledge management (KM). The movement to today's service centric economy is seen to be predicated on the use of knowledge as the critical competitive resource. The review identifies a life cycle for knowledge from its generation and discovery through to its application for business benefit. Complementary to the study of KM is the study of intellectual capital (IC). IC could be viewed as the asset that is created through effective sharing of knowledge. It is mostly associated with the firm level of analysis and presents an alternative explanation for the valuation for the firm than the traditional accounting treatments.

The relevance of this intelligent enterprise treatment to IT Governance and multi-sourcing is the recognition that it is principally services that are being sourced and governed. Unlike tangible goods, services are often knowledge based and therefore an appreciation of how value is generated through knowledge and intellectual capital is central to the IT Governance decision.

Chapter V: Corporate SC and the Intelligent Enterprise

This chapter individually references the foundation literature underpinning Corporate SC and the intelligent enterprise. The two fields are then synthesised through the author's own research into Corporate SC and its application to the IT industry. The linkage between multi-sourcing strategies, IT Governance and Corporate Social Capital are reinforced here.

Chapter VI: Personal Network Competencies

This chapter explores the maturation of the IT industry and the growing importance of relationship skills for IT professionals. Relationships between IT providers and their business clients, or peer relationships with alliance partners, are requiring IT professionals to move beyond the comfort of a technical discipline and into the soft skills areas of networking cultures and reciprocity. The open source movement is a good example of "development by networks" and this is where the personal skills of IT professionals in building trust in the network become critical. Ultimately inter-organisational relationships can all be brought down to the personal level and hence this is the best place to start when exploring relationships.

Chapter VII: Intra-Organisational Networks

Inside organisations the IT function is often viewed as a "support" or "staff" function, providing services to the core lines of business. Business alignment or business integration of the IT function has been in the top three IT success criteria for decades. With organisational structures evolving towards greater use of matrix and network management, how IT positions itself within the network of the other lines of business will become critical. This chapter explores some different models of IT/Business alignment based on the network paradigm.

From the vendor's point of view, organisational networks also have a part to play in the development and integration of service lines to provide an integrated picture to the customer and/or potential alliance partners. How networks are configured to assist with the representation of the intellectual and social capital of the vendor firm will be explored.

Chapter VIII: Research Linking Corporate Social Capital and Performance in the IT Global Market Place

This chapter presents research results identifying the links between a firm's Corporate SC and its overall performance in terms of ROI, market to book values and total shareholder returns. A network representation of the global IT outsourcing market is developed. The data was drawn from a data base of outsourcing contracts signed globally over the past decade and the Factiva business information service. The results identified the impact of the different elements of Corporate SC on firm performance. Financial soundness was found to be the most predictive element of Corporate SC for firm performance, followed by investments in human capital and centrality in the market place. Interestingly, investments in internal capital and R&D were found to have a negative impact on performance if the firms making these investments were not financially sound.

Chapter IX: ITIL and Value Networks

The Information technology Infrastructure Library (ITIL) is fast becoming the IT industry's de facto best practice guide for the provision of IT services. The latest version of ITIL has acknowledged the evolution of value chains into value networks. This chapter provides a detailed description of how value networks can be applied to IT services provision. The chapter will draw from the value network practitioner's own "best practice" guides[1]. Value networks provide a more holistic interpretation of business value over the traditional business process and value chain interpretations, through the inclusion of intangible or Intellectual capital flows. Value networks can exist as intra-organisational networks or bridge inter-organisational boundaries as is the case with outsourcing arrangements. A sample value network developed for a multi-sourcing situation is presented and analysed.

Chapter X: The Global IT Outsourcing Market: A Network Perspective

This chapter traces the evolution of the global IT outsourcing market from a network perspective. Using Social Network Analysis tools, market representations show graphically how the nature of the marketplace has evolved over the past decade. This is accompanied by a commentary identifying the growth in multi-sourcing networks and identifying the main global players in this evolution. A review of an individual vendor/client relationship is then made from a network perspective, highlighting potential shortcomings of a traditional governance structure.

This chapter will also address the controversial topic of innovation and outsourcing. The outsourcing industry has largely not delivered on the innovation challenge, with the majority of outsourcing CIOs disappointed in the lack of innovation provided by their outsourcing partners. In this chapter the innovation question is addressed from a multisourcing and network perspective, shedding some light on the innovation conundrum.

Chapter XI: Technology, Web 2.0 and Beyond

Technology developments over the past few decades have presented ongoing challenges to IT governors. Emerging technologies, popularly labeled Web 2.0, will provide fuel to the networking fire by putting advanced communications tools in the hands of individuals within the business. The current suite of social software tools like blogs, wikis and discussion lists are finding their way from the public domain to inside organisations. Web 2.0 technologies are complementing the business process centric technologies embodied in ERP systems, enabling knowledge based business practices to be effectively shared via collaboration, rather than documentation. This chapter looks at the issues and opportunities afforded by Web 2.0 and current net mining research, which promises to be the next generation of business intelligence. How will Web 2.0 impact on the multi-sourcing marketplace? Will it lead to greater transparency in transactions and interactions and what will this mean for the competitive environment? A framework for identifying organisational collaboration requirements is provided to close the chapter.

Chapter XII: Guidelines for IT Governance and Multisourcing in the Networked Economy

The previous chapters were rich in terms of research, case studies, technologies and methods for working with business networks in the IT discipline. In this chapter the threads will be synthesised into some specific guidance for what individuals, IT executives and business executives can do to improve their collective performance in a networked economy where multi-sourcing has become the norm. The chapter closes with a commentary on the interdependency of compliance and business alignment approaches to IT Governance.

REFERENCES

Annesley, C. (2006, June 6th). ING Bank signs 274m deal in multisourcing initiative. *Computer Weekly*.

Fenn, J. (2007). Understanding Gartner's Hype Cycles. Retrieved 1/12/07, from http://www.gartner.com/DisplayDocument?doc_cd=144727

Gibson, S. (2005). Multisourcng Best Practices; Sound outsourcing management-always critical to success-is multiplied in importance when several outsourcing partners are chosen. *eWeek, 22*(20), 18.

Gibson, S. (2006). P&G Strikes Balance in Multisourcing. *eWeek, 23*(2), 49.

Gorg, H., & Hanley, A. (2004). *Does Outsourcing Increase Profitability?* (No. IZA DP No. 1372): Institute for the Study of Labor.

Gorzig, B., & Stephan, A. (2002). *Outsourcing and firm-level performance* (No. Discussion Paper No. 309, DIW Berlin).

Kern, T., & Willcocks, L. (2001). *The Relationship Advantage*. Oxford University Press.

Lacity, M., & Willcocks, L. (2000a). *Global IT Outsourcing: Search for Business Advantage*. Chichester: Wiley.

Lacity, M., & Willcocks, L. (2000b). *Inside IT Outsourcing: A State-of-the-Art Report*. Oxford: Templeton College, Oxford.

Lacity, M., & Willcocks, L. (2001). *Global information technology outsourcing: in search of business advantage*. Chichester; New York: Wiley.

Leenders, R., & Gabbay, S. (Eds.). (1999). *Corporate Social Capital and Liability*. Boston: Kluwer Academic Publishers.

Quinn, J. B. (1992). *intelligent enterprise: A Knowledge and Service Based Paradigm for Industry*. Free Press.

Snowden, D., & Boone, M. (2007). A Leader's Framework for Decision Making. *Harvard Business Review, November*.

Thibodeau, P. (2005). Multivendor Outsourcing Wins Some Fans; Others Not Sold. *Computerworld, 39*(15), 7.

Thibodeau, P. (2006, April 3rd). Outsourcing Market now Favours Multisourcing, CIO Says. *Computer Weekly,* (p. 59).

ENDNOTE

[1]   http://www.value-networks.com/

Chapter II
IT Governance

With the title of this book being IT Governance in a Networked World, there is the strong suggestion that governance in this environment is different to the way traditional IT Governance is conducted. The arguments presented in this book are in support of this view. However to set the platform for this discussion it is important to identify just what is "traditional" IT Governance. In this chapter a selective review of current IT Governance practice is provided. The intent is to provide a context for future chapters rather than to act as a comprehensive review. Hence the review only covers the major developments. It starts by looking at the empirical research on IT Governance with the focus being on Weill and Ross (2004), who in research terms have written "the book" on IT Governance. This is followed be a review of the two most dominant public IT Governance guidelines and frameworks in COBIT and ITIL.

Given that governance is mostly to do with decision making; who should make them and how they should be made, a section is included on this topic. Again, this is not intended as a comprehensive review of the field, but more of a selective review to assist in setting the foundation for future chapters. Finally a section is included to introduce the concept of cooperative governance, contrasting the approach with the traditional compliance driven approaches.

CURRENT STATE OF THE ART

A good place to start in understanding IT Governance is with some definitions. As well as providing an assessment of the level of maturity in the area by the level of commonality found, it can also provide some insight into the context in which the author views this area.

IT Governance is considered a subset of corporate governance. A basic definition of IT Governance is:

The primary goals for information technology governance are to (1) assure that the investments in IT generate business value, and (2) mitigate the risks that are associated with IT[1]

Weill & Ross , (2004, p8) offer:

Specifying the decision rights and accountability framework to encourage desirable behaviour in the use of IT

which provides more of a focus on the decision makers and their accountability to some pre-defined objectives.

A more detailed definition is provided by the IT Governance Institute through the public organisation ISACA, established over 40 years ago to support IT Governance professionals:

IT Governance is the responsibility of the board of directors and executive management. It is an integral part of enterprise governance and consists of leadership and organisational structures and processes that ensure that the organisation's IT sustains and extends the organisation's strategies and objectives.[2]

This more detailed definition extends beyond the "what" of IT Governance and begins to detail some of the "hows". The definition reflects the auditing heritage of ISACA (Information Systems Audit and Control Association) and is consistent with the current views on corporate governance, especially in light of the Enron, Arthur Andersen and Worldcom collapses, that led to the establishment of a new compliance regime around the Sarbanes-Oxley Act in the USA.

The latter definitions infer a compliance approach with the establishment of defined processes, organisational structures and procedures as being the way to achieve effective IT Governance. How successful are such approaches? Do they guarantee business success if applied diligently? In the next section a review of empirical research linking IT Governance practices to business performance is provided.

BEST PRACTICE RESEARCH

The book on IT Governance by Weill and Ross (2004) was the culmination of extensive research on linking IT Governance practices to business performance at the MIT Sloan School of Management Center for Information Systems Research (CISR). Their research involved over 300 enterprises in over 20 countries during the period of 1999-2003. It represents the most extensive research conducted to date on IT Governance and its effects on business performance.

In conducting their research Weill & Ross developed a number of frameworks to support their search for best practice IT Governance. The lack of a standard way of describing an IT Governance arrangement no doubt contributed to their finding that fewer than 50 % of senior executives could accurately explain their IT Governance approach. To fill this gap, they developed a Governance Arrangement Matrix with the key IT decisions/activities (IT Principles, IT Architecture, IT Infrastructure Strategies, Business Application Needs, IT Investment) on one axis and typical arrangement archetypes that they had observed (Business Monarchy, IT Monarchy, Feudal, Federal, Duopoly, Anarchy) on the other. Using this framework they were able to classify the governance patterns of the different organisations they studied, and then draw inferences about which governance patterns were most associated with good business performance.

Overall their research found that the top performing organisations were differentiated from their competitors by up to 40% in terms of returns on their IT investments. There was however no dominant pattern of IT Governance that was clearly associated with superior business results. In fact success was related to how well the organisation articulated their business strategies, how well they set and monitored their business performance goals and then how well they linked their IT Governance arrangements with their strategies and performance goals. They found that poorly articulated business strategies and business accountabilities in general were typically associated with poor IT Governance performance. In other words, it was hard to "shine" with IT Governance if the rest of the business was poorly run. A clearly articulated business strategy e.g. customer intimacy, operational excellence, product leadership, sets the foundation for the establishment of an appropriate governance arrangement.

In looking to articulate IT Governance best practices emerging from their research, Weill & Ross identified a set of design principles and indicators for crafting an effective IT Governance scheme:

Engagement with the Business

- Can more than 50% of managers accurately describe their governance approach?
- How well is the governance approach communicated across the organisation?
- Are senior managers actively involved?
- Are there clear business objectives for IT investments?
- Are the business strategies clearly articulated?
- Are there fewer renegades and more formally approved exceptions?
- Is the governance scheme relatively stable i.e. are minimal changes being made?

Starting Point for Governance Arrangements (Then Adapted to Suit the Context)

- Federal approach for input to IT decisions.
- Duopoly arrangements for IT principles and investment decisions.
- Avoid federal approach for decision making.
- Joint business/IT decisions for business application investments.

General Principles

- Top performers on asset utilisation typically use duopoly (IT and Business unit) arrangements.
- Top performers on profit apply more centralized arrangements i.e. business monarchies for decision making.
- Top performers on growth, balance entrepreneurial needs of the business units with firm-wide strategies and principles i.e. decentralised IT organisation, principles supporting innovation and growth, critical infrastructure identified centrally.
- Further customise these principles for unique strategies and desired behaviours.

As much as this research was focused on the identification of replicable best practices, the authors were always careful to emphasise the need for organisations to use these suggestions as a starting point and to customise them to suite their distinctive competitive situations. They also acknowledge that while the appearance of the IT Governance scheme is a top-down compliance driven one, that in practice, it is far from a command and control situation. They identify a number of

communication approaches from senior management pronouncements, formal committees, coaching of non-conformists, information portals and the like. Perhaps the
true nature of the communication challenge is reflected in the quote they reported
from a systems architect that, "We are seeing ourselves more as architectural social
workers than architecture police" (Weill & Ross, 2004, p107).

GUIDELINES AND STANDARDS

While the research has indicated that for most organisations a majority of business
executives cannot articulate their own IT Governance mechanism, there exists
ample availability of formal guidelines and standards publications. A number of
cooperative IT Governance efforts have resulted in substantial guidelines being
developed and aligned with national and international quality standards.

Figure 5 identifies the IT Governance standard AS 8015 published by Standards
Australia with an overlay added for publicly available guidelines aligned to the
standard. An international standard ISO 38500 has now been created based on AS
8015. While there are overlaps between the COBIT, ITIL and CMM frameworks,
they are largely complementary frameworks that cover the breadth of IT activities. The COBIT framework plays an overarching audit like role for controlling

Figure 5. IT Governance framework (adapted from AS 8015-20053)

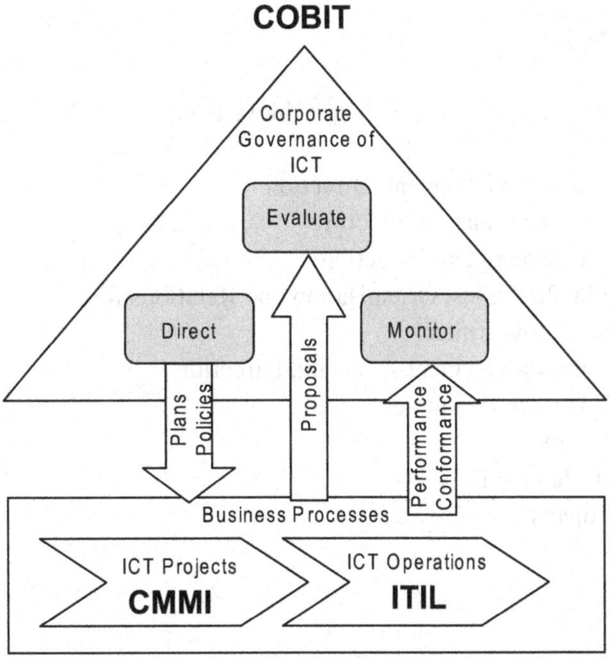

IT activities in line with business objectives. CMM was designed to support the development of software applications. CMM has now evolved into CMMI with a broader process improvement charter, and therefore a more significant overlap with ITIL and COBIT. ITIL was developed to support IT operations and service delivery. Other frameworks exist to specifically support project management and security activities that are not shown here.

A brief review of each of the identified key frameworks will now be provided.

COBIT[4]

The ISACA organisation was formed over 40 years ago from the collaborative efforts of a small number of information systems auditors. Previously referred to as the Information Systems Audit and Control Association, it now prefers to be called by its acronym only to reflect the broader audience that it now serves. It serves over 75,000 members in over 160 countries. ISACA is the source of the COBIT (Control Objectives for Information and related Technology) IT Governance framework and toolset. COBIT reflects its auditing heritage by emphasising regulatory compliance. COBIT version 4.1 has 34 high level processes that cover 210 control objectives categorised into four domains: Planning and Organisation; Acquisition and Implementation; Delivery and Support; and Monitoring and Evaluation.

To provide a flavour of the granularity of the guidance provided by COBIT these four domains are broken down to the next level of processes / activities:

Plan and Organize

This domain covers the use of IT to help achieve the company's key objectives:

1. Define a Strategic IT Plan and Direction
2. Define the Information Architecture
3. Determine Technological Direction
4. Define the IT Processes, Organisation and Relationships
5. Manage the IT Investment
6. Communicate Management Aims and Direction
7. Manage IT Human Resources
8. Manage Quality
9. Assess and Manage IT Risks
10. Manage Projects

Acquire and Implement

The Acquire and Implement domain identifies the procurement and implementation processes:

1. Identify Automated Solutions
2. Acquire and Maintain Application Software
3. Acquire and Maintain Technology Infrastructure
4. Enable Operation and Use
5. Procure IT Resources
6. Manage Changes
7. Install and Accredit Solutions and Changes

Delivery and Support

The Delivery and Support domain deals with business application and/or services implementation and support.

1. Define and Manage Service Levels
2. Manage Third-party Services
3. Manage Performance and Capacity
4. Ensure Continuous Service
5. Ensure Systems Security
6. Identify and Allocate Costs
7. Educate and Train Users
8. Manage Service Desk and Incidents
9. Manage the Configuration
10. Manage Problems
11. Manage Data
12. Manage the Physical Environment
13. Manage Operations

Monitor and Evaluate

The Monitoring and Evaluation domain deals with responsibilities seen typically as the auditing function.

1. Monitor and Evaluate IT Processes
2. Monitor and Evaluate Internal Control

3. Ensure Regulatory Compliance
4. Provide IT Governance

The COBIT guidance is provided in the form of hardcopy manuals and online tools. COBIT is aligned with several international quality standards and is recommended to those firms requiring compliance with the Sarbanes-Oxley Act.

ITIL[5]

Initially referred to as the Information Technology Infrastructure Library, ITIL was originally developed by the British Central Computer and Telecommunications Agency to develop a best practice library of IT processes. Now known as the Office of Government Communications (OGC), this organisation has overseen the development of ITIL into one of the most respected sources of information on IT services management. An independent management community called the IT Service Management Forum (ITSMF) has grown up around ITIL to support its international clientele.

ITIL is now in its third version and is delivered through a core set of publications:

*   **Service Strategy:** provides guidance on how to design, develop and implement service management. Distinctively, the service strategy module aims to answer the question about *why* something is being done, more so than *how*. The focus on business alignment and business performance overlaps with the objectives of COBIT.
*   **Service Design:** guides the design and development of services and service management processes. It includes the development and management of the services portfolio and the establishment of service levels and standards for conformance.
*   **Service Transition:** guides the transition of new or changed services into operations. The publication helps place release management, program management and risk management into a practical context of service management. The objective is to ensure a smooth and trouble free transition to a new or improved services situation.
*   **Service Operation:** provides guidance on achieving efficiency and effectiveness of the existing services. Maintaining stable operations while allowing for changes in scale, scope and service levels is a principal objective. Guidance is provided on demand management, optimising capacity utilisation, scheduling operations and problem fixes. Alternative service models like shared service units, utility computing, web services and mobile commerce are also covered.

- **Continual Service Improvement:** guides the quality management processes. It provides the principles, practices and methods for change management and capability improvement. Guidance is provided on linking improvement activities to business outcomes using the Plan, Do, Check, Act (PDCA) cycle.

A more detailed review of ITIL, together with Value network analysis is provided in Chapter IX.

CMMI[6]

Capability Maturity Model Integration (CMMI) evolved from the Capability Maturity Model (CMM) developed at the Software Engineering Institute at Carnegie Mellon University in the USA for assisting organisations develop successful software projects. CMMI has the more expansive objective of process improvement beyond software development.

CMMI has three core components:

- **CMMI-Dev:** provides guidance for managing, measuring and monitoring development processes. This component incorporates the previous CMM practices for software project development and has now expanded to generic product developments and life cycle management.
- **CMMI-SVC:** provides guidance for delivering services within organisations and out to external customers. There would be overlap in this component with ITIL.
- **CMMI-ACQ:** provides guidance to enable informed and decisive acquisition leadership.

The overall framework is still based on the maturity model concept and organisations managing their improvement through definable maturity levels.

Figure 5 may be a somewhat simplified view of the respective roles that COBIT, ITIL and CMMI play and the levels of overlap may in fact be increasing. However, the heritage of each of these frameworks suggests that COBIT is best suited to establishing the control objectives for IT activities in meeting business objectives overall; ITIL is best suited for providing detailed guidance on the business process for services management and likewise CMMI provides the same level of detailed processes for applications development.

What is common across all frameworks is that guidance in decision making, be it business alignment, service management or product development, is a critical component of each framework and therefore critical to the whole IT Governance framework. The next section therefore looks at decision making in the IT Governance context.

GOVERNANCE DECISION MAKING

The definition of IT Governance offered by Weill and Ross (2004) emphasises decision rights and accountabilities. In their governance matrix they specifically identify who is accountable for decisions regarding IT principles, architectures, IT infrastructure, IT applications and IT investment. They also indicate who has input into each decision type. Other than identifying who is accountable for IT related decisions and who might have input into these decisions, the actual process of how decisions are made is largely left to the individual. One might ask if identifying decision rights and accountabilities is enough to ensure good decisions are being made? As a form of management decision making IT Governance decisions often requires balancing many competing objectives across multiple criteria. In this section a brief review of the different approaches to management decision making is provided, leading into a discussion on compliance driven vs. cooperative approaches to IT Governance.

Management Decision Making Models

The usual starting point with decision models is to look at the rational decision making model (Kepner & Tregoe, 1965). Inspired by the idea of systemising decision making to provide a more logical and transparent result, the process typically proceeds through four stages:

1. Defining the decision objective
2. Identifying all the alternative options or choices
3. Identifying the criteria by which the options will be assessed and weighting these criteria according to relative importance
4. Assessing the options against the criteria and making the decision choice.

In the context of IT Governance one could envisage that decisions relating to the acquisition of new products or services, the selection of alternative architectural standards or prioritising IT investment options, might all be candidates for a rational decision making process.

In practice however, it can be difficult to formulate many management decisions easily into the rational decision making model. For example, it is often difficult to articulate all potential decision options and decision criteria. With a large number of options and criteria, the application of the rational decision making model can prove quite tedious as decision criteria need to be accurately weighted against one another and each option assessed against each criteria. For the more qualitative criteria the assessment of each option can be subject to personal bias. Even when the process is completed it is not unusual for several choices to be evaluated as of similar merit and therefore the manager is still left with more work to do.

Nobel prize winning researcher Herbert Simon is credited with many contributions to both economics and science, but it is for his work on organisational decision making and decision making under uncertain conditions that he is best known (Simon, 1947, 1979, 1987, 2001). Simon coined the term "bounded rationality" to describe how human decision makers are limited in how far they can apply the rational decision making process. The bounds are defined as the limits to which a human decision maker can know all of the alternative options and criteria by which a decision has to be made. What happens outside these bounds forms the basis of Simon's thesis that organisational, political and relational elements are brought to bear on the decision, resulting in the search for a "satisficing" rather than optimal result.

Decision Making in Complex Environments

Simon's work identifies that management decision making, of which IT Governance decisions are a good example, require more than the simple application of a logical process. As the business environment becomes increasingly complex through the increased globalisation of the world's markets, it appears that decision making is moving even more strongly beyond the simple rational decision making model, making Simon's work even more important than ever.

When we think of decisions that have to be made under complex conditions, whether they are due to the large number of options and criteria, or the fact that they need to be made quickly, there are many precedents from which we can learn. One particular area of interest is decision making under time pressure. In this situation one does not have the luxury of being able to walk through a logical decision making process. In these situations good decisions appear to be made based on the intuition and experience of the responsible decision maker. The field of study focusing on this style of decision making has been called "naturalistic decision making" (Lipshitz *et al.*, 2001; Zsambook *et al.*, 1992). Examples of popular fields of study for naturalistic decision making researchers are; emergency services workers like fire fighters and police , and emergency medical staff and military staff under battle conditions. These situations may only infrequently relate to IT Governance situations, but the intent for introducing it here is to explore the behavioural and intuitive aspects of good decision making under pressure, that is relevant to IT Governance decision makers.

The field of naturalistic decision making was driven by the need to better understand how decisions are made in ill-structured, uncertain or dynamic environments with ill defined or competing goals, high stakes, multiple players and time constraints. Sound familiar? Over time the focus matured to simply try and understand the way people use their experience to make decisions in field situations (Lipshitz et al., 2001). It is common to think of decision makers in these situations as having good intuition or "gut feel". The research has shown however, that such intuition does need to be based on experience to achieve a good result. They have found that skilled decision makers adopt a "recognise/react" approach, rather than a logical assessment of options approach. They quickly recognise patterns from their past experiences and can imagine or "play out" potential consequences and adjust accordingly (Klein, 2000). The identification of the option can happen almost instantaneously, with the remainder of the decision making time being used to verify the option by "playing it out". Simon uses the example of a chess champion playing under tournament conditions who tends to identify their next move in seconds but then verify the move looking for potential weaknesses (Simon, 1987).

Klein and Weick (2000) show support for Simon's concept of "satisficing" by pointing out that we often agonise over decisions that might have equal merit but are based on differing criteria. The rational decision making models may help us to articulate the conditions by which they have become options of equal merit by showing the respective strengths and weaknesses, but ultimately they are of equal merit and either choice would satisfy the need. Therefore this should be the easiest, rather than hardest decision to make. They go on to emphasise that for the manager the important learning from naturalistic decision making is for them to expose themselves to as many experiential learning opportunities as possible. They emphasise that decision making is a skill that has to be continually developed and enhanced through every new experience.

In the context of the IT Governance decision making, one can see many situations where the optimal solution is being sought and much time and energy is spent trying to differentiate between equally meritorious options, be they IT investments, architectural options or infrastructure directions. Perhaps the greatest learning for IT governors from naturalistic decision making research is the need to build decision making skills through practical experience. In effect this is saying that better IT Governance decisions will come from the key decision makers building their personal decision making skills through being exposed to multiple situations and scenarios, more so than blindly following best practice guides where the true learning experiences have been filtered out in favour of pristine presentation.

The Cynefin Decision Making Framework

The previous sections traced the evolution of decision theories from where decision making could be clearly rationalised in economic terms to organisational decision making and the concept of bounded rationality and "satisficing", and finally to naturalistic decision making and experience based learning and application. At the firm level one could identify a similar transition from the transaction based theories (Williamson, 1981) for sourcing decisions through to the resource based theory of the firm (Holcomb & Hitt, 2007). The term "resource" can have a multitude of soft interpretations like "knowledge", "competency" and now "corporate social capital". The differing theories of the firm will be addressed in more detail in Chapter III. The interplay or equilibrium between governance mechanisms of explicit contracts, implicit contracts, reputation and trust have been described as influential in outsourced ERP implementation success (Wang & Chen, 2006). At this point it is worth reflecting on how this increasingly complex business world may be impacting on the world of IT Governance. To facilitate this discussion a decision making framework developed by David Snowden, called the Cynefin framework is provided (Snowden, 2002; Snowden & Boone, 2007).

The Cynefin framework was born out of Snowden's studies in knowledge management (KM). Snowden showed an early appreciation of how simple KM methods were failing to meet the early expectations of the organisations adopting them. He subsequently developed the Cynefin framework to introduce the application of "sense making" to management and organisational practice and to create an open source movement for methods on management consultancy.

Through the use of the Cynefin framework, some of the challenges in IT Governance become clearer. The journey through the framework is best commenced at the area to the lower right, labeled "Simple" and "Best Practice". This domain is meant to identify the simple contexts where the environment is relatively stable and

Figure 6. Cynefin decision making framework (Reproduced with permission)

clear cause and effect relationships exist. Managers in this domain typically practice a sense, categorise and respond (S-C-R) approach which eventually develops into a "best practices" suite of standard processes to be applied on the occurrence of a pre-determined event. The "Simple" domain could aptly be applied to many of the operational domains of an IT outsourcing contract. For example, the best practice Information Technology Infrastructure Library (ITIL) (ITIL.org, 2007b) was initially established by the UK government to help standardise best IT management processes to international quality standards. The latest upgrade to ITIL (version 3) acknowledges the need to move beyond the internal IT management processes.

ITIL looks for the first time at some business fundamentals and relationships between all players in modern organisations using IT—Sharon Taylor, Chief Architect (ITIL.org, 2007a).

ITIL and multisourcing value networks are explored in more detail in Chapter IX. However it is suffice to say that the combination of the ITIL learning and the checkered history of IT outsourcing suggests that the IT outsourcing context is more than "Simple". Moving to the upper right context labeled "Complicated", the domain is characterised by potentially multiple "right" answers. There is no one best process so this domain is labeled with "good practice" as the aspiration. Cause and effect relationships still exist though they are not clearly apparent to all. Examples of complicated domains include oil exploration, aircraft manufacture or possibly IT outsourcing. In complicated domains critical reliance shifts from managers to "experts". The response to particular events is to sense, analyse and then respond (S-A-R). This situation adequately describes the typical help desk service, where operators field calls (sense), analyse the problem (analyse) and then hopefully provide a solution (respond) through a combination of documented processes and their own personal expertise. Help desk problems that are escalated rely on service technicians with higher levels of expertise and consequently less reliance on documented practices.

The IT outsourcing context as we know it today would sit in the "Complicated" domain. There is no single "best practice" as to how it should be done. Decisions on outsourcing also now go beyond the simple economic argument, though this will always be present. There is now substantial experience and expertise available to assist those embarking on an outsourcing initiative for the first time.

Now if we up the ante to a multisourcing context, it has been previously argued that the level of increased complexity goes beyond simply scaling up current single sourcing strategies and practices. Leaders need to also understand the relationships between their multi-sourced providers, as do the providers themselves. Moving to the top left context labeled "Complex", the ability to identify a single "right" answer is no longer possible. This context is contrasted with the "Complicated" context by comparing the deconstruction and reconstruction of a sophisticated piece of machinery like a racing car or aircraft, with say managing the future of a Brazilian rainforest (Snowden & Boone, 2007). Experts are able to successfully work with complicated machinery, but the ecosystem of a rainforest is sufficiently complex to suggest that comprehensive analytical processes are still insufficient. Solutions are however achievable through a probe-sense-respond approach. This is an emergent process where a level of experimentation is undertaken before a specific direction for action is decided. Could the multisourcing context be seen as "Complex"? The ecology of the IT market place will be explored in some detail in Chapter X, but it is suffice to say here that it shows some similar elements to a Brazilian rainforest, so the notion can't be dismissed entirely. In embarking on a multisourcing strategy both early adopter clients and providers will need to experiment to some extent. In fact the early BP exploration experience with multisourcing could be considered as one such experiment (Kern & Willcocks, 2001).

The final context identified in the Cynefin framework is "Chaos". This domain is described as one of turbulence; with no consistent patterns of cause and effect, and where any level of analysis would prove worthless. The guidance for firms operating in this context is to act-sense-respond. Acting first to restore order in even a single area provides the basis for working to transform the situation from "Chaos" to "Complex" and hopefully to some identifiable patterns that can be worked with. It would be harsh to identify current IT outsourcing experiences as Chaotic, though no doubt many an IT executive may have felt they had been in that situation at times.

In summary, it has been argued that current IT outsourcing arrangements largely fit within the "complicated" business decision making context with the risk of moving to the "complex" domain as multisourcing strategies evolve. In terms of IT Governance, this will mean a progression from the ideas of "best practice" compliance to one where some level of experimentation is welcomed. This is not to say that all IT Governance decisions will be in the "complex" or "complicated" domains. The portfolio of decisions undertaken within a typical IT management context may spread across all of the Cynefin framework domains. What is important to understand from this section is that there is no "one size fits all" solution and that governing a multisourcing context may require decision making strategies from all four Cynefin domains at some time or other.

Compliance vs. Cooperative IT Governance

The dominant logic of IT Governance today is one of compliance. The unit of analysis is focused on the single firm or organisation. The ultimate responsibility and accountability is identified as the top of these organisations, be it the CEO and/or the board of directors. The best practice research reported on here identifies how firms are establishing their IT Governance standards by which they are asking all of the business units to comply, with minimal exceptions. The formal IT Governance frameworks are providing comprehensive guidance and document processes on how businesses can establish effective IT Governance objectives and business processes to increasingly higher levels of granularity. The previous section on decision making models was designed not so much to challenge the current dominant logic for IT Governance, but to create an opportunity to extend the thinking around IT Governance beyond the current compliance approaches to accommodate more cooperative approaches. Such moves will be needed as the business environment becomes increasingly complex and the unit of analysis moves beyond the single firm to multi-firm alliance situations. If indeed the IT Governance situations evolve into truly complex environments, as identified through the Cynefin framework, the current compliance approach to IT Governance will no longer be effective.

So what is "Cooperative IT Governance"? Essentially a cooperative approach to governance, in contrast to a compliance approach, exists when there is no single higher authority accountable for its conduct. Governance in these situations has to be negotiated and agreed upon essentially between peers. While standards and guidelines may still be in place and operational, the agreement on which guidelines to use and how stringently they should be abided by is negotiated at a peer to peer level. No endorsement and support for the senior executive is available.

In terms of current practice, this archetype does not exist. Using the (Weill & Ross, 2004) IT Governance framework, the closest archetype is associated with the "not for profit" sector. The authors describe not for profits as having a broader definition of value which incorporates "public good". They also have to develop externally sourced capabilities and participate in co-production of business results. They have cultural norms which focus more on consensus, transparency and equity which impact on their approach to IT Governance. Their success tends to rely more on partnerships, joint decisions between business and IT leaders and the heavier use of committees. They also tend to have a broader external representation on their governance boards to reflect their broader definitions of value add.

The IT Governance pattern identified by Weill & Ross (2004) for "not for profit" organisations had input for IT Governance decisions coming from federal or duopoly sources with decisions made by the business monarchy. For cooperative governance the decisions would have to emanate from the federal or duopoly sources, a new pattern that did not exist in Weill & Ross's extensive research, but would have to exist in a cooperative governance regime. It is not uncommon to find such situations outside the IT domain when one raises the unit of analysis beyond the single firm to say a whole market sector or the business environment as a whole (Gerencser *et al.*, 2008). In these cases one could identify the independent market regulators, supported by the legal frameworks of the countries that support them as the ultimate authorities. In terms of corporate governance there exists a global "generally accepted" accounting standard which has been extended to broader regulatory mechanisms of which Sarbanes-Oxley is an example for USA registered firms. In the IT domain however, no such legal authority exists. Many of the public IT Governance frameworks identify themselves with the spirit of these legally enforceable corporate governance schemes, but in fact there is no single authority to enforce compliance to any given IT Governance arrangement once one moves beyond the scope of a single firm or organisation. Therefore as the business world increasingly adopts partnering, joint ventures and alliances as the mode for conducting business then the demand for peer to peer cooperative arrangements will materialise.

Case Study

Outsourcing by Consortia

Not all organisations are of sufficient scale to afford the services of top tier outsourcing providers. On this premise a group of five government agencies in Australia decided to band together to procure the services of a global IT provider to build and maintain a new suite of core business applications. By banding together they would have the size and scale to leverage a competitive deal with a major provider, while at the same time reduce their overall costs through the cost sharing arrangement. A competitive tendering process achieved a 10 year outsourcing contract with a major global IT provider, with the provider seeing the opportunity to on-sell the resultant systems to other agencies as an additional sweetener for the deal.

Regrettably the results half way into the term had fallen far short of expectations for all parties. Governance of the consortia was very much reliant on goodwill rather than strong financial commitment, as each agency still maintained a direct contracting arrangement with the vendor. The complex decision making processes for the consortia led to inevitable delays in the system specification and build stages to the extent that the system was now considered more of a legacy, rather than leading edge technology. Life hadn't been easy for the vendor either as delays impacted their own profitability and the on-sell opportunity had virtually disappeared. Thin or disappearing margins led to a drop in service quality. A required, but expensive, licensing upgrade for a key technology component had not received uniform consortia support, putting the whole arrangement at risk, as each of the agencies had taken time out to review their options.

So what went wrong? How could the vicious downward cycle where all parties are now in a lose-lose situation be turned to a virtuous win-win situation. When analysing the current predicament with the CIO of one of the agencies involved, it was apparent that the cooperative was probably doomed from the start. With no history of cooperation and only a high level perception of shared commonality of requirements, it was highly unlikely that the cooperative could operate successfully from day one. The research on alliances tells us that the most successful alliance partnerships are those where a previous relationship has existed. These agencies had been used to being masters in their own domain, so the give and take required for consortia participation would take some time to learn; including the need to build trust amongst the participants. On the service provider side, as experienced outsourcers they perhaps should have seen the warning signals earlier and insisted on stronger formal governance mechanisms being in place from the start.

Looking forward the CIO took some small steps working directly with the IT provider. Through these small initiatives he found that the two critical factors that appeared to be missing from the work to date were the lack of experienced business analysts able to effectively map business processes ahead of specifying requirements, and secondly paying attention to the relationship itself. When both were in place he found that good progress and return on investment could be achieved. Scaling these two key lessons to the consortia level is however, a significant task.

What we see from this case is the importance of balancing the tangible, the detailed understanding of the business processes underpinning new application development, with the more intangible, trust and relationship aspects. This allows progress to be made unhindered by factional issues. If the consortia were to survive and the current vicious cycle be reversed, it would require a "back to basics" re-think of the overall objectives and then re-negotiated value exchanges between all stakeholders to achieve a workable forward moving governance arrangement.

The trade-off between compliance and a cooperative approach to IT Governance is not as stark as one might initially think. Many IT Governance practitioners operating under the guise of a compliance model will testify to the level of "cooperation" they need to facilitate, as opposed to simple enforcement. The previously mentioned quote which equates the governance role to social work rather than policing, is insightful in that it identifies the tension that IT Governance practitioners are experiencing from the flattening of organisations, and the distribution of decision making authorisation to lower levels of management. The CEO mandate no longer has the immediate impact that it might have had in previous generations. Even senior management needs to operate more by influence and facilitated cooperation rather than simple mandate.

Figure 7. Balancing compliance and cooperation

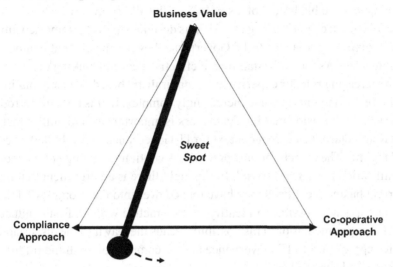

Figure 7 identifies the contrasting approaches to IT Governance as end points on a continuum. There will be compliance approaches that will have to rely heavily on facilitating cooperation and there will be cooperative approaches that will negotiate compliance standards by which the partners will choose to comply. As the business environment moves increasingly toward networked business models one would expect the pendulum to swing more strongly toward cooperative approaches to IT Governance to achieve maximum business benefit from IT. However, one would anticipate that the "sweet spot" will exist in the astute balancing of these approaches.

SUMMARY

This chapter began by providing a brief review of the current status quo for IT Governance. Current research on best practices for IT Governance found no single dominant pattern but several best practice themes that could be associated with the different business contexts in which they were practiced. The review of the industry level frameworks like COBIT, ITIL and CMMI supporting IT Governance illustrated the depth and breadth of the practices and processes that are being adopted by the industry. With all frameworks, including the audit inspired COBIT framework, they fall short of claiming to be standards to be complied with and are presented as best practice guides to be taken advantage of. Indeed this is appropriate as the research has shown that the differing business contexts and increasing business complexity works against the establishment of a single "one fits all" approach.

The section on decision making models was designed to evoke some new thinking into alternative approaches to IT Governance beyond the current compliance driven approaches. As the understanding of effective decision making evolves, one can see an increasing role for experienced or naturalistic based decision making as our business environments become increasingly complex. In this light the introduction of the Cyenfin decision making framework is important as it identifies that the evidence would place the current context for IT Governance squarely in the "complicated" regime. The search for best practices is continually being conducted but their identification is far from trivial. In this light there is an argument that many of the current business contexts may have moved over into the "complex" domain where in fact it is not possible to identify a best practice without first conducting some level of experimentation. This possibility leads the way into the discussion on cooperative approaches to IT Governance and its comparison with the traditional compliance based approaches.

The next chapter takes the discussion from the topic of IT Governance to an important component of governance, being the sourcing of IT. In particular the chapter addresses the topic of multisourcing and multisourcing networks. Differing theories of the firm are used to identify how supply chains have now evolved to supply networks and their ultimate impact on IT sourcing practices.

REFERENCES

Gerencser, M., Lee, R. V., Napolitano, F., & Kelly, C. (2008). *Megacommunities: How Leaders of Government, Business and Non-Profits Can Tackle Today's Global Challenges Together.* Palgrave Macmillan.

Holcomb, T., & Hitt, M. (2007). Toward a model of strategic outsourcing. *Journal of Operations Management, 25,* 464-481.

ITIL.org. (2007). *Information technology Infrastructure Library.* Retrieved 9/12/07, from http://www.itil.org.uk/

Kepner, C., & Tregoe, B. (1965). *The Rational Manager: A Systematic Approach to Problem Solving and Decision Making.* McGraw-Hill.

Kern, T., & Willcocks, L. (2001). *The Relationship Advantage.* Oxford University Press.

Klein, G. (2000, June 2000). Decisions. *Across the Board, 37.*

Lipshitz, R., Klein, G., & Orasanu, J. (2001). Taking Stock of Naturalistic Decision Making. *Journal of Behavioural Decision Making, 14*, 331-352.

Simon, H. A. (1947). *Administrative Behaviour.* New York: Macmillan.

Simon, H. A. (1979). Rational Decision Making in Business Organizations. *The American Economic Review, 69*(4), 493-513.

Simon, H. A. (1987). Making Management Decisions: the role of intuition and emotion. *The Academy of Management Executive, 1*, 57-64.

Simon, H. A. (2001). Complex Systems: The Interplay of Organizations and Markets in Contemporary Society. *Computational and Mathematical Organizational Theory, 7*(2), 79-85.

Snowden, D. (2002). Complex Acts of Knowing: Paradox and Descriptive Self Awareness. *Journal of Knowledge management, 6*(2).

Snowden, D., & Boone, M. (2007). A Leader's Framework for Decision Making. *Harvard Business Review, November.*

Wang, E., & Chen, J. (2006). The influence of governance equilibrium on ERP project success. *Decision Support Systems, 41*, 708-727.

Weill, P., & Ross, J. W. (2004). *IT Governance.* Boston, MA: Harvard Business School Press.

Williamson, O. (1981). The Economics of Organization: The Transaction Cost Approach. *American Journal of Sociology, 87*(3), 548-576.

Zsambook, C. E., Beach, L. R., & Klein, G. (1992). *A literature Review of Analytical and Naturalistic Decision Making.* Klein Associates.

ENDNOTES

[1] http://en.wikipedia.org/wiki/IT_governance (accessed 11th June 2008)

[2] http://www.isaca.org/Content/ContentGroups/ITGI3/Resources1/Board_Briefing_on_IT_Governance/26904_Board_Briefing_final.pdf (accessed 11th June 2008)

[3] Standards Australia "Corporate governance of information and communications technology" www.standards.com.au

[4] See http://www.isaca.org/

[5] See http://www.itil-officialsite.com/home/home.asp

[6] See http://www.sei.cmu.edu/cmmi/

Chapter III
Multisourcing Networks

So how did multisourcing networks come about?

It is worth taking some time to trace the evolution in business that has brought us to this point of multisourcing networks. In terms of sourcing, one can look through the three eras of pre-industrial, industrial and information/knowledge identified in Figure 8. This helps the reader to gain some insight into the overall trends that are taking place, and therefore hopefully helps to predict what actions one will need to take, to be successful.

Looking back to the pre-industrial era, people were typically employed in agricultural or craft based activities. Their principal means of survival depended on their own labour efforts. Their material input requirements were minimal and prior to the widespread use of monetary exchange procurement were via the barter system. Those individuals who positioned themselves as trade facilitators were often able to build their wealth beyond the norm. Interestingly those individuals were likely to have developed their individual social capital skills, which would continue to be reinforced in a virtuous cycle as their wealth built.

The industrial era was heralded in the late 18th century by machines beginning to supplant human labour. Along with the scientific management techniques introduced by Frederick Taylor, industrialisation brought to sourcing, market based procurement. Procuring firms were now able to play potential suppliers off against each other to achieve the lowest price for inputs and hence lower the cost of

Figure 8. Eras of sourcing

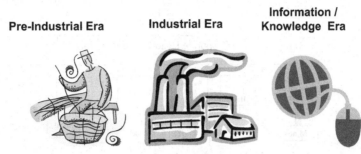

	Pre-Industrial Era	Industrial Era	Information / Knowledge Era
What is sourced?	Basic materials	Supply materials	Products and services
Who from?	From other individuals	Other manufacturers or raw material suppliers	Firms, Individuals, Government Agencies, Internet
How?	Barter / Trade	Procurement contracts	Procurement contracts, Alliances, Agencies

the resulting manufactured product. The scientific method favoured an economic rationalist approach, to the extent that social capital (SC) aspects were minimised or actively removed from the procurement decision. Industrialisation saw the growth of the mega corporation, or conglomerate aimed at "owning" their sources of supply. A typical organisational structure of a large industrial conglomerate is shown in Figure 9.

As conglomerates grew larger decision making became more unwieldy. The concepts of competitive advantage through value chains (Porter, 1985) and business process reengineering (Hammer & Champy, 1993) forced a re-think around what activities the organisation should "own" and what activities should be externally sourced. The result has been a gradual disintegration of many of the major conglomerates and a refocus on their core vertical market while outsourcing all non core activities (Quinn, 1992). Supply chain management was therefore born to manage the cooperation of organisations participating in what might previously have been an internal sourcing process (Poirier, 1999), as illustrated in Figure 10.

The information or knowledge era is a term often applied to the present, where the procurement of services sits alongside physical goods in terms of importance. The growth in firms specialising only in services has been dramatic, with the majority of the wealthiest firms on the world's stock markets now relying on non-physical assets for wealth creation. Services now account for nearly 80% of the USA gross domestic product (Basole & Rouse, 2008; Chesbrough & Spohrer, 2006), a significant proportion being in the IT sector. Powered by the Internet and increased globalisation, options for sourcing, especially for services, exploded. Like

Figure 9. Example of a conglomerate

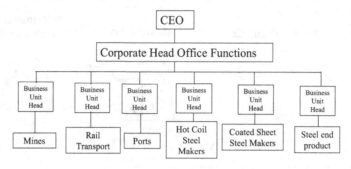

Figure 10. Supply chain management

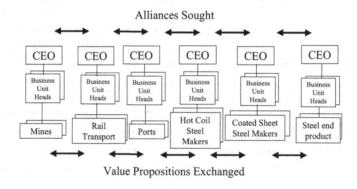

the transition into the industrial era, the major wealth generators increasingly came from the traders or facilitators of value exchanges, more so than those providing the core products. What began as supply chains became supply networks and now value networks and value shops as additional business configurations have become apparent (Allee, 2003; Stabell & Fjeldstad, 1998), facilitated by e-business applications and the Internet. The natural implication from having a network of organisations collaborating within value networks is multisourcing, where organisations will not only be sourcing from multiple organisations but at times working in business partnerships with them. A case in point is the relationship between British Aerospace and its IT outsourcer Computer Sciences Corporation. Both organisations provide services to the defense industry and have now collaborated as alliance partners in winning multi-million dollar contracts.

Case Study

DuPont: Purposeful Multisourcing

Chemicals giant DuPont was already seen to have a highly capable IT function prior to deciding to outsource its IT service requirements to two major global IT providers in Accenture and Computer Sciences Corporation. The 10 year, $4 billion alliance partnership signed in 1997, resulted in some 3,000 DuPont employees being transferred to the outsourcing providers. While DuPont had made the decision that IT was not a core function for the business it wanted to achieve a flexible IT resource capable of supporting a dynamically changing business portfolio and innovative core business solutions, while sustaining best practice cost performance. From the start DuPont decided to use two, rather than a single outsourced provider. It also retained the right to source new project work beyond the two main providers to enable it to keep some competitive tension in the arrangement.

A review of the DuPont outsourcing experience was reported on by Willcocks and Feeny (Winter 2006). Half way through the contract DuPont had been successful in achieving several of its business objectives which included reducing its fixed IT costs by 40%, gaining access to a broader skill base, some increases in speed of service and flexibility and modest cost reductions. A retained IT staff of some 70 people dealt with strategic planning, architecture, security, emerging technologies and enterprise wide projects. A further 47 staff were allocated to managing the outsourcing alliance. Several hundred additional employees were providing regional and specialised services oversight.

Despite the early gains made, DuPont began to question whether it had outsourced too much of its technical and management expertise. Willcocks and Feeny applied their own IT capability framework which confirmed some of DuPont's concerns. Specifically the operational capabilities for managing technology work, contract facilitation and relationship building were under resourced, resulting in local CIO's having to deflect their attention away from more strategic, business oriented activities. The longer term impact was that the strategic partnering of IT and the core businesses was being negatively impacted and the potential for innovative IT driven solutions reduced.

This case study shows that DuPont did many things right in setting up their outsourcing alliances. From the start DuPont had adopted a multi-sourcing strategy. However, by under resourcing in some key operational areas, their ability to sustain IT leadership and governance, technical planning and informed sourcing was being compromised. As organisations move more strongly into multi-sourcing arrangements they will no doubt learn the lessons of DuPont in the need to "right size" their internal IT capabilities, which invariably will mean retaining more, rather than less.

Figure 11. The changing face of DuPont (Reproduced with permission)

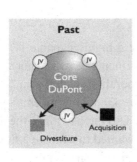
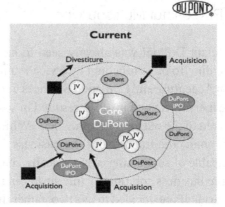

The increased reliance on alliances and joint ventures brings into question traditional definitions of what constitutes "the firm". Figure 11 provides a perspective from one of DuPont's executives as to how the company has evolved from a typical large conglomerate to a firm which now primarily achieves its business objectives through partnerships.

This short account of the business evolution toward multisourcing sheds a little light onto why it has happened. To gain some insight into the reasons for this evolution it is necessary to explore some of the fundamental organisational theories at play. The next section explores the socio-economic theories that underpin the business evolution described above.

SOCIO-ECONOMICS AND THE THEORY OF THE FIRM

This section provides a review of the research literature around the different theories of the firm. Whereas the industrial revolution saw economic rationalism persist over sociological issues, the increasing relevance of relationship networks has brought the sociological aspects back into focus. The interdependence of sociological and economic themes can be traced back to prehistoric times. Karl Polanyi was an economist who studied economies throughout history (Polanyi, 1944). According to Polanyi, every human society has had some form of economy. Early tribal economies were governed by social norms of reciprocity and redistribution. Humans sought material gains to increase their social standing within the tribe, more so than for personal gain. Polanyi therefore claims that early economies were driven by social relationships, in contrast to today's economies which are largely driven by markets. Markets themselves are not devoid of sociological dimensions. White (1981, p518)

Figure 12. "Theory of the Firm" literature themes

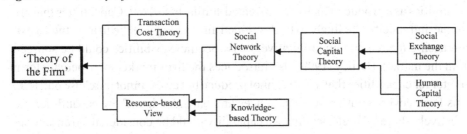

proposes the embedding of economists' neoclassical theory of the firm within a sociological view of markets by claiming: *"Markets are self-reproducing social structures among specific cliques of firms and other actors who evolve roles from observations of each other's behavior."*

The remainder of this section synthesises the literature related to the theory of the firm into three subsections, as identified in Figure 12: selected fundamental theory of the firm literature; theory of the firm from a Social Capital (SC) perspective; and theory of the firm from an intellectual or knowledge perspective.

The fundamental element of the economic market is the transaction between a buyer and a seller. It is therefore not surprising that an economic theory based on Transaction Cost Economics (TCE) plays a foundational role in discussions of markets and economies (Williamson, 1981). Using TCE as an anchor, a selection of fundamental studies representing both the transaction cost and resource-based views of the firm are reviewed with the intent of demonstrating where a Corporate SC theory might fit within the theory of the firm literature.

The fundamental premise of TCE is that the boundaries of the firm will be determined by the relative cost of a transaction. If a transaction involving the development of a new product is being considered, a decision as to whether to make the product inside the firm or source it from outside the firm will be determined by the relative cost of completing the transaction. Conditions that would favour internal production would include the uniqueness or specificity of the product. The more complex the transaction with the market, the more costly it will be to govern the transaction using market mechanisms, in contrast to the authoritarian procedures existing within a firm's hierarchy. Williamson (1981) identifies that transactions are undertaken by human agents who are susceptible to bounded rationality (Simon, 1979) and opportunism. The more uncertain the environment the more susceptible the human agent is. Simon argues for the effectiveness of hierarchies in governing decision-making under uncertainty by reducing the negative impacts of opportunism.

Barney (1999) extends Williamson's (1981) view of TCE to include firm capabilities as a product which can be treated similarly to TCE. Capabilities that are unique and specific are likely to be developed and kept inside the firm as the cost of purchasing them could be prohibitive. Less specific capabilities could be sourced from the market. Barney (1999) also introduces the firm/market intermediate form to cater for capabilities that a firm cannot produce but also cannot purchase outright. This form covers joint ventures, alliances and partnerships where capabilities are effectively shared. While acquiring a capability could be considered a transaction, a capability itself is a resource that constitutes a different view of a firm (Barney, 1991). Beyond capabilities are a whole suite of firm resources, some of which are largely intangible. Barney counts as a source of competitive advantage a firm's unique vision and purpose that could have been established over generations, or a unique suite of capabilities. These are called socially complex resources and are unique, interdependent, immobile and heterogeneous. Implicit firm-specific routines (Nelson & Winter, 1982) are included in Barney's resource-based view of the firm. The resource-based view has also been contrasted with a product view of the firm. Wernerfelt (1984) argues that strategies formulated with a focus on firm resources such as brands, technical knowledge, procedures, machinery and capital, provide a much richer field for designing competitive strategies than those that focus purely on a product portfolio.

Zingales (2000) has explored the impact of the changing nature of the firm away from a reliance on physical assets to corporate finance. The traditional corporate finance view of the firm is a nexus of contracts. This is consistent with TCE where a contract represents a transaction. However, Zingales (2000) expands this view to include implicit as well as explicit contracts. Once implicit contracts are introduced into the discussion, reputation effects are introduced that might impact implicit contracts. Once reputation is introduced then other organisational assets or capital are introduced, including the unique Human capital (HC) that is necessary to develop the growth options that eventually result in higher market values for the firm. Zingales's (2000) arguments essentially support Barney's (1991) resource-based view of the firm.

One criticism of TCE is that it assumes that hierarchical governance mechanisms are based on authoritarian control. Ghoshal and Moran (1996) challenge this view as unrealistic and potentially leading to bad management practice. They introduce the importance of social controls as a balance against rational controls. Additionally, with Zingales (2000), Ghoshal and Moran (1996) challenge the view of humans as automata under hierarchical control to operate physical assets, and promote human capability to exploit a firm's unique purpose, diversity and innovation as a resource in its own right.

The above literature has focused on characteristics of the firm whether they are based on a transaction or a resource-based view. The market view has simply been seen as those transactions or resources that aren't suited to being managed inside the firm. Baker (1984) focuses on the market and, in particular, on the social characteristics of the national securities market. Baker sees that the concepts of bounded rationality and opportunism that underpin TCE are also present with marketplace actors. Actors working in uncertain environments where price volatility is high will tend to trade with those in closer proximity to themselves. Also, opportunism in the marketplace is one of the causes of market price volatility. The importance of Baker's (1984) work is that it introduces the concept of the market as a network which is subject to all of the social norms, controls and patterns that one might also find inside the firm. As firms become less hierarchical and more networked, one can see a situation in which the blurring of the boundaries of a firm become more acute as social structures become prevalent inside the firm, between firms and in the open marketplace.

THEORY OF THE FIRM FROM A SOCIAL CAPITAL PERSPECTIVE

SC theories of the firm build directly on the perceived shortcomings of TCE. The concept of embeddedness, meaning that all economic actions are embedded in social constructs, suggests a theory of the firm that centres on social, rather than rational hierarchical structures (Carroll & Stanfield, 2003; Granovetter, 1985; K. Polanyi, 1944). In critiquing Williamson's (1981) interpretation of TCE, Granovetter (1985) highlights the over-estimation of the efficacy of hierarchies within firms and the degree to which managers can make individual rational decisions in the absence of social interaction. Granovetter's (1985) claim that all economic transactions are embedded in social constructs is a form of colonising economics as a branch of sociology. This contrasts with claims that economic theorists are colonising disciplines like sociology as a sub-branch of economics (Fine, 2001). This simply continues the debate and interplay between sociology and economic theorists that can be traced back to the roots of sociology and the works of Durkheim and Marx (Carroll & Stanfield, 2003).

A social capitalist's view of the firm could therefore define the firm as a "nexus of relationships". The relationships internal to the firm could be defined in terms of social exchange theory whereby micro-level dyadic exchange relationships form larger networks of exchange relationships at a macro level (Blau, 1964; Cook, 1982). Lin's, (1982) social resource theory for instrumental action speaks of the resources embedded in one's social network. However, Lin's (1982) vision is a social structure which is hierarchical in nature, with actors higher up in the hierarchy having greater levels of social influence on others lower in the hierarchy for resource accumulation (i.e. instrumental action). While the "nexus of relationships view" of the firm might provide a viable theory of operations within the firm, a potential weakness is in how such a theory can explain the boundary conditions separating what is internal and what is external to the firm. Pioneering SC proponent James Coleman (Coleman, 1988, pS98), in his statement *"purposive organizations can be actors ("corporate actors") just as a persons can, relations among corporate actors can constitute social capital for them as well"*, does not distinguish between individual actors and corporate actors (i.e. firms).

The assignment of SC to the collective of individuals who constitute a firm is generally accepted in the literature without critique. The SC definitions and literature move comfortably between analyses of SC at a personal and organisational level, inside the firm to outside the firm, and into marketplaces as social structures (Adler & Kwon, 2002; Alder & Kwon, 2002). Little attention is given to potential difficulties with assigning essentially human attributes of individuals to a potentially heterogeneous collective, being the firm. Rather than being able to define a boundary to the firm, SC theory tends to further blur the boundaries. If anything, SC theory identifies the interconnectedness of firms even in the open market environment with common studies on interlocking corporate directorates (Burt, 1978/9; Fennema & Schijf, 1978/9) and the marketplace as a network (Baker, 1984; White, 1981). Coleman (1998) also introduces a theory around how SC facilitates HC using an example of how SC facilitates a lowering of the dropout rate of high-school students.

Yli-Renko et al. (2001) argue that the relational view is an extension of the resource-based view. Capabilities embedded in difficult-to-imitate networks of relationships provide the same competitive advantages described by the resource-based view. The ability to form unique relationships can be viewed as a capability and a resource to be drawn on and therefore has parallels to the resource-based view, even if it is not totally consistent with it (Marti, 2004). However, differences occur in that the capabilities and resources described in the resource-based view can be seen as wholly contained within the firm, whereas the relationships that form the basis of SC are not necessarily wholly contained in the firm. In fact, the relationships which form a unique capability could be shared between firms.

The intermediate level between the firm and the market introduced by Barney (1999) to cater for hybrid situations like joint ventures and alliances is squarely where SC theory is placed. Therefore, the relationship that exists between firms in an alliance or joint venture structure differs in nature to those that exist within the firm. One would anticipate that the degree of explicit purpose and alignment inside the firm would be stronger than what might exist within an alliance or joint venture arrangement. Barney (1999) identifies the boundary between the firm and an intermediary structure as being determined by the inability of the firm to appropriate capabilities through direct acquisition. A similar argument around the appropriation of relationships or SC is more difficult to determine.

In summary, SC theories' contribution to the theory of the firm is one of blurring the boundaries between what is inside or outside the firm. The network of exchange relationships that constitute SC can move from inside the firm to between firms and into the marketplace. There are obstacles to the free movement of SC from inside the firm to within alliance partnerships and out into the marketplace, though current SC theory does little to identify them. However, there are parallels with a resource-based view of the firm, in that relationships and the ability to form them can be seen as a competitive capability and resource.

Case Study

Cisco Networking: Not Just Hardware

Cisco is famous for its networking products, products which took it at the height of the dotcom boom, to be the world's most valuable company by market capitalisation. What is perhaps less known is Cisco's partnering capabilities. From its earliest beginnings in the 1980s, founders Sandy Lerner and Len Bosack had viewed their early customers as partners by allowing them to make changes to the source code for their routers. A form of open source development, the partnering perspective allowed Cisco to achieve a loyal client base and the beginnings of the journey to what Cisco is today. In the intervening years Cisco has fine tuned its partnering skills. As well as leading to several high profile and profitable acquisitions of firms like Stratcom, Scientific-Atlanta, Linksys and Webex, it also operates a highly successful alliance program. More than 10% of the company's revenue is now derived from strategic alliances with ROI of more than 30%. Cisco has developed a number of leading practices in the management of alliances. It was also an early adopter of the Value network analysis(VNA) technique for understanding the network ecosystem within which the company operates (Allee, 2003).

As an active member of the IT marketplace network, Cisco has undoubtedly had to build its Corporate SC in order to achieve the alliances success it has enjoyed. Being a large and financially successful firm clearly contributes substantially to its social standing in the market place. However, despite its dominance in the market and its financial clout, Cisco concedes that not all the technical knowledge that it might need will exist in-house or be easily bought. Corporate SC also requires the appropriate market place relationships and an attitude for sustainable win-win partnerships, to be a truly valued asset.

THEORY OF THE FIRM FROM AN INTELLECTUAL OR KNOWLEDGE-BASED PERSPECTIVE

The models of intellectual capital (IC) that typically deconstruct IC into sub-classes of human capital (HC), internal capital (INC) and external capital (EC) or relational capital, were largely inspired by the work of Swedish scholars who were looking for a better accounting mechanism for service companies (Edvinsson et al., 1997; Sveiby, 1997). Over time this form of analysis has been taken to constitute a theory of IC. This is largely not a theory at all, but simply the deconstruction of a complex concept to aid understanding and analysis. Several authors have argued that the act of deconstruction in fact hides the integrative power of HC, INC and relational capital, which in itself is the power and value of IC (Andriessen, 2001; Sanchez et al., 2000). Attempts to build a theory of IC or intangible capital have been somewhat preliminary. Sanchez et al. (2000) have proposed a theory for the management of intangibles based on their identification, measurement and monitoring. However, the theory is not targeted and contributes little to an intellectual or intangible theory of the firm. Other authors have identified the linkage between IC and Knowledge management (KM) as one of a "breadth of view". Largely, KM has been heavily tied to an internal "inside the firm" view, whereas IC promotes an enterprise view of the firm and the role it plays in its environment, be it a marketplace or society at large (Petty & Guthrie, 1999; Wiig, 1997).

The interchangeable terms of IC and intangible capital can also cause conceptual problems. The term "Intellectual capital" ties neatly with "Knowledge management", both terms sharing a connection with human cognition. The term "Intangible Capital" is more readily linked to an accountancy interpretation which incorporates KM, as well as non-intellectual assets like brands, trademarks and reputation, and therefore could be seen as a superset of KM. That said, the literature provides far more coverage on knowledge-based theories of the firm than IC or IA theories of the firm. Knowledge-based theories of the firm will therefore be explored from here on.

A knowledge-based theory of the firm has been proposed as an extension to the resource-based view of the firm (Barney, 1991). In defining the unique capabilities or resources of the firm, specialised knowledge or know-how that is unique to the firm is proposed. A survey of CEOs found that employee know-how and reputation were viewed as the most critical intangible resources for the firm (Hall, 1992). Such know-how is seen as valuable, rare and not easy to replicate and use, and therefore meets the criteria proposed by Barney (1991) as a competitive resource. Firm-specific factors of the degree of informal networking, and individual and firm-level research and development, have been found to most positively impact knowledge creation inside firms (Soo *et al.*, 2002). In fact, it has been argued that only intangible resources can meet all the criteria proposed by Barney (1991) therefore leaving the intangibles-based theory of the firm as the only viable interpretation of the resource-based view of the firm (Sanchez et al., 2000).

From here, several lines of argument are presented as to how knowledge is used to form a theory of the firm. Grant (1996) identifies the integration of specialised knowledge as the defining capability of a firm. Drawing on the notion of explicit and tacit knowledge (M. Polanyi, 1967), Grant (1996) identifies explicit knowledge as more readily transferable and therefore not a defining capability of the firm. However, tacit knowledge is not readily transferred, so it is the capability of the firm to integrate and/or share specialised tacit knowledge that is the defining capability. The boundary of the firm is therefore dictated by ease of transfer or integration of specialised knowledge. The degree of tacitness and teachability of knowledge has been found to determine firm boundaries within multinational corporations (Kogut & Zander, 1993), reinforcing Grant's (1996) theory. Grant's (1996) knowledge-based theory also takes the position that knowledge creation only occurs with the individual and therefore forms a capability to coordinate and encourage cooperation between individuals as a competitive resource. Grant (1996) is more concerned with knowledge application than creation, while other authors are more comfortable with a view of knowledge creation being either an individual or a collective pursuit (Nelson & Winter, 1982; Spender, 1996).

Spender's (1996, p59) knowledge-based view of the firm is a *"dynamic, evolving, quasi autonomous system of knowledge production and application"*. This action-oriented view of knowledge is in contrast to the resource or asset/object view of knowledge. The boundary conditions identified by Spender (1996) are less crisp, identifying all management decisions in a dynamic action-oriented firm as being potentially firm boundary affecting. This is contrasted with static non-action-oriented firms whose boundaries become obvious. In contrast to Spender's (1996) dynamic view of the firm is the more evolutionary perspective of Nelson & Winter (1982), who identify the development of organisationally specific routine as collectively developed knowledge that constitutes the core capability of the firm. Such routines, which are tightly intertwined with the culture and tradition of the firm and hence difficult to replicate outside the firm, are not developed overnight, with some taking generations to emerge.

What is common amongst each of the perspectives on a knowledge-based theory of the firm is the view that it is the tacit and/or implicit knowledge that defines the firm. Such knowledge may be used to generate explicit knowledge for competitive use, using integrative and synthesis capabilities identified in a knowledge creation spiral (Nonaka & Takeuchi, 1995). It is not the explicit knowledge or information ownership that defines the firm but the capabilities to generate, share, integrate and combine specialist knowledge that fundamentally defines the firm's competitive position.

The other impact of a knowledge-based view of the firm is on decisions around organisational design. Transaction cost theory took the view that the internal structure of a firm is hierarchical and therefore directed largely through authority from the top down. This view was promoted by Simon (1947) as a consequence of his theories on bounded rationality and how humans deal with uncertainty. The hierarchy, it was argued, was the most efficient means for making decisions under uncertain complex conditions; collating and escalating decisions up through the hierarchy to come up with a "satisficing", rather than optimal, solution. The development of thinking underpinning the knowledge-based view of the firm moves from a focus on individual decision-making capabilities to one where knowledge is co-opted from multiple sources to support decision making. The knowledge-based view of the firm goes hand in hand with a view of the firm as a social community, with knowledge needing to be co-opted rather than conscripted (Spender, 1996). Spender (1996) proposes that managers are becoming less rule makers and employees less rule followers, with both tending towards facilitation of common goals they have agreed upon. If specialist knowledge is not always contained at the top of the hierarchy, it is argued that coordination might be better served by a flatter team-based structure where specialised knowledge could be flexibly shared by a multi-team membership of specialists (Grant, 1996).

In summary, a theory of the firm from the intellectual and intangibles perspective largely centres on knowledge-based theories of the firm. Knowledge is seen as a competitive capability and resource, consistent with the resource-based view of the firm, but extends this view by articulating the how, what and why a resource such as knowledge provides a unique competitive advantage, and how it defines the boundaries of the firm. It also introduces a process view of a capability, in contrast to seeing a resource as purely a tangible asset. Treating knowledge as an action-oriented, dynamic resource introduces a further dimension to the task of defining a theory of the firm. The act of coordinating, integrating and co-opting knowledge has implications for the organisational structures that are best suited to its use. The view that firms are simply hierarchies is challenged by the knowledge-based view of the firm.

The following schematic illustrated in Figure 13 identifies the main themes around theories of the firm relevant to this review. The concept of human constraints around bounded rationality in dealing in uncertain environments helped to inspire the development of transaction cost theory. The resource-based theory acknowledged that capabilities and resources enrich the view on what constitutes the firm. Building on the resource-based view, two schools of thought have independently emerged, one focusing on a knowledge-based view and another around SC. The increasing reliance on intangibles within firms will ensure that the knowledge and SC based views will endure for some time. Surprisingly, there is scant evidence in the literature

Figure 13. Theories of the firm literature themes

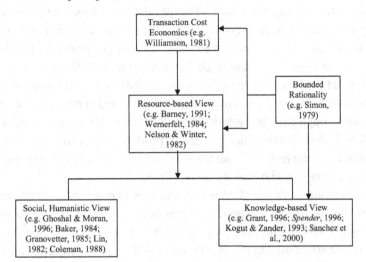

of integration between the SC view and the knowledge-based view, despite their obvious interdependencies. The focus on tacit or implicit knowledge and how it is integrated and deployed internally and externally to a firm is achievable only when the social context is addressed. While the literature from both schools acknowledges the importance of knowledge and social context respectively, the depth of analysis is minimal. The general integration of these two schools of thought is a focus for this book.

The underpinning theories of the firm play an important role in this review. This is evidenced by what is currently playing out with supply chains and their evolution toward supply networks, which is addressed in the next section. A more detailed treatment of Knowledge management, Intellectual capital and Social Capital are provided in Chapters IV and V.

SUPPLY CHAIN EVOLUTION

It is not the intent of this section to review in detail the supply chain management literature. However, having established the fundamental theoretical bases for the growing interdependency between firms, it is useful to understand how the procurement function has evolved through to a supply chain management function and now a multisourcing network function.

The term "supply chain management" (SCM) was developed in the 1980s in response to the need for organisations to manage and integrate business processes from the original source material or service provider right through to the eventual consumer. As sources of supply began to increasingly move beyond the walls of the organisations, the coordination and eventual optimisation of the supply chain was being driven more by partnerships and collaboration, than dictated by a single member of the chain. The automotive industries have been seen as leaders in the art of procurement and now supply chain management. Indicative of the change from contracted procurement to collaborative supply is Toyota's approach to how it now works with its suppliers. Toyota has demonstrated superior supply network performance through embracing tight and collaborative learning networks with its key suppliers. Toyota shares its highly regarded production expertise with its suppliers in recognition that the improved performance of its suppliers will eventually flow through to the company (Dyer & Nobeoka, 2000).

What is now apparent for SCM practitioners is that achieving integration and optimisation across the supply chain is ultimately more about managing networks of relationships between interdependent suppliers than a mathematical formulation. The challenge is best articulated by Charles Poirier's SCM maturity model (Poirier, 1999; Poirier & Bauer, 2001), as shown in Figure 14. The level 1 "Enterprise Integration" phase accurately describes the tasks that an organisation may undertake prior to releasing an outsourcing procurement tender. In essence, prior to undertaking any outsourcing activities, an organisation needs to, at a minimum, gain agreement from its internal business units on what can be outsourced and what benchmark costs the services would need to achieve to meet the cost reduction targets. The focus at this stage is nearly always on cost, and prospective vendors are largely judged on this dimension. The second level of maturity has been labeled the "Corporate Excellence" phase. The key differential from the previous phase is the introduction of a continuous improvement ethic. Using techniques like TQM, business process re-engineering, benchmarking and Six Sigma, the enterprise is looking to drive out cost adding variations in the business processes of both acquisition and use of IT services. Often cost improvements are gained by moving cost of asset responsibility outside the organisation, for example, having vendors take financial responsibility for the IT asset. The objective of organisations at this level of maturity is to ensure that their own business is optimised for performance, perhaps at times to the detriment of their partners and therefore also potentially to the longer term sustainability of their own performance.

Poirier identified the passage from level 2 to level 3 as a "cultural wall". Those to the right of the wall have come to the realisation that to fully satisfy their customers and ultimate consumers, they need to expand their supply chain thinking from "what's best for me". Through partnerships with those with complementary strengths, they can create value far beyond what is possible with an internal only view. Poirier speaks of "value chain constellations", where mutual efforts and joint resources can achieve closer to an optimal supply chain result than any single firm, no matter how large or entrenched in a market.

Figure 14. SCM maturity (Reproduced with permission, Poirier, 1999)

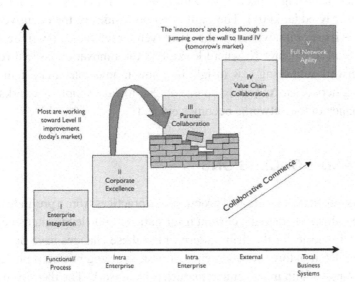

From an Information Technology Outsourcing (ITO) perspective this sows the seeds of multisourcing. To achieve a close to optimal supply chain performance it is highly unlikely that sourcing from a single vendor will be successful, hence the emergence of "best of breed" IT procurement. However, unlike a traditional manufacturing supply chain, IT outsourcing is mostly about services. The migration from level 3 to level 4 could be seen as the migration from partnerships as a "one to many" relationship to networks of relationships, which are inherently "many to many". In other words, as well as considering the single client / vendor relationship, the client also considers the relationships between the vendors that it chooses to bring into its organisation to provide services. Currently few firms could be considered to be at this phase, but not for the want of trying, as evidenced by the BP Exploration case study described in the previous chapter.

The final phase described in the Poirier framework is labeled "Full Network Agility". This phase could be interpreted in the IT sense as the achievement of true innovation through the network of partners. The perceived lack of innovation by vendors has plagued outsourcing contracts since their inception (Overby, 2007). Using the Poirier framework one can see why this is so. Essentially most IT outsourcing clients are operating at level 1 or level 2 where operating excellence is the main driver. The vendors are cooperating by similarly driving out variation through a focus on standardised procedures and behaviours of their staff. Client expectations for innovation are jumping right to level 5, having not been through the nurturing intervening phases with its vendors as true partners. Vendors for their part are making promises or setting expectations with respect to innovation that they are not able to deliver (Gedda, 2007). The fault is on both sides of the client/vendor relationship. The issue of innovation in the client /vendor relationship will be dealt with in more detail in Chapter X, where looking at the innovation issue through the lens of a network will bring new insight into how innovation can be achieved in multisourcing networks. As supply chains evolve toward supply networks the issue of governance of the networks becomes evident.

SUMMARY AND CONCLUSIONS

This chapter has traced the evolution of procurement practices from a pre-industrial era through the industrial era to the current information / knowledge intensive era. The fundamental theories of the firm underpinning these changes have been addressed in some detail before the emergence of multisourcing has been placed in the frame of a supply chain management maturity framework. The theories of the firm analysis identified that transaction cost economics is an insufficient theory to explain what we are seeing in today's markets, and that the resource based theory of the firm is more applicable to the understanding of today's markets. The increasing separation between the market valuation and accounting valuations of firms today provides strong evidence of the tangible value that may be attributable to intangible non-physical assets. What is yet to be addressed is the identification of the non physical resources that are affecting current firm valuations and their sourcing practices.

The next chapter is devoted to exploring the intangible resources that are driving firm valuations and business practices today. It is entitled "The Intelligent Enterprise" in recognition of J.B. Quinn's (1992) influential publication of the same title. As well as reviewing Quinn's key concepts around the burgeoning service economy and knowledge as a core competency, the chapter explores how his concepts of Knowledge management and Intellectual capital have played out in the nearly two decades since this work was published.

REFERENCES

Adler, P., & Kwon, S.-W. (2002). Social Capital: Prospects for a New Concept. *Academy of Management Review, 27*(1), 17-40.

Alder, P., & Kwon, S.-W. (2002). Social Capital: Prospects for a New Concept. *Academy of Management Review, 27*(1), 17-40.

Allee, V. (2003). *The Future of Knowledge: Increasing Prosperity through Value Networks*: Butterworth-Heinemann.

Baker, W. (1984). The Social Structure of a National Securities market. *American Journal of Sociology, 89*(4), 775-811.

Barney, J. (1991). Firm Resources and Sustained Competitive Advantage. *Journal of Management, 17*(1), 99-120.

Barney, J. (1999). How a Firm's Capabilities Affect Boundary Decisions. *Sloan Management Review* (pp. 137-145).

Basole, R., & Rouse, W. (2008). Complexity of service value networks: Conceptualization and empirical investigation. *IBM Systems Journal, 47*(1), 53-70.

Burt, R. (1978/9). A Structural Theory of Interlocking Corporate Directorates. *Social Networks, 1*, 415-435.

Carroll, M., & Stanfield, J. R. (2003). Social Capital, Karl Polanyi, and American Social and Institutional Economics. *Journal of Economic Issues, 37*(2), 397-403.

Chesbrough, H., & Spohrer, J. (2006). A Research Manifesto for Services Science. *Communications of the ACM, 49*(7), 35-40.

Fennema, M., & Schijf, H. (1978/9). Analysing Interlocking Directorates: Theory and Methods. *Social Networks, 1*, 297-332.

Gedda, R. (2007). Customs CIO throws cold water on vendor "innovation". Retrieved 2/12/07, from http://www.computerworld.com.au/index.php?id=1422765697

Ghoshal, S., & Moran, P. (1996). Bad for Practice: A critique of the transaction cost theory. *Academy of Management Review, 21*(1), 13-47.

Granovetter, M. (1985). Economic Action and Social Structure: The Problem of Embeddedness. *American Journal of Sociology, 91*(3), 481-510.

Grant, R. (1996). Toward a Knowledge-Based Theory of the Firm. *Strategic Management Journal, 17*(Winter Special Issue) 109-122.

Hall, R. (1992). The Strategic Analysis of Intangible Resources. *Strategic Management Journal, 13*, 135-144.

Hammer, M., & Champy, J. (1993). *Reengineering the Corporation: A Manifesto for Business Revolution.* New York: HarperCollins.

Kogut, B., & Zander, U. (1993). Knowledge of the firm and the evolutionary theory of the multinational corporation. *Journal of International Business Studies, 24*(4).

Marti, J. M. V. (2004). Social capital benchmarking system. *Journal of Intellectual capital, 5*(3), 426-442.

Nelson, R., & Winter, S. (1982). *An Evolutionary Theory of Economic Change.* Cambridge, MA: Harvard University Press.

Nonaka, I., & Takeuchi, H. (1995). *The Knowledge Creating Company.* Oxford, New York: Oxford University Press.

Overby, S. (2007). *What Price Innovation?* Retrieved 2/12/07, from http://www.cio.com.au/index.php?id=477547616

Petty, R., & Guthrie, J. (1999). Managing intellectual capital: From theory to Practice. *Australian CPA, 69*(7), 18-20.

Poirier, C. (1999). *Advanced Supply chain management*: Berrett-Koehler.

Poirier, C., & Bauer, M. (2001). *E-Supply Chain: Using the Internet to Revolutionize Your Business*: Berrett-Koehler Publishers.

Polanyi, K. (1944). *The Great Transformation: The Political and Economic origins of our Time.* Boston: Beacon Press.

Polanyi, M. (1967). *The Tacit Dimension.* New York: Doubleday.

Porter, M. (1985). *Competitive Advantage: Creating and Sustaining Superior Performance.* New York: The Free Press.

Quinn, J. B. (1992). *intelligent enterprise: A Knowledge and Service Based Paradigm for Industry.* Free Press.

Simon, H. A. (1947). *Administrative Behaviour.* New York: Macmillan.

Simon, H. A. (1979). Rational Decision Making in Business Organizations. *The American Economic Review, 69*(4), 493-513.

Soo, C. W., Devinney, T. M., & Midgley, D. F. (2002). *Knowledge Creation in Organisations: Exploring Firm and Context Specific Effects.* Fontainebleau: Insead.

Spender, J. C. (1996). Making Knowledge the Basis of a Dynamic Theory of the Firm. *Strategic Management Journal, 17 (winter Special issue)*, 45-62.

Stabell, C., & Fjeldstad, O. (1998). Configuring Value for Competitive Advantage: on Chains, Shops, and Networks. *Strategic Management Journal, 19*, 413-437.

Wernerfelt, B. (1984). A Resource based View of the Firm. *Strategic Management Journal, 5*, 171-180.

White, H. (1981). Where do Markets Come From? *American Journal of Sociology, 87*(3), 517-547.

Wiig, K. (1997). Integrating Intellectual Capita and Knowledge management. *Long Range Planning, 30*(3), 399-405.

Willcocks, L., & Feeny, D. (Winter 2006). IT outsourcing and Core Capabilities: Challenges and lessons at DuPont. *Information Systems Management* (pp. 49-56).

Williamson, O. (1981). The Economics of Organization: The Transaction Cost Approach. *American Journal of Sociology, 87*(3), 548-576.

Zingales, L. (2000). In Search of New Foundations. *The Journal of Finance, LV*(4), 1623-1653.

Chapter IV
The Intelligent Enterprise

J.B. Quinn's influential book on *The Intelligent Enterprise* was published in 1992 and joined a small cadre of scholars and practitioners reacting to the growth in the services sector and the decline of traditional manufacturing as the dominant source of employment. In 1992, the Swedish Coalition of Service Industries[1] established a project entitled the "Valuation of Service Companies", in recognition of the need to develop more appropriate valuation and reporting mechanisms for firms whose major assets were intangible. The genesis of this activity can be traced back to the 1980s and the work on the "invisible balance sheet" by the Swedish KONRAD group, several of whose members are credited with pioneering the concepts behind Intellectual capital (IC) reporting and management. The publishing of the "Valuation of Service Companies" report provided the basic framework on which subsequent researchers and business practitioners developed IC reports[2]. This report describes a "new annual report" with four key indicators: market position; human resources/ knowledge; structural value; and financial indicators.

At the time of writing *The Intelligent Enterprise*, Quinn quoted figures showing some 77% of all employment in the USA was in the services sector and that even in the Manufacturing sector, 65-75% of jobs were service related. In the intervening period, the trends identified by Quinn and the Scandinavian researchers have continued. Quinn argues convincingly that in the services economy competitive advantage comes from "best in class" competencies. For firms to optimise their performance, they should stop undertaking activities in which they are not considered to be "best in class", but instead outsource those activities to those who are. Unlike the manufacturing firm, whose links to external entities are typically supply chain oriented, the services company's links to external partners are more network oriented. The outsourcing relationship may be both a supply based one, as well as an alliance. For example Computer Sciences Corporation (CSC) is an outsource provider of IT services to British Aerospace Systems (BAE).It is also an alliance partner for generating new business for both organisations in the Defence industry market, for which both firms can claim "best in class" expertise.

In terms of organisational structures Quinn also speaks of the "inverted organisation". In contrast to the traditional organisational hierarchy with the CEO at the top and the "workers" as the base with instructions filtering from top to bottom, the services organisation should have the customer facing workers at the top, with the layers of management providing "support" to these workers.

While in practice, the services company CEO no doubt still retains hierarchical power and direction over the customer facing staff, the image of the inverted organisation identifies the changing nature of management. Unlike factory workers, the customer facing staff in a services firm is the lens through which customers assess a firm. The reputational assets of the firm that contribute significantly to its value are largely in their hands. This staff is also in the best position to provide customer feedback on the firm's performance. Therefore the role of management becomes more focused on supporting and facilitating staff performance rather than purely providing directions and instructions. Knowledge sharing both up, down and across the organisation becomes a critical activity in the services firm, hence the emphasis on Knowledge management. The changing nature of management will impact on the style of governance that is appropriate. One would anticipate that the style of governance appropriate for a manufacturing firm may therefore not necessarily be as appropriate to the services firm.

During the 1990s the field of Knowledge management (KM) emerged to build on the work of these pioneers. Substantial bases of scholarly work around KM,

Figure 15. The "inverted" organisation

including several dedicated academic journals on the topic, have emerged. In the business world KM experienced the peak of the typical hype curve toward the end of the 1990's with many organisations appointing "Chief Knowledge Officers" and dedicating substantial funds to KM programs.

In parallel with the development of KM a somewhat smaller and focused field emerged around what is typically labeled "Intellectual capital" (IC) or "Intangible Asset Management". In contrast to KM, which is typically adopted inside organisations, IC aims to report on firm performance from an external perspective. A critical driver of this focus was the accounting community, which was becoming concerned that their traditional accounting reports were losing relevance to business executives, as share values began to substantially exceed accounting book values and therefore reduce the balance sheet to an historical report, rather than a tool for managing into the future (Collins *et al.*, 1997; Baruch Lev & Zarowin, 1999; Wallman, 1995).

So what relevance do KM and the intelligent enterprise have to IT Governance? A key theme for this book is the changing nature of the firm from an industrial era where manufacturing businesses dominated along with their top down hierarchical management structures. For this era a top down compliance approach to governance was a good fit. However the emergence of the "intelligent enterprise" flags a greater focus on services, people, competence and knowledge sharing. In this environment potential fit for a top down compliance approach to governance is not guaranteed. In order to better assess how effective governance can be achieved in a services dominated economy it is important to understand the foundations for the knowledge based economy, and that means a closer look at KM and IC.

In this chapter some of the key underpinning theories for KM and IC will be reviewed together with the provision of a series of short case studies to illustrate how the business world has reacted to the developments in KM and IC.

KNOWLEDGE MANAGEMENT

Perhaps the greatest challenge for KM scholars is the shear breadth of topics that KM influences, or is influenced by. The breadth of literature on KM is overwhelming. For this review, KM will be viewed as a substantial suite of literature located under the umbrella of IC/IA (Wiig, 1997).

For an overview, Jashapara's integrated approach to Knowledge management (Jashapara, 2004) is selected. Jashapara approaches the broad topic of Knowledge management through the following knowledge life cycle model: Definitions of KM invariably identify processes like creating, assessing, sharing and leveraging for organisational advantage. KM researchers also invariable acknowledge its multi-

Figure 16. Knowledge management: and integrated approach (adapted from Jashapara, 2004)

disciplinary nature. Therein lays both the power, as an integrating discipline, and the weakness, as a discipline lacking a clear identity. Writings on KM have been drawn from disciplines as broadly spread as anthropology, artificial intelligence, psychology, information science, accounting, philosophy, human resource management, sociology, management strategy and operations research. A framework is necessary to analyse KM, to enable the different disciplinary views to flow through in an ordered fashion.

The Jashapara framework for KM identifies knowledge discovery, knowledge generation, knowledge evaluation, knowledge sharing and leveraging knowledge as the key dimensions. Selected literatures representing these dimensions are discussed in the following sections.

DISCOVERING KNOWLEDGE

Fundamental studies of "knowledge" can be traced back to the early philosophers and the "capture" of ideas and knowledge, initially through oration and story telling, and then to evolving forms of written media. While knowledge has always been important to human development the advent of the post industrial age has been the key driver for the intense interest in KM. Management guru Peter Drucker provided a strong impetus in the business world with his writings on the new knowledge based society:

In this society, knowledge is the primary resource for individuals and for the economy overall. Land, labor, and capital—do not disappear, but they become secondary. (Drucker, 1992p.95)

This was supported by rising separation of market values from firm book values from the late 1970s. A new knowledge based theory of the firm has been proposed by several authors (Grant, 1996; Kogut & Zander, 1993; Spender, 1996). Kogut and Zander call for the boundaries of the firm to be defined by the tacitness of the knowledge that is being transferred. In contrast to the traditional hierarchy, they identify firms as:

Firms are social communities that specialize in the creation and internal transfer of knowledge. (Kogut & Zander, 1993, p.625)

Their empirical research results show that the less codifiable the knowledge of the firm is, the more likely the knowledge will be only transferred within wholly owned operations. Spender (1996) argues for knowledge to be seen as a process rather than an object or resource. In addressing the needs of management Spender argues for management as a facilitation of alliances between independent knowledge creating entities, rather than management as rule makers and employees as rule followers. Like Kogut and Zander, the organisational forms emerging look more like networks than hierarchies. Grant (1996) identifies the unique integration of a firm's specialised knowledge sources as a key competitive differentiator. He argues that the ability to integrate specialised knowledge sources becomes a core competency defining the firm.

What is common to all knowledge based formulations of the firm is that they reflect an organisational structure more fluid and adaptable than the traditional hierarchy. They also identify boundaries of the firm from an operational or pragmatic perspective more so than a legal entity one. This would suggest that firm boundaries are moving faster than the legal system for defining them. The inference is that governance structures in the knowledge era may need to rely on social norms and reciprocal relationships ahead of the availability of legal instruments becoming available to support them. The role of social capital (SC) in governing inter-organisational relationships becomes more visible in such situations.

Beyond theory of the firm discussions, of more fundamental interest to firms has been how knowledge is shared for organisational advantage. Early efforts in KM, often called first generation KM, relied on sharing explicit knowledge or

Figure 17. SECI model (Nonaka and Takeuchi, 1995)

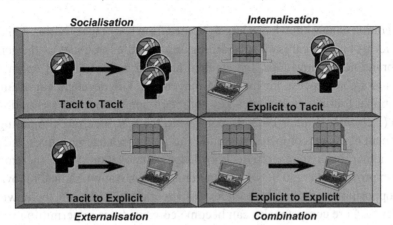

information, using technology to assist with moving information around the firm. Second Generation KM focussed on the conversion of tacit knowledge to explicit knowledge for subsequent distribution (L. Edvinsson & Malone, 1997; Snowden, 2002). Perhaps the best known process model for knowledge conversion was provided by Nonaka and Takeuchi (1995).

The so called SECI model identifies the knowledge conversion spiral for the sharing of knowledge through a tacit to explicit and explicit to tacit conversion spiral. The work was inspired by the earlier work of Polanyi (1967) and his study of the tacit nature of knowledge. This work has since been criticised by Snowden (2002) as understating the complexity of knowledge and knowledge processes. According to Snowden, knowledge is highly contextual and only contains meaning at the point of use. He also argues that *"We can always know more than we can tell, and we will always tell more than we can write down"* (p102).

Despite the management impetus provided by Drucker and others, the successful application of KM has proven elusive to many. The early emphasis on leveraging knowledge was focused on sharing explicit knowledge through the use of information technologies or developing large information repositories through attempts to codify as much tacit knowledge as we could. This approach has provided limited success. Discovering what important knowledge exists is one thing. Successfully generating new knowledge and then assessing, sharing and leveraging this new knowledge requires more than the simple application of Newtonian principles.

GENERATING NEW KNOWLEDGE

The generation of new knowledge largely comes from learning activities. This may take the form of new organisational learning around better practices, or the generation of brand new innovations. Incremental learning and refining of operational practices is a core process for the TQM movement. The development of unique organisational routines is seen as a key source of competitive differentiation for the firm (Nelson & Winter, 1982). In contrast to the KM literature promoting the development of a core competency around unique knowledge resources and processes, another major source of new knowledge is innovation. While incremental process improvement could be seen as incremental innovation, radical innovation and the opportunities it provides paradoxically requires the opposite to knowledge convergence. Core competencies can become core rigidities in permitting radical new ideas and knowledge to infiltrate the closed thinking of a tight knowledge community (Leonard-Barton, 1992). The consequence for management is the requirement to continually challenge the status quo. Fundamentally an emphasis on organisational learning is required. The continual challenge of organisational norms can be viewed as "double loop learning" (Argyris & Schon, 1978).

The organisational learning literature has been conscripted by KM researchers to explain how new forms of knowledge can be generated through an organisational wide approach to learning. Inherently, learning is about sharing experiences from a past activity. Learning is both contextual and dependent on the frames of experiences of the receptor; meaning that the successful communication of shared learning can require quite a range of methods of varying sophistication. At the simpler end are "lessons learned" repositories which typically provide "tips and hints" described for specific situations. "After action reviews" draw from the traditional military practice of post exercise de-briefings (Collison & Parcell, 2001). De-contextualising a situation specific learning into an organisational wide learning has been achieved through the use of archetype characters and systems models to articulate complex cause and effect situations (Senge, 1990). Narrative processes have also been employed to help generate and communicate learning. Learning histories make use of investigative journalistic methods to tease out the subtle experiences and learning from mostly successful activities, for example, completing the design of a new car in record time (Kleiner & Roth, 1997).

EVALUATING KNOWLEDGE

In concert with the generation of new knowledge goes the evaluation of its importance to the organisation. The evaluation of the potential benefits of new knowledge can take a number of forms. The development of a Knowledge management strategy has been promoted by KM practitioners. KM strategies are aimed at identifying the KM activities that are likely to be most beneficial to the firm. Hansen, Nohria et al (1999) identify the classification of KM strategies as either a codification strategy, where efforts are focussed on the conversion of tacit knowledge to explicit forms, or personalisation strategies, where the focus is on leveraging unique areas of expertise. Which strategy to use will depend on whether the firm's business model relies on the franchising of a proven model for growth or the use of unique or boutique skills. The Balanced Scorecard (R. S. Kaplan & Norton, 1992) includes an innovation and learning perspective for aligning activities with an existing strategy. Identifying the critical knowledge supporting decision making within core business processes is another method for evaluating where knowledge has the greatest impact on a business (Lock Lee, 2005).

An alternative view is to use competitive knowledge to directly impact the development of the business strategy, rather than aligning activities with a pre-existing strategy. Centred on the knowledge based view of the firm, business strategies could be developed around the unique integration of specialised pockets of unique expertise (Grant, 1996). A business model based on shared knowledge through alliances (Spender, 1996) suggests a business strategy based on a core competency for leveraging the extended knowledge based resources from a cooperative of partnerships and alliances.

The multi-faceted nature of KM have caused many firms to struggle with definitions and identifying the interdependencies with competing theories, tools and technologies. Binney (2001) provides a KM spectrum which characterises potential KM applications with enabling technologies and tools against the following dimensions:

- Transactional;
- Analytical;
- Asset Management;
- Process;
- Developmental; and
- Innovation and creation.

The proposed use of the spectrum is to assist in either supporting an existing business strategy with selected KM investments or helping to design a business strategy around KM investments.

In summary, evaluation of knowledge and its importance to the firm can be viewed as the selection and alignment of KM activities to a pre-existing business process or strategy. Alternatively, KM activities could be the focus of a business strategy, consistent with a knowledge centred view of the firm.

SHARING KNOWLEDGE

Unlike oil and iron, knowledge and information grow when shared; an idea or skill shared with someone else is not lost but doubled. (K. E. Sveiby, 1997, p.22)

Knowledge management and knowledge sharing could be considered one and the same. While many of the early KM efforts relied on a codification strategy for capturing and sharing knowledge, the most effective means for sharing knowledge has been through human interaction and tacit to tacit knowledge sharing (K. Sveiby, 1996). Human to human knowledge sharing is a socialisation process (Nonaka & Takeuchi, 1995). The motivation for sharing knowledge in this way inside organisations is impacted by the knowledge sharing culture which exists in the firm or organisation. Organisational hierarchies are designed to effectively communicate information across the organisation. It does not follow that knowledge sharing would occur in the same way. In fact, effective knowledge sharing often occurs across the traditional organisation boundaries reflected by the formal hierarchy. Knowledge sharing cultures vary between organisations. The instigation of a formal KM programme is therefore typically accompanied by an organisational change program.

The change process for developing the vision and strategy, and communicating the change vision (Kotter, 1996), is well illustrated by the CEOs of two leading KM adopting organisations. Jim Wolfensen's vision of turning the World Bank into the "Knowledge Bank" was used to launch the successful World Bank KM programme in 1996. Likewise the head of BP, John Browne, articulated his KM vision in the Harvard Business Review (Prokesch, 1997). Both organisations have now followed through on the vision. For both organisations and many others world wide, the major organisation vehicle for achieving effective knowledge sharing has been the Community of Practice.

Figure 18. The knowledge sharing cycle

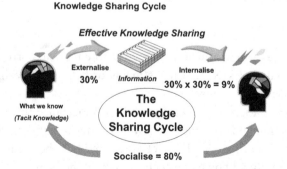

Communities of Practice are groups of people who share a concern, set of problems, or a passion about a topic, and who deepen their knowledge and expertise in this area by interacting on an on-going basis. (Wenger et al., 2002, p.4)

Communities of Practice (CoPs) provide an alternate vehicle for sharing knowledge to the more structured top down knowledge flows of the formal hierarchy. For large globally distributed organisations a CoP is a vehicle for sharing practices across geographies without the need to overcomplicate the formal structures. CoPs are typically non-hierarchical and more collegial in their operations, demonstrating a contrast in culture from the formal hierarchy.The success of CoPs primarily depends on the passion for the practice by the membership. The challenge for organisations is to avoid pushing formalised processes to the extent that little "space" is left for CoPs to develop their practices (Lock Lee, 2005; Seely Brown & Duguid, 2000). A more extended coverage of CoPs is provided in Chapter VII in the study of intra-organisational networks.

Developing successful mechanisms for sharing complex tacit knowledge continues to present significant challenges to organisations. As reflected in Nonaka and Takeuchi's SECI knowledge sharing spiral model, the sharing of tacit knowledge is a socialisation process. How humans communicate with each other about complex topics is invariably through dialogue. The art of story telling has been reinvigorated for the purposes of sharing subtle knowledge or lessons with a broader audience. Denning (2001), identifies with storytelling methods which not only led to more effective knowledge sharing at the World Bank, but also provided the platform for joint discovery of new ideas and knowledge. In a business context, purposeful stories can capture and hold the attention of an audience, be self propagating to develop a life of their own and develop a new language for new forms of understanding (Snowden, 1999, 2002).

In summary, the art of knowledge sharing is seen to be substantially grounded in human to human interaction. The development of an appropriate supporting culture for knowledge sharing is seen as a key requirement for effective knowledge sharing. Communities of Practice are seen as providing the organisational and cultural environment for effective knowledge sharing. Long standing CoPs can develop a heritage of their own, rich with anecdotes and stories reinforcing the tradition of effective knowledge sharing and practice development. Effective knowledge sharing is seen as the key driver of Intellectual capital development (Wiig, 1997; Zhou & Fink, 2003).

LEVERAGING KNOWLEDGE

The Knowledge management literature is substantially focussed on mechanisms inside the firm or organisation. The ultimate impact of leveraging knowledge within an organisation is the impact it has on the environment outside the firm, be it a market place or the community at large. Commonly when one talks about Knowledge management at the firm or organisation level, it is usually in terms of Intellectual capital. In effect, Intellectual capital (IC) represents an enterprise view of knowledge use, whereas Knowledge management represent the more tactical internal view (Wiig, 1997). The linkage between Knowledge management and Intellectual capital therefore could be seen as KM being the internal process that develops the IC assets for external leverage (Zhou & Fink, 2003).

A pragmatic example is the management of intellectual property in the form of patents and licences. Patents are in effect the externalisation of knowledge created inside the firm. They are one of the few forms of knowledge that can be traded in the marketplace in the same way as physical assets. Dow Chemicals was one of the first firms to benefit from a more rigorous process for managing knowledge reflected in its patents, saving millions of dollars spent on sustaining patents of little leverage to the firm (Petrash, 1996).

Case Study

Leveraging Knowledge across a Global Petroleum Company (Balnaves & Busch, 2002)

The petroleum industry has been a ripe field for the successful leveraging of the quite specialised and sophisticated technical knowledge associated with the exploration and production of crude oil. The medium sized, yet global petroleum firm had launched its KM program in the late 1990s with the objective of making a bottom line contribution through the global sharing of specialist knowledge. A number of communities of practice were formed, principally along discipline lines like exploration, production engineering and geophysics. Specific targets were set, for example the production engineering community committed to a 5% above budget profitability increase. This target was achieved through a number of knowledge sharing initiatives. The global deployment of an "expert team" across the major prospects led to above budget recovery rates and hence improved profitability. On the cost side a potential shutdown of a production field due to increases of H_2S in the gas stream was avoided through extensive consultation across the communities of practice. The potential loss of revenue from a shutdown would have been in excess of $700,000 / day.

By introducing shared learning and peer review as routine practices the Communities of Practice were able to introduce new process efficiencies. For example, one shared learning session led to the acceleration of the production simulation studies undertaken on a new field creating efficiency gains in the hundreds of thousands of dollars. Another session facilitated a more thorough and rapid risk assessment for a joint venture prospect, leading to an earlier progression to a valued project than would have previously been possible. This case study provides an example of how scarce expertise can be effectively leveraged through cross divisional and geographic boundaries for the overall benefit of the organisation.

In summary, Jashapara's integrated approach to Knowledge management traces a cycle from discovery, generation, evaluation, sharing and finally leverage. From the philosophical perspective of what knowledge is, the generation of knowledge is seen as akin to how organisations learn. New knowledge has to be evaluated for usefulness and criticality, with several categorisation style frameworks and scorecards supporting this process. The sharing of knowledge is substantially a human to human activity necessarily supported by an enabling knowledge sharing culture and the more informal organisation vehicles like Communities of Practice. Finally Knowledge management is seen largely as processes conducted inside the firm or organisation. Its external incarnation or leverage is described as Intellectual capital. In effect Knowledge management at the enterprise level becomes Intellectual capital management.

A second source Knowledge management literature review used is a compendium publication on classic and contemporary works in Knowledge management (Morey *et al.*, 2000). The editors have divided the contributions into:

a. **Strategy:** leading with the classic organisational learning work of Peter Senge and covering more contemporary knowledge strategy work of David Skyme (2000)and IC strategies of Patricia Seeman et al.(2000);

b. **Process:** leading with the classic works of Takeuchi and Nonaka and their theory of organisational knowledge creation and their now famous SECI (Socialisation, Externalisation, Combination and Internalisation) knowledge spiral (Nonaka & Takeuchi, 1995); and

c. **Metrics:** leading with the classic works of Kaplan and Norton and the Balanced Scorecard (BSC) and Sveiby and the Intangible asset monitor (IAM), through to contemporary works around metrics for communities of practice.

In reviewing these contributions as a representative microcosm of the available KM literature, the KM strategy elements that relate to IC and the KM metrics contributions are all relevant to this review. KM processes have largely been concerned with how new knowledge is created, shared and deployed for organisational advantage. New knowledge in this context also covers new learning from past activities. A theme of networks and Communities of Practice pervades the KM process literature (Pena, 2002; Wenger, 1998; Wenger et al., 2002). The relationship between networks, communities and SC is a close one and therefore deserves some attention. The KM metrics literature is either related to Communities of Practice and social networks (Lock Lee, 2000) or is substantially the same as IC metrics literature (Liebowitz, J. and C. Y. Suen ,2000; Malhotra, Y., 2003; Mouritson, J., P. N. Bukh, et al. ,2002). KM Networks are seen as related to, but not identical with, the SC and Alliance Management elements. A theoretical treatment of knowledge networks will be covered in a later section on Human Networks and its practical application in the section on Communities of Practice.

In essence, knowledge within the firm can be seen as a fundamental resource to be drawn on and leveraged in the marketplace as IC. In some sectors this could be viewed as a company's core competence (Prahalad and Hamel, 1990). The outward looking view of how knowledge is leveraged outside the firm has been labelled IC. At the enterprise level many authors have now helped formulate the concepts around IC and its core components of external capital, internal capital and human competence (Sveiby, 1997; Stewart, 1997; Edvinsson and Malone, 1997). IC is now explored in more detail in the next section.

INTELLECTUAL CAPITAL

The growth in the market value of publicly-owned corporations has accelerated well beyond the tangible book values of these corporations over the past 15 to 20 years (Baruch Lev, 2001). The widening gap between market and book values has been labeled the "intangible asset gap" which has now grown to the extent that, on average, only one in every five dollars of market value can be found on company balance sheets (Brebbia, 2000; Baruch Lev, 2001). The intangible asset gap has been attributed to a firm's Intellectual capital (IC) and the terms IC and Intangible Assets (IA) are often used interchangeably (Stewart, 1997). The trend towards the knowledge-based firm and the rapidly growing services sector is seen as the reason for this phenomenon (Basole & Rouse, 2008; Chesbrough & Spohrer, 2006). Comparing the top ten companies by market capitalisation of ten to fifteen years ago with those that fill the same lists today, there is an obvious shift, with service companies replacing industrial sector companies (Guthrie & Petty, 2000; Lock Lee, 2004; Wurzburg, 1998). Fama et al. (2001) point out that the percentage of public firms paying dividends had dropped from 68% in 1978 to only 21% in 1999. The reduction was attributed to the increase in small growth-oriented firms that prefer to reward investors through share price capital appreciation. Many of these firms are services companies. Services or knowledge-based companies have relatively few tangible assets, with the majority of their assets being intangible (e.g. company brand, staff competencies, business models (K. E. Sveiby, 1997)).

Traditional accounting methods generally refer to intangibles as goodwill. The inadequacy of traditional accounting methods in catering for modern knowledge-based corporations has led to a plethora of research aimed at generating a more appropriate method of accounting and valuation (Bontis *et al.*, 1999; Baruch Lev, 2001). Alternative IC balance sheets (K. E. Sveiby, 1997) have been designed and the BSC (R. S. Kaplan & Norton, 1992) has been used to report on non-financial metrics. New financial and non-financial indices have been derived in an attempt to correlate intangible performance with market performance (Baruch Lev, 1999; Low, 2000; Strassmann, 1999), and many versions of IC statements have been designed to inform company executives and investors of the intangible value drivers possessed by a company (Unerman & Guthrie, 2007). Despite the intangible accounting efforts of the past decade, the success in penetrating mainstream management thinking can best be summed up as a general ambivalence to published IC indicators by capital market actors (Holland, 2006; Johanson, 2003; Mouritson, 2003).

Another identifiable change in the marketplace is the growth in interdependencies between firms. These interdependencies are not simply value chain examples, but more complex value networks (Allee, 2003; Ebers, 1997; Gulati *et al.*, 2000; Stabell & Fjeldstad, 1998). With firms becoming more networked a higher percentage of staff is required to manage interactions and relationships with other firms. Butler et al.(1997) claim that over 50% of labour activity in the USA is now applied to searching, coordinating and monitoring relationships and interactions. The increased importance of inter-firm relationships indicates a need for staff and firms to demonstrate increased levels of social skills in order to maximise the value of these relationships. SC has its roots in civic or "public good" applications (Putman, 1995), but in recent times the concept of SC has entered the corporate arena (D. Cohen & Prusak, 2001; S. Cohen & Fields, 1999; Leenders & Gabbay, 1999; Uzzi, 1997) as another form of intangible asset.

INTELLECTUAL PROPERTY

As a research area, Intellectual Property (IP) in terms of patents, copyrights, trademarks and trade secrets pre-dates the KM and IC literature. The increased attention IP has gained in recent years could be attributed to the growing interest in KM, and the fact that IP forms one of the few intellectual assets that are explicitly transacted in monetary terms. Being a tradeable commodity, patents and copyright are among the few intellectual assets that can stand alongside physical assets, receiving management attention to best leverage the inherent value available (Maxwell, 2002). The Technology Broker Model for IC (Brooking, 1996) specifically identifies IP as one of two components of a firm's structural capital. The other component is infrastructure assets like processes, methods and technologies. While patents and copyright have played a significant role in both creating and protecting wealth generated around significant inventions, from a KM perspective IP is often used as an example of how inadequate current valuation systems are for valuing IC.

Petrash (1996) provides a good example of the management of explicit knowledge assets at the Dow Chemicals company. Better management of the Dow patent portfolio was selected as the first initiative of their newly launched intellectual asset management programme. Dow Chemicals employs over 4000 R&D scientists, and has some 25,000 patents costing around $US30 million to sustain. Through an analysis of the knowledge flows underpinning current patents and by looking for complementary and competing themes of knowledge use and alignment with business strategy, Dow was able to claim a 25% reduction in their patent maintenance costs.

The Dow experience is a tangible example of how the management of knowledge can add directly to annual earnings, through cost savings achieved. However, by reducing the number of active patents, and therefore perhaps the value of "accounting intangibles" held on the Dow balance sheet, it is in fact lowering Dow's book value. Is this a good or a bad thing? In the industrial era, this may have been viewed as a bad thing (i.e. an asset one has invested in being written off at zero value), in effect reducing the size of the company. However, in a knowledge era, the book value of companies is becoming less of a determinant of company value (Baruch Lev & Zarowin, 1999). Responsible management of intellectual assets of an "industrial" firm like Dow is a pointer to a "changing of the guard" with respect to physical and intangible assets.

MEASURING AND MANAGING INTELLECTUAL CAPITAL

To facilitate an effective governance arrangement it is important that measurement schemes exist for business value and the factors contributing to its generation. In this section a review of measurement schemes for IC and IA is provided.

The terms "Intellectual capital" (IC) and "intangible assets" (IA) are often used interchangeably within the literature. While one could argue that not all intangibles (e.g. brands and corporate reputation) are adequately defined as IC (Petty & Guthrie, 2000), the literature covering these topics generally treats the terms interchangeably (Kaufmann & Schneider, 2004), and this is the stance taken in this review. The accounting literature has tended to favour the term "intangibles" when describing the growing gap between accounting book values and share market valuations. The accounting research community has also focused on the diminishing value relevance of financial accounting measures and market efficiency developments (Beaver, 2002). On market efficiencies, researchers have been interested in whether market-to-book ratios are a measure of market inefficiency (Lev, 2001; Smithers & Wright, 2000). For example, firms with high market-to-book ratios could be viewed as overpriced. However, the market-to-book gap cannot be fully explained in terms of traditional accounting measures like earnings and even forecasted earnings levels (Hand & Lev, 2003).

The loss of the value relevance of financial accounting measures suggests that the usefulness of earnings, cash flows and book values to predicting Total shareholder return (TSR) has diminished over the past 25 years (Ball, 1992; Baruch Lev & Zarowin, 1999). The inference from these claims is that financial accounting reports are missing important information that could better inform managers and investors of potential share market returns. The initial studies used statistical techniques to demonstrate a reduced level of share price variations that could be explained by traditional accounting measures like earnings, book values and cash flows (Baruch Lev & Zarowin, 1999). These findings have been challenged and extended in different directions from a methodological perspective (Collins et al., 1997). Francis & Schipper (1999) argued that increased volatility in the market can bias simple statistical regressions to over-emphasise the loss of relevance. They analysed firms from high volatility technology sectors and low volatility industrial sectors to find an increase in balance sheet and book value relevance, but continuing support for a decline in the relevance of earnings information. Liu & Thomas (2000) demonstrated that value relevance can be enhanced by the inclusion of forecast earnings into the regression equations. Analyst consensus on earnings forecasts and their accuracy has been found to be highly dependent on the level of intangibles a firm possesses. The higher the level of intangibles, the lower the level of consensus and accuracy (Barron *et al.*, 2002).

While there have been various challenges to the detail of the "loss of relevance" of accounting measures in predicting share values, the general tenet of the studies is that there has been a loss of relevance, particularly in respect to earnings reports. In trying to explain the growing gap between market and book values, researchers have been calling for higher levels of disclosures on known intangibles. Common intangibles like R&D and advertising have been shown to have a strong correlation with share price in certain industries (Chauvin & Hirschey, 1993; Johnson *et al.*, 2002; B. Lev & Sougiannis, 1999). An intriguing study of IA effects on share prices in the pre-Securities and Exchange Commission (SEC) era, when regulations were less strict on the capitalisation of intangibles, found no evidence that increased capitalisation of intangibles impacted share prices. In fact, investors inferred that by increasing the capitalisation of intangibles, firms were overstating their earnings, resulting in a loss of relevance of earnings statements when high levels of intangible capitalisation had occurred (Ely & Waymire, 1999). In contrast, Barth & Clinch (1998) found a positive effect on share price when the value of accounting intangibles was re-stated. A correlation was found between high levels of IC, as measured by Tobins Q (TOBQ), and sustained profitability, but also sustained losses, as firms either locked into a sustainable competitive position through their IC or sustained losses through a loss of reputation (Villalonga, 2004).

Accounting researchers have largely viewed IC from an "assets and liabilities" perspective, exploring a number of accounting options to explain the growing gap between market and book values, called the "intangibles gap". The "intangibles gap" can be volatile but still show an upward trend. The relevance of traditional financial accounting reports continues to be challenged. The following sections explore the literature around IC, which tends to exist largely outside accounting, but is ultimately intertwined with it.

IC as a research topic is still in its infancy, with a concerted focus on the topic beginning in the mid- to late 1990s. The topic attracted the interest of the OECD in 1999 through its international symposium for measuring and managing IC, which provided further impetus to IC research into the new millennium (OECD, 1999). An early review of the literature (Petty & Guthrie, 2000) identified two stages of development of IC research. The first stage related to the development of frameworks for IC and general consciousness-raising, which carried through to the mid-1990s. This level of research was largely focused on the presentation of new conceptual models, supported by academic argument. Examples of first-stage IC literature have successfully targeted the general business community in raising the awareness of non-physical and non-financial capital (Kaplan & Norton, 1992; Lev, 2001; Stewart, 1997; Sveiby, 1997). The linkage between foundational literature on theories of the firm and organisational knowledge with IC has been explored through a comprehensive literature review (Bontis et al., 1999). Bontis et al. (1999) identified the business appeal of the IC concept as a critical resource enacted through organisational learning flows. However, they cautioned that IC would never be measured in traditional monetary terms. Rather, customised metrics may be disclosed as addenda to traditional annual financial reports (Leif Edvinsson, 1997).

The second-stage IC research relates to the impact of IC on the behaviour of markets and labour, supported by empirical research (Brennan & Connell, 2000). A review of European IC management and reporting practices has been undertaken, which identifies issues with voluntary disclosure of IC elements and standard forms of IC reporting still having some way to go (Zambon *et al.*, 2003). Content analysis measures have been used to identify intellectual reporting practices from annual reports (Guthrie & Petty, 2000). Others, such as Bond and Cummins (2003), have developed comprehensive economic models of intangibles in an attempt to quantitatively explain the market-to-book value gap. Also, Bukh (2003) has undertaken empirical research to understand the ambivalence market analysts have to IC reports. A comprehensive review of toolsets for measuring and managing intangibles is provided by Bontis et al. (1999). The IC taxonomies specifically target IC, while other related tools like Economic Value Added (EVA), the Balanced Score Card (BSC) and human resource models are also reviewed in the context of IC.

Kaufmann et al. (2004) concentrated on the literature post-1997. These authors indicated that the field of IC research was still struggling with an ambiguity of terms and definitions, and a variety of views and interpretations, as there were no dominant schools of thought. They pointed to the significant amount of literature on the reporting of IC, and the comparatively small amount on the ensuing "management of intangibles". The allocation of resources to intangibles was also identified as an area of neglect. In addition, research on IC appeared to differ based on whether the focus was on internal management issues or external stakeholder issues. Often, the focus was either mixed or poorly defined. The authors proceeded to identify a lack of an underpinning theory required to base management action around intangibles. The initial research aimed at identifying such an underpinning theory had focused on the resource-based view of the firm (Garcia-Ayuso, 2003; Ordonez de Pablos, 2003; Sanchez *et al.*, 2000).

In locating IC in the literature, Petty and Guthrie (2000) identified its rise in importance to business today as driven by the general acknowledgement of a "new economy" era. The revolution in IT, Knowledge management (KM) and the knowledge-based economy, the networked society and the emergence of innovation as a key competitive driver, have all contributed to the increased attention IC research has enjoyed. The inter-relationship of IC and KM literature also attracts discussion, with KM literature being significantly more prolific than that of IC. Petty and Guthrie (2000) take the view that KM is about the management of IC and therefore could be seen as subsidiary to, or supporting of, the IC object. This view is also strongly agued by Sanchez et al. (2000), who claim that IC is a much broader concept than KM, and that KM is just one intangible attribute of IC.

What is apparent from a review of both conceptual and empirical research studies is the variety of IC topics being addressed and methods being used. This is symptomatic of the early stages that these research studies are in. The exploratory nature of the empirical research would indicate that researchers are currently building a broad base of research experience with IC, which will necessarily underpin future, more focused research, as the critical theoretical and practical issues of the importance of IC emerge.

Two dominant themes in IC research: the measurement and management of IC, and KM and its relationship to IC, are now explored in more detail. The measurement and management of IC to date has largely focused on IC reporting. These IC reports have been the major vehicle for informing market actors of the value inherent in IC-intensive firms. As early as 1995, Skandia Insurance had attached an IC supplement to their annual report (Leif Edvinsson, 1997). The increasing importance of intangibles was identified by Swedish researcher Karl-Erik Sveiby in his seminal work on "company know-how" (Sveiby et al., 1986). Since this time a plethora of literature has been published in support of methods for measuring and managing intangibles (L. Edvinsson & Malone, 1997; Johanson *et al.*, 1999; Baruch Lev, 2001; K. E. Sveiby, 1997). From Sveiby's "Intangible asset monitor" (Sveiby, 1997) and Kaplan and Norton's BSC (R. Kaplan & Norton, 1996), increasingly sophisticated scorecards have been built (Liebowitz & Suen, 2000; Mouritson *et al.*, 2001; Wall & Doerflinger, 1999). IC has been broken down into subsidiary concepts like structural capital, human capital, customer capital, innovation capital, external capital, stakeholder capital and knowledge capital, for the purposes of measurement and reporting for management. In 1999, the OECD commissioned several projects to explore the spread of IC reporting across several continents (OECD, 1999). More recent developments have recognised that IC metrics alone are not effective in communicating value propositions to the marketplace. The Danish Government has published guidelines for IC reporting which encourages the inclusion of "knowledge narratives" to better communicate value creating challenges and initiatives (Mouritson *et al.*, 2002; Pakhus, 2000).

Despite the significant development activities around IC valuation and reporting from around 1995 to 2000, anecdotally it appears that progress has slowed. The anticipated increase in IC reporting, following Skandia's lead, has not eventuated. Attempts to develop single indices for IA performance (Bontis et al.,1999; Lev, 1999; Low, 2000; Strassman, 1999) have also struggled to gain acceptance. This lack of progress led Johanson (2003) to report on potential reasons for market actors' ambivalence to IC information. Johanson (2003) offers five primary reasons: a lack of understanding of intangibles; a lack of trust in the measures; an exaggerated risk of losing the intangible resource; a lack of confidence in management to take action with respect to intangibles; and the mentality of market actors to softer intangibles. Also, Holland (2003) points to a rift between what company executives, fund managers and analysts believe is relevant IC information. Holland (2003, p46) identifies dysfunctions in the information value chain from company executive to market actors, that are presenting real barriers to progress with IC.

IC reporting has both an internal and external effect. The internal reporting aspects of the BSC and/or IAM can provide support for effective management decision-making (R. S. Kaplan & Norton, 1992; K. E. Sveiby, 1997). The external reporting aspects of IC reporting can contribute to the externally focused executive management element in influencing market actors.

Figure 19. Scorecard example

The Celemi Intangible Assets Monitor 1996

		Knowledge Capital		
Our Customers (External Structure)		**Our Organization** (Internal Structure)		**Our People** (Competence)

Our Customers (External Structure)	1996	1995	Our Organization (Internal Structure)	1996	1995	Our People (Competence)	1996		1995	
Growth/Renewal			**Growth/Renewal**			**Growth/Renewal**				
Revenue growth	**50%**	44%	IT investment			Average professional				
Image enhancing			% Value added (15)	**6%**	11%	experience (7)	**8.0**	**2%**	7.8	–25%
customers (2)	**46%**	40%	Organization enhancing			Competence enhancing				
			customers (2)	**44%**	44%	customers (2)		**46%**		43%
			Product R&D			Total competence,				
			% Value added	**8%**	18%	experts (4,7)	**343**	**15%**	298	43%
			Total investment in org.			Average education level				
			% Value added	**14%**	33%	all employees (3)	**2.3**	**0%**	2.3	0%
Efficiency			**Efficiency**			**Efficiency**				
Sales/customers (12),			Change i proportion of			Value added per expert				
change	**39%**	4%	admin. staff (1,8)	**–3%**	4%	(4,15) TSEK	**816**	**–6%**	867	–13%
			Growth in sales per			Value added per employee				
			admin. staff (11)	**5%**	–20%	(15) TSEK	**643**	**–3%**	665	–13%
Stability			**Stability**			**Stability**				
Repeat orders (9)	**61%**	66%	Admin staff turnover(1,14)	**8%**	0%	Expert turnover(4,14)		**16%**		10%
Five largest			Admin staff seniority(1,13)	**3**	3	Expert seniority(4,13)	**3.4**	**47%**	2.3	79%
customers (5)	**34%**	41%	Rookie ratio (10)	**32%**	64%	Median age all employ	**34**	**0%**	34	–12%

Case Study

Celemi: Reporting on Intellectual Capital

The IAM report shown in Figure 19 was developed by the Swedish training company Celemi. The report is a result of a knowledge audit, reporting on the intangible assets of the firm (K. E. Sveiby, 1997). As a services rather than manufacturing firm, Celemi identifies its strategic assets as their customers (external structure), their organisation (internal structure) and their people (competence). What is evident when comparing this intangible asset report to the conventional balance sheet, is that not only are the measures substantially different i.e. these are no financial or physical asset valuations like borrowings or plant & equipment valuations, but how forward looking the measures are. For example, revenue from "image enhancing" clients, staff turnover and staff professional experience are more relevant to a service company than the financial and physical asset measures.

Better known in the management literature is the Balanced Scorecard (BSC) by Kaplan and Norton (1992). The key dimensions of the BSC are: customer perspective; innovation and learning perspective; internal business perspective; and financial perspective. While containing many of the same characteristics as IC reports, the intent of the BSC is to guide companies in aligning performance with their business strategy. The BSC does not identify itself with a "knowledge-based" view of the firm, a central tenet of IC reports (Mouritson *et al.*, 2005). IC reporting has been inspired by people, and knowledge is the central resource for value creation[3]. The BSC has strategy alignment as its central value creating tenet. With this in mind, while the surface metrics may look similar, the interpretation and actions identified from their reporting may be entirely different. For example, a poor internal efficiency result within the BSC might prompt an investment in new IT systems. An IC report showing a similar deficiency may identify a knowledge problem, for example, poor training or development support.

What both the IAM and the BSC demonstrate is that the traditional forms of accounting measurement, being the balance sheet and profit and loss statements, are no longer sufficient for both reporting on and predicting performance in a service based economy. As the objective of IT Governance is to ensure that a firm's IT investments are adding business value to the firm, one needs to recognise how "value" is determined. IT investments are often difficult to justify using traditional accounting measures of value. However, if one looks to IAM or BSC measures as indicators of business value, then the justification of IT investments may take on a whole new perspective. For example, an IT system which enhances customer experience and enhances the firm's reputation might be easily justified through its contribution to intangible or non-financial measures found in the IAM or BSC, but not easily justified by the traditional ROI measures.

SUMMARY

In summary, this chapter has addressed the change from an industrial / manufacturing dominated economy to an intangible asset services centric economy. With knowledge being the key resource for a services economy a comprehensive review of the KM state of the art was included to provide some insight into how firms and organisations are dealing with an asset that has now become central to their performance. The section on IC provides a view of how performance measurement systems are now evolving to accommodate this change in focus. While these changes are more evolutionary than revolutionary, one can see that what constitutes business value in the services / knowledge based business environment can vary significantly from an environment where physical assets were the central measure of value.

This chapter started with a review of Quinn's book on the intelligent enterprise. A central tenet for Quinn was for organisations to identify their "best in class" competencies and to focus their attention on building and sustaining them as their competitive advantage, while outsourcing all other activities. Outsourcing invariably leads to an escalation in alliances and partnerships as a core business activity for all firms. As has been identified in the introductory chapter, this has certainly been the case over the past decade or more. Therefore the ability to build and sustain effective relationships becomes a necessary competency for all organisations. The next section therefore addresses a new class of asset called "Corporate Social Capital", which centres on one's ability to form effective business relationships. In this section a view of IT Governance will be developed from a sociological view point.

REFERENCES

Allee, V. (2003). *The Future of Knowledge: Increasing Prosperity through Value Networks*. Butterworth-Heinemann.

Argyris, C., & Schon, D. A. (1978). *Organizational Learning: A Theory of Action Perspective*. Reading, MA: Addison-Wesley

Ball, R. (1992). The Earning-price anomaly. *Journal of Accounting and Economics, 15*, 319-345.

Balnaves, C., & Busch, B. (2002). *Creating and Nurturing a Knowledge Sharing Culture in a High Performance Technical Group*. Paper presented at the Society of Petroleum Engineers Inc. International Conference on Asia Pacific Oil & Gas on Creative Solutions for Maturing Basins and New Frontiers.

Barron, O. E., Byard, D., Kile, C., & Riedl, E. J. (2002). High Technology Intangibles and Analysts' Forecasts. *Journal of Accounting Research, 40*(2), 289-312.

Barth, M., & Clinch, G. (1998). Revalued Financial, Tangible, and Intangible Assets: Associations with Share Prices and Non-Market-Based Value Estimates. *Journal of Accounting Research, 36(Supplement)*, 199-233.

Basole, R., & Rouse, W. (2008). Complexity of service value networks: Conceptualization and empirical investigation. *IBM Systems Journal, 47*(1), 53-70.

Beaver, W. (2002). Perspectives on Recent Capital Market Research. *The Accounting Review, 77*(2), 453-474.

Binney, D. (2001). The Knowledge management Spectrum—understanding the KM landscape. *Journal of Knowledge management, 5*(1), 33-42.

Bontis, N., Dragonetti, N. C., Jacobsen, K., & Roos, G. (1999). The Knowledge Toolbox: A Review of the Tools Available to measure and Manage Intangible Resources. *European Management Journal, 17*(4), 391-402.

Brebbia, C. (2000). *Intellectual assets account for 78% of total value of S&P500.*

Brennan, N., & Connell, B. (2000, 29-31 March). *Intellectual capital: current issues and policy implications.* Paper presented at the 23rd Annual Congress of the European Accounting Association, Munich, Germany.

Brooking, A. (1996). *Intellectual capital, Core Assets for the Third Millennium Enterprise.* International Thomson Business Press.

Bukh, P. N. (2003). The relevance of intellectual capital disclosure: a paradox? *Accounting, Auditing & Accountability Journal, 16*(1), 49-56.

Butler, P., Sahay, A., Hall, T., Mendonca, L., Manyika, J., Hanna, A., et al. (1997). A Revolution in Interaction. *McKinsey Quarterly*(1), 4-23.

Chauvin, K., & Hirschey, M. (1993). Advertising, R&D Expenditures and Market Value of the Firm. *Financial Management, 22*, 128-140.

Chesbrough, H., & Spohrer, J. (2006). A Research Manifesto for Services Science. *Communications of the ACM, 49*(7), 35-40.

Cohen, D., & Prusak, L. (2001). *In Good Company: How Social Capital Makes Organizations Work.* Boston: Harvard Business School Press.

Cohen, S., & Fields, G. (1999). Social Capital and Capital Gains in Silicon Valley. *California Management Review, 41*(2), 108-129.

Collins, D. W., Maydew, E. L., & Weiss, I. S. (1997). Changes in the value-relevance of earnings and book values over the past 40 years. *Journal of Accounting and Economics, 24*(1), 39-67.

Collison, C., & Parcell, G. (2001). *Learning to Fly: Practical Lessons from one of the World's leading Knowledge Companies*: Capstone Publishing.

Denning, S. (2001). *The Springboard: How Storytelling Ignites Action in Knowledge-Era Organizations*: Butterworth Heinemann.

Drucker, P. (1992). The New Society of Organizations. *Harvard Business Review*(September—October).

Ebers, M. (1997). *Explaining Inter-Organisational Network Formation.* Oxford, New York: Oxford University Press.

Edvinsson, L. (1997). Developing Intellectual capital at Skandia. *Long Range Planning, 30*(3), 366-373.

Edvinsson, L., & Malone, M. S. (1997). *Intellectual capital—realizing your company's true value by finding its hidden brainpower*: New York: Harper Business Publisher.

Ely, K., & Waymire, G. (1999). Intangible Assets and Stock Prices in the Pre-SEC era. *Journal of Accounting Research, 37*, 17-44.

Fama, E., & French, K. (2001). Disappearing dividends: changing firm characteristics or lower propensity to pay? *Journal of Financial Economics, 60*, 3-43.

Garcia-Ayuso, M. (2003). Factors explaining the inefficient valuation of intangibles. *Accounting, Auditing & Accountability Journal, 16*(1), 57-69.

Grant, R. (1996). Toward a Knowledge-Based Theory of the Firm. *Strategic Management Journal, 17*(Winter Special Issue), 109-122.

Gulati, R., Nohria, N., & Zaheer, A. (2000). Strategic Networks. *Strategic Management Journal, 21*, 203-215.

Guthrie, J., & Petty, R. (2000). Intellectual capital: Australian annual reporting practices. *Journal of Intellectual capital, 1*(3), 241.

Hand, J., & Lev, B. (2003). *Intangible Assets: Values, Measures and Risks*. Oxford: Oxford University Press.

Hansen, M., Nohria, N., & Tierney, T. (1999). What's Your Strategy for Managing Knowledge? *Harvard Business Review, 77*(2), 106-116.

Holland, J. (2006). Fund Management, Intellectual capital, Intangibles and Private Disclosure. *Managerial Finance, 32*(4), 277—316.

Jashapara, A. (2004). *Knowledge management: An Integrated Approach*. Prentice-Hall.

Johanson, U. (2003). Why are capital market actors ambivalent to information about certain indicators on intellectual capital? *Accounting, Auditing & Accountability Journal, 16*(1), 31—38.

Johanson, U., Martensson, M., & Skoog, M. (1999). *Measuring and Managing Intangibles: Eleven Swedish Qualitative Exploratory Case Studies*. Paper presented at the International Symposium on Measuring and Reporting Intellectual capital: Experience, Issues and Prospects, Amsterdam.

Johnson, L., Neave, E., & Pazderka, B. (2002). Knowledge, innovation and share value. *International Journal of Management Reviews, 4*(2), 101-134.

Kaplan, R., & Norton, D. (1996). *The Balanced Scorecard: Translating Strategy into Action*. Boston: Harvard Business School Press.

Kaplan, R. S., & Norton, D. P. (1992). The Balanced Scorecard—measures that drive performance. *Harvard Business Review, 70*(1), 71-79.

Kaufmann, L., & Schneider, Y. (2004). Intangibles: A synthesis of current research. *Journal of Intellectual capital, 5*(3), 366-388.

Kleiner, A., & Roth, G. (1997). How to Make Experience Your Company's Best Teacher. *Harvard Business Review, September-October*.

Kogut, B., & Zander, U. (1993). Knowledge of the firm and the evolutionary theory of the multinational corporation. *Journal of International Business Studies, 24*(4).

Kotter, J. P. (1996). *Leading Organisational Change*: Harvard Business School Press.

Leenders, R., & Gabbay, S. (Eds.). (1999). *Corporate Social Capital and Liability*. Boston: Kluwer Academic Publishers.

Leonard-Barton, D. (1992). Core Capabilities and Core Rigidities: A Paradox in Managing New Product Development. *Strategic Management Journal, 13*, 111-125.

Lev, B. (1999, February, 1999). Seeing is Believing: A better approach to estimating knowledge capital. *CFO*.

Lev, B. (2001). *Intangibles: Management, Measurement, and Reporting*. Washington, D.C.: Brookings Institution Press.

Lev, B., & Sougiannis, T. (1999). Penetrating the book-to-market black box: The R&D effect. *Journal of Business and Finance Accounting, 26*, 419-449.

Lev, B., & Zarowin, P. (1999). The Boundaries of Financial Reporting and How to Extend Them. *Journal of Accounting Research, 37*(2), 353-385.

Liebowitz, J., & Suen, C. Y. (2000). Developing knowledge management metrics for measuring intellectual capital. *Journal of Intellectual capital, 1*(1), 54-67.

Liu, J., & Thomas, J. (2000). Stock Returns and Accounting Earnings. *Journal of Accounting Research, 38*(1), 71-101.

Lock Lee, L. (2000). Knowledge Sharing Metrics for Large Organizations. In D. Morey, M. Maybury, & B. Thuraisingham (Eds.), *Knowledge management: Classic and Contemporary Works*. MIT Press.

Lock Lee, L. (2004). Social Capital Measurement as a Proxy for Intellectual capital Measures. In M. Rao (Ed.), *Knowledge management Tools and Techniques: Practitioners and Experts Evaluate KM Solutions*: Butterworth-Heinemann.

Lock Lee, L. (2005). Balancing business process with business practice for organizational advantage. *Journal of Knowledge management, 9*(1), 29-41.

Low, J. (2000). The Value Creation Index. *Journal of Intellectual capital, 1*(3), 252-260.

Maxwell, R. (2002). Smart Patents: is your intellectual capital at risk? *Harvard Business Review, 80*(4), 18-19.

Morey, D., Maybury, M., & Thuraisingham, B. (Eds.) (2000). *Knowledge management: Classic and Contemporary Works*: MIT Press.

Mouritson, J. (2003). Intellectual capital and the capital market: the circulability of intellectual capital. *Accounting, Auditing & Accountability Journal, 16*(1), 18-30.

Mouritson, J., Bukh, P. N., Larsen, H. T., & Johnson, M. R. (2002). Developing and Managing Knowledge through Intellectual capital Statement. *Journal of Intellectual capital, 3*(1), 10-29.

Mouritson, J., Larsen, H. T., & Bukh, P. N. (2005). Dealing with the knowledge economy: intellectual capital vs. balanced scorecard. *Journal of Intellectual capital, 6*(1), 8-27.

Mouritson, J., Larsen, H. T., & Bukh, P. N. D. (2001). Intellectual capital and the 'capable firm': narrating, visualising and numbering for managing knowledge. *Accounting Organizations and Society, 26*(7-8), 735-762.

Nelson, R., & Winter, S. (1982). *An Evolutionary Theory of Economic Change*. Cambridge, MA: Harvard University Press.

Nonaka, I., & Takeuchi, H. (1995). *The Knowledge Creating Company*. Oxford, New York: Oxford University Press.

OECD. (1999). Measuring and Reporting Intellectual capital: Experience, Issues and Prospects: Results of an International Symposium, Amsterdam 9-11 June 1999, OECD, Paris,[online] Available: http://www.oecd.org/document/15/0,2340,en_2649_201185_1943055_1_1_1_1,00.html (2nd April 2007).

Ordonez de Pablos, P. (2003). Intellectual capital reporting in Spain: a comparative view. *Journal of Intellectual capital, 4*(1), 61-81.

Pakhus, D. (2000). *A Guideline for Intellectual capital Statements*: Danish Agency for Trade and Industry.

Pena, I. (2002). Knowledge networks as part of an integrated knowledge management approach. *Journal of Knowledge management, 6*(5), 469—478.

Petrash, G. (1996). Dow's journey to a knowledge management culture. *European Management Journal, 14*(4), 365-373.

Petty, R., & Guthrie, J. (2000). Intellectual capital Literature Review: Measurement, Reporting and Management. *Journal of Intellectual capital, 1*(2), 155-176.

Polanyi, M. (1967). *The Tacit Dimension.* New York: Doubleday.

Prokesch, S. (1997). Unleashing the Power of Learning: An Interview with British Petroleum's John Browne. *Harvard Business Review, 75*(5), 146-162.

Putman, R. (1995). Bowling Alone: America's Declining Social Capital. *Journal of Democracy, 6*(1), 65-78.

Sanchez, P., Chaminade, C., & Olea, M. (2000). Management of intangibles: An attempt to build a theory. *Journal of Intellectual capital, 1*(4), 312-327.

Seely Brown, J., & Duguid, P. (2000). Balancing Act: How to Capture Knowledge Without Killing It. *Harvard Business Review, May-June.*

Seemann, P., Long, D. D., Stucky, S., & Guthrie, E. (2000). Building Intangible Assets: A Strategic Framework for Investing in Intellectual capital. In D. Morey, M. Maybury, & B. Thuraisingham (Eds.), *Knowledge management: Classic and Contemporary Works*: MIT Press.

Senge, P. (1990). *The Fifth Discipline: The Art & Practice of the Learning Organization.* New York: Currency Doubleday.

Skyme, D. (2000). Intangible Performance Measures. *I3 Update/Entovation,* (41).

Snowden, D. (1999). Story telling: an old skill in a new context. *Business Information Review, 16*(1).

Snowden, D. (2002). Complex Acts of Knowing: Paradox and Descriptive Self Awareness. *Journal of Knowledge management, 6*(2).

Spender, J. C. (1996). Making Knowledge the Basis of a Dynamic Theory of the Firm. *Strategic Management Journal, 17 (winter Special issue),* 45-62.

Stabell, C., & Fjeldstad, O. (1998). Configuring Value for Competitive Advantage: on Chains, Shops, and Networks. *Strategic Management Journal, 19,* 413-437.

Stewart, T. A. (1997). *Intellectual capital: The New Wealth of Organizations.* New York: Doubleday.

Strassmann, P. (1999, October 1999). Calculating Knowledge Capital. *Knowledge management*.

Sveiby, K. (1996). Transfer of Knowledge and the Information Processing Professionals. *European Management Journal, 14*(4), 379-388.

Sveiby, K. E. (1997). *The New Organizational Wealth: Managing & Measuring Knowledge-Based Assets*: Berret-Koehler Publishers, Inc.

Unerman, J., & Guthrie, J. (2007, 25-27 April). *UK Account Preparers' Perspectives on the Role of Intellectual capital Reporting.* Paper presented at the 30th Annual Congress of the European Accounting Association, Lisbon, Portugal.

Uzzi, B. (1997). Social Structure and Competition in Interfirm Networks: The paradox of Embeddedness. *Administrative Science Quarterly, 42*, 35-67.

Villalonga, B. (2004). Intangible resources, Tobin's q, and sustainability of performance differences. *Journal of Economic Behaviour & Organization, 54*, 205-230.

Wall, B., & Doerflinger, M. (1999). Making Intangible Assets Tangible. *Knowledge management Review*(10), 28-33.

Wallman, S. (1995). The Future of Accounting and Disclosure in an Evolving World: The Need for Dramatic Change. *Accounting Horizons, 9*(3), 81-91.

Wenger, E. (1998). *Communities of Practice: Learning, meaning, and Identity*: Cambridge University Press.

Wenger, E., McDermott, R., & Snyder, W. M. (2002). *Cultivating Communities of Practice.* Boston: Harvard Business School Press.

Wiig, K. (1997). Integrating Intellectual Capita and Knowledge management. *Long Range Planning, 30*(3), 399-405.

Wurzburg, G. (1998). Markets and the Knowledge Economy: Is Anything Broken? Can Government Fix It? *Journal of Knowledge management, 2*(1), 32-46.

Zambon, S., Abernethy, M., Wyatt, A., Bianhi, P., Labory, S., & Lev, B. (2003). *Study on the Measurement of Intangible Assets and Associated Reporting Practices*: Commission of the European Communities—Enterprise Directorate General.

Zhou, A., & Fink, D. (2003). The intellectual capital web: A systematic linking of intellectual capital and knowledge management. *Journal of Intellectual capital, 4*(1), 34-48.

ENDNOTES

[1]   See http://www.sveiby.com/Portals/0/articles/SwedishCoP.htm (accessed 22/7/07).

[2]   See Swedish Coalition of Service Industries (1995), *Valuation of Service Companies*, Publication No. 10, Master Samuelsgatan 51, S-11157 Stockholm, Sweden.

[3]   See http://www.sveiby.com/Portals/0/articles/BSCandIAM.html (accessed 22/7/07) for a discussion on this topic.

Section II
A Sociological View of Governance

Chapter V
Corporate Social Capital and the Intelligent Enterprise

This chapter is concerned with building up the concept of Corporate Social Capital (SC) as a critical firm resource in terms the governance of multisourcing relationships. The establishment of Corporate SC as a performance related concept draws from the related concepts of Social Networks (SN), Intellectual capital (IC) and Corporate Reputation (CR). The relevance of the relationship aspects of SN has been established in chapter III (Figure 12). Also addressed in that review was the knowledge based theory of the firm, that will be developed in more detail through an exploration of the IC literature and the CR literature, each seen as contributing to a foundation for Corporate SC and ultimately impacting IT Governance and multisourcing relationships.

While the importance of the relationship aspects of Corporate SC to IT Governance is well established (Kern & Willcocks, 2001; Willcocks & Cullen, 2006), the impact of IC and CR on IT Governance is less understood. If one reflects on the key objective of IT Governance, being to maximise the business value achieved through investments in IT (PriceWaterhouseCoopers, 2007; Williams, 2007), then it becomes clear that "business value" can have a far broader interpretation than has traditionally been viewed for IT. The traditional use of IT has been to help streamline or automate business processes and hence achieve business value through improved efficiencies. To a large extent IT has been able to achieve this. However, as the business value equation moves toward a greater reliance on intangibles and

Figure 20. Corporate social capital, IT governance and business value

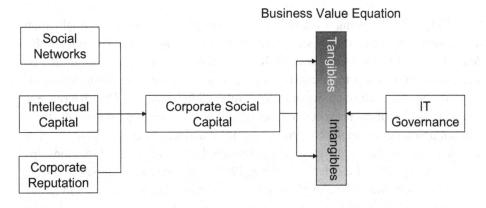

intangible valuations, restricting IT applications to process improvement will substantially limit its ability to generate significant business value in the future. For example, much of today's business value is captured within the IC of firms. Early shareholders in companies like Google, Microsoft, Yahoo and eBay have grown wealthy on the back of the IC that these firms have developed, more so than the efficiency of their internal systems. Therefore this begs the question of how can IT contribute to the business value of IC and CR development?

Figure 20 provides an overview of the linkages between Corporate SC and IT Governance and their common focus on generating business value. The impact of IT to a firm's IC developments, and the consequent relevance to IT Governance, is a significant movement from traditional thinking in which IT is only seen as a vehicle for process efficiency, and even worse, as a commodity utility service (Carr, 2004). The evolution of IT as a process efficiency aid to the facilitation of collaborative relationships and new forms of IC, and hence business value, is addressed in more detail in Chapter XI. In this chapter however, the theoretical foundations are being established for the remainder of the book. Initially a formulation for Corporate SC is built and then used as a framework for exploring the literature around Social Capital, Corporate Reputation, Alliance Networks and Human Networks. This is followed by a section on the measurement and valuation of intangibles, specifically, SC. For IT Governance to be effective, value measurement schemes for intangibles like Corporate SC will be important. Finally the integration of Intellectual capital and Social Capital literature is achieved through reviewing the major "schools of thought" credited with their respective development. The value of viewing IC through the lens of SC is then argued, prior to completing the chapter with a linking of Corporate SC to multisourcing governance.

CORPORATE SOCIAL CAPITAL FORMULATION

With Corporate SC being a relatively new concept for research and application the opportunity exists to take some license in developing a formulation for it. By definition there is significant overlap between the concepts of Corporate SC, IC and CR when it comes to discussing intangibles. Each could be defined to comprehensively cover all of an organisation's intangible resources. The difference is largely in the historical perspective from which the given area approaches the topic of intangibles. For example, Corporate Social Capital has its genesis in the field of sociology and tends to view intangibles through the lens of personal relationships (Adler & Kwon, 2002; Leenders & Gabbay, 1999). Corporate Reputation has largely been developed through the marketing literature and a focus on brand and image (Fombrun & Shanley, 1990), though with an argument that it represents much more than this (Jackson, 2004). Intellectual capital is seen by many to be represented by an organisation's intellectual property in the form of its patents and licenses (Petrash, 1996). However, like the other concepts there are many arguments for broadening the definition to encompass the full scope of intangibles (Brooking, 1996; Edvinsson & Malone, 1997; Roos, 2003).

Given that the topic of interest is governing relationships, Corporate SC is put forward as the most appropriate lens for the evaluation of multisourcing relationships. Therefore, for this analysis the concept of Corporate SC will be built up through the incorporation of concepts like Intellectual capital and Corporate Reputation via a critical review of the literature.

The study of Social Capital (SC) as it relates to business and markets is still a relatively recent phenomenon with the majority of the research being of a nor-

Figure 21. The different perspective on intangible resources

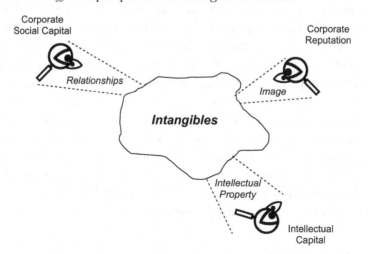

Figure 22. Corporate social capital and intellectual capital

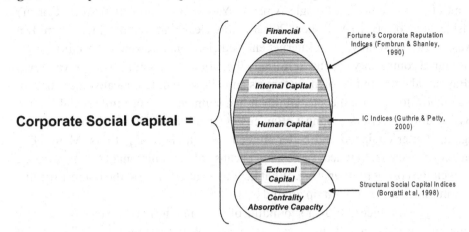

mative, rather than an empirical nature (Florin *et al.*, 2003; Leenders & Gabbay, 1999). The linkage between SC and Intellectual capital (IC) performance has been largely neglected but this could simply be attributed to the disparate disciplines from which these concepts have emerged, that is, sociology and accounting. The organisational theorists' approach to intangibles could identify SC as a component of External capital (EC), though in many cases EC is typically defined more narrowly as relationships with customers and suppliers (Sveiby, 1997).

However, SC can have a broader interpretation which can be relevant at the individual, firm or market level. As such, it can be argued that Corporate SC plays a role across all of the identified components of IC, as illustrated in Figure 22:

The above formulation of Corporate SC incorporates the accepted formulation of IC made up of Human capital (HC), Internal capital (INC) and External capital (EC) (Guthrie & Petty, 2000). It also acknowledges the overlap between formulations of corporate reputation and an expanded formulation of EC to incorporate the structural aspects of relationships. The model shown in Figure 22 identifies an overlap between the structural aspect of SC and the EC component of the IC formulation. It identifies corporate reputation as equivalent to the IC concept, with the addition of financial soundness.

Case Study

Story of eBay: Building Social Capital With and Between Customers

eBay is undoubtedly one of the biggest success stories to come out of the dotcom boom and is continuing to thrive. In terms of market capitalisation over its 10 year life, eBay has consistently and significantly outperformed the market, including some of the big names like Google, Amazon, Yahoo and Microsoft. In Adam Cohen's inside story of eBay (A. Cohen, 2002) it was clear that founder Pierre Omidyar was not driven simply by an Internet enabled electronic transaction facility, but to also build community around it. Initially the rationale was pragmatic, it was a way eBay could conscript its own customers and allow them to educate other customers on how to best use the site. Omidyar had stumbled on corporate social capital. By building a network amongst eBay customers eBay had actually fortified itself against better equipped and better funded auction site competitors. Many eBay customers were loath to leave eBay, not because of the functionality of its software or even the cost of participating. What kept them at eBay were the interest specific communities that had built up around eBay.

Many years since Omidyar's founding of eBay and the handing over of the CEO reins to a professional business executive, Meg Whitman, the same principles of building social capital with its customers has helped sustain eBay's success. On their growth journey Whitman admits to making a few mistakes and diverging slightly from their community principles with a few of their changes. Invariably the business suffered as a consequence leading Whitman to reflect:

The number one thing is to think about how an event affects community ... community has always been central

eBay is a living example of the value of Corporate SC and its impact on firm performance.

The commonality between IC elements and Corporate SC include, for example, an individual's social network (SN), a firm's alliance structures and stakeholder relationships. These are both Corporate SC and IC elements and provide a tangible linkage between Corporate SC and IC. Other IC elements like reputation, patents, skills and experience that may not be explicitly defined as part of Corporate SC, do contribute to Corporate SC by acting as "attractors" for potential connections, and therefore Corporate SC development. For example, a firm looking to develop an alliance arrangement will be attracted by elements like reputation, brand and the skills and experience of the staff in prospective organisations.

The terminology of Corporate SC was promoted by Leenders and Gabbay (1999). They note that SC theory has mainly been applied to individual actors and that Corporate SC studies address the question of how social structure is related to the attainment of the objectives of corporations and their members. In addition, Social Network Analysis (SNA) has been applied to marketplaces to better understand the structure and dynamics of competition in a networked economy (Bueno & Salmador, 2004; Ron Burt, 2003; Ronald Burt *et al.*, 2002). It is therefore appropriate to consider Corporate SC as an important influence in the networked economy and to concentrate on the use of SNA as a core investigative technique.

Whether growth in market-to-book ratios is related to the increased level of networking in the marketplace, is still an open question. While the economic impact of SC has been studied extensively (Carroll & Stanfield, 2003; Fine, 2001; Mark Granovetter, 1985; Holmlund, 2001; White, 1981; Windolf, 2002; Woolcock, 1998), research focused at firm level is scarce. The IC literature typically acknowledges the existence of "relationship capital" (Marr & Chatzkel, 2004; Roos & Roos, 1997), but only more recently has acknowledged the richer SC terminology (Bueno & Salmador, 2004; McElroy, 2002). This recognition is still normative in nature and has yet to develop into empirical research relating SC to IC performance.

The practical significance of this analysis becomes evident when one considers the growth of "what went wrong?" literature around high profile corporate collapses of recent years, the most infamous being that of the Enron Corporation and its auditor Arthur Andersen (Toffler, 2003). As financial information becomes less effective as a forecasting tool for future value (Ballow *et al.*, 2004; Lev, 2001), the market is relying on other tools which might include SC elements like IC, social and environmental responsibilities, corporate reputation and the like. In the case of Enron, the core issue could be ascribed to a mismanagement of intangibles, as Enron moved its business model from a physical asset-intensive to an IC-intensive model. The lack of an identifiable value creation path, from IC use and financial performance, left room for inappropriate external reporting (Chatzkel, 2003). The impact of public trust and reputation on the firm's future prospects is no better illustrated by the collapse of accounting firm Arthur Andersen which lost the confidence and trust of the marketplace through a series of reputation destroying events (Toffler, 2003). One could argue that the negative aspects of SC (D. Cohen & Prusak, 2001; Portes, 1998) contributed to a financially successful global firm,

Figure 23. Structure of theoretical literature overview

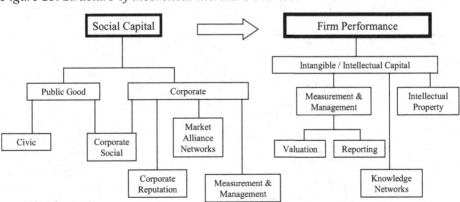

collapsing into non-existence in a few short years. A strong internal culture and social norms within Arthur Anderson had blinded it from seeing the negative impacts of its actions (Toffler, 2003). Figure 23 provides an illustration of the relevant topics to be reviewed.

The above taxonomy identifies how each of the themes and sub-themes in the literature relate to the two core concepts of SC and IC. Each of the themes contributes to the overall objective of researching the linkage between Corporate SC and firm performance.

SOCIAL CAPITAL

The foundation literature on SC is summarised in Figure 24, which identifies the principal themes (represented as boxes) acknowledged in the literature on SC. Associations are indicated by arrows connecting the identified themes.

SC as a concept has its roots in the field of sociology, where it was largely used to describe organisational effects developed through socially derived connections in broader communities, societies and cultures (Baker, 2001; R. S. Burt, 1992; Nahapiet & Ghoshal, 1998; Robert Putman, 1995). While the genesis of the term is somewhat unclear, a majority of scholars attribute the first systematic analysis of SC to Bourdieu (1980). Bourdieu (1986) wrote about SC in conjunction with

Figure 24. Social capital: Foundation literature themes

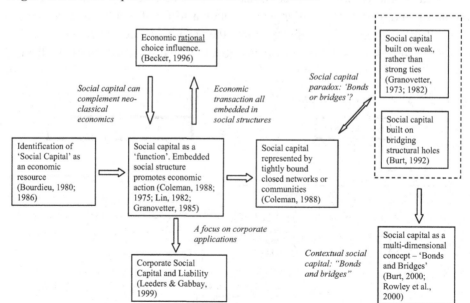

cultural and symbolic capital and its conversion to economic capital. Bourdieu (1986, p248) defined SC as:

the aggregate of actual or potential resources which are linked to possession of durable networks of more or less institutionalized relationships of mutual acquaintance and recognition.

Bourdieu (1986) focused on the benefits accruing to the individual from membership of a group or collective, and the social mechanisms required to achieve such membership. While Bourdieu's definition does not necessarily limit the benefits of SC to the individual, as did most writings on SC at the time, its applicability at the level of the group, firm or enterprise was not specifically acknowledged.

Bourdieu's theoretical treatment of SC has been acknowledged by SC critics, Fine (2001) and Portes (1998). The majority of scholars have presented a positive view of SC (J. Coleman, 1988; Lin, 1982; Robert Putman, 1995). However, Fine (2001) decries the lack of scholarship on SC, claiming that the term has been used by economists to conveniently explain away the shortcomings in rational choice economic theory. He describes this as the colonisation of the social sciences by economists. While acknowledging the early contribution of Bourdieu, Fine (2001) is concerned with Bourdieu's (1986) loose use of the term "capital" *viz* social, cultural and symbolic capital. Other authors have similarly identified negative aspects of SC (Adler & Kwon, 2000; Portes, 1998), including the risks involved in being too heavily connected, and potentially constraining independent action.

Portes (1998) also decries the faddish use of the term "social capital". Several scholars identify problems with the economic rational choice arguments. Becker (1996) argues that it ignores the social context in economic choice situations (see also Coleman, 1988; Fine, 2001; Granovetter, 1985; Portes, 1998). And Portes (1998) identifies the negative aspects of SC when it leads to communities that are so tightly bound by social norms and traditions that individual freedom and openness to external interventions are critically compromised. This effect has been similarly identified with respect to constraining innovation (D. Cohen & Prusak, 2001; Florida *et al.*, 2002). Additionally, Portes (1998) warns against the conceptual extensions of SC, for example, extending SC concepts from the individual to communities and even nations. He also warns against circularity in arguments being presented. For example, a common assertion is: "high civic pride leads to good social capital and better outcomes", but could good outcomes actually have generated civic pride? (Portes, 1998, pp20-21).

Following on from the initial work of Bourdieu is Coleman (1975, 1988), who positions SC as an economic resource for action. Coleman (1988, pS98) claims SC is:

... defined by its function. It is not a single entity, but a variety of different entities, with two elements in common: they all consist of some aspect of social structures, and they facilitate certain actions of actors—whether persons or corporate actors—within the structure.

Coleman (1988) also identifies three forms of SC: obligations and expectations; social norms; and information channels. The first two forms are seen as essential for achieving the closed networks that Coleman sees representing high levels of SC. Additionally, Coleman, in his definition, makes claims that SC is interpretable at both the individual and group (corporate) levels. This has largely been accepted by other SC researchers, although the lack of critical analytical support has attracted criticism from Portes (1998).

Coleman's (1998) thesis of tightly bound communities or networks constituting high SC is in contrast to Granovetter's (1973) strength of weak ties theory and Burt's (1992) structural holes theory. Granovetter argues that one benefits from weaker, or more distant ties, which provide more opportunities than closer ties. Burt (1992) identifies a related argument: that unique advantage accrues to those who provide a unique link between disparate communities (i.e. bridging a structural hole). Granovetter and Burt therefore argue that high SC is attached to "bridging" communities, rather than "bonding" communities. However, Burt (2000) does concede that the arguments could be complementary: while open networks increase the opportunity to identify new value creating opportunities, closed networks may be required to exploit these opportunities. This situation has since been supported by empirical research conducted on the semiconductor and steel industries, contrasting the "exploration" and "exploitation" characteristics of the respective industries (Rowley et al., 2000). SC is therefore a multi-dimensional concept, whose interpretation will depend on the context within which it is used.

In summary, the development of SC as a concept is centrally placed in the nexus of sociology and economics. Sociologists are seeing SC as a vehicle for promoting sociological concerns into the realms of economics and business. Likewise, economists have adopted SC as a mechanism for explaining and interpreting non-economic factors that might explain the practical shortcomings of neo-classical economic theory.

The SC paradox contrasts the tightly bound or closed networks identified by Coleman (1998) with the "strength of weak ties" and "structural holes" arguments of Granovetter (1973) and Burt (1992). This has led to the acceptance of SC as a context dependent concept, with both the "bonds" of close ties and the "bridges" (Adler & Kwon, 2002) over weak or disparate ties representing good SC, depending on the context. Of particular relevance to this review is whether the SC paradox plays out at the firm level, as well as the individual or personal level, as described in the literature to date.

The following sections explore in more detail the sub-components of SC as described in Figure 23, that is, public good SC, Corporate SC, CR, market alliance networks and SC measurement and management.

PUBLIC GOOD SOCIAL CAPITAL

Early SC literature was substantially focused on civic, or public good applications. Sociologists were principally concerned with the connection between "good neighbourhoods" and economic prosperity (Coleman, 1988; Putman, 1995; Woolcock, 1998). Putman's (1995) paper on the loss of civic mindedness in the USA attracted wide public attention, including a presidential meeting for Putman. Putman (1993) had also identified how differing levels of SC between the north and south of Italy was responsible for the respective differences in regional development rates. Also, the World Bank embraced SC as a concept for fighting poverty in third world countries (World_Bank, 2007).

SC survey instruments have been developed to assess the level of civic goodwill that exists in the community to inform interventions to improve the levels of SC, and hence economic prosperity (Krishna & Shrader, 1999; Spellerberg, 2001). For instance, Woolcock (1998) developed a policy framework, in conjunction with the World Bank, for embedding autonomous social relations within communities, between communities and civil society; between civil societies and the state; and within corporate enterprises.

Although the connection between civic mindedness and regional economic prosperity is well established, we must not suppose that all forms of SC leading to regional economic prosperity are civic-related. In the case of Silicon Valley, SC is related more to the collective of universities, venture capitalists and law firms specialising in intellectual property (Cohen & Fields, 1999). The level of economic prosperity is undoubted, despite the quite low levels of civic mindedness in the region.

CORPORATE SOCIAL CAPITAL

Traditionally, SC for private sector firms comprises of their contributions (usually financial) to the communities within which they operate (Allee, 2000). Figure 25 provides an overview map of several key themes in the Corporate SC literature to be covered in this section.

While often seen as corporate philanthropy, good corporate citizenship can also contribute to improved business performance (Allee, 2000; Hancock, 2005; Ro-

Figure 25. Corporate social capital literature themes

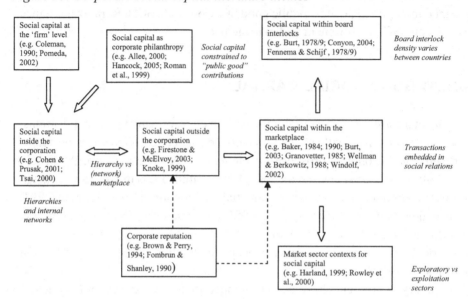

man *et al.*, 1999; Waddock & Graves, 1997). Discussions on this traditional view of SC can be labelled "industrial era" thinking. Many commentators have argued that there is a transition from the industrial era to a knowledge era (Drucker, 1992; Savage, 1996) where the traditional factors of production of land, labour and capital are being replaced by the creation of value through knowledge. In the knowledge era the boundaries between firms, governments and society at large are becoming increasingly blurred. Firms are becoming embedded within a complex web of inter-connections that span markets, governments and communities, rather than simply managing the interface between private and public sectors. In this knowledge era the concept of SC can take on a different dimension for the "firm".

For instance, Corporate SC is now much more than the social responsibility item in triple bottom line reporting[1] (Elkington, 1999). Leenders and Gabbay (1999) offer four levels of analysis for Corporate SC: the individual human being; groups or departments where individuals work together; the organisation itself (being the collection of groups or departments); and the inter-organisational network of organisations. These authors emphasise that Corporate SC can also become a li-ability whereby strong reciprocal ties can effectively close off the opportunity for exploring weaker ties. Therefore, relationships inside the firm, as well as external to the firm, can be seen as forms of SC.

Pomeda et al. (2002, p15) define the term "business social capital" to separate it from civic mindedness, which they call "relational capital". Business SC includes factors like productive infrastructure, productive behaviour and international commercial exchanges. Also, Pomeda et al. (2002) discuss the micro/macro aspects of SC initially established by Coleman (1990), who described the behaviour of a "firm" actor as constituted by the interdependent action of the individuals making up the firm. However, Pomeda et al. (2002) add an analysis of HC and how incentives can impact behaviours of individuals who, in their interactions with each other, are defining the SC of the firm. Knoke (1999) builds the linkages between organisational networks and Corporate SC and notes that network dynamics have reshaped corporate practices even to the level of the employment contract between the firm and its employees.

SC of "the firm" therefore can be represented both inside and outside the firm (Firestone & McElroy, 2003). A firm's external SC can be represented by its position in a marketplace. The study of marketplaces as networks has attracted significant research attention (Baker, 1984, 1990; Ron Burt, 2003; Mark Granovetter, 1985; Tsai, 2000; Wellman & Berkowitz, 1988; Windolf, 2002). The study of market boundaries from a network perspective has been contrasted with traditional methods of defining industry sectors on individual firm attributes (Berkowitz, 1988). The complex web of inter-relationships between firms in the marketplace provides the opportunity to study the competitive advantage available through the structure of a networked marketplace and a firm's positioning in the network (Burt, 2003). Burt argues that information benefits are maximised for firms that maintain relationships which span structural holes within a diverse network or marketplace. Granovetter (1985) also argues strongly that all market transactions are embedded in social relations and structure, whilst Baker's (1984) empirical research studies of option traders, and firm relationships with investment bankers, (Baker, 1990), supports Granovetter's assertions.

Granovetter (1985, p501) goes further to claim that the relationships between firms are more effective than internal hierarchies in delivering economic benefits. Simon (2001) provides a counter argument for critical, complex and time critical functions requiring hierarchies to execute effectively (e.g. war efforts). Internal hierarchies vs. (networked) markets are a fundamental issue faced by all firms considering the outsourcing of internal functions, for example, Information Technology Services (ITS) (Barney, 1991; Glassman, 2000; Thorelli, 1986; Williamson, 1981).

Inter-firm relationships based on common directorships known as "board interlocks" have attracted interest through the inferred influence that directors may have over inter-firm alliances (Ronald Burt, 1978/9; Conyon & Muldoon, 2004; Fennema & Schijf, 1978/9). For smaller firms, "board interlocks" are often related to shared ownership dating back to when the majority of companies were family-owned. A country's heritage for family-owned corporations and interlocks reflecting family-based relationships has shown through in studies on board interlocks at a national level. For example, France and Germany have much higher concentrations of board interlocks than the USA and the UK (Windolf, 2002).

Case Study

Companies Connections through Board Interlocks
(Analysis by Cai Kjaer, Optimice Pty Ltd)

It is not uncommon for company directors to sit on multiple boards. Two companies sharing a single board member could be considered interlinked, as the common board member could feasibly employ knowledge and experiences gained from one company in the other, and visa versa. If these companies shared more than one director then one could consider the interlinking between them even stronger. If we extend this logic to a whole market place, one could envisage a vast network of interlinked firms. It could be anticipated that the actual behaviour of firms could be influenced by the level of interlinking with other firms as facilitated by common directors.

Map 1 shows how firms listed on the Australian Stock Exchange are interlinked via common board members. The size of the nodes reflects the relative number of interlocks a firm has.

Map 1.

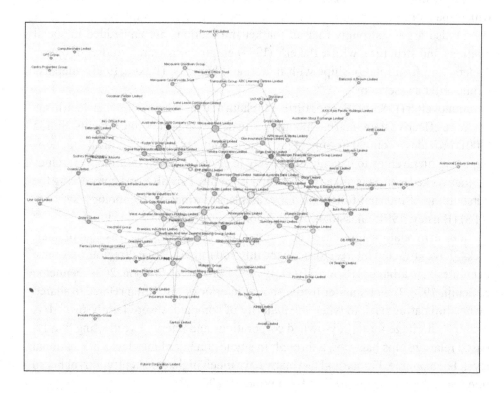

Several authors have noted that high SC can be detrimental to company performance. Florida, Cushing et al.(2002) state that highly cohesive groups can be blind to the sorts of new innovations that unconnected sources might bring. Along the same theme, others (D. Cohen & Prusak, 2001; Knoke, 1999; Locke, 1999) express concerns about the dangers of "group think" or "herd mentality". This is contradicted, in a definitional sense, by several other authors (ABS, 2004), who include "tolerance for diversity" or "diversity of friendships" as one of the key themes of SC. Burt (2000) argues that SC is more a function of brokerage across "structural holes" than closure within a network.

Other researchers have argued that SC of market sectors and, in particular, SN structures, differs between industries. Rowley et al. (2000) have demonstrated that exploratory industry sectors, like the semiconductor industry, require a broader and more diverse network of alliances, in contrast to the steel industry, where exploitation is the key focus requiring much tighter and focused networks. Harland (1999) explores the SC and liabilities that exist within supply networks. She notes that firms like Benetton and Toyota have pursued specific strategies to establish themselves as a network hub to gain key marketplace advantages. The use of different forms of networks in achieving decisions in banking firms is another example (Han & Breiger, 1999; Mizruchi & Stearns, 2001).

In summary, Corporate SC has emerged to describe SC from a corporate, rather than a public good, perspective. While a characterisation of SC exists which refers to corporate activities that contribute to the public good, the substantial literature that exists addresses the issues of SC inside the firm and external to the firm.

The characterisation of the marketplace as a SN has attracted substantial interest from SN researchers. As markets become more complex and interconnected the relevance of such studies will increase. Board interlocks through common directorships have also attracted attention, with public websites now exposing the patterns of interlocks that exist[2]. Finally, the multi-dimensional character of SC is now surfacing through empirical research on market sectors. Industrial sectors are now seen as benefiting from tightly bound exploitive networks, in contrast to new economy sectors like bio-technology and IT which demonstrate benefits from more open and diverse networks.

Corporate reputation is introduced here as a potential SC contributor. While corporate reputation has largely been developed within the marketing literature (Brown & Perry, 1994; Dollinger *et al.*, 1997; Fombrun & Shanley, 1990), one could argue that reputations, like SC, can be measured or assessed by external actors. As such, reputations are socially constructed and therefore deserve to be considered as a form of SC operating in the marketplace.

CORPORATE REPUTATION

Corporate reputation can be related to SC and/or public good investments made by corporations. As mentioned earlier, this is now considered more than purely corporate philanthropy, and a direct link to improved business performance is now being claimed. In one sense, corporate reputation can be thought of as either a sub-set of Corporate SC, representing the public good aspects, or one could argue that the terms are equivalent. Hall (1992), in a survey of 100 UK CEOs, identified company reputation, product reputation and employee know-how as the most important contributors to a company's success. Together with culture and networks, these attributes were valued more highly than physical assets.

Like SC, corporate reputation becomes important in incomplete information environments, where pre-purchase evaluations of quality could be vague or incomplete, for example, with law firms, accounting firms and other like service companies (Weigelt & Camerer, 1988). Linkages between Corporate SC and corporate reputation have been identified (Preston, 2004). Reputations are built from perceptions of a firm's relative structural position in the marketplace, its financial performance, its perceived conformity to social norms and its stated strategies (Fombrun & Shanley, 1990). Podolny et al. (1996) analysed networks and niches in the semiconductor industry between 1984 and 1991 and found that status was important, especially in crowded niches. The supporting empirical research conducted by the authors also indicated that high market-to-book ratios and low dividend yields induced a higher reputation to firms than profits, advertising intensity, size and risks. This has interesting implications for a company's investments in intangibles. Other benefits identified from a good corporate reputation include attractiveness for joint venturing and lower transaction costs (Dollinger et al., 1997). However, the authors indicate that "reputational" capital is multi-dimensional, with product and management reputation being the most important components.

Reputation can also be seen as an enhancer of relationships (Jackson, 2004). De Castro et al. (2004) define "reputational" capital as a sub-set of relational capital which in turn is a sub-set of SC. They split relational capital into direct relationships with suppliers, customers, partners and shareholders and indirect relationships with the community, government, trade unions and the mass media. "Reputational" capital is recognised as an influence on the development of both forms of relationships.

Fortune magazine's annual list of "most admired" companies, compiled since 1983[3], has been the source of several research studies on "reputational" capital (Brown & Perry, 1994; Dollinger et al., 1997; Fombrun & Shanley, 1990). The index uses eight attributes: quality of management; quality of products and services; value as a long-term investment; innovation; soundness of financial position; ability to attract and retain talented people; responsibility to the community and the environment; and wise use of corporate assets (Brown & Perry, 1994). The only explicit SC attribute is responsibility to the community and the environment. Surprisingly, this list does not include the SC attribute of relationships. Other researchers have built the links between corporate reputation and SC (De Castro et al., 2004; Jackson, 2004).

The *Fortune* list of eight criteria has six intangible attributes of which only one could be explicitly attached to SC and perhaps two others indirectly (i.e. innovation and ability to attract and retain talented people). The research based on this index has introduced other attributes such as relationship capital, joint ventures and alliances, and the ability to lower transaction costs, all of which are regularly mentioned in the literature on SC. In summary, corporate reputation should be at least considered as a concept which overlaps SC in a definitional sense, but could also be seen as a contributor to SC and vice versa.

Case Study

KAZ: Growing a Business through Building Corporate Social Capital

KAZ computer services was founded by Peter Kazacos in 1988 to provide outsourcing IT services to the Australian IT market place. From its fledgling start, KAZ grew to become one of the largest Australian owned IT services firms, prior to its acquisition by Telstra, Australia's principal telecommunications provider, for $333million in 2004. From the start KAZ tuned its corporate social capital through astute partnering with larger global IT firms as well as building a large number of medium to large client accounts across the country.

Sociogram 1 shows the Australian IT outsourcing market in 2007, with the outsourcing providers identified as circles and the clients as squares. The relative size relates to the number of outsourcing contracts a provider or client has entered into. One can see that KAZ has by far the largest number of contracts, though the overall value of the contracts (identified by the thickness of the links) is less than the major global providers like IBM, EDS and CSC. The data indicates that KAZ was following a strategy of building "customer capital" in the market place through its large number of separate clients as well as providing complementary services to major clients by partnering with some of the larger global providers. In this way KAZ was developing its business through building corporate social capital in the market place, which no doubt played a role in its acquisition by Telstra in 2004. Peter Kazacos was able to confirm this interpretation when he was first presented with this data in 2007.

Sociogram 1.

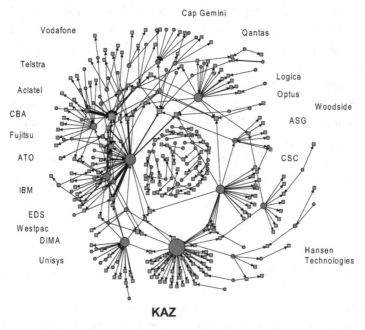

KAZ

MARKET ALLIANCE NETWORKS

The alliance literature relevant to this literature review is related to the human/social aspects of alliance management and its relative contribution to management decision-making and market performance. However, alliances can take many forms, with the level of formality ranging from a new legal entity, through to an "arm's length" informal arrangement (Lorange & Roos, 1992). The continuum of alliance structures is represented in Figure 26.

Alliances can be seen as one of the three major economic governance mechanisms, the other two being the firm and the market (Ebers, 1997). Typically, alliances are formalised through varying degrees of legal formality. While sociological research indicates that contracts can work against the development of a good business relationship (Macauley, 1963), alliances between major corporate entities are formalised to some degree. The primary intent of the alliance literature is the identification

Figure 26. Alliance forms (source: Lorange & Roos, 1992, p3)

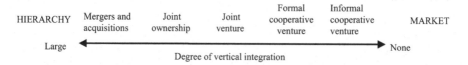

HIERARCHY	Mergers and acquisitions	Joint ownership	Joint venture	Formal cooperative venture	Informal cooperative venture	MARKET

Large ←——————— Degree of vertical integration ———————→ None

of appropriate partners and the on-going management of the alliance (Chan *et al.*, 1997; Dyer & Nobeoka, 2000; Gittel, 2003; Hoang *et al.*, 2003; Lyons, 1991; Mc-Cutcheon & Stuart, 2000; More & McGrath, 2001). However, there is recognition that the management of people and competencies in multicultural and multinational settings is likely to have a large impact on the overall, long-term operations and effectiveness of an alliance (Lorange & Roos, 1992). Empirical research on alliances has shown that complementary requirements and social and cultural compatibility are pre-cursers to a successful alliance (Sarker *et al.*, 2001). Firm valuations are also seen to be impacted by alliances (Chan et al., 1997). In particular, smaller firms have been shown to be able to significantly grow their firm valuation through technical alliances, typically with larger firms (Das *et al.*, 1998). Marketing alliances were seen to be less value enhancing than technical alliances.

The alliance literature mostly focuses on the single deal; however, the sheer growth in the number of alliances being formed will naturally lead to discussions of "alliance networks", beyond simple partnerships (Dyer & Nobeoka, 2000; Gulati *et al.*, 2000; Uzzi, 1997). The SC available to firms within a network will depend on how they identify and execute network connections as well as how attractive they are for potential partners. SN become valuable conduits for information and knowledge flows, providing access to new opportunities, but can also be constraints on independent action (Portes, 1998). SC becomes even more important in uncertain environments (Gulati & Gargiulo, 1999), when firms fall back to their trusted partners, with whom they typically have some history (Gulati et al., 2000; McCutcheon & Stuart, 2000).

The choice of network partners is most influenced by a prior contact or experience (Gulati, 1995). A number of empirical research studies on alliance networks have highlighted the importance of a rich supply network of relationships. For instance, Koka & Prescott (2002) use the steel industry to illustrate these points. Toyota has also demonstrated superior supply network performance through embracing tight and collaborative learning networks with its key suppliers (Dyer & Nobeoka, 2000). Talmud & Mesch (1997), in their study of Israeli firms, found a negative relationship between corporate instability and SC.

Relationships within market networks are not always equal. Highly regarded organisations (i.e. those with high levels of SC) are likely to be meticulous in their due diligence prior to selecting an alliance partner. For a newly established firm, successfully negotiating an alliance with a highly regarded organisation may enable them to benefit from a reflected reputation (Stuart, 2000). A market characterised by dominant actors reduces the uncertainty in the marketplace, leading to stable supply chain alliances. In contrast, in marketplaces where no dominant players exist, the market is uncertain, leading to many structural holes and therefore diverse opportunities. Podolny (2001) refers to the different network styles as "pipes and prisms", reflecting the multi-faceted nature of network relationships.

From a globalisation perspective, the motivation for alliance formations can be predicated on differing cultural foundations. For multinational enterprises, SC based on relationships is even more critical in the Asian firms where guanxi (China), kankei (Japan) and inmak (Korea) provide the framework for business arrangements (Hitt *et al.*, 2002).

The success or failure of alliances, with respect to improved profitability and/or market performance, is continually under review (Chan et al., 1997). Alliance success or otherwise is seen to have both a tangible and intangible impact on market perceptions. Indeed, market valuations have reacted immediately to the public announcement of alliances. The effect of alliances in terms of Corporate SC is therefore an important aspect for consideration.

HUMAN NETWORKS

Human networks are a central concept in this study forming a bridge between KM, SC, alliances and IC. Figure 27 provides an overview of several key human network themes that will be explored in this sub-section: The differences between the classes of human networks are related to the different levels of structure or formality. Typically, Communities of Practice (CoPs) and SN are largely intra-organisational and are seen to be less formal, while inter-enterprise and alliance networks infer a higher degree of formality. In the KM literature, human networks are synonymous with CoPs, defined as "groups of people who share a concern, a set of problems, or a passion about a topic, and who deepen their knowledge and expertise in this area by interacting on an on-going basis" (Wenger *et al.*, 2002). These groups are typically informally connected and operated (E. Lesser & Prusak, 1999; E. L. Lesser &

Figure 27. Human network literature themes

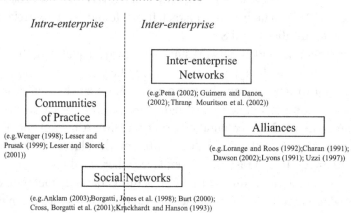

Storck, 2001; Wenger, 1998). "Networks" is a term used to describe more formally established groups. Within organisations, networks may be formally recognised and funded; however, typically, networks describe inter-enterprise groups (Guimera *et al.*, 2002; Pena, 2002). More commonly, inter-enterprise networks are covered in the literature on alliances (Charan, 1991; Dawson, 2002; Lorange & Roos, 1992; Lyons, 1991; Thrane *et al.*, 2002; Uzzi, 1997). The other major source of literature on human networks is the SN literature pertaining to SC. SN can be thought of as the structural components of SC. There is substantial literature on the analysis and measurement of SN and their relationship with IC and KM (Anklam, 2003; Borgatti *et al.*, 1998; Ronald S. Burt, 2000; Rob Cross *et al.*, 2001; Krackhardt & Hanson, 1993).

There are overlapping definitions for networks, the common denominator being that they are all human-based and involve relationship building and sharing of knowledge. Knowledge networks in the KM literature emphasise the knowledge sharing aspects particularly inside the firm. Effective knowledge networks within a firm are seen as a key mechanism for sharing best practices across the enterprise for organisational advantage (i.e. lower costs, faster cycle times, higher revenues).

MEASURING AND MANAGING SOCIAL CAPITAL

With the acceptance of SC as a concept that potentially provides benefits to individuals, communities, organisations, firms and even nations, the need to measure and manage it is a progression. Methods for measuring SC have taken two distinct paths. The first is through survey methods, which identify particular dimensions of SC, and typically use Likert-type scales to achieve a measure of quantitative evaluation. The development and application of this style of measurement has been largely inspired by Putman's critique of civic mindedness in the USA (Putman, 1995), and it has mainly been used to assess whole communities or nations. The second path is through the use of SNA techniques (Scott, 2000; Wasserman & Faust, 1994). This method is inspired by a definition of SC as the quality of relationships between individual actors (Burt, 1992; Coleman, 1988). SNA surveys collect information about ties or links between individuals, and then interpret the network patterns into different dimensions of SC.

With regard to the first path, the majority of survey-based measures for SC have been generated as national responses to the perceived decline in civic pride, community and wellbeing in the USA (Putman, 1995). For instance, measurement frameworks for national level measures of SC have been developed in Australia (ABS, 2004), New Zealand (Spellerberg, 2001), the UK (Harper, 2001) and the USA (R. Putman, 1993). These measurement frameworks are looking to develop a global benchmark measurement tool for understanding the SC of different nations. The typical dimensions of SC that are included in these benchmarking tools include participation in networks, reciprocity, trust in the community, social norms, tolerance of diversity, personal empowerment, trust in government, altruism and philanthropy, and demographic information.

The World Bank has been active in promoting the value of SC in support of its mission to fight poverty. It has developed a social capital assessment tool (SCAT) to assess SC levels in the countries and regions within which it operates (Krishna & Shrader, 1999). SCAT provides a framework for macro and micro assessment. At the macro level, formal relationships and structures such as legal rules, political regimes and participation in policy formation are assessed. At the micro level, the assessments are split into cognitive and structural dimensions. The cognitive dimension is concerned with many of the dimensions studied in the national SC surveys mentioned previously *viz* values of trust, reciprocity, solidarity, social norms and attitudes. The structural dimensions assess horizontal network structures, and the formal and informal modes of decision making within these networks. The application of SCAT and like tools often makes use of composite indices of SC. Fukuyama (1999) and Hjollund & Svendsen (2000) have synthesised SC survey tools into a standard questionnaire with a recommended suite of statistical approaches for analysing the results.

Qualitative survey methods have also been used for organisational SC applications. For instance, Glaeser et al. (2000) developed a survey instrument to measure trust and trustworthiness, elements that the authors consider to be key components of SC. In their empirical research, the survey respondents were also invited to participate in experimental "trust" games to further develop an understanding of trustworthy behaviour. The findings indicate that social proximity is closely related to trust and trustworthiness. Glaeser et al. (2000) also found that individuals of high status, a component of SC, are able to elicit more trustworthiness in others. The experimental approach to the measurement of SC has also been applied to predict future financial decisions, for example, repaying a loan (Karlan, 2002). The results indicate that those identified as trustworthy by the trust game are more likely to pay back loans. The impact of social interactions and network ties on knowledge acquisition and exploitation in young technology-based firms has been shown to be positive (Yli-Renko *et al.*, 2001). These authors, in their survey, asked simple questions about the degree of social interactions between company members and their customers, as an indication of SC.

A SC benchmarking system has been designed to assess the market performances of geographic clusters (Marti, 2004; Viedma, 2003). Marti (2004) considers six key factors in assessing possible network formation: resources and capabilities; demand; suppliers and other related industries; firm strategy; culture and structure;

and competitors and government. This framework enables clusters to benchmark their SC in terms of network construction.

Also, Youndt et al. (2004) used a survey instrument to measure SC, along with HC and organisational capital in assessing their impact on investments. The authors constructed five questions to elicit a SC profile from the respondents. The questions focused on factors that might encourage collaborative behaviour.

In summary, concerning the first path, survey-based SC benchmarking systems have proved to be a popular development activity for SC researchers. At the national level, the benchmarking tools do appear to be converging to the extent that a standard toolset is probably within reach. Outside national or regional SC assessments, other SC survey designs are still at the exploratory or emergent stage. The work of Marti (2004) and Viedma (2003) appears to be the genesis of a SCAT with applications to firms and markets, but it is still at a preliminary level, and has yet to attract the SC research community at large.

Regarding the second path, SNA has developed into a sociological discipline of its own, since its genesis in the early work of social psychologist Dr. J.L. Moreno and his work with sociograms in the 1930s (Jacobs, 1945). A plethora of graph theoretic measures have been designed to describe social constructs, positions and/or roles within SN. SNA methods have matured to the extent that a number of texts and reference books have been produced (e.g. Scott, 2000; Wasserman & Faust, 1994), and a professional society has been formed to support its development[4]. Network measures have been related to several SC interpretations. The SC concepts of trust, reciprocity, diversity and network participation can be inferred from the interpretations of the SN representation of the community or population under study.

Typical SNA surveys will contain directives like: "nominate those colleagues that you have the most trustful relationship with" (Rob Cross & Parker, 2004). Demographic information like business unit membership, nationality and geographic location can be captured as attributes of each respondent. Bounded surveys (i.e. where the population under study is constrained to nominating only those that belong to the group under study) can identify reciprocity if actor A and actor B nominate each other as trustworthy ties.

There are some SC dimensions that cannot be easily captured with SNA. For example, altruism or philanthropy and levels of personal empowerment would be difficult to interpret from a relationship map. If attributes like these are important to the application at hand, then SNA may need to be complemented by more traditional techniques. While there are some areas where SNA methods are deficient, the power of the technique is in its ability to analyse the complexity of the interrelationships that exist within a community, organisation or marketplace, down to the individual (R. Cross *et al.*, 2002; Gulati & Gargiulo, 1999; Krackhardt & Hanson, 1993; W. Tsai & Ghoshal, 1998; Wellman, 1990).

Table 1. SNA measurement construct examples

Measurement Construct	Description
Network Size and Density	Measures the size of the network by the number of actors in the community under study. Density is determined by the number of interconnections as a proportion of the maximum possible number of interconnections.
Degree Centrality	Measures the centrality of an actor in the community, based on the number of other actors connected to it. Generally, the degree is defined as either "inward" or "outward", reflecting the relationship direction.
Reciprocity	Measures the two-way connections between actors.
Betweenness Centrality	Measures the degree to which an individual actor is on the path of connections between other actors.
Closeness Centrality	Measures the degree to which an actor is connected to every other actor in the network, i.e. the distance required (number of indirect connections) to reach other actors.
Cliques and Sub-groups	Groups that can be distinguished by the density of connections between the members compared to the rest of the network.

The visual representation of a network is a graph of nodes or actors connected by one or more links. The links may optionally be directional, that is, have a specific direction of influence. In mathematical terms, the graph can be analysed via a number of measurement constructs that make use of properties of network graphs. Some examples of key constructs developed by SNA researchers (Wasserman & Faust, 1994) are shown in Table 1.

Different constructs have different SC interpretations for individuals interacting within or between groups or for groups interacting with other groups (Borgatti et al., 1998). For example, SC connections between two firms (groups) may indicate high degree centrality (i.e. many connections). A low closeness measure (i.e. minimal distance between members of two firms) would also indicate a central position in a network.

In conclusion, for path two, the SNA methods for measuring SC could be seen as complementary to the more qualitative survey techniques. Some of the limitations of SNA measures for SC include the inability to provide reasonable interpretations for some of the SC concepts like altruism and personal empowerment. The ability to undertake an analysis at the individual relationship level provides a degree of granularity that cannot be achieved with broad-based qualitative surveys. In particular, the advantages related to the structure of a community and the position of actors within the community network can be studied in some detail. The ability to make visible the invisible networks that exist in an organisation provides a powerful instrument for measuring and managing the SC in and between organisations.

SCHOOLS OF THOUGHT: IC, IA AND SC

This critical review of the literature finds authors clustered around particular "schools of thought", which are illustrated in Figure 28: The schools of thought reflect clusters of authors who have cited the thought leaders in that cluster. The clusters reflect the level of overlap, or lack thereof, between the schools of thought under focus. The majority of authors from those selected for detailed review fall within one of the three identified schools of thought. The schools of thought are: the Scandinavian School of Intellectual capital; the New York School of Intangible Assets; and the Chicago School of Social Capital. Each school will now be discussed in more detail.

The Scandinavian School of Intellectual capital

The pioneers of this school of thought are arguably Karl Erik Sveiby (1997) and Leif Edvinsson (1997). These authors led the Swedish concentration on research around IC and KM. Other researchers from Scandinavian countries like Denmark and Finland have joined this school and there is now a growing membership from outside Scandinavia. This school has largely been concerned with developing means for reporting IC performance. In particular, it is concerned with identifying

Figure 28. Schools of thought across IC, IA and SC

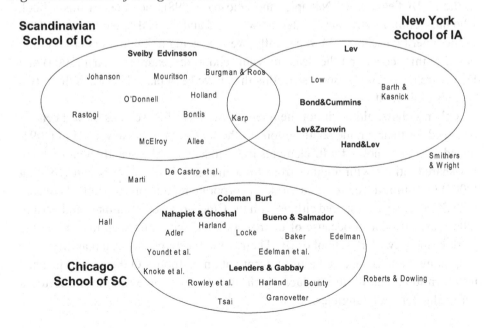

measures and metrics around IC attributes, how to organise IC elements, and how to communicate them to market actors.

The New York School of Intangible Assets

This school of thought is accounting-based and is focused on the accounting treatment of IA. The leader of this school of thought is Baruch Lev, along with colleagues from the Brookings Institute Project on Intangible Assets. The largely quantitative research is looking for explanations for the growing gap between market values and net tangible asset values. This gap has led to a growing concern around the on-going relevance of traditional accounting measures. The Scandinavian school overlaps the New York school in its interests in growing market-to-book values as evidence of the growth in the knowledge-based economy.

The Chicago School of Social Capital

While the concept of SC has a long history, it is perhaps the work of John Coleman and Ron Burt from the University of Chicago that has proved central to the development of SC in a corporate context. This school has looked at markets as social constructs, identifying SC as a key source of economic value. The school has been largely unconnected with the schools of IC/KM and IA. Leenders & Gabbay (1999) further developed the SC theme into Corporate SC and liability in their edited volume, but none of the papers submitted explicitly referenced key authors in the IC/IA fields. Even Nahapiet and Ghoshal (1998), members of this school, who have built the strongest bridge between SC and IC, had failed to cite authors in the other two schools. More recently, we are seeing a few authors cross citing between this school and the Scandinavian school, for example, Marti (2004) and De Castro et al. (2004). Because of this they have been placed between these two schools of thought.

Other authors, although not members of the identified schools, have been introduced for their unique contributions to the focus of this review. R. Hall (1993) introduced a taxonomy for IC elements independently of the Scandinavian school, but shared citings with authors from the Chicago school. Roberts and Dowling (2002) were introduced for their work on corporate reputation, an aligned concept with SC and they also shared citings with the Chicago school. Smithers and Wright (2000) are introduced because of their work which could be seen to critique the work of the New York school of IA. Their work questions the sustainability of an IA premium and is based on a full interpretation of Tobin's Q theory and its need to return to an equilibrium value, which would see at some time in the future a zero value for net intangibles.

The rationale for categorising the selected references into three schools of thought is to highlight the large gap in the literature connecting SC with IC and IA. The remainder of this critique of the literature is focused on critically analysing the identified schools of thought and taking the opportunity to identify knowledge from an integration of their ideas. In the following sections, literature from within and between the identified schools of thought is selected for detailed discussion.

FROM SOCIAL CAPITAL TO INTELLECTUAL CAPITAL

The long pedigree of SC and its interplay with the field of economics was discussed in Chapter III on Socio-economics and the theory of the firm. The current section takes an analytical view of important works that have led to the connection between SC and IC e.g. (Nahapiet & Ghoshal, 1998).

Granovetter (1985), in his paper on the embeddedness of economics in social structure, argues convincingly about how just about every economic or commercial transaction can be shown to be influenced by social structure. He uses examples of power held by boards of directors, supply chain transactions dictated more by relationships than price, and the absence of litigation when strong networks exist.

One of the early commentators on SN as it pertains to corporate performance is Burt. His (2003) work on the social structure of competition forms the basis for the argument that SC is intimately related to market performance. Burt (2003) sees SC, along with financial capital and HC, as the basis of competition. In fact, SC acts as a mediating influence on financial capital and HC in a competitive environment. By characterising the marketplace as a SN, Burt (2003) identifies particular positions of actors within the network as conferring competitive advantage. These positions place the actor at an advantageous location with respect to information and knowledge flows. Burt is recognised for his concept of "structural holes" in a network or marketplace which could be compared with gaps in the market. Actors placed across "structural holes" have the advantage of early insights into opportunity and therefore first mover advantages accrue to them.

Burt has conducted numerous experiments and research studies in support of his proposition around "structural holes" (Burt, 1992; 1997; 2000; Burt, et al., 2002) and its relationship to profit generation. The largely quantitative studies have drawn correlations between SN performance and personal performance, promotions and compensation received. At the organisational level, Burt (2003) identifies examples of advantage gained from spanning "structural holes", but concedes that closed networks (Coleman, 1990) become important when looking to pursue the advantage created through spanning the more open, exploratory networks.

Both Burt (2003) and Granovetter (1985) tend to work with individual actors rather than at the corporate level, though there are claims that the principles are equally relevant to firms as they are to individuals (J. Coleman, 1988). The weakness when concentrating on individuals is that correlating the relationship between SC, as measured by SN characteristics, and quantitative market measures like ROA, earnings or market values are only notional or based on surveyed opinions of performance. The cognitive jump between individual and corporate entities is also a big one, with little empirical research support. These weaknesses have been partially addressed through several empirical studies (Bounty, 2000; Rowley *et al.*, 2000; W. Tsai, 2001; Youndt et al., 2004).

Rowley et al. (2000) have pursued the different utility of open and closed networks in their analysis of the steel and semiconductor industries. Using comprehensive quantitative techniques, they were able to confirm that for fast changing industries like the semiconductor industry, characterised by exploration for the next opportunity, open networks are beneficial. Their networks show a preponderance of weak ties developed through partnerships and alliances. Alternatively, the firms in this industry operating within closed networks, with many strong and redundant ties, perform poorly. The situation was reversed when the mature and slow changing steel industry was studied. In this industry it is in the exploitation of best practices, rather than in their discovery, that the advantage lies. Closed networks were seen as most beneficial for exploitation applications.

Youndt et al. (2004) surveyed some 200 organisations looking for intangible factors of SC, organisational capital, R&D, HC and IC impacts on firm performance, as measured by TOBQ and ROA. Their findings indicate that organisational capital does not contribute to the same degree as HC, IT investments and SC. They found that, overall, IC was highly related to TOBQ and ROA measures. While this research is important from the perspective of linking SC and IC to TOBQ measures, it is limited by the fact that SC is only measured internal to the firm, and therefore ignores attributes like corporate reputation. The study was also limited by the short longitudinal period of two years.

Bounty (2000) addresses the externalities of SC and the study of R&D workers and how they balance the protection of their firm's IC against the generation of new knowledge through external relationships (i.e. external SC). On balance, the findings indicate that the firm benefits more from building its EC and capturing new ideas from external sources than concentrating on protecting what they have generated internally (Bounty, 2000, p63). The study indicates that some 40% of new ideas are from sources outside the firm, and therefore are reliant on good external SC to access them.

Tsai (2001) studied business units within a large petrochemical company and also a food manufacturing company. His research identified that the interaction between absorptive capacity (AC) and network position had a significant impact on innovation and business performance. The introduction of the concept of "absorptive capacity" (Tsai, 2001, p997), measured by Tsai as R&D intensity (RES), is important as it identifies a firm's attribute that is a precondition for successful SC development at the firm level. From this point on in the book, absorptive capacity (AC) may be referred to interchangeably with its proxy, RES.

The SC and IC research themes had developed independently until the late 1990s, when Nahapiet and Ghoshal published their seminal (1998) work. In this work they proposed that a firm's capability to create SC provides a condusive environment for IC creation. They posit that firms are better placed to create SC than markets, with consequential organisational advantages. Nahapiet and Ghoshal (1998) had drawn their interests in SC from the work of the Chicago School of SC, led by Coleman (1990) and Burt (1992).

The ability of firms, as social communities, to specialise in creating and sharing knowledge was seen as offering a contrasting "theory of the firm" to the traditional transaction cost theory. The "theory of the firm" discussion relates to what should be kept inside the organisation and what should be left to the market. The authors draw on the work of Nobel Laureate Herbert Simon (Simon, 1947), who agrees that efficiency of communications, rather than transactions, should be the determinant. In his seminal (1947) work, Simon argues strongly for the merit of the management hierarchy and the communications it affords. Simon (2001) also acknowledges the important role that social and behavioural dimensions play in efficient communications and hence organisational performance.

Nahapiet and Ghoshal's (1998) developed a model for linking SC to the creation of new IC through the combination and exchange of knowledge. SC provides the mechanism that maximises knowledge combination and exchange. This model highlights the characterisation of IC as more related to general Knowledge management concepts than the particular characterisations of IC that have emerged from the Scandinavian School on IA (e.g. Sveiby, 1997). Interestingly enough their deconstruction of SC into structural, cognitive and relational dimensions in building their arguments is not dissimilar to Sveiby's deconstruction of IC into HC, INC and EC dimensions used to build an argument for IC's impact on organisational performance. While they disregard the emerging mainstream IC literature, Nahapiet and Ghoshal's (1998) SC/IC linkage has been the foundation work for a plethora of related research. However, until recently, the link to the Scandinavian and New York Schools of IC and IA in the literature was tenuous.

The pioneering work of Nahapiet & Ghoshal (1998) has not escaped criticism. For instance, Locke (1999) points out that there is also a dark side to SC and that more is not always better. Locke identifies the common criticism that closed networks can become insular and impervious to new ideas. They can be the source of value destroying politics within firms and Locke (1999) uses the examples of the collapse of the Japanese banking system and IBM's pre-1990s culture as an example of too much SC. Locke (1999, p8) also argues that knowledge creation is an individual pursuit and does not in itself generate SC and in fact could do the reverse. This criticism is perhaps a little misguided as Nahapiet & Ghoshal (1998, p251) do agree that knowledge or IC does result from SC elements. The issue of closed networks and negative effects that can arise from them is real and points to the need to build a balance or establish a limit to how far one might look to build up SC.

MULTISOURCING GOVERNANCE

The preceding sections have explored, through the literature, the concepts of social capital, corporate reputation and Intellectual capital as intangible resources for the firm. A comprehensive formulation of Corporate SC has been proposed which subsumes the concepts of Intellectual capital and Corporate Reputation within its definition. Multisourcing governance is about managing networks of relationships amongst firms. The value to the participating firms can and should be measured in terms other than return on investment (ROI). The growing discrepancy between firm market and book values is a stark demonstration that value can be generated through non financial means i.e. through the application of non-financial resources, of which Corporate SC is one. Looking back to the supply chain maturation framework provided in chapter III (Figure 14), one could envisage that firms operating at level 5 would be achieving value well beyond optimising the cost of supply. An agile network of suppliers with complementary skill bases and the motivation to create new value through innovation, will create new value for its participants, potentially well beyond the value for which they were originally assembled.

For the business manager facilitating a multisourcing arrangement to the supply firm executive, the message from this chapter is that by carefully building a network of complementary skilled firms the value generated could far exceed the traditional supply chain optimisation goals. The Corporate SC implicit in a network of cooperative and reciprocating members is a resource that can be leveraged to generate new opportunities well beyond the scope of the original alliance.

SUMMARY AND CONCLUSIONS

The conclusion from the contextual literature review is that Corporate SC could justifiably be identified as a resource that could contribute to defining the boundaries of the firm and that the research could be located along with other resource-based theories of the firm (e.g. knowledge-based view of the firm).

Citation analysis identified that the literature could be largely partitioned into three "schools of thought": the Scandinavian School of IC; the Chicago School of SC; and the New York School of IA. Of particular interest, however, was the intersection between SC and IC, one of the bridges that this review aims to build.

The core phenomenon addressed by the literature reviewed in this chapter is the sustained growth in market-to-book ratios of publicly listed firms over the past 25 years. This has led to a reduction in the usefulness of traditional financial measures such as earnings, cash flows and book values, in predicting share market performance. Ultimately, this can lead to excessively high cost of capital for intangible-intensive firms, systematic undervaluation of these firms, more insider trading opportunities and the potential for manipulation of financial results (Lev, 2001). Explanations of this phenomenon have been largely referred to as the growing "intangibles effect" (Stewart, 1997). Quantitative accounting-based studies using available data on specific intangibles like R&D and advertising have not been able to fully explain the intangibles effect.

The review of the IC research included many theoretical frameworks for describing intangibles and measuring and managing them from an individual firm perspective. IC indices suffer from the need to collate a multitude of component parts with no assurance that these components can be measured in a standardised manner, or that the descriptors for the components can be applied consistently by different firms.

The following research issues are put forth as a means for building a platform for viewing SC as a primary lens for viewing a firm's IC. In this way, SC is positioned to play a central role in addressing the identified gap in the literature relating SC to IC and firm performance. The proposed construct linking SC to the traditional IC elements is discussed below.

Figure 29. Social capital and IC

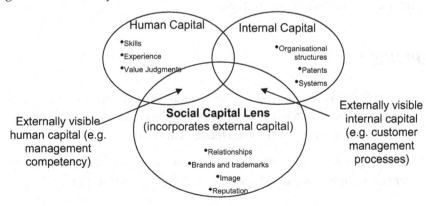

Figure 29 illustrates the relationship between IC (as its traditional components of HC, INC and EC) and SC. Some elements of IC are commonly defined as part of SC (e.g. an individual's SN), but a firm's alliance structures and stakeholder relationships are both SC and EC elements to the extent that one could argue that SC totally encapsulates the EC component of IC. Other IC elements, like patents, skills and experience that may not be explicitly defined as part of SC, do contribute to SC by acting as "attractors" for potential connections, and therefore SC development. For example, a firm looking to develop an alliance arrangement with another firm will be attracted by elements like reputation, brand and the skills and experience of the staff in these prospective organisations. Strictly however, a SC lens into a firm's HC and INC elements would only see what is externally visible (e.g. a customer service process or senior management competency). An organisation, however, achieves excellent SC by collectively maximising its EC, INC and HC. As such, the potential exists for SC to act as a proxy measure for IC.

The use of SC as a proxy measure for IC performance is an unexplored area. However, the increasing networked nature of the marketplace suggests that market-level SC measures could indeed provide a better gauge of IC performance than current IC measures that rely on composition from parts drawn from quite diverse sources (e.g. human competency, business processes, brands). SC is a network measure which can provide a single focus on socially constructed relationships. A collective measure for SC based on relationships could provide a single concept to explain variations in market-to-book ratios, or the so called "intangibles effect".

The relevance of the intangible effect for multisourcing networks is the intangible resource, in the form of Corporate SC. Corporate SC accrues to networks that have successfully melded into an effective cooperative, potentially generating value for its members far beyond the original reasons for its formation. The following chapters move from theory to practice in terms of IT Governance from a sociological perspective. The application of corporate social capital within personal and intra-organisational networks is explored specifically, highlighting the implications for IT Governance and multisourcing strategies.

REFERENCES

ABS. (2004, 11/2/2004). Measuring Social Capital—An Australian Framework and Indicators. Retrieved 10/5/07, from http://www.abs.gov.au/AUSSTATS/abs@.nsf/Lookup/1378.0Main+Features12004?OpenDocument

Adler, P., & Kwon, S.-W. (2000). Social Capital: The Good, the Bad, and the Ugly. In E. Lesser (Ed.), *Knowledge and Social Capital*: Butterworth-Heinmann.

Adler, P., & Kwon, S.-W. (2002). Social Capital: Prospects for a New Concept. *Academy of Management Review, 27*(1), 17-40.

Allee, V. (2000). The Value Evolution: Addressing larger implications of an intellectual capital and intangibles perspective. *Journal of Intellectual capital, 1*(1), 17-32.

Anklam, P. (2003). KM and the Social Network. *KM Magazine, 6*(8).

Baker, W. (1984). The Social Structure of a National Securities market. *American Journal of Sociology, 89*(4), 775-811.

Baker, W. (1990). Market Networks and Corporate Behaviour. *American Journal of Sociology, 96*(3), 589-625.

Baker, W. (2001). Social Capital. *Future—the Aventis Magazine, 2*, 52-56.

Ballow, J., Burgman, R., & Molnar, M. (2004). Managing for shareholder value: intangibles, future value and investment decisions. *Journal of Business Strategy, 25*(3), 26-34.

Barney, J. (1991). Firm Resources and Sustained Competitive Advantage. *Journal of Management, 17*(1), 99-120.

Becker, G. (1996). *Accounting for Tastes*: Cambridge: Harvard University Press.

Borgatti, S., Jones, C., & Everett, M. G. (1998). Network Measures of Social Capital. *CONNECTIONS, 21*(2), 1-36.

Bounty, I. (2000). Interpersonal and interaction influences on informal resource exchanges between R&D researchers across organizational boundaries. *Academy of Management Journal, 43*(1), 50-65.

Bourdieu, P. (1980). Le capital social:notes provisoires. *Actes Rech Sci. Soc., 31*, 2-3.

Bourdieu, P. (1986). The Forms of Capital. In J. G. Richardson (Ed.), *Handbook of Theory and Research for the Sociology of Education*. New York: Greenwood Press.

Brooking, A. (1996). *Intellectual capital, Core Assets for the Third Millennium Enterprise*: International Thomson Business Press.

Brown, B., & Perry, S. (1994). Removing the Financial Performance Halo from Fortunes "Most Admired" Companies. *Academy of Management Journal, 37*(5), 1347-1359.

Bueno, E., & Salmador, M. P. (2004). The role of social capital in today's economy. *Journal of Intellectual capital, 5*(4), 556-574.

Burt, R. (1978/9). A Structural Theory of Interlocking Corporate Directorates. *Social Networks, 1*, 415-435.

Burt, R. (2003). The Social Structure of Competition. In Rob Cross, A. Parker & L. Sasson (Eds.), *Network in the Knowledge Economy* (pp.13-56). New York: Oxford University Press.

Burt, R., Guilarte, M., Raider, H., & Yasuda, Y. (2002). Competition, Contingency, and External Structure of Markets. *Advances in Strategic Management, 19*, 167-217.

Burt, R. S. (1992). *Structural Holes*: Cambridge: Harvard University Press.

Burt, R. S. (2000). The Network Structure of Social Capital. In R. I. Sutton & B. M. Shaw (Eds.), *Research in Organizational Behaviour, 22*, 345-423. Greenwich: JAI Press.

Carr, N. G. (2004). *Does IT matter? information technology and the corrosion of competitive advantage*: Harvard Business School Press, Boston.

Carroll, M., & Stanfield, J. R. (2003). Social Capital, Karl Polanyi, and American Social and Institutional Economics. *Journal of Economic Issues, 37*(2), 397-403.

Chan, S. H., Kensinger, J., W., Keown, A. J., & Martin, J. D. (1997). Do strategic alliances create value? *Journal of Financial Economics, 46*, 199-221.

Charan, R. (1991). How Networks Reshape Organizations—For Results. *Harvard Business Review, 69*(5), 104-115.

Chatzkel, J. (2003). The Collapse of Enron and the role of intellectual capital. *Journal of Intellectual capital, 4*(2), 127-143.

Cohen, A. (2002). *The Perfect Store: Inside eBay*. London: Piatkus.

Cohen, D., & Prusak, L. (2001). *In Good Company: How Social Capital Makes Organizations Work*. Boston: Harvard Business School Press.

Coleman, J. (1975). Social Structure and a Theory of Action. In P. Blau (Ed.), *Approaches to the Study of Social Structure*: New York: Free Press.

Coleman, J. (1988). Social Capital in the Creation of Human capital. *The American Journal of Sociology, 94 Supplement*, S95-S120.

Conyon, M., & Muldoon, M. (2004). *The Small World Network Structure of Board of Directors*: Warton school, University of Pennsylvania.

Cross, R., Borgatti, S., & Parker, A. (2001). Beyond answers: dimensions of the advice network. *Social Networks, 23*, 215-235.

Cross, R., Borgatti, S. P., & Parker, A. (2002). Making invisible work visible: Using social network analysis to support strategic collaboration. *California Management Review, 44*(2), 25-46.

Cross, R., & Parker, A. (2004). *The Hidden Power of Social Networks*: Harvard Business School Press, Boston, MA.

Das, S., Sen, P., & Sengupta, S. (1998). Impact of Strategic Alliances on Firm Valuation. *Academy of Management Journal, 41*(1), 27-41.

Dawson, R. (2002). *Living Networks: Leading Your Company, Customers, and Partners in the Hyper-Connected Economy*: Prentice-Hall.

De Castro, G. M., Saez, P. L., & López, J. E. N. (2004). The role of corporate reputation in developing relational capital. *Journal of Intellectual capital, 5*(4), 575-585.

Dollinger, M., Golden, P., & Saxton, T. (1997). The Effect of Reputation on the Decision to Joint Venture. *Strategic Management Journal, 18*(2), 127-140.

Drucker, P. (1992). The New Society of Organizations. *Harvard Business Review*(September—October).

Dyer, J., & Nobeoka, K. (2000). Creating and Managing a High Performance Knowledge-Sharing Network: The Toyota Case. *Strategic Management Journal, 21*, 345-367.

Ebers, M. (1997). *Explaining Inter-Organisational Network Formation*. Oxford, New York: Oxford University Press.

Edvinsson, L., & Malone, M. S. (1997). *Intellectual capital—realizing your company's true value by finding its hidden brainpower*: New York: Harper Business Publisher.

Elkington, J. (1999). *Cannibals with forks: the triple bottom line of 21st century business*: Oxford: Capstone.

Fennema, M., & Schijf, H. (1978/9). Analysing Interlocking Directorates: Theory and Methods. *Social Networks, 1*, 297-332.

Fine, B. (2001). *Social Capital vs. Social Theory*. London, New York: Routledge.

Firestone, J., & McElroy, M. (2003). *Key Issues in the New Knowledge management*: Butterworth-Heinmann.

Florida, R., Cushing, R., & Gates, G. (2002). When social capital stifles innovation. *Harvard Business Review.*

Florin, J., Lubatkin, M., & Schulze, W. (2003). A Social Capital Model of High-Growth Ventures. *Academy of Management Journal, 46*(3), pp.374-384.

Fombrun, C., & Shanley, M. (1990). What's in a Name? reputation Building and Corporate Strategy. *Academy of Management Journal, 33*(2), pp.233-256.

Fukuyama, F. (1999). *Social Capital and Civil Society*: George Mason University.

Gittel, J. H. (2003). *The Southwest Airlines Way: Using the Power of Relationships to Achieve High Performance.* New York: McGraw-Hill.

Glaeser, E., Laibson, D., Scheinkman, J., & Soutter, C. (2000). Measuring Trust. *THe Quarterly Journal of Economics, August.*

Glassman, D. (2000). *IT outsourcing and Shareholder Value*: Stern Stewart Research.

Granovetter, M. (1973). The strength of weak ties. *American Journal of Sociology, 78*, pp.1360-1380.

Granovetter, M. (1985). Economic Action and Social Structure: The Problem of Embeddedness. *American Journal of Sociology, 91*(3), pp.481-510.

Guimera, R., Danon, L., Diaz-Guilera, A., Giralt, F., & Arenas, A. (2002). The real communication network behind the formal chart: community structure in organisations. from http://galadriel.ffn.ub.es/articles/emal_networks.pdf

Gulati, R. (1995). Social Structure and Alliance Formation Patterns: A Longitudinal Analysis. *Administrative Science Quarterly, 40*, pp.619-652.

Gulati, R., & Gargiulo, M. (1999). Where do Interorganizational Networks Come From? *American Journal of Sociology, 104*(5), pp.1439-1493.

Gulati, R., Nohria, N., & Zaheer, A. (2000). Strategic Networks. *Strategic Management Journal, 21*, pp.203-215.

Guthrie, J., & Petty, R. (2000). Intellectual capital: Australian annual reporting practices. *Journal of Intellectual capital, 1*(3), pp.241.

Hall, R. (1992). The Strategic Analysis of Intangible Resources. *Strategic Management Journal, 13*, pp.135-144.

Hall, R. (1993). A Framework linking Intangible Resources and capabilities to sustainable competitive advantage. *Strategic Management Journal, 14*(8), pp.607-618.

Han, S., & Breiger, R. (1999). Dimensions of Corporate Social Capital: Toward Models and Measures. In R. Leenders & S. Gabbay (Eds.), *Corporate Social Capital and Liability* (pp. pp. 118-133): Boston: Kluwer.

Hancock, J. (2005). *Corporate Social Responsibility*: Kokan page.

Harland, C. (1999). Supply Network Strategy and Social Capital. In R. Leenders & S. Gabbay (Eds.), *Corporate Social Capital and Liability* (pp. pp. 409-430): Boston: Kluwer.

Harper, R. (2001). *Social Capital: A Literature Review*: Social Analysis and Reporting Division Office for National Statistics, UK.

Hitt, M., Lee, H., & Yucel, E. (2002). The Importance of Social Capital to the Management of Multinational Enterprises: Relational Networks Among Asian and Western Firms. *Asia Pacific Journal of Management, 19*, pp. 353-372.

Hjollund, L., & Svendsen, G. T. (2000). Social Capital: A standard method of measurement.

Hoang, H., Rothaermel, F., & Simac, S. (2003). *The Impact of General and Partner-Specific Alliance Experience on Joint R&D Project Performance* (No. 2003/28/ENT). Fontainebleau: INSEAD.

Holmlund, M. (2001). The D&D Model—Dimensions and Domains of Relationship Quality Perceptions. *The Services Industries Journal, 21*(3), pp.13-36.

Jackson, K. (2004). *Building Reputational capital: Strategies for Integrity and fair Play That Improve the Bottom Line*. New York: Oxford University Press.

Jacobs, J. H. (1945). The Application of Sociometry to Industry. *Sociometry, 8*(2), pp. 181-198.

Karlan, D. (2002). *Using Experimental Economics to Measure Social Capital and Predict Financial Decisions*: Princeton University, Dept. of Economics.

Kern, T., & Willcocks, L. (2001). *The Relationship Advantage*: Oxford University Press.

Knoke, D. (1999). Organizational Networks and Corporate Social Capital. In R. Leenders & S. Gabbay (Eds.), *Corporate Social Capital and Liability* (pp. pp. 17-42): Boston: Kluwer.

Koka, B. R., & Prescott, J. E. (2002). Strategic alliances as social capital: A multi-dimensional view. *Strategic Management Journal, 23*(9), 795-816.

Krackhardt, D., & Hanson, J. R. (1993). Informal Networks: The Company Behind the Charts. *Harvard Business Review, 71*(4), pp.104-111.

Krishna, A., & Shrader, E. (1999, June 22-24, 1999). *Social Capital Assessment Tool.* Paper presented at the Conference on Social Capital and Poverty Reduction, Washington.

Leenders, R., & Gabbay, S. (Eds.). (1999). *Corporate Social Capital and Liability.* Boston: Kluwer Academic Publishers.

Lesser, E., & Prusak, L. (1999). *Communities of Practice, Social Capital and Organisational Knowledge*: IBM Institute of Knowledge management.

Lesser, E. L., & Storck, J. (2001). Communities of practice and organizational performance. *IBM Systems Journal, 40*(4), pp.831-841.

Lev, B. (2001). *Intangibles: Management, Measurement, and Reporting.* Washington, D.C.: Brookings Institution Press.

Lin, N. (1982). Social Resources and Instrumental Action. In P. Marsden & N. Lin (Eds.), *Social Structure and Network Analysis* (pp. pp.131-145). Beverly Hills, CA: Sage.

Locke, E. A. (1999). Some reservations about social capital. *Academy of Management Review, 24*(1), pp.8-9.

Lorange, P., & Roos, J. (1992). *Strategic Alliances: formation, implementation and evolution.* Oxford: Blackwell Publishers.

Lyons, M. P. (1991). Joint-Ventures as Strategic Choice—A Literature Review. *Long Range Planning, 24*(4), pp.130-140.

Macauley, S. (1963). Non-contractual relations in Business: A preliminary Study. *American Sociological Review, 28*(1), pp.55-67.

Marr, B., & Chatzkel, J. (2004). Intellectual capital at the crossroads: managing, measuring, and reporting IC. *Journal of Intellectual capital, 5*(2), pp.224-229.

Marti, J. M. V. (2004). Social capital benchmarking system. *Journal of Intellectual capital, 5*(3), pp.426-442.

McCutcheon, D., & Stuart, F. I. (2000). Issues in the Choice of Supplier Alliance Partenrs. *Journal of Operations Management, 18*, pp.270-301.

McElroy, M. (2002). Social Innovation Capital. *Journal of Intellectual capital, 3*(1), pp.30—39.

Mizruchi, M., & Stearns, L. B. (2001). Getting Deals Done: The Use of Social Networks in Bank Decision-Making. *American Sociological Review, 66*(5), pp.647-671.

More, E., & McGrath, M. (2001). *Strategic Alliances as Collaborative Strategy or a Method of Implementing Strategy: A Case Study in Australia's Communications Sector.* Paper presented at the Communications Research Forum.

Nahapiet, J., & Ghoshal, S. (1998). Social Capital, Intellectual capital, and the organizational Advantage. *Academy of Management Review, 23*(2), pp.242-266.

Pena, I. (2002). Knowledge networks as part of an integrated knowledge management approach. *Journal of Knowledge management, 6*(5), pp 469—478.

Petrash, G. (1996). Dow's journey to a knowledge management culture. *European Management Journal, 14*(4), pp.365-373.

Podolny, J. (2001). Networks as Pipes and Prisms of the Market. *American Journal of Sociology, 107*(1), 99.33-60.

Podolny, J., Stuart, T., & Hannan, M. (1996). Networks, Knowledge, and Niches: Competition in the Worldwide Semiconductor Industry, 1984-1991. *American Journal of Sociology, 102*(3), pp.659-689.

Pomeda, J., Moreno, C., Rivera, C., & Martil, L. (2002, 25-26th November, 2002). *Towards an Intellectual capital Report of Madrid: New Insights and Developments.* Paper presented at the The Transparent Enterprise. The Value of Intangibles, Madrid, Spain.

Portes, A. (1998). Social Capital: Its Origins and Applications in Modern Sociology. *Annual Review of Sociology, 24*, pp.1-24.

Preston, L. (2004). Reputation as a source of corporate social capital. *Journal of General Management, 30*(2), pp.43-49.

PriceWaterhouseCoopers. (2007). IT Governance in Practice: Insight from leading CIOs. Retrieved 4/1/08, from http://www.pwc.com/extweb/pwcpublications. nsf/docid/790d48a25a3505008525726d00567783

Putman, R. (1993). *Making Democracy Work: Civic Traditions in Modern Italy*: Princton: Princeton University Press.

Putman, R. (1995). Bowling Alone: America's Declining Social Capital. *Journal of Democracy, 6*(1), pp.65-78.

Roman, R., Hayibor, S., & Agle, B. (1999). The relationship between social and financial performance. *Business and Society, 38*(1), pp.109-125.

Roos, G. (2003). *An Intellectual capital Primer*: Cranfield University.

Roos, G., & Roos, J. (1997). Measuring your Company's Intellectual Performance. *Long Range Planning, 30*(3), pp.413-426.

Rowley, T., Behrens, D., & Krackhardt, D. (2000). Redundant Governance Structures: An Analysis of Structural and Relational Embeddedness in the Steel and Semiconductor Industries. *Strategic Management Journal, 21*, pp. 369-386.

Sarker, M., Echambadi, R., Cavusgil, S. T., & Aulakh, P. S. (2001). The Influence of Complementarity, Compatibility, and Relationship Capital on Alliance Performance. *Journal of the Academy of Marketing Science, 29*(4), pp.358-373.

Savage, C. (1996). *Fifth Generation Management*: www.kee-inc.com.

Scott, J. (2000). *Social Network Analysis* (2nd ed.): Thousand Oaks, CA: Sage.

Simon, H. A. (1947). *Administrative Behaviour*. New York: Macmillan.

Simon, H. A. (2001). Complex Systems: The Interplay of Organizations and Markets in Contemporary Society. *Computational and Mathematical Organizational Theory, 7*(2), 79-85.

Spellerberg, A. (2001). *Framework for the Measurement of Social Capital in New Zealand*. Statistics New Zealand.

Stewart, T. A. (1997). *Intellectual capital: The New Wealth of Organizations*. New York: Doubleday.

Stuart, T. (2000). Interorganizational Alliances and the Performance of Firms: A Study of Growth and Innovation Rates in a High Technology Industry. *Strategic Management Journal, 21*, 791-811.

Sveiby, K. E. (1997). *The New Organizational Wealth: Managing & Measuring Knowledge-Based Assets*: Berret-Koehler Publishers, Inc.

Talmud, I., & Mesch, G. (1997). Market Embeddedness and Corporate Instability: The Ecology of Inter-industrial Networks. *Social Science Research, 26*, 419-441.

Thorelli, H. (1986). Networks: Between Markets and Hierarchies. *Strategic Management Journal, 7*, 37-51.

Thrane, S., Mouritson, J., & Johnson, M. R. (2002). *Networks, Intellectual capital and the Management of Knowledge: Performing the 'New Economy'*: Copenhagen Business School.

Toffler, B. (2003). *Final Accounting*: Doubleday.

Tsai. (2000). Social Capital, Strategic Relatedness and the Formation of Interorganizational Linkages. *Strategic Management Journal, 21*, 925-939.

Tsai, W. (2001). Knowledge Transfer in Intraorganizational Networks: Effects of Network Position and Absorptive Capacity on Business Unit Innovation and Performance. *Academy of Management Journal, 44*(5), 996-1004.

Tsai, W., & Ghoshal, S. (1998). Social Capital and Value Creation: The Role of Intrafirm Networks. *Academy of Management Journal, 41*(4), 464-476.

Uzzi, B. (1997). Social Structure and Competition in Interfirm Networks: The paradox of Embeddedness. *Administrative Science Quarterly, 42*, 35-67.

Viedma, J. M. (2003). SCBS Social Capital Benchmarking System: Profiting from Social Capital when Building Networked Organisations. *Journal of Universal Computer, 9*(6), 501-509.

Waddock, S., & Graves, S. (1997). The Corporate Social Performance-Financial Performance Link. *Strategic Management Journal, 18*(4), 303-319.

Wasserman, S., & Faust, K. (1994). *Social Network Analysis: Methods and Applications*: UK: Cambridge University Press.

Weigelt, K., & Camerer, C. (1988). Reputation and Corporate Strategy: A Review of Recent Theory and Applications. *Strategic Management Journal, 9*, 443-454.

Wellman, B. (1990). Different Strokes for Different Folks: Community Ties and Social Support. *American Journal of Sociology, 96*(3), 558-588.

Wellman, B., & Berkowitz, S. D. (1988). *Social structures: a network approach*: New York, Cambridge University Press.

Wenger, E. (1998). *Communities of Practice: Learning, meaning, and Identity*: Cambridge University Press.

Wenger, E., McDermott, R., & Snyder, W. M. (2002). *Cultivating Communities of Practice*. Boston: Harvard Business School Press.

White, H. (1981). Where do Markets Come From? *American Journal of Sociology, 87*(3), 517-547.

Willcocks, L., & Cullen, S. (2006). The Outsourcing Enterprise: The Power of Relationships. Retrieved 20/11/07, from http://www.logicacmg.com/r/8000/the+outsourcing+enterprise%3a+the+power+of+relationships/400009147

Williams, P. (2007). IT Governance Roundtable. Retrieved 4/1/08, from http://www. itgi.org/

Williamson, O. (1981). The Economics of Organization: The Transaction Cost Approach. *American Journal of Sociology, 87*(3), 548-576.

Windolf, P. (2002). *Corporate Networks in Europe and the United states.* Oxford, New York: Oxford University press.

Woolcock, M. (1998). Social Capital and economic development: Toward a theoretical synthesis and policy framework. *Theory and Society, 27,* 151-208.

World_Bank. (2007). World Bank [Online], Available: http://web.world-bank.org/wbsite/external/topics/extsocialdevelopment/exttsocialcapital/ 0,menuPK:401021~pagePK:149018~piPK:149093~theSitePK:401015,00.html [4th April 2007].

Yli-Renko, H., Autio, E., & Sapienza, H. J. (2001). Social Capital, Knowledge Acquisition and Knowledge Exploitation in Young Technology-Based Firms. *Strategic Management Journal, 22,* 587-613.

Youndt, M. A., Subramaniam, M., & Snell, S. A. (2004). Intellectual capital profiles: An examination of investments and returns. *Journal Of Management Studies, 41*(2), 335-361.

ENDNOTES

[1] The three dimensions of triple bottom line reporting are: social responsibility; environmental responsibility; and financial performance.

[2] For instance, see http://www.theyrule.net/. (accessed 17/9/07)

[3] see http://money.cnn.com/magazines/fortune/mostadmired/2007/index.html (accessed 21/7/07) for 'most admired' companies list along with the methodology used for its compilation.

[4] See http://www.insna.org/ (accessed 21/7/07) which is the community site for academics and practitioners working with SNA techniques.

Chapter VI
Personal Network Competencies

Traditionally the competency of an IT worker has been largely measured in technical terms. The ability to understand and deploy complex technology was seen as the critical skill required. However, the environment is changing. The time where applications could simply automate tried and tested manual processes with the confidence that immediate benefits to the business would result, is now past. The industry has matured to the extent that current IT applications need to develop and evolve hand in hand with the business. The ability to fully specify the requirements for an application, and then have them passed "over the wall" to the IT department for delivery has gone. Even with so-called packaged ERP software, instances where the software can be deployed without customisation or significant configuration are few and far between. With customisation comes relationship requirements with the business users, and therefore increased governance requirements (Wang & Chen, 2006). A recent study of staff interaction requirements found that up to 80% of staff job descriptions now require significant levels of personal interactions (Johnson *et al.*, 2005). What is clear is that relationships between IT staff members, and between IT staff and their business clients have become a critical success factor.

The Open source software (OSS) movement has uncovered another IT worker competency, and that is to be able to work in a network consisting essentially of volunteers. Open source software development has now been legitimised by the industry through the support and adoption of many of the major market players like Sun Microsystems, IBM and HP. OSS is largely developed by large teams of volunteer programmers, cooperating virtually via e-mail and the Internet to develop an end product. Companies like IBM have contributed large amounts of previously proprietary software code to OSS development projects. OSS is a significantly different organisational model for the development of software to the traditional corporate model. Workers in OSS projects may have similar technical competencies to their corporate worker colleagues, but the organisational competencies required to be effective in the given organisational context is substantially different. In fact the "good corporate IT worker" could be seen as the antithesis of the good OSS IT worker in terms of organisational effectiveness. As more corporations adopt the OSS model the need for the IT worker to learn new organisational competencies becomes paramount.

For the IT executive, the contrast between working in a traditional one to one governance arrangement, to one where the governance is more about personal influence than legal contracts, challenges traditional executive competency requirements. One on one negotiation skills are no longer enough. To effectively operate in a networked environment the IT executive will need to learn new political influencing skills and also learn to effectively manage their own personal networks.

This chapter looks at a number of contradictions in the IT industry in terms of the competencies required to operate effectively. Underpinning the new emerging competencies is the ability to work in a network. Whether they are multisourcing networks, open source development networks or alliance networks, the required competencies are similar. The coexistence of sole sourcing and multisourcing, corporately developed software and open source software, and corporate IT infrastructure with public IT infrastructure, each provide a contradiction in terms of competency requirements to be resolved.

The science of social networks is used to help identify the competency requirements for the networked world. Each of the above contradictions emphasises the need to be able to manage within networks. A basic tutorial on Social Network Analysis (SNA), the key analytical technique used for studying social networks, will be provided. This will be followed by two sections looking at management competencies and then IT worker competencies. Finally a section will be provided on linkages between personal networking competencies and performance.

Tutorial

Social (Organisational) Network Analysis: An Overview

The invention of the sociogram is often credited to a social psychologist, Dr. J.L. Mareno, who used it to map "liking" and "disliking" relationships between New

York schoolgirls in the 1930s. The technique has since evolved into a commonly accepted sociological tool, but it is only recently that sociograms have come to the attention of the corporate world. Social Network Analysis (SNA), also called Organisational network analysis (ONA) describes the collection of analytical techniques that can be applied to networks as visualised through the sociogram. As the term implies, SNA was principally invented for studying social relationships between people in the broader communities and neighbourhoods. Its application to business situations has been relatively recent, as workplaces have evolved from industrial command and control situations of the past, to today, where individual workers have much higher levels of discretion and empowerment (Scott, 2000; Wasserman & Faust, 1994).

A typical SNA collects data on relationships from nodes or "actors" in the network. Traditionally this has been done via survey, where respondents are asked to identify those people to whom they are closely connected i.e. that they have "ties" to. The nature of the connections can be determined by the survey, though usually they indicate advice flows, information flows, friendship, working connections and the like. Actors do not necessarily have to be at the personal level. They can describe firms or organisations. Linkages or ties between firms could represent contractual, joint venture or alliance relationships. Once the connections information has been obtained from the survey data, specialised computer software can be used to display this network of connections. Both nodes and ties can be given attributes, For example, if nodes are people they could be identified by their geographic location, their departmental membership in the organisation, their seniority, age, gender and so forth. Likewise ties can be given attributes like strength of relationship, frequency of communication and nature of relationship.

The analysis of the network can take many forms. Visual inspection of the sociogram can provide a quick assessment of the dominant patterns that might exist. Are the relationships clustered around geographic locations, inside departments, or within seniority bands? Are there disconnected groups? In mathematical terms the network representation is a graph. Graph based measures have been developed to identify clusters or cliques, measure the relative density of the network, identify longest and shortest paths between nodes and to identify different centrality measures for individual nodes. The key centrality measures and their relationship with social capital (SC) are shown in Table 2.

The measure of market positioning in a networked market place requires some assessment and measurement of the value of different roles and positions held within the network. SNA is by far the most mature and objective method for measuring market positioning or structural SC. SNA measures typically treat the network as a graph, independent of the context within which it exists. The measures developed are objective and context free. Knowledge of the context for the network is then

Table 2. Centrality measures

Measure	Description	Relation to SC
Degree	Number of direct ties to a node	Increases SC
Closeness	Total distance to all members	Decreasing SC with larger distances
Betweenness	Times that the shortest paths pass through this node (potential boundary spanner)	Increases SC. Few redundant ties

applied to the way network measures are interpreted. For example, what does a high centrally connected node mean in the context of the IT marketplace? Context can also be used to select from the plethora of available SNA metrics, the ones which are most appropriate. For example, if one is studying a community of traders, the betweenness measure may be appropriate, as traders that are on the path between firms are placed in an advantageous position for facilitating a trade. In the consulting market high "in degree" measures would indicate which companies are most sought after, as "in degree" measures those firms that are most nominated by client firms. The high fidelity analysis provided by SNA, in assessing a firm's structural SC makes it unlikely that other superior methods could be found for this part of the analysis.

The application of SNA to firm level analysis is less familiar than those conducted at the personal level. Berkowitz (1988) has analysed networks of firms in order to identify a more appropriate classification of industry sectors based on the nature of who firms are networked with, rather than the individual firm attributes. Here the firms are being analysed more for their individual pattern of connections i.e. the firm's ego network and how their individual network may provide advantages over other competitive firms in the market place.

Computer software programs are generally used to support SNA, both in terms of visualising the network as well as calculating SNA metrics. This visualisation software has functions to display nodes and links in different forms, for example, node shapes or link thicknesses, depending on the attributes being analysed. A simple example is shown to illustrate processing of network data. The matrix below shows the internal presentation of a network with nodes labeled "A", "B", "C" and "D". The cells denote a linkage if a "1" is present. Note that links can be bi-directional e.g. A-B and B-A.

Figure 30. Matrix representation of a network

	A	B	C	D
A	0	1	1	1
B	1	0	0	0
C	0	1	0	0
D	0	1	1	0

Figure 31. Sociogram representation of a network

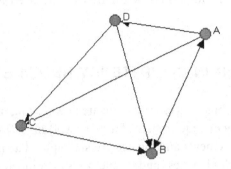

The software draws the sociogram that is represented by the matrix. One can see that the bi-directional links are shown with arrow heads at both ends of the link.

The relationships being analysed with SNA are largely qualitative. The ties identified are therefore determined through proxies which may or may not effectively represent the relationship under analysis. For example, does a contractual relationship adequately represent the closeness of a partnership or relationship? Are R&D partnerships a better representation of a close relationship than a marketing relationship?

SNA centrality measures are also just mathematical proxies for positioning within a network of actors. For example, a dominant network position is often quantified as the number of inward ties. Is this an accurate representation? Is it always true? Much of the sociological research around SNA is focused on testing the viability of mathematical network centrality measures as proxies for the true power of network positioning.

Data collection is another limitation. Data for SNA is normally collected through surveys. Such surveys suffer the limitations of most survey instruments in terms of the effectiveness of the survey instrument in providing a consistent and robust response from respondents. Data sourced from indirect sources like data bases or electronic logs can avoid the individual bias that may occur with human respondents, but suffers from the need to infer relationships indirectly, rather than directly from the human respondents. Where the actors in the study are firms rather than individuals, limitations exist in finding representative data sources, whether they are human or electronic sources.

Despite the limitations identified above, SNA is the tool of choice when analysing network effects. Many of the limitations can be minimised through the use of data triangulation techniques to assess relationship existence and strengths using multiple data sources. Future chapters will provide many examples of SNA applied to the analysis of relationship networks. As the use of SNA in business contexts has grown, its application in business areas is now being regularly called Organisational network analysis (ONA). The terms SNA and ONA are used interchangeably in this book.

A CONTRADICTION IN COMPETENCY REQUIREMENTS

Current trends in the IT business environment are now putting into question traditional views of competency requirements for those working in the industry. While the technical skill requirements and the need to stay up to date remain a constant, it is the increasing need for business and people skills as competency requirements, which are presenting the main challenges. In other words, the occupation of IT is changing, therefore to succeed, new occupational competencies (McClelland, 1973) need to be developed. Even for technical staff, the boundaries between previously distinct technical areas are beginning to blur as technologies become more integrated at the point of use. For example, the end use device for IT consumers used to be a fixed terminal or PC, whereas now a plethora of mobile devices are exercising the same needs for connectivity, applications, security and usability aspects of fixed terminal devices. IT security, applications, hardware and telecommunications support staff now have to build effective partnerships with their technical service brethren if a seamless support service is to be achieved. In measuring competencies and firm effects in the pharmaceutical research, Henderson and Cockburn (1994) distinguished between "component" and "architectural" competencies. Component competencies were described as local abilities fundamental to day-to-day work, for example, technical work. Architectural competencies described the compe- · tencies needed to make use of content competencies organisationally i.e. being able to integrate the technical work into the overall development which includes competencies in working with interpersonal relationships, organisational systems, cultures and value systems.

To make matters more complex the business of IT is evolving with new and very different business models now challenging the old and traditional ones, causing confusion over how best to train and prepare staff for working in the industry. These emerging contradictions are now addressed.

Contradiction No. 1: Open Source vs. Closed Source Software

Until fairly recently, software development had been a "behind closed doors" activity. Whether the applications were developed as products for sale or as in house custom developments, software development teams are typically hired to work in teams to develop the application or product. This closed sourced approach to software development called for tight procedures for managing the life cycle development exposing the eventual end users to the development through carefully managed releases. Beyond technical skills (content competency), software developers were often hired for their ability to work in a team and to meet strict deadlines (architectural competency). Familiarity with the given software development methodologies and the ability to work effectively within them is another common trait sought after for closed source developments.

The growth in acceptance of OSS has been something of a revelation to the software development community. Many observers were somewhat puzzled by why highly skilled software developers would continue to donate their time to such initiatives, without the availability of explicit economic rewards. Closer study of the motivations of OSS developers has indicated that there are rewards available beyond the altruistic rewards (Lerner & Tirole, 2002). Many of the motivations indicate a longer term view for returns to the OSS developer and include:

- Being a visible and effective contributor to an Open Source project can provide new job opportunities. For the recruiter of software developers it is rare to be able to assess talent at the level of software code development or problem identification;
- Skill development with current technology. OSS projects regularly make use of the newest development tools and techniques and therefore it is a means for a developer to tune their skills, making themselves more marketable;
- There is a growing number of examples of developers being offered venture capital to progress their work in the commercial world; and
- Peer recognition and reputation enhancement, which is more of a reward for the ego, rather than a direct economic one.

In recognition that networks underpin OSS developers, a number of scholars have made use of SNA measures and techniques to study the nature of OSS projects (Grewal *et al.*, 2006; Long & Siau, 2007; Tuomi, 2000). The studies found that a typical OSS project will commence around a single hub, but over time multiple hubs may generate, eventually leading to what is called a "core/periphery" structure where a tightly networked core of developers act as a governing and central development group with a less structured and less connected periphery of a larger number of contributors, many who may be once off contributors (Lerner & Tirole, 2002; Long & Siau, 2007). The organisational structure for OSS projects resemble different communities informally formed around practices and particular technologies used in these practices (Tuomi, 2000).

For the OSS project initiators and core developers, the ability to influence a direction, rather than mandate one is a key differentiator for OSS projects (Lerner

Table 3. Contrasting competencies

	Closed Source	Open Source
Leadership / Management	• Project / commercial management skills • Team management • Client management	• Influencing / motivational skills • Large scale design skills • Technical skills • Community building skills • Altruistic
Individual Contributors	• Technical skills • Team participation skills • Developer methodology process skills • Ability to focus and sustain attention	• Technical skills • Community participation skills • Exploratory / inquisitive • Altruistic

& Tirole, 2002). This includes having exceptional design skills to enable the astute assessment of the value of the different contributions volunteered to the OSS project (Ljungberg, 2000). For peripheral developers, their contributions add breadth and number to the "number of eyes" evaluating the software and at the same time they are taking advantage of a learning opportunity through their participation.

The Table 3 compares and contrasts competency requirements for close sourced and open sourced software projects: One can see that the closed source situation calls for commercially oriented competencies that can be focused at the task on hand for on time, on budget delivery. The open source situation is not explicitly commercially focused and therefore relies more on competencies for developing and working in widespread communities, often with people you will never physically meet. For some individuals the contrast in competency requirements will have them dedicated to one form or the other. For others, they can be complementary, where skills built in the open source world could be profitably applied by the same individuals in the closed source world, perhaps by way of the integration of OSS products with complementary commercial products (Lerner & Tirole, 2002).

Contradiction No. 2: Private vs. Public IT Infrastructure

It is now some 25 years since personal computers were introduced into the consumer market. Over this period the cost of personal computing has reduced significantly compared to the cost of corporate computing, to the extent that today a majority of employees enjoy far more powerful computers, faster communications and a broader base of applications at home than they do at work. What's more, what they pay for the use of these facilities at home is a fraction of what their employers pay for an apparently less functional service inside their company firewalls. The justification for this extraordinary situation is regularly put down to the additional security required to protect the firm's intellectual assets and the need to standardise on a lowest common denominator to keep support costs to a minimum. These arguments have been able to sustain the substantial cost premium over home based systems, but the situation is being challenged from a number of fronts. Consumer markets ISPs are becoming larger, more mature and more sophisticated in their security offerings. Their consumer service processes and cost models have become fine tuned through working in the competitive consumer market. Even the major software providers like Microsoft and Oracle now complement their own support staff with public forums to help answer difficult support questions; a form of open source help desk. CIOs must now be asking why can't my ISP do the same job for me at work as it does at home? The corporate IT market is also now under attack from software as a service (SaaS) providers offering solutions at a fraction of the cost of an in-house corporate application (O'Reilly, 2004).

The increased consumerisation of IT will undoubtedly have a major impact on the way corporate computing will be conducted in coming years (Neal, 2005). BP have led the way with their digital allowance scheme which allows employees to source their own preferred PCs and ISP provider as long as they can demonstrate self sufficiency in its support and compliance to a minimum security level. The net cost to BP is substantially lower than the cost of the traditional corporate support environment (Neal, 2005). As end users take more responsibility for their own IT equipment, its selection and support, the role of IT and the competencies required may have to change from troubleshooter to coach and/or partner. The changes in required corporate IT competencies, should the transactional IT support be left to consumer market providers, are identified in Table 4.

For firms running their own private infrastructure the required competencies are consistent with those required to run a profitable IT service. For the executive, this means commercial client management skills. For the individual IT worker this means delivering to predefined Service Level Agreements (SLA), usually by way of adherence to predefined and standardised support processes. The ability to follow a process, work in teams and respond to customers is the key skill requirements.

Table 4. Private / Public infrastructure competencies

	Private Infrastructure Use	**Public Infrastructure Use**
Leadership / Management	• Commercial Management skills • Cost Management • Client Management	• Business alliance skills • Employee negotiation skills • Public affairs skills • Auditing skills
IT staff Contributors	• Customer service skills • Team participation skills • Process adherence • Ability to focus and sustain attention	• Coach • Community participation skills • Exploratory / inquisitive

The public infrastructure scenario could see in-house IT taking no direct responsibility for IT infrastructure or applications. End users are encouraged to use their own personal computers, email and collaborative software, with some predefined security provisos. The business departments will become responsible for standardisation rather than IT. Where non-standardisation is hurting the business the business leaders will negotiate the level of standardisation they will want, with consulting advice from IT. Implementations will be directed by the business, not IT. Applications are bought by the business as a service (SaaS) or through participation in OSS developments. Only applications that are deemed to provide a distinct competitive advantage remain in-sourced. The role of IT changes significantly in this scenario. IT staff become expert advisors and partners to the business rather than a separate service arm. IT executive require employee relationship skills and public affairs skills to help staff migrate to IT self sufficiency. They also need auditing skills to ensure that the self sufficiency arrangements, which will evolve with the market for IT commodities, are not exposing the firm to undue risk. They will need to become expert advisors on technical developments in the public arena which could be leveraged to gain a further advantage for the firm or expose the firm to new risks. They will communicate this directly to staff through public communication channels rather than through the traditional governance hierarchies. For the individual IT staff member the role becomes one of coach and partner in development, rather than problem solver. The IT staff member will use their expert knowledge of the technology to work with their business colleagues in pursuing new business opportunities. Structurally these staff may re-join the business departments that they may have previously been taken from to join a centralised IT function. The centralised function will no longer be needed as the cost efficiency responsibilities have been moved outside to the market place. In summary, the IT staff move from being service providers to technical brokers. As technical experts embedded in the business they will be the prime vehicle for brokering innovations into the business. The ability to network effectively will be a core competency requirement.

Contradiction No. 3: Single Sourcing vs. Multisourcing

A single sourcing scenario describes a total IT outsourcing situation where the office of the CIO acts as the contract manager and governance leader with the sole IT vendor. This situation describes many of the early IT outsourcing deals of the 1990s. The required competencies of the retained IT was one of contract and commercial management as well as acting as the prime channel for access to the business clients. IT Governance was achieved typically through the "hourglass" structure, where the vendor was expected to appoint a single point of contact, or account executive, who ultimately was accountable for the contracted services. Likewise the CIO

Figure 32. Single sourcing vs. multisourcing

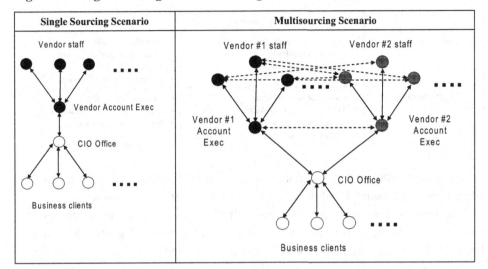

became the single point of contact for the business clients. Relationships between the service delivery personnel and the business end-users were managed through the hourglass, which usually resulted in overloaded CIOs and account executives.

Today the above scenario is less common as firms move toward selective sourcing (Lacity & Willcocks, 2000b) or multisourcing. Multisourcing adds complexity and subsequently more sophisticated skills and competencies in managing them (Annesley, 2006). The selective sourcing scenario suggests that the firm retains some services in- house. The effect is the same as the multisourcing scenario, which in effect introduces a third dimension of management responsibility for the CIO. As well as dealing with the additional individual vendor (or in-house) service contracts, he or she will also have to be concerned about the relationships between the different service providers if a seamless service is to be provided to the business clients. The extent to which such relationships can be mandated in service contracts is questionable, especially if the multisourced vendors actively compete in the market place. The business development executives from the participating vendors will be looking for any weaknesses in the contract structures which could enable them to increase their revenues.

The two scenarios in Figure 32 are somewhat idealistic. In practice there will also need to be direct relationships between the service delivery staff and the business users to ensure that the services aren't overburdened with bureaucratic overheads. The multisourcing scenario intimates that the responsibilities and therefore competencies of the individual players go far beyond adherence to the commercial and legal terms of the contract. The leadership for both the client and vendors is moving

Table 5. Single and multisourcing competencies

	Core Single Sourcing	Core Multisourcing
Leadership / Management	• Commercial management skills • Cost management • Client management	• Facilitation skills • Complex negotiation skills • Political skills • Community development skills
IT staff Contributors	• Customer service skills • Team participation skills • Process adherence • Ability to focus and sustain attention	• Relationship skills • Community participation skills • Exploratory / inquisitive

toward orchestration and facilitation. The individual IT staffs need "architectural" competencies to complement their technical or "content" competencies.

The concentration on networks and soft skill relationship competencies in no way obviates the importance of the commercial and legal frameworks. These frameworks provide the "bones or skeleton" on which the "flesh" of the softer skill competencies is added to achieve a healthy multisourcing arrangement. Without the bones the sourcing arrangement would collapse into a morass of cultural niceties with no business benefits. Without the "flesh" there are also little or no business benefits as valuable resources become engaged in legal or commercial conflicts while the end business user suffers.

Unlike the previous competency comparison tables it is likely that in the multi-sourcing scenario the identified competencies are additional to, rather than instead of the competencies required for sole sourcing.

This section has provided three emerging contradictory situations. Within these we may asses the changing competency requirements for IT staff involved in, or with, outsourcing arrangements. The next section takes a more holistic view of IT Governance and the challenges the traditional modes of IT Governance face as scenarios like those above begin to substantially play out in the market place.

Case Study

Operating in the IT Bazaar

To help illustrate the evolution to a networked IT market place I want to relate a personal experience of bazaar style governance in the procurement of a new personal computer for home. I had grown up in an IT world where brand names mattered. In the 1970s and 1980s the PC revolution had thrown up a number of entrepreneurial start-ups, but the movement of traditional brands such as IBM and HP into the world of PCs ensured that the corporate world could continue to operate under the adage of "No-one ever got fired for buying IBM". The corporate IT world was a cathedral. The rapid changes in technology were met with a carefully crafted governance regime for procurement biased against moving away from the proven brands. Despite lower cost alternatives the risk premium was considered too high and more often than not, these decisions were vindicated as many of the PC start-up companies disappeared leaving their clients with unsupported hardware.

The world was changing however for home PC users. The open PC architecture pioneered by IBM had spawned a massive number of PC component companies, providing plug in pieces for multiple branded and unbranded PCs. By the late 1990s the commoditisation of the PC and its components was pushing prices down to the extent that the risk to the personal buyer was sufficiently low enough to encourage one to assemble a custom PC from "best of breed" components. I was now prepared to make the leap and assemble a custom PC for my specific needs. I was confident in being able to identify the most appropriate components I would require, using the plethora of literature and Internet forum sites evaluating competitive components. My one personal concern was my systems integration skills. What happens if I purchase all of these carefully identified components and fit them into the PC frame and it doesn't work? Who am I going to blame? The thought of having a high end PC at a low end price was sufficient however to put these thoughts aside and venture into the bazaar.

The bazaar at that time and still is today, the weekend computer market. Computer markets have emerged along with the commoditisation of IT hardware and now can be found in most mid to large sized towns and cities. They are invariably populated by vendors of Asian heritage, a heritage rich in bazaar style trading. On my first pass of the bazaar stalls I was pleased to find all of my first choice components available. Unfortunately though, no single stall could provide all of the components on my list. It looked like I was in for a long and tedious bargaining program with multiple stall owners. While bemoaning my situation to one particular stall holder, let's call him Han, who happened to have about 60% of my desired components, he quickly responded "No problem, just wait here". Han then proceeded to run around to those stalls that had my desired components that he did not have on his own stall. Having collected the components Han then proceeded, between serving other customers, to assemble my PC with my selected components. Within three hours I walked out of the bazaar with my custom PC, assembled and tested. I saw no money change hands as my vendor "procured" components from the other stalls. I was not charged a systems integration fee nor paid a premium for any of the components. I was a very happy customer!

What I had been able to observe first hand was the power of the bazaar. No doubt there would have been a "settling up" process between Han and the other stall holders after the bazaar. The system however worked on the community traits of trust and reciprocity. No doubt Han would have similarly assisted his other stall holder colleagues in the past. Despite the fact that they were operating competitive stalls within the bazaar, they knew the value of cooperation when it mattered and that a happy customer can be good for everyone involved.

The bigger question from this short anecdote is whether the personal procurement experiences of the bazaar scale up to the needs of the corporate world as IT becomes increasingly commoditised?

IT GOVERNANCE: THE CATHEDRAL AND THE BAZAAR

Eric Raymond's heavily cited essay on "The Cathedral and the Bazaar" contains his personal musings on his experiences with open source software development which had radically changed his thinking about how complex software can be successfully developed (Raymond, 2000). Raymond presents the traditional software development perspective that "too many cooks spoil the broth" which is exemplified in the context of software by Brooks's Law which predicts that the complexity and communication costs of a project rise with the square of the number of developers, while work done only rises linearly (Brooks, 1978). The traditional "Cathedral" approach to developing software was therefore one using a dedicated team of craftsmen working within carefully crafted guidelines to develop new software releases. This typically results in the long release intervals and the inevitable disappointment when long-awaited releases are not perfect. Subsequently end users seem to be constantly awaiting the next release to resolve their business problems.

In contrast, Raymond offers the law of the Bazaar and attributes it to Linus Torvalds, the founder of arguably the most successful OSS project to date, the Linux operating system. Linus's law of "Given enough eyeballs, all bugs are shallow" essentially indicates that software flaws are best identified by the masses, more so than the selected skilled few. Its corollary for action is "Release early and release often" to provide the greatest opportunity for rapid development and stability.

In the true spirit of open source development, the tag line "The Cathedral and the Bazaar" will now be conscripted to provide some insight into the changing world of IT Governance. The decade or more of IT outsourcing governance experience could be comfortably compared with the building of the cathedral.

In the early days of IT outsourcing, the legal and commercial frameworks were often borrowed from other procurement fields, for example major construction or development projects. In this way, they provided a start to the building of the IT Governance cathedral. The cathedral however is under constant renovation. With failure rates of greater than 30% (Lacity & Willcocks, 2000a), both the parishioners and owners are looking to improve the situation. New integrated governance frameworks are being designed to hopefully enable both clients and vendors to achieve a

greater level of success (Cullen & Willcocks, 2003). However the wild card in the governance scheme is the management of relationships (Kern & Willcocks, 2001; Weill, 2004; Willcocks & Cullen, 2006). Like the aesthetics of the cathedral, meeting the need of a multitude of stakeholders can be complex and elusive. Looking back to the Cynefin framework (Snowden & Boone, 2007), one can see that the Cathedral approach to IT Governance places it in the "complicated" domain. Specialist craftsmen in the form of lawyers and commercial managers are the major contributors to the governance scheme. Changes are slow to be developed and implemented. Paralysis by analysis is common place, and like the closed software development scenario reported on by Raymond, the performance track record is not good.

In parallel to the software development situation, IT Governance suffers from a plethora of processes: detailed procurement and delivery contract terms, service level agreements and the like, but still has a less than acceptable track record. The most compelling parallel however is the impact of human behaviour. Just as the success of open source software (OSS) has exposed some positive human traits that are more akin to a bazaar than the cathedral, perhaps the IT Governance world could benefit from a little bazaar type thinking. The emergence of multisourcing threatens a parallel to Brook's Law that would go something like "the complexity of your multisourcing governance arrangement will increase by the square of the number of vendors you choose, while your performance will only improve linearly". This could be an alarming reality for the many firms now undertaking a multisourcing strategy. Moving from the cathedral to the bazaar will require fewer legal and commercial skills but an increased dose of socialisation skills.

Raymond's criticism of Brook's mathematics is that it assumes that everyone has to communicate with everyone else in the provider network, though he does concede that the core group of OSS developers would be affected by Brook's Law. For the multisourcing situation it is also true that not all suppliers will need to communicate intensely with each other. However, it is likely that multisourcing arrangements may fall within the Cynefin "complex" domain which means that traditional management processes are likely to be ineffective. Some level of probing or experimentation, within agreed boundaries, will be required before settling on an optimal path. For example, a client may choose to try different combinations of suppliers in different parts of the firm to assess how effective the combination, including interfacing with in-house IT, will be. For non-competitive applications a firm may choose to join an open source consortia, providing opportunities for individual developers to demonstrate their skills through their volunteered contributions and the prospects of a paid job at the end of it. Once a client is embedded in the bazaar as a regular client, providers may more easily self organise to meet their needs, all without the need for legal, commercial or supervisory overheads. In terms of IT infrastructure, the BP digital allowance scheme described earlier is an example of bridging the "at home/at work" divide for the benefit of all, as individuals get to use their PC of choice and the company gets the benefit of bazaar level pricing without the risks.

What we know about bazaars is that vendors are highly networked, whether through family or long term friendships. For the unsuspecting buyer wandering through the bazaar, the word of mouth network appears to work faster than an e-mail,

with vendors uncannily knowing of conversations you may have had with a vendor on the other side of the market. Perhaps the IT market has yet to reach the networking capacity of Turkish carpet sellers, but it is certainly heading in that direction. Its vendors will need to become more collaborative to survive and buyers will need to be aware that this is the case and not treat them as independent vendors. For the buyer the complexity of the bazaar is too much for any one firm to comprehend. Buyers will also need to collaborate and share their market intelligence to ensure that they are receiving competitive products and services.

In this chapter the common theme has been that to be successful in the new IT sourcing regime one has to develop his/her relationship management skills. The requirement is equally relevant to both management and individual contributors for both the client and supplier. But what about the value of relationship management and networking skills today? Are they as valuable today as they will be tomorrow? This next section will review some research that draws a clear association between networking and performance. Organisational network analysis (ONA) techniques are used in the reported research to identify particularly important networking attributes and the individuals who occupy them (see SNA/ONA side bar). The association between networking attributes and performance are then demonstrated.

THE RELATIONSHIP BETWEEN NETWORKING AND PERFORMANCE

"It's not what you know but who you know" is the often quoted phrase for describing, usually with some cynicism, the successful promotion of a colleague or acquaintance. However, along with the cynicism is clearly an element of truth. The connection between networking and performance has been well researched. Typically the research has shown that high performers tend to be centrally located within networks, they invest in the careful selection and nurturing of their relationships and their behaviour patterns are one of exploration and engagement in quality relationships.

Measuring the value of a good relationship can be problematic. SNA is a tool for analysing and measuring the value of relationships. Through SNA a variety of measures are available for assessing relative positions within a network, whether they are personal or market level networks. The most common measure is centrality, which in essence measures how well connected an individual or entity is within a given network. The correlation between centrality measures and performance is commonly used to identify the links between relationships and performance. It should be noted though that being "too central" can also have negative effects on performance. Being too close knit can result in the loss of access to fresh ideas and innovations. Therefore optimal performance is usually associated with the "right" level of centrality. As indicated in Chapter V, there are two roles within networks that are seen to be particularly advantageous. The centrally connected actor is identified as being a sought after resource; for advice, information, friendship or the like. The bridging or brokering role is identified with actors who connect disparate communities. These actors are seen to be ideally placed to introduce new innovations and progress new and profitable ideas into the community. Both roles are seen as being rich in SC. The connections between these roles and personal performance will now be illustrated.

BROKERAGE AND INNOVATION

Entrepreneurs and inventors are no smarter, no more courageous, tenacious, or rebellious than the rest of us—they are simply better connected. (Hargadon, 2003)

Innovation is a much talked about, much written about and much studied topic. It is also seen by many as a critical vehicle for achieving extraordinary success in business. Yet organisations regularly struggle to meet the innovation expectations of their stakeholders, be they their clients, management team or even their own employees. Innovation is regularly associated with breakthrough technologies and hero worshipped inventors. However, as Andrew Hargadon points out, even Edison wasn't a lone inventor, but was involved in a web thick with ties to other people, ideas and objects, that together made up his particular "invention", the electric light bulb. Innovation is as much social as it is technical.

Structural holes and brokerage proponent, Ron Burt has undertaken a number of empirical research studies looking to identify connections between SC and innovation (Ronald Burt, 2003; Ron Burt, 2005).

The result of Burt's research is illustrated in Figure 33. The left hand side shows that the two idea judges tended to rate ideas coming from individuals in brokerage positions in the network more highly. The right hand side of the figure shows the probability that an idea will be rejected or that an individual will offer no ideas at all. The results showed that for those individuals who are more tightly constrained within their networks i.e. centrally located, the probability of them coming up with a new idea is lowest, or if they do have one, the chance of having it dismissed is significantly higher than for those in less constrained positions.

It is not enough however, for a broker to simply be in a position to identify a good idea. Brokers or bridges need to also have the influencing skills to firstly argue the merits of the ideas with his or her peers and then ultimately with management. Kelley's study of star performers at AT&T's research laboratories identified that the

Figure 33. Connection between brokerage and idea acceptance (Ronald Burt, 2003 by permission of Oxford University Press)

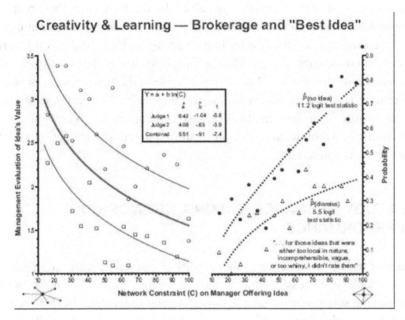

skills of initiative, networking, small-L leadership, organisational savvy and show and tell capabilities were required to turn good ideas into successful innovations (Kelley & Caplan, 1993).

Of course identifying promising ideas and successfully engaging management in their funding is only part of the journey. To be classed as a successful innovation, the ideas have to be productive in practice. New ideas do not come with tried and tested recipes. This is where the exploitation teams need to be effective in the sharing of the adaptations and improvisations commonly required to make something work in practice. The characteristics of exploitation teams are substantially different to exploration teams. Research by March (1991) indicated that a concentration on exploitation over exploration can have a short term beneficial effect on organisational learning, but in the long term is destructive. He and Wong (2004) showed empirically that firms that could effectively balance the competing demands for exploration and exploitation achieved higher levels of innovation success. Conversely, most firms struggle with innovation precisely because they fail to effectively balance exploration and exploitation initiatives. In summary, social network theory suggests that successful innovation is best achieved through careful management of the interaction between exploration and exploitation activities. From a personal competency perspective, this means that the brokers will need to influence and engage with those centrally connected, if the good ideas are to be converted into successful innovations.

In practice the exploration and engagement practices are best facilitated by the bridge or broker with what Kelley calls "star performer" characteristics. The transition to exploitation might typically take the form of a "best practice" implementation. In many organisations today cross divisional "communities of practice" are used as a mechanism for implementing a global best practice across organisational boundaries. Again, while a star performer broker could help initiate the exploitation process the "high contact" style of the tight clusters or cliques that make up effective exploitation teams could quickly alienate the exploratory style of the broker. Therefore, the broker must have the ability to recognise when it is time to retreat from the activity and let the exploitation team get on with the implementation unhindered.

CASE STUDY RESEARCH LINKING NETWORKING AND PERFORMANCE

The previous section has illustrated the network characteristics and competencies required to achieve successful innovations. Achieving successful innovations is however not the sole predictor of a high performing individual. In this section a selection of research identifying associations between networking attributes and individual performance is presented.

Case 1: Social Network Efficiencies and White Collar Worker Productivity (Bulkley & Alstyne, 2006)

Bulkley and Alstyne (2006) undertook a substantial empirical analysis using e-mail communication patterns and targeted surveys to assess individual productivity within a mid sized recruitment consulting firm. The researchers hypothesised that during the course of a career individuals will move from an exploration style of networking, where building new contacts takes primacy, to an exploitation style of networking where more mature workers tend to work with their existing network. A second hypothesis relates to the efficiency with which information moves through the network, proposing that frequent short communications outperforms infrequent and lengthy communications.

As one means of validating the use of e-mail as a proxy for informal communication the authors were able to confirm the social network theory that centralisation, in terms of central connectors and brokers, do predict performance, in this case, revenue generation. The hypothesis relating to the evolution of networking patterns throughout a career was tested using data from senior staff (partners) as opposed to more junior consultants. The effect was evident by visualising the frequency of email communications conducted over the 24 hour day.

The results showed that junior consultants' email patterns can spread over 20 hours of the day, which is indicative of the exploration focus of junior consultants. In contrast the senior partners tended to concentrate their e-mail activities around the working day only, indicating a concentration of informal communication with pre-existing contacts. Of significance is that both situations were found to be pre-dictive of revenue generation and therefore performance.

In terms of information flow efficiencies the results confirmed the hypothesis that smaller emails and faster response times were on average positively related to performance. In other words it's not only who you are connected to but also how you communicate with them that is important. A complementary finding from the research was that efficient internal networks and communication used to leverage external networks appeared more effective than the traditional "size of the rolo-dex" that any individual may possess. So in summary, the research confirmed that achieving a central position either as a central connector or broker matters within networks. How you achieve centrality may depend on your stage in your career. Also your style of informal communication also matters. Faster, shorter and more regular responses outperform longer and less regular communications.

Case 2a: Personal Attributes and Centrality (Klein *et al.*, 2004)

The previous case reinforced the social network theory that centrality matters when it comes to performance. This research study looks at personal attributes that may predict how successful or not one might be in achieving centrality based on personal attributes. The research analyses three types of networks; advice, friendship and adversarial networks, reflecting the diversity in the types of relationships around which a network can form. Of particular note is the adversarial network, which is not well addressed in the social network literature, but is important for the negative affects it can have on actors participating within it (Labianca *et al.*, 1998). The value of knowing the adversarial network is being able to recognise who to avoid more so than who to seek out. The personal attributes selected for study were: education, activity preference, conscientiousness, extraversion, agreeableness, neuroticism, together with attributes of similar demographics and similar value systems. The empirical work involved surveys with a residential team based national service pro-gram. The International Personality Item Pool (IPIP) survey instrument (Goldberg, 1992) was employed to identify personality attributes of the respondents.

The results indicated that highly educated individuals who are low in neuroti-cism are high in advice and friendship centrality and low in adversarial centrality. "Activity preference" i.e. liking to be busy, was positively correlated with advice

Figure 34. Network entrepreneur personality index (Reproduced with permission)

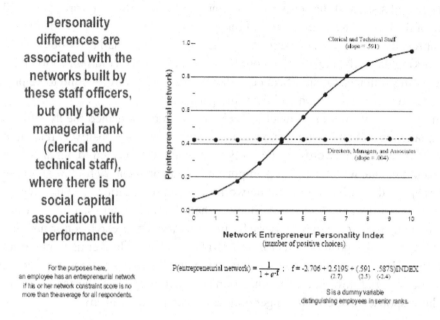

Personality differences are associated with the networks built by these staff officers, but only below managerial rank (clerical and technical staff), where there is no social capital association with performance

For the purposes here, an employee has an entrepreneurial network if his or her network constraint score is no more than the average for all respondents.

$$P(\text{entrepreneurial network}) = \frac{1}{1 + e^{-f}} : \quad f = -2.706 + 2.519S + (.591 - .5875)\text{INDEX}$$
$$(2.7) \quad (2.5) \quad (-2.4)$$

S is a dummy variable distinguishing employees in senior ranks.

and friendship networks. Hedonism (fun loving) and tradition (similar histories) were also positively correlated with advice and friendship networks.

"Openness to experience" i.e. being intellectual, open minded, unconventional, was found to be negatively correlated with friendship networks and positively correlated with adversarial networks. In other words, others may find these types of individuals irritating to be with. Another attribute that predicted membership of an adversarial network was extraversion. Interestingly one might expect extraverted people to be welcomed into friendship networks, if not advice networks. Extraversion was not found to be correlated with either of these networks. As one might expect, the other strong predictors for membership of the adversarial network are neuroticism and disagreeableness.

Case 2b: Personality Correlates of Structural Holes (R. Burt *et al.*, 1998)

Like the above research, this research explores personality correlates, however this time with brokering, rather than centrally connected roles. The authors used a personality questionnaire designed to characterise an individual's personality traits. A network entrepreneur personality index was measured using a short 10 question survey. The expectation was that those individuals with a high entrepreneur personality index would be members of entrepreneurial networks rich in structural holes. The empirical study was conducted with several hundred employees from employment, information and training services backgrounds.

The results, as shown in Figure 34 describe the anticipated relationship, but only for the staff classifications below the managerial rank. Typically these are clerical, technical or junior staff. The dashed line above shows that no association exists for the middle to senior management ranks. The inference is that independent of whether a manager has an entrepreneurial personality or not, their networks become an integral part of their work and therefore become a necessary learned trait for senior managers.

In summary, competence in relationship formation and management is a skill required at all levels of the organisation. At a personal level, one needs to be aware of how one can use their network to help build their own competence levels as well as helping others to build theirs. At the organisational level the supervisor or manager needs to build the skills to be able to effectively balance work relationships within and between teams. At the market place level having the skills and competence to manage an effective client or supplier relationship or negotiate an effective alliance agreement will be much sought after.

In terms of multisourcing and Corporate SC the interest would be in generating a healthy advice network between the partners while hopefully avoiding the emergence of an adversarial network. This research would indicate that the most important personal attributes to look for in staff who will be participating in the partnership are that they are highly educated and have no neurotic tendencies. People who have a preference for being busy, who enjoy work and share some work traditions with the other partners are also seen to demonstrate the positive personal attributes for generating a productive advice network.

For junior staff looking to move into leadership roles within an alliance partnership, the evidence from the research indicates that an entrepreneurial personality is useful in generating networks in the first place, but for more experienced managers an entrepreneurial personality is not a requirement.

Case 3: The Relationship Between Brokerage and Performance (Ron Burt, 2005)

As indicated in Chapter V a network duality exists when it comes to describing SC benefits, broadly defined as brokerage and closure. At the individual level a broker occupies a bridging position between largely disconnected network clusters or communities and is therefore privy to the diversity of ideas and information which are the foundations for innovation and growth. In a closed network those individuals most centrally connected are associated with the highest levels of SC. Up until the early 1990s it was the central connectors that garnered most attention. Ron Burt introduced the theory of "structural holes" at this time (R. S. Burt, 1992) and this case review is of the subsequent empirical work demonstrating the linkage between brokerage and personal performance.

Figure 35 shows the results of an empirical study showing the relationship between an individual's network constraints (high constraint means tightly embedded in a closed network, low constraint means high opportunity for brokerage). The data was drawn from study populations of salesmen and supply chain managers. The vertical axis is a measure of performance relative to peers. A score of zero indicates a typical level of performance for a given job rank, location, experience and work type. A score of 1 is 1 standard deviation above one's peers. The results clearly indicate that those individuals who act as brokers by spanning structural holes enjoy higher performance rewards than those locked into tight networks. This result is exactly the same when judging innovation and the generation of good ideas as described previously.

These results beg the question: Who benefits most from employing people with brokerage capabilities within their IT Governance teams? Should a multisourcing governance network look like a closed network where each participant is connected with the other? Alternatively, should the governance network leave room

Figure 35. Relationships between brokerage and performance (Ron Burt, 2005, by permission of Oxford University Press)

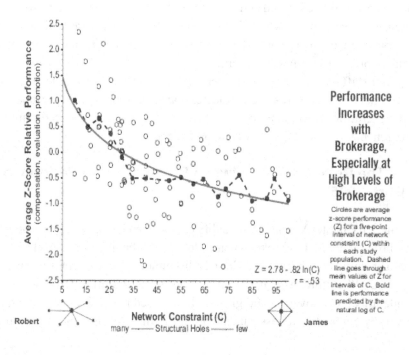

for brokerage opportunities by being more open? Entrepreneurship may in fact not be a desired capability for sourcing relationships that are looking for cost savings alone. If however the client is looking for business advantage through the innovation of its sourcing partners, then entrepreneurship and brokerage become more important. Therefore, the strategic vision for the multisourcing arrangement will play an important role in how the governance teams are staffed.

The next case looks at research conducted with an IT services vendor and the relationship between networking and performance for a global sales force.

Case 4: The High Performance Sales Force (Lock Lee & Kjaer, 2006)

The network below has been extracted from an ONA looking at how well connected the sales and business development staff were across a global services firm. One question used in the ONA survey was to ask the respondent to identify who in the organisation had helped them win deals valued at greater than $50million. The lighter coloured nodes identify those nominated. The shape of the nodes indicates that indeed those high value nodes were often well connected and were often senior officers in the company. There are therefore two interpretations one could make from this. Either the formal position in the hierarchy is dictating who gets approached for assistance on major tenders, or alternatively those employees most sought after for their personal characteristics are also the high performers who get promoted to the most senior positions. While both positions are viable interpretations of the data, informal interviewing of selected subjects, in concert with other research described in this section would suggest the latter interpretation is the most viable.

Consistent with the previous research presented on the connections between centrality and performance this research provides additional data to reinforce these results.

Figure 36. IT vendor global sales force network

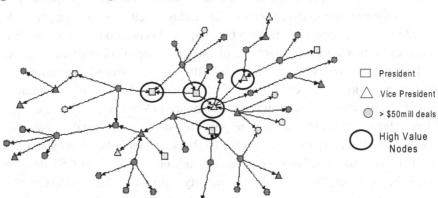

IMPLICATIONS FOR IT GOVERNANCE AND MULTISOURCING

On the surface one might conclude from this chapter that there are two extremes in choosing competencies to support IT Governance and multisourcing activities. One either looks for law makers and policing, or social workers and mediators. From a governance compliance perspective, good law makers can generate effective IT standards to uphold, leaving it to the IT police to ensure compliance. From a governance cooperation perspective the social workers and mediators would use their softer relationship skills to influence the constituency in following an agreed approach to IT Governance and multisourcing. In reality the analogy is a strong one. The world in which we live can be both complicated and complex. While the police do have a set of laws to enforce, they often cannot be crisply defined to the extent that their interpretation is obvious in all contexts. Even when the interpretation is clear, the police may choose not to apply them in certain contexts. The gap between policing and social work is closing. The skills and competencies required of a police worker today would have many overlaps with those required of the social worker.

The IT context is no different. The comment by the IT architect feeling more of a social worker than a police officer reflects the true challenge facing organisations in conducting effective IT Governance and multisourcing arrangements. Relationship skills do matter, and they matter not only at the management level, but also down to the individual IT contributor. It is no longer possible for IT workers to work individually in silos. As our business environments become more global and complex the core competencies required of the IT worker will require a healthy dose of soft skills to complement the technical skills and competencies that currently exist.

SUMMARY AND CONCLUSIONS

This broad ranging chapter has addressed the emerging personal competency requirements for working in the IT outsourcing industry, either as a manager/leader or an individual participant, from both the client and vendor perspective. With IT Governance as an anchor, the chapter explored a number of contradictions arising around competency requirements as the industry evolves beyond sole sourcing to multisourcing. Initially the emergence of OSS changed the sourcing relationship for new IT applications. The growth in acceptance of OSS will guarantee that it will form a larger part of the applications portfolios of companies in the future. The competency requirements for closed sourced software (either in-house or outsourced) contrast significantly with those required to work effectively with OSS developments. A key differential is that the community nature of OSS teams requires a more collaborative and influencing style of operation than the traditional project management focus of closed sourced software developments. On the infrastructure side, the emergence of public IT infrastructure used as a viable alternative to in- house or limited outsourced infrastructure could change the nature of the IT infrastructure competencies of retained IT staff. By shifting the IT support responsibilities to the individual staff member and their personal public infrastructure providers, internal IT staff responsibilities shift to becoming expert or specialist consultants to the business. As a business partner the competency requirements are substantially different to that of a service provider. The final contradiction arises when one moves from a substantially single sourced situation to a multiple source arrangement. A complex systems argument was used to demonstrate how a simple scaling up of single source processes is not sufficient. The competency requirements move from a process centric and process adherence capability to one of influence, facilitation and political astuteness. The sections on IT competency contradictions as they relate to IT Governance are highlighted in the section on the cathedral and the bazaar, to emphasise the change in how culture and capability for IT Governance in the new IT world might look.

The inference from the first part of this chapter was that networking skills and personal SC were going to be important attributes for working in the new IT world. The second part of this chapter addressed the linkages between networking competencies and performance. The initial section addressed the acknowledged "bug bear" of current outsourcing relationships, being the lack of perceived innovation (Gedda, 2007; Overby, 2007). The networking concept of brokerage and the competencies required to be an effective broker were introduced. This section demonstrated how brokerage skills were essential for successful innovation to be achieved and in this way inferring which competencies may be missing from current IT Governance teams. The final sections in the chapter provided a selective literature review of case study research linking networking and the development of SC to performance. The case studies covered the areas of white collar worker productivity, through to the personality traits of individuals with high personal SC, to the key linkages between brokerage capability and performance rewards and finally to the networking capabilities of high performance IT sales staff. The implications for organisations in conducting IT Governance and multisourcing were then addressed.

The common theme of this chapter is the evolution in the competency needs of the IT worker toward more non-technical "people" oriented skills. As well as the accepted commercial, legal and process skills, governance teams will now need to achieve more through influence, facilitation and, if you like, personal SC. These softer skills are likely to exist in current governance teams more through good luck than careful selection. It is also likely that these skills would not be regularly found in a single individual and therefore governance team competencies and the blending of skills into an effective governance "network" will become critical.

Having now addressed the individual competencies required to meet the changing governance requirement in the IT world, the next chapter is devoted to stepping up to the level of the organisation or firm and the intra-organisational relationships that need to exist to achieve an effective governance arrangement and SC at the departmental level.

REFERENCES

Annesley, C. (2006, July 18th). Skill need changing as banks adopt multisourcing. *Computer Weekly*.

Berkowitz, S. D. (1988). Markets, market-areas, and enterprises. In B. Wellman & S. D. Berkowitz (Eds.), *Social structures: a network approach*. New York: Cambridge University Press.

Brooks, F. (1978). *The Mythical Man-Month*. Boston, MA: Addison-Wesley Longman Publishing Co.

Bulkley, N., & Alstyne, M. V. (2006). *An Empirical Analysis of Strategies and Efficiencies in Social Networks*. Paper presented at the SUNBELT 2006, Vancouver.

Burt, R. (2003). Structural Holes and Good Ideas. *American Journal of Sociology?*

Burt, R. (2005). *Brokerage and Closure: An Introduction to Social Capital*. Oxford: Oxford University press.

Burt, R., Jannotta, J., & Mahoney, J. (1998). Personality correlates of structural holes. *Social Networks, 20*, 63-87.

Burt, R. S. (1992). *Structural Holes*: Cambridge: Harvard University Press.

Cullen, S., & Willcocks, L. (2003). *Intelligent IT Outsourcing*: Butterworth-Heinemann.

Gedda, R. (2007). Customs CIO throws cold water on vendor "innovation". Retrieved 2/12/07, from http://www.computerworld.com.au/index.php?id=1422765697

Goldberg, L. R. (1992). The development of markers for the big five factor structure. *Psychological Assessment, 4*, 26-42.

Grewal, R., Lilien, G., & Mallapragada, G. (2006). Location, Location, Location: How Network Embeddedness Affects Project Success in Open Source Systems. *Management Science, 52*(7), 1943-1056.

Hargadon, A. (2003). *How Breakthroughs Happen: The Surprising Truth About How Companies Innovate*. Harvard Business School Press.

He, Z.-L., & Wong, P.-K. (2004). Exploration vs. Exploitation: An Empirical Test of the Ambidexterity Hypothesis. *Organization Science, 15*(4), 481-494.

Henderson, R., & Cockburn, I. (1994). Measuring Competence? Exploring Firm Effects in Pharmaceutical Research. *Strategic Management Journal, 15*(Winter Special Issue), 63-84.

Johnson, B., Manyika, J., & Yee, L. (2005). The next revolution in interactions. *McKinsey Quarterly*.

Kelley, R., & Caplan, J. (1993). How Bell Labs Creates Star Performers. *Harvard Business Review*.

Kern, T., & Willcocks, L. (2001). *The Relationship Advantage*. Oxford University Press.

Klein, K., Lim, B., Saltz, J., & Mayer, D. (2004). How Do They Get There? An Examination of the Antecedents of Centrality. *Academy of Management Journal, 47*(6), 952-963.

Labianca, G., Brass, D. J., & Gray, B. (1998). Social networks and perceptions of intergroup conflict: The role of negative relationships and third parties. *Academy of Management Journal, 41*(1), 55-67.

Lacity, M., & Willcocks, L. (2000a). *Global IT Outsourcing: Search for Business Advantage*. Chichester: Wiley.

Lacity, M., & Willcocks, L. (2000b). *Inside IT Outsourcing: A State-of-the-Art Report*. Oxford: Templeton College, Oxford.

Lerner, J., & Tirole, J. (2002). Some Simple Economics of Open Source. *The Journal of Industrial Economics, L*(2), 197-233.

Ljungberg, J. (2000). Open source movements as a model for organising. *European Journal of Information Systems, 9*, 208-216.

Lock Lee, L., & Kjaer, C. (2006). Relationship management: The new IT core competency? *CSC Leading Edge Forum Journal*(December).

Long, Y., & Siau, K. (2007). Social Network Structures in Open source software Development Teams. *Journal of Database Management, 18*(2), 25-40.

March, J. (1991). Exploration and Exploitation in Organizational Learning. *Organization Science, 2*(1).

McClelland, D. C. (1973). Testing for competence rather than for "intelligence". *American Psychologist, 28*, 1-14.

Neal, D. (2005). Your employees and your customers are growing up—what are you going to do? *CSC Leading Edge Forum Journal* June 2005. Retrieved 9/12/2007, from http://www.lef.csc.com/foundation/library/publicationdetail02.asp?aID=2087&ptID=2001

O'Reilly, T. (2004). *Open Source Paradigm Shift.* Retrieved 9/12/07, from http://tim.oreilly.com/articles/paradigmshift_0504.html

Overby, S. (2007). *What Price Innovation?* Retrieved 2/12/07, from http://www.cio.com.au/index.php?id=477547616

Raymond, E. (2000). The Cathedral and the Bazaar. Retrieved 5/12/07, from http://www.catb.org/~esr/writings/cathedral-bazaar/cathedral-bazaar/

Scott, J. (2000). *Social Network Analysis* (2nd ed.). Thousand Oaks, CA: Sage.

Snowden, D., & Boone, M. (2007). A Leader's Framework for Decision Making. *Harvard Business Review, November.*

Tuomi, I. (2000). *Internet, Innovation, and Open Source: Actors in the Network*: SITRA—The Finnish National Fund for Research and Development.

Wang, E., & Chen, J. (2006). The influence of governance equilibrium on ERP project success. *Decision Support Systems, 41*, 708-727.

Wasserman, S., & Faust, K. (1994). *Social Network Analysis: Methods and Applications*. UK: Cambridge University Press.

Weill, P. (2004). Don't Just Lead, Govern: How Top-Performing Firms Govern IT. *MIS Quarterly Executive, 8*(1).

Willcocks, L., & Cullen, S. (2006). *The Outsourcing Enterprise: The Power of Relationships.* Retrieved 20/11/07, from http://www.logicacmg.com/r/8000/the+outsourcing+enterprise%3a+the+power+of+relationships/400009147

Chapter VII
Intra–Organisational Networks

The growing interest in internal networks within organisations has been spawned by the apparent ineffectiveness of the traditional hierarchical organisational structures to deal with the complexity of today's business environment. Even with matrix structures, which can generate their own operational complexities, there is always an extra dimensional lever that executives would like to have access to. In designing organisational structures executives can choose to design around product or service lines, geographies, business processes, supply chain flows, customers, core competencies and the like. With the desire to facilitate faster decision making, executives are looking to flatten organisational structures, pushing accountability further down the line. The consequences are that hierarchical power and the power of position is now being eroded. The proportion of work activities needing to be achieved through influence and negotiation, rather than direction, is continually growing. As identified in the previous chapter, this is having a major impact on the competency requirements of managers operating in a more networked environment.

Inside organisations we will see the traditional organisation chart showing the hierarchy of departments and their hierarchical reporting relationships to the CEO. The organisation chart is meant to be a representation of how the firm is organised and therefore how it goes about its business. Unfortunately such representations only give a hint as to how things are done. Those who have been part of the organisation for some time will know how things "really get done". There will exist a hidden organisation that better reflects this, which is something that old-timers intuitively know and have learnt and what newcomers desperately want to know. Much has been written about the so called "hidden organisation" over the past decade (Baker, 2000; Rob Cross & Parker, 2004; Mizruchi & Stearns, 2001; Tsai & Ghoshal, 1998; Wellman *et al.*, 2001). This is now extending to the Asian economies and the appreciation of Asian culture within organisations (Wellman et al., 2001). The "hidden organisation" is a network largely formed by volunteers. Like the OSS movement described in the previous chapter, the bonds that form the network are not necessarily formed along the lines of a formal hierarchy. Network leaders tend to self select and are sustained in their roles by a network membership that voluntarily chooses to work with the leader to achieve agreed common goals. The network leaders make use of their social capital (SC) within the organisation to achieve their objectives by firstly attracting like minded individuals to their cause and then coordinating them to deliver on their objectives. For many it is this SC that provides the lubrication for the formal organisation to achieve its goals (Cohen & Prusak, 2001). Several practical guides on how networks are created and sustained have now been published (Anklam, 2007; Collison & Parcell, 2001; Wenger *et al.*, 2002).

In this chapter, the IT Governance of multisourcing relationships will be viewed from inside the organisation. For the IT function the challenge is not only to present a unified face for the IT service, but to be able to service their internal clients that present themselves in increasingly complex guises. There is no single point representation for business needs. There is no easy means for gaining agreement on enterprise wide IT initiatives. There is also typically a heterogeneous base of end-users that range from the super user with skills comparable to the experts within the IT function, through to technology shy novices who might need to be nurtured and coached into using the technology beneficially. To be effective the IT function needs to understand how to become authentic members of the firm's networks to understand how IT can more effectively contribute to the firm's activities.

For the vendor the task is potentially more complex. Inside their own firms the organisational matrix will be stretched to cover product and service lines, geographic markets, competencies and skill bases, industry specialisations and the like. Depending on the firm's strategy, the customer base is also likely to be heterogeneous, providing challenges to the organisation to provide "best in class" standard products and/or services while at the same time offering a tailored service or product suite to the end client. For large global vendors, the challenge is to be able to leverage the vast knowledge base that they have within their ranks without overloading the organisation with bureaucratic overheads. Again global networks appear to be the preferred organisational vehicle for achieving this objective (Lesser & Prusak, 1999; Lock Lee & Neff, 2004).

The next section will review the use of networks within organisations i.e. the "hidden organisation". This will be followed by a section on communities of practice (CoPs), the preferred organisational vehicle for leveraging organisational knowledge. Networks will then be addressed from both the client and vendor perspectives.

THE HIDDEN ORGANISATION

The rise in the informal organisation can be traced through articles on the topic published in the business press over the past decade or more. The impetus for the work has been the acknowledgement that company executives can no longer rely on giving directives and expecting staff to obediently follow orders. Many a new CEO has discovered to their chagrin the "organisational immune system" that can frustrate attempts to institute organisational change. In 1993 Krackhardt and Hanson (1993) wrote about the informal organisation behind the formal company organisation chart. The authors liken the formal organisation to a skeleton and the informal organisation as the central nervous system. The informal organisation is uncovered through a Social Network Analysis survey, asking respondents who they go to for advice, who their trusted friends are and who they communicate with the most. The responses can then be used to map the advice, trust and communication networks operating in the firm as previously illustrated in Chapter VI (SNA tutorial). The authors reported on a CEO who experienced a lack of progress with a special task force that he had convened. An SNA survey identified that the task force leader had only a peripheral position in the firm's trust network. By appointing someone who was central to the trust network to the task force, the CEO was able to avoid having to close down or substantially restructure the task force, and the change in group dynamics, for the better, was obvious within weeks.

In terms of IT Governance, could that be just like the task force mentioned above? Could members of the governance team share no trust network connections? How can trust be built within the governance team if they are only exposed to each other at the periodic review meetings? How can the governance team members become part of the trust networks existing in the business? How can vendors join this trust network? How much more effective would they be if they were? While the IT Governance team may be formally identified under the CIO in the organisation chart, unless it is also identified with the informal organisation, its task could become "mission impossible".

The communication network reflects how information flows through the organisation. Again one would anticipate that information would flow through the formal hierarchy, which is designed to communicate the intent of the executive through to the staff charged with delivering on the mission. Large investments are made

Figure 37. Survey of a global IT services firm (n = 550)

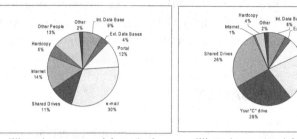

Where do you source information?	Where do you store information?
•E-mail dominant	•89% Unstructured
•87% Unstructured Repositories	•49% Private

in developing corporate data bases and data warehouses to facilitate rapid access to operational information to all concerned. At least this is a formal organisation's process view of the world. Reality as revealed by SNA studies of communication patterns can often be quite different. Firstly, when asked where they source their information from, invariably the sources are from unstructured repositories like e-mail, the Internet, face-to-face, telephone or SMS. Only a small proportion is sourced from the designed information sources like data warehouses, data base applications and Intranets.

The above survey is symptomatic of several similar surveys of organisations across different industry sectors, both in the public and the private sector. The message is clear. People prefer to source and share their information informally. In other words, information has a social life (Seely Brown & Duguid, 2000), such that it cannot be easily separated from the people that create it, add value to it and eventually share it. Often the added value of receiving information from a trusted partner rather than sourcing it from a data base is the qualification that often comes with the delivery. For example, "I would be careful how you used this as the source is suspect", or "you can trust this data, it has been verified several times by our group".

Figure 38 describes a communications network for a government utility which included not only individuals, but also groups and systems. What is evident from the map is that a number of individuals are playing information brokering roles to several of the corporate systems and external information systems. The greater efficiency in sourcing information through the brokers, rather than having to learn the intricacies of a system that one might only use spasmodically, is just too attractive to ignore. Much of the information shared is conveyed in an uncontrolled fashion, via e-mail. This example further emphasises the social life of information. The information brokers are playing a critical role, but their efforts are normally invisible to the executive and the formal organisation.

Figure 38. Information brokers

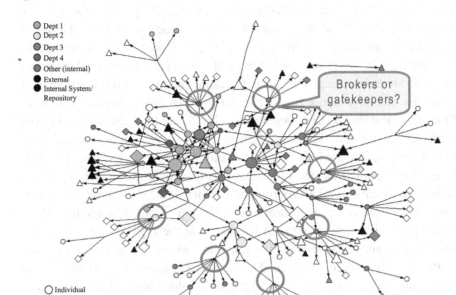

What is becoming apparent is the hidden power of the informal organisation. It can act to thwart well intentioned management initiatives, or alternatively be used to accelerate a difficult organisational change through leveraging the key opinion leaders found in the informal organisation. In their Harvard Business Review article in 2002, Cross and Prusak (2002) identified the particular roles within the formal networks that individuals play and how these roles can be used to great effect when implementing organisational change. The central connector role is most evident as the "go to" people. Central connectors are the "opinion leaders" and therefore can be either a positive or negative influence in terms of their alignment with the intent of the executive. "Boundary spanners" play the important role of bridging perspectives between disparate groups. It is often the brokers who are engaged as the change agents, moving between groups to broker cooperation. The other identified role is the "peripheral specialists", who tend to intentionally sit on the fringes of the network, often as technical specialists, potentially providing deep expertise not typically found in the other roles. Understanding the roles that individuals can play in the informal organisation provides an added dimension to the organisational change management challenge. Sponsorship cascaded through the formal lines of authority is clearly a requirement for successful change. However, being able to enlist particular roles in the informal organisation could be the difference between a successful change and an energy draining failure.

For the IT function their activities are almost synonymous with organisational change. Invariably IT initiatives will change the way people operate, either through making routine jobs redundant, or institutionalising processes within which staff must operate, or providing a competitive lever in the marketplace. The complexity of providing an effective IT service has led to the need for sophisticated processes to be installed to help manage the demand. Despite the increased formalisation of the IT service and governance functions it has its own hidden organisation, with all of the roles identified by Cross and Prusak (2002). Central connectors will exist in the lines of service of desktop management, networks and telecommunications, server management and the like. Business clients will prefer to go directly to their connectors for expedited service. IT is a technically complex discipline. Peripheral specialist will exist in the technical strongholds, whether they be experts in security, the resolution of complex communications or desktop problems. Sometimes these peripheral specialists will be sourced from outside the organisation. They may not be as visibly active as others in the function, but come into their own when the really difficult problems surface. The "boundary spanners" will provide the important integrating roles between the technical silos and the business clients. In terms of IT Governance, it is therefore a much bigger task than simply having the appropriate processes and organisational structures in place. The interaction between the formal and informal aspects of an IT service will be addressed more comprehensively in chapter IX under value networks.

Having introduced the hidden informal organisation the task now is to understand how organisations can leverage the informal organisation for beneficial purposes. Many of the operating aspects of informal organisations have been captured in the Knowledge management (KM) literature. The interest in the field of KM peaked in the late 1990s and with it an understanding about how organisations were effectively sharing knowledge across the formal lines of business. The term "communities of practice" (CoPs) was coined (Wenger, 1998) to describe informal organisational groups formed with the express purpose of sharing knowledge. In the next section CoPs will be reviewed as an alternate source of value in linking across the organisational silos.

COMMUNITIES OF PRACTICE

Communities of Practice (CoPs) is a term used to describe groups that form informally around a particular discipline or skill to enable their members to share and learn from each other. Informal CoPs have always existed in the modern organisation (Wenger, 1998). Popular Knowledge management programs began appearing in the mid 1990s, invariably with CoPs as their central platform. Most of the activity has been led by the large global organisations, with a majority of the global Fortune Top 10 companies prominent in the literature. Benefits to the business have been expressed in a variety of ways. They range from savings attributed to sharing a best practice, receiving quick advice for pressing operational problems, right through to generating innovative products or services.

The maturing of the field has led to several attempts to standardise the terminology. The term "Communities of Practice"(CoPs) has now largely been accepted as the umbrella term for describing, "informal groups bound together by shared expertise and passion for a joint enterprise". Under this umbrella exists a number of terms to describe different incarnations of a CoP. The most common sub-categorisation is to distinguish between formally supported, top-down, business aligned CoPs and the more informally established, bottom up, interest based CoPs. Different companies have adopted many different terms for formally supported CoPs. In BHP Billiton they are called "Networks" (Lock Lee, 2000), in the World Bank "Thematic Groups" in Daimler Chrysler "Tech Clubs", "Learning groups" in HP (Wenger et al., 2002) and "Delivery Networks" in BP (Collison & Parcell, 2001). Others suggest that CoPs and knowledge networks are the same thing (Anklam, 2007). Seely Brown and Paul Duguid (Seely Brown & Duguid, 2000) have chosen to distinguish "Knowledge Networks" from CoPs, not on the basis of the degree of business alignment or formality, but on the level of potential cohesiveness. Networks are defined as geographically broader and less cohesive than CoPs, whose role is more one of information sharing than true knowledge sharing. The argument Seely Brown and Duguid makes is that the levels of trust required to achieve true knowledge sharing and shared practice can only come from regular, intense and reciprocal interactions. This is largely not possible with widely distributed networks. The implications for organisations wanting to achieve true knowledge sharing through networks is how these networks can appropriately nurture and align local CoPs, where true knowledge sharing is more viable.

One can see from the breadth of definitions that there can exist a continuum for the degree of formalisation of network/CoP structures. The left had side of Figure 39 shows the traditional formal organisational forms of functional business and matrix organisations. Moving to the right we have various views of organisational elements that might complement the formal structures. CoPs and networks exist beyond the life of the single initiative and therefore must necessarily be distinguished from project or ad-hoc teams that are formed for a single purpose, with the intent of disbanding once the task has been completed.

Rather than treating these entities as distinct vehicles one can see that ad hoc teams and project teams could be vehicles employed by CoPs and networks (Figure 40) to deliver their results, whether it be devising and documenting a new practice, developing a training program or even organising a company conference.

Figure 39. Networking models

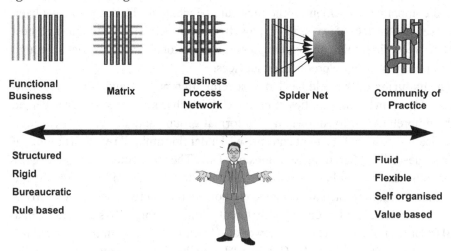

Figure 40. Interactions between CoPs, networks and teams

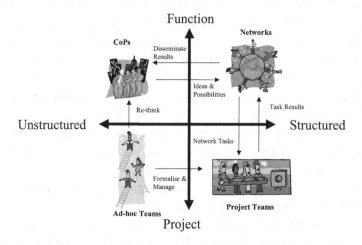

Perhaps the most compelling experiences with CoPs and networks over the past decade has centred on organisations trying to balance the desire to more formally harness the power of these informal, cross enterprise CoPs, without destroying them or driving them further underground. For the more industrially focused businesses there is a clear trend to embed formal support for CoPs into the organisation's business improvement or operational excellence programs (e.g. Xerox, Raytheon, BP, Ford, DaimlerChrysler, BHP Billiton). For the more service oriented companies there have been greater attempts at having CoP participation embedded in personal job descriptions and goals (Ernst & Young, IBM, Schlumberger, Computer Sciences Corp).

Table 6. Line vs. network responsibilities (source: Parry Norling, DuPont)

Practice Network Responsibilities	Line Management Responsibilities
Effectiveness	Efficiency
"Possibility seeking" arm	"Implementing" arm
"Doing the right thing"	"Doing it right"
To tell the line management the possibilities	To tell the network its needs
Understand operational needs, look for the right members, facilitate, be an agent for discovery	Provide direction and optimal resource allocation
Assist with paradigm shifts, systems, processes and capabilities (like a trusted consultant)	Be open to collaborative decision making with a wider group

Another common challenge faced by CoPs and networks is accountability. Like the formal lines of management, CoPs and networks are usually tasked with organisational objectives. However, given the cross organisational roles that CoPs often have there are inevitably clashes on who is accountable for what. The characterisation of the respective roles of CoPs and line management (Table 6) were provided by DuPont. As one can see the line management accountability for delivery of the business result is not diluted by the presence of CoPs and networks, which become trusted advisors and sources of inspiration and innovation for the line management.

For CoPs as a source of innovation, organisations need to be mindful that CoPs developed around a particular specialisation can suffer from the SC liability problem where the community becomes so tightly bound that it becomes impervious to new ideas and paradigms. Seeley Brown and Duguid (1991) argue that true innovation is achieved at the intersection of these communities, or where members have overlapping interests, and in effect act as bridges between the communities, as argued by Burt (2003).

Given the informal nature of CoPs it can be difficult to identify how they are working? Whether they are being effective or not? Who is participating and who is playing a leading role? For large organisations overt management could in fact harm their operation, so monitoring activities can be problematic. Monitoring activities need to be as non-intrusive as possible. The following example illustrates such a non-intrusive analysis of a significant CoP programme operating globally within the Computer Sciences Corporation (CSC). The firm operates a company wide portal which supports the development of CoPs (Lock Lee & Neff, 2004). Staff is able to launch their own CoP using the portal as a shared space. Staff can join any CoPs that interest them. The number of CoP shared spaces numbered in the hundreds with close to 20,000 members when this analysis was conducted. The technique was to use membership data to identify affinity networks between individual members and also between CoPs. For example, if two staff members choose

Figure 41. Communities of practice "Organisation Chart"

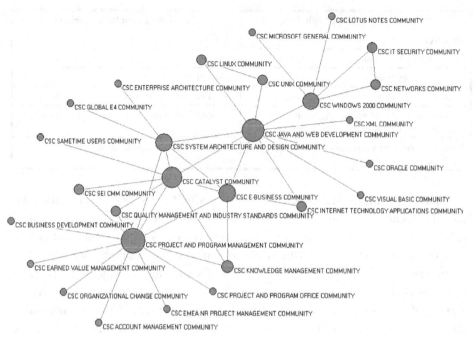

Figure 42. CSC broker network?

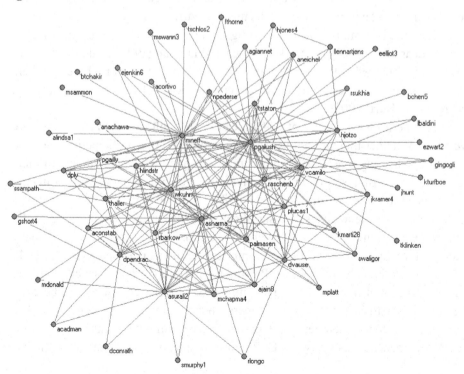

to be members of several of the same CoPs then a relationship would be inferred between them, with a strength of relationship related to the number of their common CoP memberships. Likewise for CoPs, an affinity relationship between CoPs would be inferred by the degree of overlapping memberships, with the strength of relationship being related to the degree of common membership. The following maps show the strongest affinity relationships identified.

Figure 41 could be described as an organisational chart for Computer Science Corp.'s core competencies at the time of the study. The identified communities are those with the highest membership. The relationships show how these competencies are related. One can see two cliques at the top of the figure showing linkages between the windows 2000, IT security and Networks communities. The second clique is between the Unix, Linux and Web development communities. The clique with the largest membership however joins the project and program community, Catalyst (CSC's development methodology), the e-business community, Architecture and Design and Knowledge management.

Figure 42 identifies those individuals who have volunteered to be members of many communities. The affinity linkages between them indicate a degree of common interest. There are a number of interpretations that can be made from a map like the one shown here. They could simply reflect those people who are inquisitive and like to have a window into many worlds. If activity within the communities were also monitored together with the data here, one might infer that some of these people would make excellent knowledge brokers. As identified in the previous chapter, these staff could be effective vehicles for implementing major organisational changes or leveraging new innovation opportunities by being at the intersection between communities (Brown & Duguid, 1991).

This section and the previous one have provided an overview of the most common informal or hidden organisational structures that operate to different degrees in all organisations. Some organisations have recognised their existence and are attempting to leverage them for greater business benefit. Others choose to ignore them or to even stamp them out, which usually leads to them going further underground. However if an organisation's management chooses to work with their internal networks, one thing is certain. The internal networks can either act as catalysts for change, or effective immune systems against change, and therefore need to be catered for. This warning is equally valid for the IT Governance function in its role of brokering multiple vendors into their distributed client base. The next sections therefore address the relevance of internal business networks and the IT function from both the internal IT Governance and the multisourced vendors' perspective.

BUSINESS NETWORKS AND IT GOVERNANCE

This chapter has so far identified the characteristics of the informal organisation as a suite of networks formed around topics of common interest. Often the rallying points for these networks or communities reflect the core competencies held within the organisation, but not formally recognised in the organisation charts. The IT function itself can be viewed as a network of competencies as illustrated in Figure 41. Where IT services are outsourced these CoPs could extend outside the formal organisation to the outsourcing partners. From an IT Governance perspective however, it is not sufficient to simply manage the IT focussed CoPs. There needs to be some mechanisms for connecting the IT CoPs and networks with the networks and CoPs that exist in the business at large. In terms of IT innovation, these bridging network connections can be critical (R. S. Burt, 2004).

Bridging networks or CoPs present some unique challenges. Core membership of CoPs is often founded on a shared educational and/or work experience. For example, the core membership of a geophysicists or electrical engineers CoP is founded on a common formal educational base followed up by a discipline centric work experience history. Members of the IT fraternity, or any other discipline for that matter, would not normally be welcome here. The typical formal organisation response of appointing relationship managers would hold no authority in the informal organisation. In fact a tightly managed CoP can become the worst form of organisational silo, impenetrable to those that have not met the unwritten prerequisite qualification criteria. Such CoPs or networks that appear closed to outside intervention have been recognised as having negative SC, or SC liabilities (Adler & Kwon, 2000; Bagley *et al.*, 2004; Cohen & Prusak, 2001; Leenders & Gabbay, 1999; Portes, 1998). In effect their cooperative strength is also their weakness. So what can the IT networks do to successfully engage with the business networks?

The insight into a resolution is to look again at the SC contradiction introduced in Chapter V on the benefits of brokerage and closure. This issue has been addressed directly by Burt (2005) in looking to rationalise these two apparently opposing concepts for SC. Burt's proposition is that if groups can demonstrate what he refers to as "structural autonomy" whereby there are dense interconnections within the group together with a diverse suite of bridging connections to other groups or networks, then performance will be maximised. Alternatively, poorest performance will result from divisive groups with few, if any, external bridges.

To achieve maximum performance the network leadership needs to be sufficiently enlightened to acknowledge that strong cohesion within the network must not be to the exclusion of external stakeholders, as shown in Figure 43. The author experienced an example of such leadership in the late 1990s in BHP Billiton, where the leader of their largest network, a global maintenance engineering network, was

Figure 43. brokerage and closure matrix (adapted from Ron Burt, 2005 Fig. 3.5, p.139)

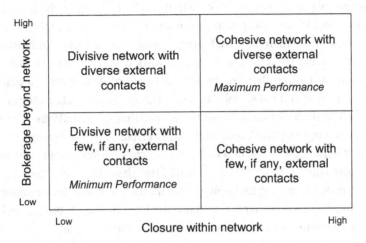

approached by some of the core membership with a request from a production manager to participate in their core leadership group. His rationale was that maintenance was the major cost in his area and he was motivated to understand more about the discipline and felt that membership in the network would provide him with this. The core members presented the proposition to the leader in a somewhat negative fashion. This person was not a maintenance engineer, nor had he been one previous to becoming a production manager. To his credit the network leader recognised the importance of engaging with someone who potentially could represent a key stakeholder group for their network. He not only welcomed him into the network but encouraged him to actively contribute from his production perspective. By this action he showed he was mindful of the SC liabilities of being in the bottom right hand quadrant of the brokerage/closure matrix.

The IT functional networks are no different to any other network. The speciality of the discipline can lead to the function being seen as a "closed shop". The first action of the IT leadership is to demonstrate structural autonomy within their own networks by ensuring that the discipline networks are cohesive internally (which may include outsource partners) as well as being receptive to external, non IT members wanting more active participation within the IT network. This will necessarily require some adjustment to network activities to accommodate contributions from those who do not have the extensive IT background of the majority of members. For example, special bridging or innovation sessions could be developed where non IT members are invited in to participate in innovation motivated brainstorming sessions. Alternatively, they could be invited into business improvement sessions to represent the "voice of the customer".

The second action is for IT function brokers to position themselves so they are invited to participate in other networks. This can be a confronting challenge, a bit like gaining an invitation to an exclusive club that you feel inadequately qualified to join. It is an advantage if the brokers can demonstrate some affinity to the membership of the network into which they are trying to gain membership. An individual who has changed careers from the area of the network of interest into IT, is a good bridging mechanism. Failing that, the brokers do need to demonstrate a genuine interest in the topic area and not simply be seen as an indiscriminate explorer. The IT brokers will also have to demonstrate some value in their contributions. This may be via assisting the target network to operate more effectively, say through the use of collaborative technologies provided by the IT function. Alternatively one could assist with the provision of other IT services like data base or record keeping services or even some leading edge technology that might contribute to the network's core project activities. In summary, the main attribute of the IT broker seeking membership into a business network, is to show enthusiasm, a genuine interest in the network's business and make a practical contribution to the effective operation of the network. Without such attributes membership of a non-IT network will be difficult, if not impossible to sustain.

This section has identified the challenges and opportunities that the IT function faces in engaging the informal organisation in IT Governance. The formal organisation can mandate a given IT Governance role and structure for the organisation. However, as most CIOs will know, such governance mechanisms can and are undermined by the informal organisation. It is not until the IT function can engage with the informal networks in the business, gaining a true insight into the impacts of governance arrangements at the working level, that a truly effective IT Governance arrangement can be achieved.

The majority of IT functions have been established as a service to the main lines of business. In fact many such "shared services" arrangements have often been established through shifting IT staff from the main lines of business into the shared function. This exercise is rarely straight forward with some lines of business claiming that their IT staff members are core to their operations and the services would be diluted if they were to be taken into a shared service arrangement. Network analysis can provide some unique insight into how "embedded" a particular function or individual may be within a core line of business. Its use could help predict potential difficulties in achieving a shared service organisational design and assist with defining where the line should be drawn in terms of services and mainstream operations. In the next section a case study is presented to illustrate how ONA can be used to assist with organisational design exercises for shared services.

NETWORK ANALYSIS AND ORGANISATIONAL DESIGN FOR SHARED SERVICES

With the advent of outsourcing in the early 1990's, much of the discussion in IT management circles was around what to keep in house and what to potentially outsource. The common theme was that commodity services that did not provide a particular competitive advantage to the firm were prime targets for outsourcing, whereas those services that were integral to a firm's competitive advantage should be retained in house (Quinn, 1992). For those firms or organisations that were not yet prepared to outsource services to external providers, a common tactic was to redesign the organisations such that commodity style services could be organised within a shared services facility and made available across the whole organisation. Such shared services are not confined to IT, but also typically include services like human resources, and finance and administration. In this way outsourcing of services could be undertaken in an incremental way with minimal disruption to the organisation as a whole.

In practice this division has never proved to be easy to determine. In fact a study of some 40 firms adopting this approach between 1991 and 1993 found that the majority of firms encountered significant problems and were largely disappointed with the results (Lacity *et al.*, 1995). The principal difficulty is gaining agreement on whether a particular competency is indeed distinctive and competitive for the organisation. For the mainstream lines of business the inclination is to label the majority of services as strategic, if only to sustain control of the resource. The situation is accentuated in firms making sophisticated use of IT services, for example, research organisations, geosciences, financial analyses, defence and aerospace organisations.

The use of ONA takes organisational analysis down to the individual level. The patterns of engagement between a given service area and the remainder of the organisation can provide some critical insight into the potential for separating the service into a shared service function, or alternatively, where there is likely to be significant, and often justified, resistance to such a move. The following case study is used to illustrate the application of ONA for shared services design.

Case Study

Organisational Design

Mark is a divisional manager for a major publicly owned transport utility. His division of over 100 staff is responsible for conducting the complex task of transport planning and scheduling. Unseen disruptions occur in the transport network on a daily basis.

Mark's department is responsible for both planning the master timetable and also designing the schedule adaptations brought about by disruptions to this timetable. The staff profile ranges from operational management levels, specialised analysts through to a significant number of clerical and administrative staff. The clerical staff is required to deal with the large amount of information that his management and analyst staff require to effectively undertake their duties. Over recent years Mark has been focussed on upgrading their information and analytical systems to better support his management and analytical staff. The systems developed were quite sophisticated and required specialist skills to both use, and maintain them to the required level. On the positive side the new systems are now successfully removing many of the labour intensive clerical and administrative activities allowing Mark to consider some structural changes to his division to better leverage the advantages offered by the upgraded systems.

On the organisational wide front a major drive was being undertaken to create a shared services division. As with most shared services initiatives the business rationale was to structure what was seen as overhead services for the organisation into a single division, which could then more flexibly adapt to the changing needs of the core lines of business. A new IT function had been established as a shared service and much of the IT infrastructure services had been outsourced to a global supplier. The initiative had already conscripted a few of Mark's staff into the shared help desk facility. The organisation was now looking at other potential overhead resources that could be conscripted into the shared services division for leveraging across the whole organisation. His executive manager had indicated to him that these considerations would need to be addressed in his planned re-organisation of his division.

Mark had some reservations about the methods used in determining what was operationally strategic and what could be considered a commodity shared service. His experience with the shared help desk service was not particularly good for some of his specialised needs, forcing him to recreate a few support positions. He was also cognisant of the potential loss of the specialised knowledge required to effectively manage the complex timetabling task. He wanted to be sure that any organisational change enhanced the sustainability of his division's knowledge base, rather than dilute it. Mark had been introduced to the ONA methods by the agency's organisational development section, which was keen to pilot the technique. Seeing the potential of the technique to assist with his organisational redesign, Mark was a willing volunteer.

The ONA survey of the department achieved close to a 100% response rate with the critical question asked being "Who do you rely on to provide you with critical advice in doing your job?" From this question alone, sociograms were developed identifying the dependency network which existed across the whole division. By also making use of attributes of each individual like the sections that they belonged to, their age, their experience in the industry, the sociograms could be used to assist with not only succession planning but also in the assessment of the criticality of the sections within Mark's division, to each other.

Figure 44 is a sociogram showing the advice dependencies that exist across the division. The two support sections that are potential candidates for splitting off into a shared services unit are coloured black and white. One can see that Support Section B, indicated by the white nodes, is relatively self contained with the majority of its interactions with the rest of the division occurring through just two of the section members. The inference is that this section could be relocated as a shared service with minimal impact. Support Section A, indicated by the black nodes, is however far more embedded into the network of other core sections. It would appear that splitting this section out into a shared service would have a more substantial impact on the existing dependencies.

Mark was encouraged by these results as they aligned well with his own perceptions. He was concerned about the possibility of losing Support Section A to the shared service and felt that he now had some data that could be used to demonstrate why such a move would be counter-productive for his division.

Organisations undertaking re-engineering to create shared service divisions are constantly faced with dilemmas such as those faced by Mark. A decade or more of

Figure 44. Sociogram identifying support divisions

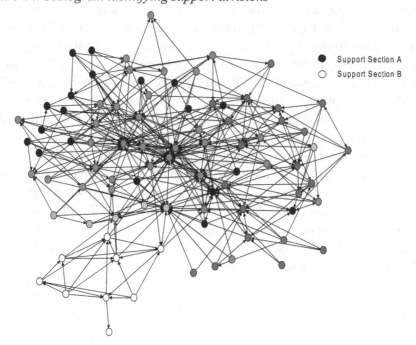

IT outsourcing experience has seen a continual oscillation of personnel between outsourced service providers, retained IT functions and staff embedded directly in the core lines of business. Without real data on which to base these decisions, actions are more often driven by emotion or dictate. The above case study provides a demonstration as to how ONA can be used to provide the relationship dependency data needed to make effective re-engineering decisions.

IMPLICATIONS FOR IT GOVERNANCE AND MULTISOURCING

Governance as facilitated by a corporate function, whether it be human resource, financial or IT policies will always experience a tension with the main operating lines of business. Tasked with identifying "best practice" standards and then facilitating their governance, these groups are often seen to be at odds with the operating groups who may often view such activities as wasteful corporate overheads. Even if the compliance policies are crisp and clear, the opportunity is always present to lobby for exceptions, particularly if the local advantage of non-compliance is attractive enough. With the growing complexity of business and globalisation impacts, which bring into effect both local and cultural factors, the cases for exceptions can only get stronger.

The major implications for IT Governance and multisourcing from a more networked business environment is that driving blind compliance to a single suite of standards is going to be increasingly difficult to achieve. As organisations like Cisco and DuPont begin to rely on an increasingly larger proportion of their revenues coming from joint ventures, even the authority for a given compliance scheme would be brought into question. By taking a network view of IT Governance and multisourced procurement, the IT function would see that to be successful it needs to become a "player" in the informal networks that pervade all organisations. Networks will often comfortably stretch beyond company boundaries without the restriction of formal legal agreements. Often the informal networks will precede and pre-qualify formal alliance agreement. To be effective the IT functions need to be prepared to become active members of these informal communities, building SC on the way. Likewise the IT function needs to open up its own communities to outsiders. By "opening up the black box" and openly discussing IT Governance issues with their business counterparts, SC and the increased trust that goes with it, can assist the function achieve more effective IT Governance in even the most complex business environments.

SUMMARY AND CONCLUSIONS

This chapter has provided an alternative view to the typical organisational structure chart. While the formal organisation is typically described in hierarchical terms, the informal organisation is described in terms of networks and communities. Such networks and communities are rarely documented in a formal sense and hence are largely hidden from the casual observer. Ignoring the hidden organisation is however, done at one's peril. The networks and communities that exist inside organisations are more often bound by trust than reporting relationships. Hence, they can act as either highly effective agents of change or alternatively an organisational "immune system" resistant to all management efforts to instigate change.

The concept of Communities of Practice informally formed around a particular discipline or practice, has been selected for particular attention. CoPs are arguably the greatest contribution made by the Knowledge management movement to date, being seen as the most effective vehicle for sharing knowledge across an organisation. Analysing CoPs using a networks paradigm identifies two areas of organisational benefit from CoPs. They are the close collaboration or closure within the CoP when developing a practice, but also the interaction or brokerage between CoPs as a key source of innovation. It was argued that optimal performance is achieved when both closure and brokerage are achieved in concert.

For the IT function and its role in IT Governance, the interaction with the informal organisation is arguably as important as the formal governance mechanisms established. The IT function itself has much to gain from developing its own IT discipline or practice networks. However, being party to an organisation's non-IT CoPs can provide the IT function with access to shop floor opinion and expertise. It could also lead to the IT innovation that has proved so elusive in many organisations. It has been argued in this chapter that achieving brokerage between IT CoPs and other business CoPs could prove particularly challenging. Identifying the appropriate broker for each business CoP needs to be carefully considered, as such brokers will need to win the trust of the CoP based on their own energy, enthusiasm and willingness to contribute. The rewards in the trust stakes can however be substantial and beyond what might be achieved through the formal relationship channels.

Finally a case study was presented to illustrate how ONA techniques can be used to assist with re-organisation and re-engineering activities. In terms of the IT function, deciding which individuals should be drawn from the core lines of business into a shared service is the most challenging task. For the core lines of business, the loss of critical knowledge or a dilution of services is the biggest fear and therefore creates the most resistance. Through the use of ONA, data can now be provided to demonstrate what the likely impact may be on the core businesses through the creation of a shared services division, so that organisational change management efforts can be targeted more effectively.

Having provided a view of IT Governance from a sociological perspective and an analysis of how networks and communities are at work within organisations the following section relates to applications and future directions. The next chapter reports on a substantial empirical research project linking Corporate SC to firm performance. This is then followed by two chapters on emerging network management practices. The first introduces the concept of value networks and their application to the IT industry. Value networks have recently been acknowledged by ITIL, the global best practice organisation for the IT services industry, as a best practice for building IT strategy. This is followed by a network analysis of the global IT services sector identifying emerging market intelligence and relationship management practices. A chapter on the impacts of technology, with a focus on the Web 2.0 phenomena, closes the section.

REFERENCES

Adler, P., & Kwon, S.-W. (2000). Social Capital: The Good, the Bad, and the Ugly. In E. Lesser (Ed.), *Knowledge and Social Capital*. Butterworth-Heinmann.

Anklam, P. (2007). *Net Work: A Practical Guide to Creating and Sustaining Networks at Work and in the World*: Butterworth-Heinemann.

Bagley, C., Ackerley, C. L., & Rattray, J. (2004). Social exclusion, sure start and organizational social capital: evaluating inter-disciplinary multi-agency working in an education and health work programme. *Journal of Education Policy, 19*(5), 595-607.

Baker, W. (2000). *Achieving Success Through Social Capital: Tapping the Hidden Resources in Your Personal and Business Networks*. San Francisco: Jossey-Bass.

Brown, J. S., & Duguid, P. (1991). Organizational Learning and Communities-of-practice: Toward a Unified View of Working, Learning and Innovating. *Organization Science, 2*(1), 40-57.

Burt, R. (2003). Structural Holes and Good Ideas. *American Journal of Sociology?*

Burt, R. (2005). *Brokerage and Closure: An Introduction to Social Capital*. Oxford: Oxford University press.

Burt, R. S. (2004). Structural holes and good ideas. *American Journal Of Sociology, 110*(2), 349-399.

Cohen, D., & Prusak, L. (2001). *In Good Company: How Social Capital Makes Organizations Work*. Boston: Harvard Business School Press.

Collison, C., & Parcell, G. (2001). *Learning to Fly: Practical Lessons from one of the World's leading Knowledge Companies*: Capstone Publishing.

Cross, R., & Parker, A. (2004). *The Hidden Power of Social Networks*: Harvard Business School Press, Boston, MA.

Cross, R., & Prusak, L. (2002). The People Who Make Organizations Go-or Stop. *Harvard Business Review, 80*(6), 104-112.

Krackhardt, D., & Hanson, J. R. (1993). Informal Networks: The Company Behind the Charts. *Harvard Business Review, 71*(4), 104-111.

Lacity, M., Willcocks, L., & Feeney, D. (1995). IT Outsourcing: Maximum Flexibility and Control. *Harvard Business Review*(May-June).

Leenders, R., & Gabbay, S. (Eds.). (1999). *Corporate Social Capital and Liability*. Boston: Kluwer Academic Publishers.

Lesser, E., & Prusak, L. (1999). *Communities of Practice, Social Capital and Organisational Knowledge*. IBM Institute of Knowledge management.

Lock Lee, L. (2000). Knowledge Sharing Metrics for Large Organizations. In D. Morey, M. Maybury & B. Thuraisingham (Eds.), *Knowledge management: Classic and Contemporary Works*. MIT Press.

Lock Lee, L., & Neff, M. (2004). How Information Technologies Can Help Build and Sustain an Organisation's CoP: Spanning the Socio-Technical Divide? In P. Hildreth & C. Kimble (Eds.), *Knowledge Networks: Innovation Through Communities of Practice*: Idea Group Inc.

Mizruchi, M., & Stearns, L. B. (2001). Getting Deals Done: The Use of Social Networks in Bank Decision-Making. *American Sociological Review, 66*(5), 647-671.

Portes, A. (1998). Social Capital: Its Origins and Applications in Modern Sociology. *Annual Review of Sociology, 24*, 1-24.

Quinn, J. B. (1992). *intelligent enterprise: A Knowledge and Service Based Paradigm for Industry*: Free Press.

Seely Brown, J., & Duguid, P. (2000). *The Social Life of Information*. Harvard Business School Press.

Tsai, W., & Ghoshal, S. (1998). Social Capital and Value Creation: The Role of Intrafirm Networks. *Academy of Management Journal, 41*(4), 464-476.

Wellman, B., Chen, W., & Weizhen, D. (2001). Networking Guanxi. In T. Gold, D. Guthrie & D. Wank (Eds.), *Social Networks in China: Institutions, Culture, and the Changing nature of Guanxi.*

Wenger, E. (1998). *Communities of Practice: Learning, meaning, and Identity.* Cambridge University Press.

Wenger, E., McDermott, R., & Snyder, W. M. (2002). *Cultivating Communities of Practice.* Boston: Harvard Business School Press.

Section III
Research, Applications and Future Directions

Chapter VIII
Research Linking Corporate Social Capital and Performance in the IT Global Market Place

In 1996 Barry Nalebuff and Adam Brandeburger published their book with the paradoxical title of "*Co-opetition*" (Nalebuff & Brandenburger, 1996). The term originally credited to Ray Noorda, the founder of the networking software company Novell, means competing and cooperating at the same time. Drawing from a background in game theory applied to business, the authors identify that to be successful does not require others to fail. Game theory has proved to be particularly effective in complex environments where many interdependent factors exist (Brandenburger & Nalebuff, 1995). Unlike most games where the result is necessarily win/lose, the authors identify that the rules of business are not so clear cut and there are many situations where win/win is not only possible but preferable. Nalebuff and Brandeburger identify the value network around a company as having roles for suppliers, customers, competitors, but also "complementors". "Complementors" are those firms whose products or services add distinctive complementary value to a company's mainstream supplier offerings. Therefore there will be many situations where "best of breed" does not produce the best result unless the individual providers also demonstrate complementary value for the client.

In this chapter a brief review of the IT industry networks is conducted followed by sections on a suite of novel research techniques that are introduced for analysing the networked market place. The techniques rely on identifying market place alliances, whether they are contractual or market development based. Ultimately they do rely on social network representations applied at the firm level and maximising Corporate Social Capital (SC) for market place actors. In this way they are very different, but complementary to traditional market research techniques. A set of research questions and hypotheses are developed around the concept of Corporate SC. For the scholar, the research methodology is described in some detail in the Appendix.

IT INDUSTRY NETWORKS

The IT industry sector (ITS) has been a rich field for identifying complementary value examples. IBM ceding the operating system software to Microsoft for its IBM PC launch is well documented. Intel profits when Microsoft develops more sophisticated software, requiring CPU upgrades. Management consulting firms profit when SAP introduces a new release of product. Many start-up IT firms have profited from associations with mainstream providers like IBM, Microsoft and Google by licensing specialised code segments into their mainstream products. Today the IT industry is a good example of the practice of "co-opetition". The challenge now is to identify methods that can be used to analyse and research the market. Traditional market research techniques that concentrate on market share, unit sales and revenues become less informing when the market place becomes more interconnected. Like the "best of breed" trap, if one doesn't know of the relationships between the market players, firms can run the risk of becoming "battlefield hosts", rather than having the cooperative environment they were hoping for.

The ITS is distinguished by the relative ease with which firms can form and disband relationships and joint ventures (Knoke *et al.*, 2002). Joint venture formation has been seen to have a positive impact on market valuations on announcement. Beyond announcement market valuations for joint ventures that strengthen a position in an existing market are positively affected, while those that assist in entering new unrelated product markets have no appreciable impact on market values (Koh & Venkatraman, 1991). These authors also found that joint ventures between large and small partners tended to favour the smaller partner in terms of increased market valuation as the smaller firm benefited from "reputation spill over" from the larger partner. This is consistent with the idea that small firms can improve their levels of SC via a successful joint venture and therefore endorsement with a well regarded partner (Das *et al.*, 1998; Stuart, 2000).

Technology development is a fundamental characteristic of the IT industry (Ferrary, 2003; Nault & Vandenbosch, 2000). The potential for growth and wealth creation has encouraged governments to play an active part in brokering partnerships at least at the basic research stages of development. The Japanese IT market and the development of computer and electronic devices have been facilitated by the powerful Ministry of International Trade and Industry (MITI). MITI encouraged the collaboration of many large corporate research laboratories of companies like NEC, Hitachi, Fujitsu and Toshiba in developing VSLI, high speed computing and fifth generation computers. The impact of such schemes appears to have reduced the technological and market uncertainty in the IT market for Japanese firms. This is advantageous, though no correlations to market valuations over time have been conducted (Fransman, 1990).

Cunningham and Culligan (1988) used the IT sector to study factors affecting competitive advantage in dynamic markets. The authors identified that a firm's ability to move between competitive groups may be more important than a static understanding of a market position in markets as dynamic as the IT market. The ability to move between groups is related to mobility barriers that may differ between entry and exit. The understanding and tracking of these movements over time was seen as critical to achieving a competitive advantage. The findings of Cunningham and Culligan (1988) are consistent with the view that the marketplace is a highly interconnected and dynamic structure, where a single snapshot of market structure is only of limited value as the IT markets rapidly change and adapt to complex competitive forces.

Knoke, Yang et al.(2002) investigated the dynamics of strategic alliance networks in the Global Information sector. In their study covering the period from 1989 to 2000, they found a general trend for accelerated rates of alliance formation. Of the 145 firms in the study, they found that a core of 30 firms were most active in the 1990s. Additionally, they found that organisations sought new connections with other organisations that have direct and indirect ties resembling their own alliance propensities. Another finding that was counter to the general globalisation trend was for the Japanese firms to retreat post-2000 to alliances concentrating on other Japanese firms.

At the firm level, the creation of SC and Intellectual capital (IC) has been demonstrated through IT career transitions (Reich & Kaarst-Brown, 2003). This case study of Clarica Life Insurance identified a stream of business enabling IT innovations achieved through more than 70 career transitions of IT people. As IT people moved from the IT function to a line business function, their SC links to the IT function remained while extending these connections into the mainstream business. The result was a more sustainable and effective use of IT in mainstream business, a form of IC. This case study identifies how SC and IC can be developed through staff movements between functions or lines of business. At the market level one could hypothesise that the movement of staff between firms within the IT sector might also build SC and IC for the sector overall. The mobility of IT staff is notorious, especially in IT hot spots like Silicon Valley in California (S. Cohen & Fields, 1999).

In summary, the literature on the IT industry has been mainly focused on how IT impacts the productivity of other sectors, more so than the IT sector itself. This could be attributed to the relative youth of the sector. The sparse literature that does exist emphasises the dynamic nature of the market, the importance of new technological innovations and the huge growth potential available through commercialising such innovations. The dynamic nature of the industry is demonstrated by the adaptability of firms in moving between different sub-groups in the market and the high mobility of human resources between firms. The literature supports the view that the IT market is an excellent platform for the study of SC and IC performance.

RESEARCH QUESTIONS

In Chapter V, Figure 22 identified the overlapping concepts for Corporate SC. IC is differentiated from Corporate Reputation through the addition of financial soundness. The IC component of EC overlaps with the structural SC constructs of "centrality" and "absorptive capacity". Corporate SC could therefore be described as a particular lens through which a firm's IA could be examined. Therefore, in formulating the research question, the overall concept of Corporate SC, as well as its component parts, is addressed.

Two primary research questions being addressed here are therefore:

1. What impact does Corporate SC have on overall firm performance?
2. To what extent do the sub-elements of Corporate SC contribute or detract from firm performance?

The empirical research literature has looked at a variety of firm performance measures. In most cases only a single performance measure is used which does not provide a balanced perspective of a firm's overall performance. For this research, three firm performance measures are used: Return on investment (ROI); Tobins Q (TOBQ) (a market-to-book value measure); and Total shareholder return (TSR). These measures were selected to provide a balance of accounting performance measures and market-based performance measures. Sales performance is used as a control variable for firm size.

The SC literature distinguishes two aspects between the quantitative or structural aspects of SC and the more qualitative aspects of SC (Borgatti & Foster, 2003; Borgatti *et al.*, 1998). A taxonomic representation of the Corporate SC formulation is illustrated in Figure 45: Concerning the first aspect, one can see from the taxonomic representation of Corporate SC that the structural SC being represented as a firm's partnership and alliance activity has been separated out for attention. A

Figure 45. Corporate social capital formulation

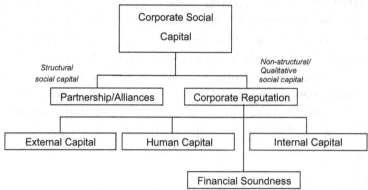

firm's positioning in the marketplace, as determined by the nature of its alliances and joint ventures and the contribution of market positioning on market performance, is a unique contribution for this research. The second aspect, the non-structural or qualitative aspects of SC, has been formulated as a firm's corporate reputation. Corporate reputation in turn is represented by externally visible IC components: External capital (EC), plus externally visible Human capital (HC) and Internal capital (INC), together with the firm's financial soundness.

RESEARCH HYPOTHESES

This section describes how the hypotheses for this research were developed and defined. The Corporate SC construct can be built up in a stepwise fashion from a narrowly focused construct like structural SC, through the increasingly more abstract constructs of IC and corporate reputation. This is illustrated in Figure 46.

Recall from chapter V that a gap in the literature exists with the integration of SC and IC and corporate reputation concepts. The above model addresses this gap. From a base formulation of network centrality (CENT), Absorptive Capacity (AC) is added to cater for the ability to absorb new knowledge from alliances. Intellectual capital (IC) is added as a status attribute for the firm. Corporate reputation can be formulated as IC with the addition of financial soundness. Collectively, the concepts of alliance networks, AC, IC and corporate reputation can be incorporated into the integrated model for Corporate SC. The advantage of the building block approach is that, as well as developing hypotheses to test the impact of the individual Corporate SC elements on firm performance, one can also assess the additional contribution each sub-element makes to the overall Corporate SC formulation using stepwise regression approaches.

Figure 46. Integrated model for corporate social capital

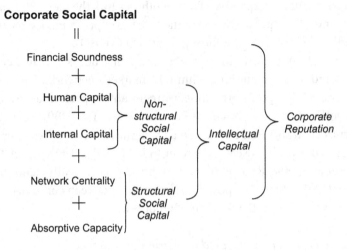

The Corporate SC representation shown in Figure 46 is therefore used to provide a context for the construction of the hypotheses for this research. A more detailed research model has been developed to describe how the contextual model has been operationalised to achieve testable hypotheses. Figure 47 summarises the linkage between the measurable elements found within the hypotheses and the Corporate SC concepts identified in Figure 45 and Figure 46.

The ovals represent latent variables, which are manifested in the observed or measured variables identified in the rectangles. The dotted connection between

Figure 47. Path model for hypotheses development

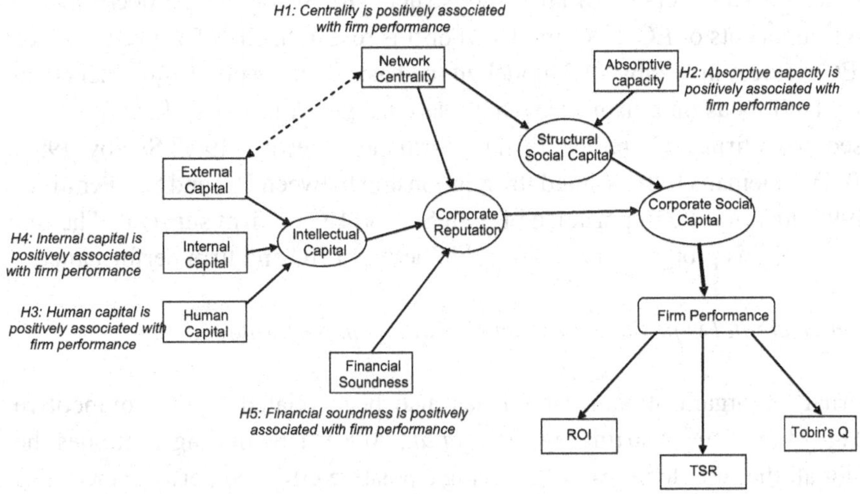

network centrality and EC identifies the potential redundancy between these elements from a conceptual perspective. The hypotheses link the measured variables, being the elements of Corporate SC, with the three firm performance measures of ROI, TSR and market to book ratio proxy, Tobins Q (TOBQ).

Addressing each hypothesis in turn, the first construct is a firm's centrality (CENT), measured by its positioning within the market's network of alliances, vs. firm performance. The proposition relating firm centrality to performance is inferred by social network researchers (Baker, 1990; Burt, 1992; Tsai, 2001). The proposition that a firm's centrality can be viewed as a significant intangible asset for the firm is conjectured here. IC researchers refer to EC (Sveiby, 1997) or relationship capital (Marr et al., 2004; Roos et al., 1997), but not specifically centrality. It is therefore expected that there is a positive relationship between centrality and firm performance as identified in the following hypothesis:

H1: *Centrality is positively associated with firm performance*

The second construct adds AC, which is operationalised as R&D intensity (RES) (W. Cohen & Levinthal, 1990; Tsai, 2001) to centrality and provides a richer concept, labelled here as "structural social capital". AC takes into account a firm's capacity to absorb knowledge or information from an alliance partner. It is expected that a firm's ability to absorb new knowledge will be positively related to its performance, which is identified in the following hypothesis:

H2: *Absorptive capacity is positively associated with firm performance*

The third construct uses elements from the IC model (Sveiby, 1997) to come up with an enriched version of an IC construct. The Sveiby model deconstructs IC into components of EC, INC and HC. For this research, CENT is used in place of the EC element in Sveiby's IC model on the basis of conceptual equivalence, in that they both focus on a firm's external relationships. A number of authors have proposed that a firm's IC predicts firm performance (Stewart, 1997; Sveiby, 1997; Lev, 2001). Coleman (1988) argued the relationship between HC and SC. Pennings et al.(1998) identify the importance of both SC and HC on firm survival. The following hypothesis proposes the relationship between HC and firm performance.

H3: *Human capital is positively associated with firm performance*

Internal, or organisational capital has also been related to the competitive advantage of the firm (Martin-de-Castro *et al.*, 2006). This finding continues the theme for all the sub-elements of IC having a positive effect on performance. The proposition that INC is positively associated with firm performance therefore constitutes the fourth hypothesis:

H4: *Internal capital is positively associated with firm performance*

The fourth construct introduces financial soundness together with IC to come up with a representation of corporate reputation. Several authors have developed theories linking corporate reputation to firm performance (Hall, 1992; Fombrun & Shanley, 1990). The importance of the financial element of corporate reputation is inferred by Brown & Perry (1994) in their claim that a firm's "financial halo" can obscure other elements of a firm's corporate reputation. It is therefore expected that financial soundness will be positively associated with firm performance as described in the fifth hypothesis:

H5: *Financial soundness is positively associated with firm performance*

In summary, the proposition that Corporate SC positively impacts firm performance is achieved through a series of hypotheses linking the sub-components of Corporate SC to firm performance. The integrated model for Corporate SC addresses the gap identified in the literature around the integration of IC and SC into an integrated concept for Corporate SC. In the course of evaluating the hypotheses, the results would also inform the impact of subsidiary constructs like CENT, AC, IC and corporate reputation.

RESEARCH RESULTS LINKING CORPORATE SOCIAL CAPITAL TO FIRM PERFORMANCE

The previous sections identified key research questions and hypotheses relating to the impact of Corporate SC on firm performance. This section provides the results of the hypotheses tests conducted on some 156 firms selected from the global ITS market. The results will identify the elements of Corporate SC that are most predictive of good firm performance.

The next section provides a description of the data being analysed. The primary data is described, along with the variables extracted from the Compustat database. A more detailed description of each variable used in the analysis then provided.

The data description sections are followed by a section highlighting the results of the hypotheses testing performed. The results of the hypotheses tests are discussed in terms of areas of support for the theories proposed, as well as unexpected results where hypotheses were not supported. A final section provides the results of some analyses that investigate scenarios where hypotheses have not been supported or only marginally supported. Specifically, the section reports on interaction analyses undertaken *post hoc,* the analysis of the main effects included in the hypotheses testing.

DATA DESCRIPTION

Table 7 identifies the labels for each variable used in the analyses with a short description. The variables generated by content analysis (CA) of the Factiva Information Service are described below. In general, business news stories are largely positive or neutral. "Negative press" tends to be polarised around a few common themes, for example, lay-offs, movement of a key executive, investigations by the securities commission, disputes or strikes. The indexes for HC, INC and EC were developed by balancing good and bad news stories according to the scheme provided in the previous chapter. Sensitivity analyses were run for indexed and non-indexed (counting all stories, good or bad) and it was found that there were only relatively minor differences on the bivariate correlations conducted. While the impact of negative stories may be minor, the indexes were still thought to be more representative of the true situation and were therefore retained for the analysis.

Table 7. Variable labels and descriptors

Variable Labels	Description
Dependent Variables	
ROI	Return on investment (%)
TOBQ	Tobins Q (ratio). Proxy for market-to-book ratio
TSR	Total shareholder return (%). Share price appreciation plus dividends
Independent Variables	
CENT	Market centrality measured as Eigenvector centrality
RES	R&D intensity = R&D/Net sales. A proxy for absorptive capacity
HC	Human capital index
INC	Internal capital index
Zscore	Altman's ZScore. Proxy for financial soundness
Control Variables	
SIZE	Sales net of credits used as a proxy for firm size.
IND	Industry Sector dummy: 1 = software and services, 0 = other IT sectors
P_L	Profitability dummy: 1 = mean earnings per share >= 0, 0 = mean earnings per share <0

DATA VARIABLES

This section provides a description of the statistical distributions found for each of the variables used in the analyses:

ROI: Return on investment

The ROI results are available directly from the Compustat database. The results were collected on an annual basis. The distribution was not normal, showing a majority of firms just below the "0" mark, with a long tail of negative ROI results. It is interesting to note that the mean ROI results for the sample used for the IT industry were negative.

TOBQ: Tobins Q

The TOBQ results were calculated from base data available from the Compustat database. The distribution was not normal, showing a majority of firms in the "0" to "5" range, with a long positive tail stretching as high as nearly 40. The distribution indicates that the majority of firms have a TOBQ value beyond "1" and therefore a significant proportion of their market value is not accounted for in their "book" values.

TSR: Total Shareholder Return

The TSR results are available directly from the Compustat database. The results were collected on an annual basis. The distribution was not normal, showing a majority of firms spanning the "0" mark with a long tail of positive TSR results. TSR results can be impacted by spurious share price movements in any given year. This may account for the extreme results at the high end of the tail.

CENT: Market Centrality Measured as the Eigenvector Centrality Measure

Joint venture associations were generated through the Factiva search of each of the companies in the sample. Only joint venture firms that were part of the sample list were included to calculate CENT. This was not seen as a major limitation as it was assumed that joint ventures with listed companies would contribute more to market positioning than the usually smaller unlisted companies.

Figure 48 shows a representation of the joint venture relationships between the sample firms in the IT marketplace. The lines reflect a joint venture arrangement.

The size of the node reflects the relative CENT of a firm. As can be seen, the firms in the centre of the map tend to have the highest centrality scores. The individual CENT scores were determined using the eigenvector CENT algorithm. The distribution of results was not normal, being strongly skewed toward the lower end, with a relatively long tail.

RES: Research Intensity: A Proxy for Absorptive Capacity

RES was measured as research activity, as determined from the Factiva search, divided by sales. This variable was used as a proxy for absorptive capacity. The distribution was not normal, being heavily skewed toward the lower scores but with a long tail.

HC: Human Capital Index

The HC index was developed around the formula described in the methodology. Unlike R&D and CENT, the index can be negative, indicating a firm with a high proportion of negative stories with respect to HC. The distribution has a majority

Figure 48. Industry map with high centrality nodes highlighted

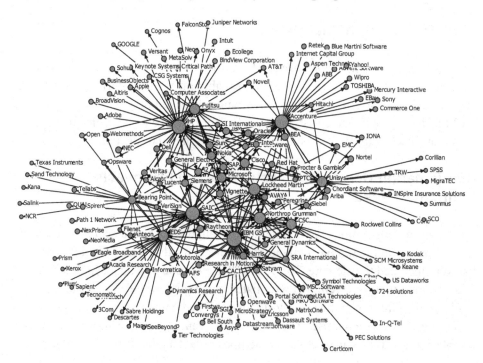

of firms with an HC index just above "0" and was not normal. There is a long tail toward the positive end of the distribution.

RESULTS OF HYPOTHESES TESTS

As identified earlier, the hypotheses were built up through four models. The first model is a simple firm centrality vs. firm performance. The second model adds RES and provides a rich concept of structural SC, taking into account a firm's capacity to absorb knowledge or information from an alliance partner. The third model adds the HC and INC elements from the IC model to come up with an enriched version of an IC model[1] which subsumes the structural SC model in place of the "external capital" construct. The fourth model adds financial soundness to come up with a representation of corporate reputation. This model is also used to represent the Corporate SC concept for the purposes of the regression analysis. Due to the non normal distributions of the majority of the variables under consideration a ranked regression approach was employed.

Figure 49 provides a graphical representation of the stepwise regression tests conducted excluding the control variables of firm size, firm profitability and software/non-software industry sector. The use of the stepwise regressions approach was to facilitate the exploration of the additional explanatory power provided as each conceptual step is added into the regression equations. As shown in Figure 46, the Corporate SC concept could be viewed as comprising a number of subsidiary concepts addressed in the literature, like structural SC, IC and corporate reputation. Models 1 to 4 represent a progression through more comprehensive models of SC. For example, Model 1 provides the simplest model, equating SC with CENT alone, through to Model 4 which contains the complete model for Corporate SC developed in this research. Note that for Model 3 both HC and IC are added at this step to represent the increment from the subsidiary concept of structural SC to the IC concept.

An hypothesis test was conducted for each of the three firm performance measures of ROI, TOBQ and TSR. Three control variables for firm size, profitability and industry sub-sector were included. The results indicated that the selected control variables were significant predictors of firm performance for most of the firm performance scenarios. Each control variable was therefore investigated for all models resulting in a further 18 tests, in addition to the three tests conducted on the full sample.

A stepwise regression approach was used to introduce each of the models from Models 1 to 4 one step at a time. Statistical significance shown in the tables is indicated at the $p < 0.01$, $p < 0.05$ and $p < 0.10$ level for two-tailed tests. As the hy-

Figure 49. Stepwise regression model

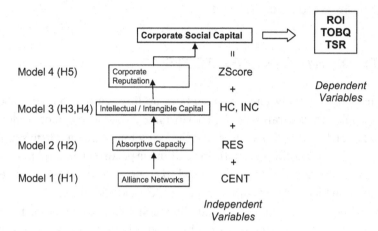

potheses predict a directional influence, the equivalent significance levels should be one-tailed tests. Therefore, the statistically significant variables shown are actually significant to at least the $p < 0.05$ level. Each of the tables shows the unstandardised coefficients with the p values in brackets below. The change in explanatory power in moving from Model 1 to Model 4 is measured through changes in the adjusted R^2. The Δ Adj R^2 for Model 1 reflects the change from the Adj R^2 for a regression model containing the control variables only (not shown). Changes that are statistically significant are indicated. The following section presents the results for each of the regression tests conducted.

Table 8 provides the regression results using the full sample according to the model shown in Figure 49. As anticipated the control variables of firm size, profitability and industry sub-sector all had a statistically significant influence on the test results, though industry sub-sector was only significant for ROI performance. Given the significance of the control variables, the regression test interpretations were made on the analyses of the sub-sets where firm size, profitability and industry sub-sector have been controlled for.

The full sample was used to explore the degree to which the explanatory power of the individual Corporate SC elements add to the influence on firm performance. The change in adjusted R-squareds was used to identify the changes in explanatory power. The results are summarised in Figure 50.

The numerical results are available in Table 8. Overall, the results show that Corporate SC significantly predicts all firm performance measures at the $p < 0.01$ level. The results show that the increased explanatory power of the Corporate SC model elements beyond the control variables differed, depending on the firm performance measure. For ROI (Panel A) the increase in adjusted R-squareds was

Table 8. Full sample: Regression test results (Unstandardised coefficients and p-values)

Model 1: $Perf_{ROI}$;
          $Perf_{TOBQ}$;
          $Perf_{TSR} = b_0 + b_1CENT + b_2SIZE + b_3IND + b_4P\_L + e$
Model 2: $Perf_{ROI}$;
          $Perf_{TOBQ}$;
          $Perf_{TSR} = b_0 + b_1CENT + b_2RES + b_3SIZE + b_4IND + b_5P\_L + e$
Model 3: $Perf_{ROI}$;
          $Perf_{TOBQ}$;
          $Perf_{TSR} = b_0 + b_1CENT + b_2RES + b_3HC + b_4INC + b_5SIZE + b_6IND + b_7P\_L + e$
Model 4: $Perf_{ROI}$;
          $Perf_{TOBQ}$;
          $Perf_{TSR} = b_0 + b_1CENT + b_2RES + b_3HC + b_4INC + b_5ZSCORE + b_6SIZE + b_7IND + b_8P\_L + e$

Panel A $Perf_{ROI}$ Variables	Model 1 Coefficient p-value	Model 2 Coefficient p-value	Model 3 Coefficient p-value	Model 4 Coefficient p-value
Controls				
IND	41.729* (0.002)	41.155* (0.002)	42.894* (0.001)	25.191* (0.018)
SIZE	0.211** (0.000)	0.193** (0.000)	0.212** (0.000)	0.158** (0.000)
P_L	242.836** (0.000)	242.015** (0.000)	236.340** (0.000)	215.368** (0.000)
Main Effects				
CENT	0.037 (0.366)	0.052 (0.210)	0.044 (0.327)	-0.005 (0.886)
RES		-0.030 (0.233)	-0.026 (0.329)	-0.046+ (0.055)
HC			0.069* (0.004)	0.044* (0.050)
INC			-0.046 (0.222)	0.009 (0.804)
ZScore				0.275** (0.000)
F-Statistic	20.07** (0.000)	19.83** (0.000)	19.97** (0.000)	20.52** (0.000)
Adj R²	0.837	0.836	0.839	0.845
Δ Adj R²	0.000	-0.001	0.003 [a]	0.006 [a]
N	550	543	543	527

** p-value significant < 0.01 (two-tailed); * p-value significant < 0.05 (two-tailed);
+ p-value significant <0.10 (two-tailed);
[a] Adjusted R-squared change is significant at p-value significant < 0.01.
See Table 7 for variable definitions.

continued on following page

Table 8. continued

Panel B Perf$_{TobinsQ}$ Variables	Model 1 Coefficient p-value	Model 2 Coefficient p-value	Model 3 Coefficient p-value	Model 4 Coefficient p-value
Controls				
IND	50.401* (0.045)	50.212* (0.047)	54.022* (0.030)	18.807 (0.398)
SIZE	-0.291* (0.001)	-0.291* (0.001)	-0.228* (0.009)	-0.339** (0.000)
P_L	78.912** (0.000)	79.048** (0.000)	78.377** (0.000)	41.609** (0.000)
Main Effects				
CENT	0.195* (0.011)	0.197* (0.012)	0.239* (0.003)	0.168* (0.021)
RES		0.002 (0.963)	0.031 (0.421)	0.015 (0.666)
HC			0.044 (0.211)	0.011 (0.728)
INC			-0.151* (0.012)	-0.100+ (0.070)
ZScore				0.494** (0.000)
F-Statistic	7.47** (0.000)	7.59** (0.000)	7.56** (0.000)	9.60** (0.000)
Adj R^2	0.636	0.642	0.644	0.706**
Δ Adj R^2	-0.001	0.006 [a]	0.002	0.062[a]
N	553	546	546	532

** p-value significant < 0.01 (two-tailed); * p-value significant < 0.05 (two-tailed);
+ p-value significant <0.10 (two-tailed);
[a] Adjusted R-squared change is significant at p-value significant < 0.01.
See Table 7 for variable definitions.

continued on following page

minimal, though statistically significant for the last two models, which add HC & INC (adds 0.3% explanatory power) and Zscore (adds 0.6% explanatory power), which is statistically significant at the $p < 0.01$ level. For TOBQ (Panel B), the increase in explanatory power added by the Corporate SC elements over the control variables is 6.2%, which is statistically significant at the $p < 0.01$ level. The majority of this increase (6%) is, however, provided by the addition of the Zscore. For TSR (Panel C) the Corporate SC elements add 13% to the explanatory power over the control variables. The increase is shared by RES adding 1.9%, HC and INC 4.2% and Zscore 7.1%, each change being statistically significant at the $p < 0.01$ level.

Table 8. continued

Panel C Perf$_{TSR}$ Variables	Model 1 Coefficient p-value	Model 2 Coefficient p-value	Model 3 Coefficient p-value	Model 4 Coefficient p-value
Controls				
IND	-19.397 (0.302)	-23.262 (0.222)	-18.548 (0.327)	-29.284 (0.133)
SIZE	-0.125$^+$ (0.085)	-0.161* (0.033)	-0.107 (0.180)	-0.163$^+$ (0.051)
P_L	147.019** (0.000)	146.888** (0.000)	131.821** (0.000)	107.852** (0.000)
Main Effects				
CENT	-0.011 (0.852)	0.180 (0.772)	0.001 (0.987)	-0.043 (0.528)
RES		-0.069 (0.101)	-0.060 (0.170)	-0.090* (0.038)
HC			0.210** (0.000)	0.207** (0.000)
INC			-0.154* (0.017)	-0.103 (0.121)
ZScore				0.229** (0.000)
F-Statistic	1.02 (0.428)	1.09 (0.251)	1.26* (0.041)	1.58** (0.000)
Adj R^2	0.006	0.025	0.067	0.138
Δ Adj R^2	-0.002	0.019 ^{a}	0.042 ^{a}	0.071 ^{a}
N	547	540	540	525

** p-value significant < 0.01 (two-tailed); * p-value significant < 0.05 (two-tailed);
$^+$ p-value significant <0.10 (two-tailed);
^{a} Adjusted R-squared change is significant at p-value significant < 0.01.
See Table 7 for variable definitions.

The above results support the view that a firm's "financial halo" tends to dominate how its reputation is viewed. Brown & Perry (1994) have shown that *Fortune* magazine's "most admired" companies list is heavily influenced by prior financial results. They provide methods for removing the financial halo in order to investigate the non-financial elements of a firm's reputation. Studies on the *Fortune* survey results have shown that financial performance explains anything from 42% (McGuire *et al.*, 1990) to 53% (Fombrun & Shanley, 1990) of the variance of the overall firm ratings. The dominating influence of financial performance found here is therefore consistent with the analyses of the *Fortune* magazine data.

Figure 50. Adjusted R-squareds for models 1 to 4

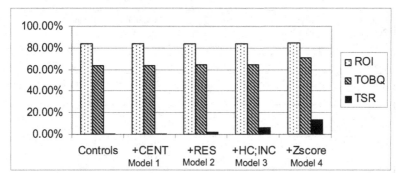

Some new results here are the differential results obtained between the more accounting-focused firm performance measures like ROI and the market-based measure of TSR. The results for TSR are worth noting for the larger relative impact of non-financial elements. Specifically, RES, HC and INC do add significant explanatory power to the relationship with TSR beyond financial soundness. This is significant, given the growing importance of market performance measures in assessing a firm's overall performance.

SUMMARY OF REGRESSION RESULTS

The results are summarised in Table 9, which shows only the significant factors (at the $p < 0.05$ *level, one tail test*). Table 9 can be used to look for any enduring patterns in the results achieved. The strongest pattern was the positive relationship between HC and both ROI and TSR, which exists across all scenarios. The exception from Table 9 was for profitable firms, which was still significant at the p <0.10; one tail test. The next strongest pattern was for financial soundness, where financial soundness only fails to predict TSR for large, profitable or non-software firms. Financial soundness predicted firm performance for all other scenarios. The negative association between RES and ROI was consistent for four of the six scenarios, with one other scenario also showing a negative, though not significant, relationship. The negative relationship between INC and TOBQ (five out of six scenarios) and TSR (three out of six scenarios) was also consistent in terms of the more market-based measures. Finally, the positive relationship of CENT with TOBQ was relatively strong (three out of six scenarios with one other at the p <0.1; one tail test level). A slightly weaker negative relationship pattern existed with TSR (two out of six scenarios with one other at the $p<0.1$; one tail test level). Table 10 summarises the general patterns found in the results.

Table 9. Summary table of results

	Controls			Main Effects				
	IND	**P_L**	**SIZE**	**CENT**	**RES**	**HC**	**INC**	**Zscore**
Full Sample								
ROI	+	+	+		−	+		+
TOBQ		+	−	+			−	+
TSR		+	−		−	+		+
Large Firm								
ROI		+			−	+		+
TOBQ	+						−	+
TSR		+		−		+		
Small Firm								
ROI		+			−	+		+
TOBQ		+					−	+
TSR		+				+	−	+
Profitable								
ROI	+		+					+
TOBQ	+		−	+			−	+
TSR	−			−		+	−	
Loss-making								
ROI			+		−	+		+
TOBQ			−	+			−	+
TSR			−		−	+		+
Software Industry								
ROI		+	+			+		+
TOBQ		+	−	+				+
TSR		+				+	−	+
Non-software Industry								
ROI		+	+		−	+	+	+
TOBQ		+	−				−	+
TSR		+				+		

The general patterns show that the Corporate SC relationships do vary depending on the firm performance dependent variable being assessed. For ROI, which could be considered an accounting-based historical measure, the results suggest that financial soundness and HC are the most predictive factors of a positive ROI result. Investments in R&D appear to be purely an expense and reduce ROI performance. TOBQ, considered a leading indicator of future performance and financial soundness and CENT ,are seen as significant predictors of a positive result, whereas INC predicts a negative result. TSR is considered a market-based historical measure. The result pattern suggests that strong financial soundness and investments in HC are rewarded by the market. On the contrary, CENT and investments in INC are seen as being penalised by the market for at least one scenario.

The general patterns shown here, however, do not tell the full story. The hypotheses test models do not include attributes for interaction effects that could provide more insight into the main effects achieved. Interaction effects are explored in the next section.

The hypotheses test results in Table 11 provide a summary of the sub-sample regression tests. The summarised results show support for three of the five hypotheses (H1, H3 and H5). Hypotheses H2 and H4 were not supported. The support for H4 for ROI in the non-software industry has been discounted as spurious owing to its marginal significance and the six other significant negative associations found for INC against firm performance.

The positive association of CENT only existed for TOBQ performance. This might suggest that market CENT, like TOBQ, is seen as a predictive rather than an historical performance measure. Firms who position themselves optimally in the marketplace would, in fact, be positioning themselves for future gains. This is consistent with the literature on Corporate SC which suggests that investments in SC are both strategic and long-term (Ron Burt, 2003; Ronald Burt *et al.*, 2002).

The support for a positive association of HC with ROI and TSR (H3), suggests that investments in HC are valued by the market in terms of shareholder return, as well as enhancing ROI. This association is well supported in the literature (Coleman, 1988; Florin *et al.*, 2003; Kaplan & Norton, 2004; O'Donnell & Berkery, 2003; Pennings et al., 1998). The HC association was consistent across all sub-samples.

Table 10. General result patterns

	CENT	RES	HC	INC	Zscore
ROI		–	+		+
TOBQ	+			–	+
TSR	–		+	–	+

Table 11. Hypothesis test results

Hypothesis	Full Sample	Large Firm	Small Firm	Profit-making	Loss-making	Software	Non-software
H1: *Centrality is positively associated with firm performance*	+	–	–	+	+	+	–
H2: *Absorptive capacity is positively associated with firm performance*	–	–	–	–	–	–	–
H3: *Human capital is positively associated with firm performance*	+	+	+	+	+	+	+
H4: *Internal capital is positively associated with firm performance*	–	–	–	–	–	–	+
H5: *Financial soundness is positively associated with firm performance*	+	+	+	+	+	+	+

+ = Hypothesis Supported —= Hypothesis not supported

The positive association between financial soundness and firm performance (H5) was the strongest predictor, predicting all firm performance measures for the majority of sub-samples. Interestingly, the only scenario where financial soundness was not found to be a significant predictor was for large, profitable or non-software firms, when predicting TSR performance (Table 9). This is potentially an interesting result. The image suggests that large, mature equipment manufacturers that are operating profitably have perhaps reached a plateau where the market is now looking for more than financial performance. These same sub-samples are also distinguished for showing the negative effects of centrality. Both large and profitable firms had negative associations between centrality and firm performance.

Non-software firms also showed a negative, though not significant, relationship. That is, the larger, mature firms could be "locked in" to long-term alliances that are delivering a financial return but not the growth and innovation that the market may be looking for. From a SC perspective this situation lends support to the structural holes argument (R. S. Burt, 1992, 2004), where the advantage from alliance networks is bridging holes in market networks, identifying new ideas and innovations as a source of new growth. The conjecture is that large, established firms in mature industries would find this style of alliance formation more difficult to achieve. But for those that can the rewards are available through improved market values.

The unsupported hypotheses were the hypothesised positive relationship between RES (H2) and INC (H4) with firm performance. For both hypotheses, significant relationships were, in fact, found in the opposite direction. The explanation for the negative relationship of RES with mostly ROI has been covered earlier (i.e. that the R&D proxy is being seen simply as an expense). The negative relationship for INC has been found against TOBQ and TSR, but not ROI. This would suggest that it is not the expense of investments in INC that is the issue. On its own the result is difficult to interpret and therefore is covered in the next section on interaction effects.

POST HOC ANALYSIS RESULTS

As a consequence of the unexpected results reported in the previous section, a *post hoc* analysis was conducted. A number of interaction effects were explored, either as a result of the unexpected prior results or results anticipated through the literature. This section describes the results of these analyses.

The previously reported regression tests indicated that financial soundness was the most predictive element of Corporate SC on firm performance. It was therefore conjectured that the interaction of financial soundness with other Corporate SC components could also have a significant impact on firm performance. Florin et al. (2003) investigated the indirect effects of social resources on high growth ventures by analysing the interaction of social resources with HC and financial capital. The argument made was that HC is a resource of the firm which is enhanced through its socialisation with other firms. The authors were principally concerned with new venture performance, with the performance metrics relating to capital raising, sales growth and return on sales. However, their analysis of post-IPO performance has some overlap with the context of this research, especially for the smaller, less profitable IT firms.

A number of interaction effects were explored to provide an explanation for the rejected hypotheses identified in Table 11. Firstly, following Florin et al. (2003), the interaction between financial soundness and centrality and its association with firm performance was explored. Lin's (1982) theory of instrumental action speaks of attributes like wealth, status and power, placing actors within a social hierarchy and dictating the level of access to social resources. Based on Lin's theory one would anticipate that strong financial performance would act as an attractor for profitable alliances and joint ventures and therefore, ultimately, firm performance.

Secondly, the interaction between financial soundness and RES and its association with firm performance was explored. The suggestion is that a firm's financial soundness mediates the relationship between RES and firm performance. This interaction analysis is in response to the unexpected negative relationships found between RES and firm performance.

Thirdly, the interaction between financial soundness and HC and its association with firm performance was explored. The suggestion is that a firm's financial soundness mediates the relationship between HC and firm performance. This proposition extends the analysis of Florin et al. (2003) who investigated the interaction between human resources and centrality and financial capital and centrality, but not human resources and financial capital.

Fourthly, the interaction between financial soundness and INC and its association with firm performance was explored. The suggestion is that a firm's financial soundness mediates the relationship between INC and firm performance. This interaction analysis is in response to the unexpected negative relationships found between INC and firm performance.

Finally, the interaction between CENT and HC and its association with firm performance was explored to see if a firm's centrality mediates the relationship between HC and firm performance. This analysis replicates that of Florin et al. (2003), who found that the interaction between a firm's social resources (CENT) and human resources had a positive effect on its performance, measured as return on sales.

The investigation was conducted using interaction plots as described by Aiken & West (1991). The scenarios selected for investigation were for each of the selected interaction variables against a firm performance measure identified in the main effects regression tests. Note that all variables shown below are ranked, not raw, variables. The selected investigations were:

1. TSR vs. Zscore x CENT

This plot investigates the negative relationship found between CENT and TSR, which was not consistent with H1, which hypothesised a positive relationship between CENT and firm performance. The hypothesis was that financial soundness may have a moderating effect on this relationship.

The interaction plot is shown in Figure 51, along with the regression equation used. Each of the variables was centered prior to running the regression.

$$TSR = (b_1 + b_3 Zscore)CENT + (b_2 Zscore + b_0)$$

In the main effects, CENT was negatively associated with TSR for large or profitable firms. The interaction effect with financial soundness was also negative for TSR. The above plot shows that the direction of association changes from low to high financial soundness. This suggests that CENT helps TSR for firms in poor financial shape, but can be a constraint for large profitable firms; in effect reducing TSR. This is consistent with the earlier conjecture that large profitable firms are potentially constrained by high CENT. The interaction plot shows, however, that building CENT can be a positive move for firms that are less profitable and looking to build TSR performance.

2. TOBQ vs. Zscore x RES

This plot investigates the negative relationship found between RES and TOBQ performance, which was not consistent with H2, which hypothesised a positive relationship between RES and firm performance. The hypothesis was that financial soundness may have a moderating effect on this relationship.

The interaction plot is shown in Figure 52, along with the regression equation used. Each of the variables was centred prior to running the regression.

$$TSR = (b_1 + b_3 Zscore)RES + (b_2 Zscore + b_0)$$

The interaction plot shows that the negative main effect of RES on TSR was not sustained for high levels of financial soundness. That is, high levels of financial soundness can reverse or moderate the strength and/or direction of the influence of RES on TSR. A possible explanation is that the market only appreciates R&D investments from firms that have the financial resources to afford it. This is consistent with the view that R&D is treated as an expense with no compensating share value appreciation. For firms that do not have the financial resources to invest in R&D, the market would penalise those that did invest their limited resources there.

3. TSR vs. Zscore x HC

This plot investigates the negative interaction effect of financial soundness and HC on TSR. A strong positive relationship was found between HC and TSR for most scenarios and therefore the negative interaction effect with financial soundness was unexpected.

The interaction plot is shown in Figure 53, along with the regression equation used. Each of the variables was centred prior to running the regression.

$$TSR = (b_1 + b_3 Zscore)HC + (b_2 Zscore + b_0)$$

The relationship between HC and TSR was strongly positive, whereas the coefficient for the interaction between HC and financial soundness was negative. For TSR it looked like the influence of HC on TSR was stronger for firms with poor financial soundness, but became weaker as financial soundness improved. This explains the negative coefficient for the interaction term. However, the relationship remains positive for all levels of financial soundness. An explanation for the above

Figure 51. CENT x Zscore interaction influence on TSR

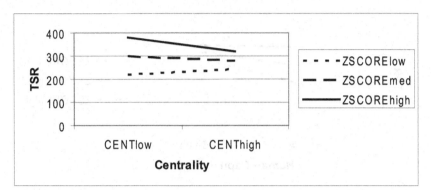

Figure 52. RES x Zscore interaction influence on TSR

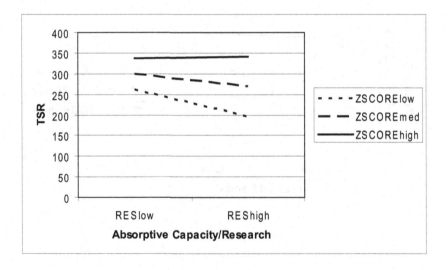

result could be that increasing HC could be seen as the best way of improving a poor financial position and is therefore rewarded in the marketplace. This effect is perhaps less prominent as firms achieve a higher level of financial soundness and the potential to explore other investment opportunities like R&D or INC exist.

4. TOBQ vs. Zscore x INC

This plot investigates the negative relationship found between INC and TOBQ performance, which was not consistent with H4, which hypothesised a positive

Figure 53. HC x Zscore interaction influence on TSR

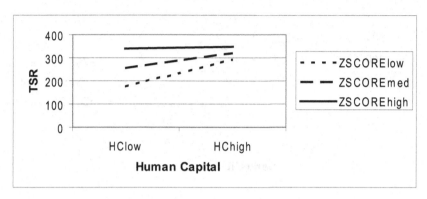

Figure 54. INC x Zscore Interaction Influence on TOBQ

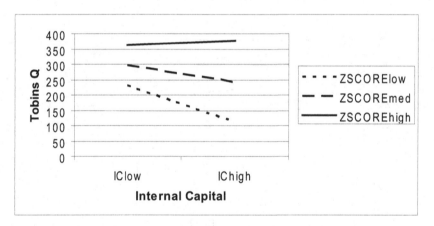

relationship between INC and firm performance. The hypothesis was that financial soundness may have a moderating effect on this relationship.

The interaction plot is shown in Figure 54, along with the regression equation used. Each of the variables was centered prior to running the regression.

$$TOBQ = (b_1 + b_3 Zscore)INC + (b_2 Zscore + b_0)$$

The main effects show INC having a negative association with TOBQ and TSR, but the interaction term of Zscore x INC is positive. The above plot shows the relationship changes from negative to positive at higher levels of financial soundness. In other words, the negative relationship does not hold if the firm has strong financial soundness. This result mimics the result for the RES and financial soundness interaction effect on TSR. The rationale could be that investments in INC, like R&D, are not rewarded if the firms do not have the financial capacity to support it. Where firms do have the financial capacity to afford an investment in INC then it is rewarded in the marketplace.

5. TSR VS. CENT X HC

This plot replicates the Florin et al. (2003) investigation of the effects of CENT on the relationship between HC and firm performance, in this case TSR. Like the Florin et al. (2003) study, a statistically significant interaction term is found for the relationship with TSR, but in this case the sign is positive.

The interaction plot is shown in Figure 55, along with the regression equation used. Each of the variables was centered prior to running the regression.

$$TSR = (b_1 + b_3 CENT)HC + (b_2 CENT + b_0)$$

The result shows that for all levels of HC, firms with lower CENT can achieve higher TSR performance than those with high CENT. The differences, however, are not large. This is in contrast with the Florin et al.'s (2003) finding that firms with higher CENT are more effective at acquiring financial capital. The minimal difference in the slope of the relationship between HC and firm performance found here is

Figure 55. HC x CENT Interaction Influence on TSR

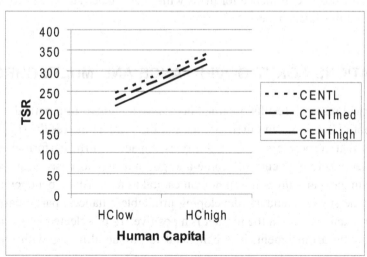

similar to Florin et al. (2003). The differences could be explained by the differences in the firm performance dependent variable, one being TSR and the other being new finance acquired by new firms. One would expect that higher levels of connectivity would assist firm human resources to gain new financial capital. On the other hand, this would not necessarily be expected for building TSR, as has been demonstrated by the negative relationship between CENT and TSR for large or profitable firms. An explanation for the above result could be that firms that have lower levels of connectivity might provide more freedom for the firm's human resources to create shareholder value in a variety of ways beyond just alliances.

In summary, the *post hoc* interaction effects analyses were able to provide viable explanations for the unexpected results obtained for the five hypothesis tests. For both RES and INC relationships with firm performance, the interactions effect analysis was able to show that financial soundness has the potential to moderate the negative effects of RES and INC on firm performance. The inference from the results suggests that R&D and INC investments are only of value to those who already have the financial resources to afford them. Firms investing in R&D or INC without the financial means to do so would be penalised by the market. However, investments in HC were seen to be a positive investment for firms at any level of financial soundness. The option would be more important to firms in poor financial shape as the influence of increased investments in HC on TSR was found to be greater for firms in poor financial shape than those that are more financially sound. Likewise, firms with lower CENT could also expect to leverage their HC more in improving TSR than more highly connected firms.

The interaction plot in Figure 51 reinforces the view that high CENT can be a liability in terms of TSR performance for firms that are performing well financially. The interaction effects show that the direction of influence of CENT on TSR can change from a positive influence for firms with poor finances to a negative one for firms in good financial shape.

IMPLICATIONS FOR IT GOVERNANCE AND MULTISOURCING

The empirical research results obtained here have a number of practical implications for both IT vendors and their clients. For the vendors the results support the hypothesis that corporate social capital does impact on firm performance. In a market place where new entrants come and go on a regular basis, sustaining financial soundness and investing in human capital as a priority is beneficial for all firms. For the smaller vendors, developing profitable alliances, particularly with the more reputable firms in the market is a positive. To be selected as a vendor in a multisourcing arrangement, it is beneficial to pursue alliances with reputable partners with whom you have clear complementary and value adding offerings. For the larger more established firms, being over-allianced can become a liability as scarce executive time and attention may be overly diverted.

For the client looking to multisourced arrangements, the research results offer some market intelligence insight into what might be driving IT vendor performance. The need to select financially sound IT vendors goes without saying. However on other dimensions close attention to the human capital available to prospective vendors will ensure that the vendor competencies will be capable of meeting client demands. More subtle is the network of alliance partners with whom vendors will engage . The full complexity is usually only available through the development of a sociogram of the market as illustrated in Figure 48. As a client, one can look to identify clusters of pre-allianced vendors with complementary offerings that suit your needs. The opportunity exists to procure from the cluster with minimal risk of having to expend valuable time and money governing relationships between vendors once they have been contracted.

SUMMARY

This chapter has provided the results of empirical research conducted relating Corporate SC and its constituent elements to firm performance. The results of the multiple regression analyses used to test the hypotheses were presented. This was followed by *post hoc* analysis of unexpected hypothesis results, using methods for testing the interaction effects between independent variables.

The hypotheses tests showed three of the five hypotheses being supported. The positive relationships between CENT, HC and financial soundness and firm performance were supported. The hypothesised positive relationships between RES and INC with firm performance were not supported. The two rejected hypotheses, together with results from similar studies from the literature, were then further analysed for interaction effects. Viable explanations were achieved for the failed hypotheses.

The significant results achieved are summarised as follows:

- Corporate SC has a statistically significant influence on firm performance, proving value relevant for all firm performance measures.
- The largest differential in explanatory power of Corporate SC was for TSR and least for ROI, suggesting that Corporate SC is more beneficial for market-based performance measures.
- Financial soundness is the most critical Corporate SC component when predicting future firm performance. The only exception is for large, profitable

or non-software firms, when predicting TSR, where other factors appear to have more influence.

- CENT positively impacts only TOBQ, suggesting that CENT is a strategic, future positioning factor for the firm. Significantly, the software industry benefits most from higher CENT.
- Large or profitable firms, especially those in the non-software sector, can experience negative impacts from being overly connected. TSR can be negatively impacted by high CENT for these firms, despite being financially sound.
- HC has a consistently positive relationship with ROI and TSR for all scenarios of firm size, profitability or industry sector.
- The investment in HC is differentially more attractive for firms with poor finances than those that are financially sound. However, all investments in HC are beneficial. For loss-making firms, investments in HC are the most beneficial in terms of TSR and ROI. The opposite is true for investments in R&D and INC for these firms, where TSR can decrease.
- Investments in R&D have a negative impact on firm performance, particularly ROI. This suggests that R&D is being treated only as an expense with no counterbalancing increase in market performance. The suggestion also is that for the sample used, R&D is not a good proxy for absorptive capacity.
- Investments in INC have a negative effect on a firm's TOBQ and TSR performance.
- Financial soundness can mediate and potentially reverse the negative relationship of R&D and INC with firm performance.

This chapter has identified how IT vendors in particular, can best leverage their Corporate SC to improve their overall performance. With two of the most critical factors being financial soundness and human capital, it is evident that the relationship with the clients must be such that the service providing firms must be able to achieve an acceptable financial return, otherwise the overall relationship and the economic case for establishing it are at risk (Kern & Willcocks, 2001).

This chapter has been devoted to a research study of IT vendors and vendor alliance networks. The next chapter looks at the emerging practice of Value network analysis and how IT vendors and clients can effectively partner to achieve communal value from the relationship.

REFERENCES

Aiken, L., & West, S. (1991). *Multiple Regression: Testing and Interpreting Interactions*. Sage Publications.

Borgatti, S., & Foster, P. (2003). The Network Paradigm in Organizational Research: A Review and Typology. *Journal of Management, 96*(6), 991-1013.

Borgatti, S., Jones, C., & Everett, M. G. (1998). Network Measures of Social Capital. *CONNECTIONS, 21*(2), 1-36.

Brandenburger, A., & Nalebuff, B. (1995). The Right Game: Use Game Theory to Shape Strategy. *Harvard Business Review, 73*(4).

Burt, R. (2003). The Social Structure of Competition. In Rob Cross, A. Parker & L. Sasson (Eds.), *Network in the Knowledge Economy* (pp.13-56). New York: Oxford University Press.

Burt, R., Guilarte, M., Raider, H., & Yasuda, Y. (2002). Competition, Contingency, and External Structure of Markets. *Advances in Strategic Management, 19*, 167-217.

Burt, R. S. (1992). *Structural Holes*: Cambridge: Harvard University Press.

Burt, R. S. (2004). Structural holes and good ideas. *American Journal of Sociology, 110*(2), 349-399.

Cohen, S., & Fields, G. (1999). Social Capital and Capital Gains in Silicon Valley. *California Management Review, 41*(2), 108-129.

Cohen, W., & Levinthal, D. (1990). Absorptive Capacity: A New Perspective on Learning and Innovation. *Administrative Science Quarterly, 35*, 128-152.

Coleman, J. (1988). Social Capital in the Creation of Human capital. *The American Journal of Sociology, 94 Supplement*, S95-S120.

Cunningham, M., & Culligan, K. (1988). Competition and Competitive Groupings: An Exploratory Study in Information technology Markets. *Journal of Marketing Management, 4*(2), 148-174.

Das, S., Sen, P., & Sengupta, S. (1998). Impact of Strategic Alliances on Firm Valuation. *Academy of Management Journal, 41*(1), 27-41.

Ferrary, M. (2003). Managing the disruptive technologies life cycle by externalising the research: social network and corporate venturing in the Silicon Valley. *International Journal of Technology Management, 25*(1-2), 165-180.

Florin, J., Lubatkin, M., & Schulze, W. (2003). A Social Capital Model of High-Growth Ventures. *Academy of Management Journal, 46*(3), 374-384.

Fransman, M. (1990). *The Market and Beyond: Cooperation and competition in Information technology in the Japanese System*. Cambridge: Cambridge University Press.

Kaplan, R., & Norton, D. (2004). Measuring the Strategic Readiness of Intangible Assets. *Harvard Business Review, 82*(2), 53-63.

Kern, T., & Willcocks, L. (2001). *The Relationship Advantage*: Oxford University Press.

Knoke, D., Yang, S., & Granados, F. (2002, July 4-6). *Dynamics of Strategic Alliance Networks in the Global Information Sector, 1989-2000*. Paper presented at the The Dynamics of Networks: 18th EGOS Colloquium, Barcelona, Spain.

Koh, J., & Venkatraman, N. (1991). Joint venture Formations and Stock Market Reactions: An Assessment in the Information technology Sector. *Academy of Management Journal, 34*(4), 869-892.

Martin-de-Castro, G., Navas-Lopez, J. E., Lopez-Saez, P., & Alama-Salazar, E. (2006). Organizational capital as competitive advantage of the firm. *Journal of Intellectual capital, 7*(3), 324-337.

McGuire, J., Schneeweis, T., & Branch, B. (1990). Perceptions of Firm Quality: A Cause or Result of Firm Performance. *Journal of Management, 16*(1), 167-180.

Nalebuff, B., & Brandenburger, A. (1996). *Co-opetition*: HarperCollinsBusiness, London.

Nault, B., & Vandenbosch, M. (2000). Research Report: Disruptive Technologies—Explaining Entry in Next Generation Information technology Markets. *Information Systems Research, 11*(3), 304-319.

O'Donnell, D., & Berkery, G. (2003). Human interaction: the critical source of intangible value. *Journal of Intellectual capital, 4*(1), 82-99.

Pennings, J., Lee, K., & VanWitteloostuijn, A. (1998). Human capital, Social Capital, and Firm Dissolution. *Academy of Management Journal, 41*(4), 425-440.

Reich, B. H., & Kaarst-Brown, M. L. (2003). Creating social and intellectual capital through IT career transitions. *Journal of Strategic Information Systems, 12*, 91-109.

Stuart, T. (2000). Interorganizational Alliances and the Performance of Firms: A Study of Growth and Innovation Rates in a High Technology Industry. *Strategic Management Journal, 21*, pp.791-811.

Tsai, W. (2001). Knowledge Transfer in Intraorganizational Networks: Effects of Network Position and Absorptive Capacity on Business Unit Innovation and Performance. *Academy of Management Journal, 44*(5), 996-1004.

ENDNOTE

[1] While the confirmatory factor analysis indicated that RES was distinct from the other proposed elements of IC, it is included as part of IC in the regression model.

Chapter IX
ITIL and Value Networks

The previous chapters have concentrated on organisational theory and management in general and identifying the linkages to IT Governance and multisourcing. In this chapter a management framework designed by and for the IT function will be reviewed from a network's perspective. ITIL (Information Technology Infrastructure Library) is the result of an initiative of the UK Office of Government Commerce to collate and publish a suite of "Best IT Management" practices. The result is a process model covering the various IT service functions like service desks, problem and incident management; configuration and change management; service level management, capacity management, security management; and IT application development, implementation and maintenance. Many organisations have embarked on the use of ITIL as a holistic management guideline for all their IT services operations, despite the OGC being careful not to promote it as such. A common criticism of ITIL is therefore the danger of organisations adopting ITIL as a "silver bullet" for IT service ills. The most recent version of ITIL, version 3, extends the framework beyond operational aspects to address business alignment issues and hence, relevance to IT Governance activities. The growing importance of networks is acknowledged in the Service Strategy publication (ITIL, 2007) through the identification of Value network analysis (Allee, 2003) as a preferred technique for designing and analysing new service provisions.

In this chapter ITIL identified governance processes will be reviewed from a network perspective. Value network analysis (VNA) will then be described as a means for facilitating IT Governance and preparing for the implementation of a multisourcing strategy.

IT GOVERNANCE AND ITIL

IT Governance has variable definitions between organisations or even continents. For some organisations IT Governance is a matter of compliance with pre-determined and approved standard processes. A more enlightened view acknowledges that IT Governance involves more than compliance. We can define IT Governance as the means by which an organisation's investment in IT is aligned with the business value achieved. That is, a concentration on "doing' the right IT" rather than "doing IT right", which is viewed as IT management, more so than IT Governance (PriceWaterhouseCoopers, 2007; Williams, 2007). The other point of contention on IT Governance is whether the function is critical enough to justify it being represented at board level. For many, the lack of board representation can be a cause for poor IT Governance due to a lack of senior executive input. For others, IT is seen as simply a utility support service and therefore does not justify representation at the most senior levels (Carr, 2004).

The following analysis was conducted using outsourcing contracts data for the Australian IT outsourcing market, together with information on the executives of the client and vendor companies involved in these contracts. Relationships between CIOs and board members of the clients' companies are shown as links. A contractual relationship is also inferred between the CIO and the vendor CEO and is shown as a link. Additional links are also inferred for executives who have either worked for the same organisation at the same time or been board members together. The nodes are identified as individuals who are either board members, CIOs or vendor CEOs. The relative size of the node reflects the number of links a particular individual has.

While the data is limited to what can be gleaned from public sources, broad patterns of relationships are identifiable. Looking at the clusters of board members, one can see that with very few exceptions, there is little intermingling between board members and CIOs and/or vendor CEOs. The data reinforces the view that IT is not currently engaged at the board level. Whether it should or not is still an open question (Nolan & McFarlan, 2005; Williams, 2007). One would anticipate that the situation won't be changed by the IT functional heads' promotion of the importance of IT to their respective boards. It is more likely that board attention might come from negative aspects of IT, like major cost overruns on IT projects, serious security

Figure 56. Relationships between executives in the Australian IT outsourcing market place (data sources: Datamonitor and One Source)

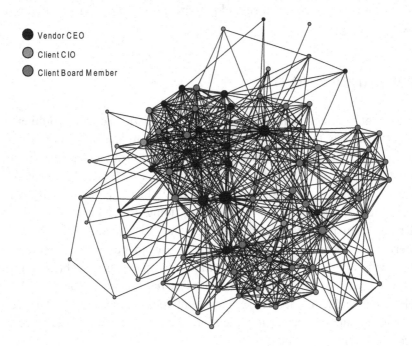

breaches or generic business risks as observed during Y2k. Therefore despite the arguments for IT Governance to be a board level concern, for the foreseeable future, IT Governance relationships will need to exist at all levels to be effective.

IT Governance surveys typically indicate a variety of support for the different IT Governance Frameworks. A common theme is the growing demand for guidance in this area. The most used IT Governance frameworks are ITIL and COBIT. COBIT (Control Objectives for Information and related Technologies) provides a governance framework for IT with an auditing flavour. Some 34 core processes are identified that relate to 318 control objectives and over 1,500 control practices are provided as guides for customization (Campbell, 2005). In this chapter the ITIL framework has been chosen for review for its closer alignment to the topic of this book, being networks and multisourcing.

The ITIL framework publications are designed to be a source of good practice in service management (ITIL.org, 2007). It is not designed as an auditing standard. It is however a source of knowledge for achieving certification to ISO/IEC 20000 service management standards. The most recent version of the ITIL library (version 3) has five core publications:

- Service Strategy;
- Service Design;
- Service Transition;
- Service Operation; and
- Continual Service Improvement.

Service strategy provides guidance on the design, development and implementation of an IT service. Service strategy is about ensuring that the services portfolio is established to achieve both cost effectiveness and distinctive business performance. Service strategy is designed to answer the *what* and *why* questions more so than the *how*. IT Governance according to ITIL is seeded in this volume.

The Service Design module is concerned with the design of the IT services portfolio to meet the organisation's strategic objectives. The module is concerned not only with new services, but with the improvement of existing services, the setting and achievement of service levels and ultimately the design capabilities for service management.

Service Transition considers the transitioning of new services into operation. In essence, service transition follows on from service strategy and service design by managing the risks of disruptions to existing services as new service releases are introduced. The module is principally concerned with the processes of release management, programme management and risk management.

Service Operation is concerned with the management of existing operations. Guidance is provided on ways to maintain stability in service operations, while allowing changes in design, scale, scope and service levels. Managing availability, controlling demand, optimising capacity utilization, scheduling operations and fixing problems are all within the scope of service operations.

Continual Service Improvement is included in recognition that customer demands are constantly changing and therefore services need to be continually assessed for incremental improvement. This module draws methods from quality management, change management and capability improvement. Linking improvement initiatives to outcomes based on the Plan, Do, Check, Act (PDCA) model is a foundation for this activity.

The ITIL Services Strategy module is the starting point for IT Governance. The service strategy is necessarily aligned with the business's strategic objectives in a way that it can be dynamically adapted to the needs of the business. Unlike the earlier versions of ITIL, the current version is business focused and is therefore concerned with how the business itself is interacting with its customers, suppliers and partners and what role IT can play in maximising business advantage. The ITIL view of governance is more aligned with concerns about business value generated through IT than compliance to standard practices. Therefore IT Governance, from an ITIL perspective, starts with sourcing governance. ITIL acknowledges that sourcing IT services from outside the organisation can create distinctive business value if executed astutely. The argument is made for outsourcing activities that are only peripherally related to the business's strategic themes. Called "context activities", these activities are typically seen as support, rather than competitive services. Sourcing structures are identified as a continuum from total internal sourcing, through to a shared service internal arrangement, to full service outsourcing, Prime contractor, Consortium and finally multi-vendor sourcing.

Figure 57 identifies alternative sourcing structures that have been commonly used. The axes show that as one moves from a totally in-sourced situation through to best of breed multisourcing, the IT capability potential increases with the breadth of choice available, but at the cost of increased complexity of governance. Totally in-sourced services was the most common structure until the early 1990s. The internal shared service model was introduced to achieve some level of accountability for in-house service providers, with services incurring a market based charge, therefore enabling profit and loss accounting to be achieved for the internal service providers. The movement to IT outsourcing began in the early to mid 1990s and usually involved a full service outsourcing to a single vendor under long term contracts. The prime contractor model is a variation of sole vendor outsourcing, where the prime vendor is expected to source other vendors to provide services, but remains fully accountable for their performance. The consortia approach looks to the client to short list a panel

Figure 57. Alternative sourcing structures

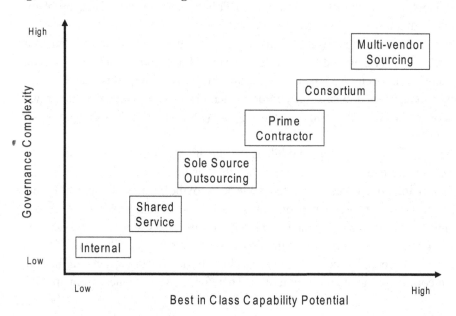

of providers who are then encouraged to collaborate with each other to provide a unified service. Finally, the multisourcing structure requires the client to take on the role of service integrator while sourcing "best of breed" suppliers.

Sourcing governance is specifically distinguished from vendor management by ITIL. IT Governance is seen as a framework of decision rights that encourage desired behaviours (Broadbent, 2002; Weill, 2004). Of particular importance is the split between decision rights for client and vendors. ITIL notes that particular problems arise when the client takes responsibility for operational decisions on behalf of the outsourcer. Inevitably, poor relationships and poor services result. ITIL recommends a governance body with all service providers represented that has the authority to act without escalation to senior management. To help clarify decision rights, ITIL recommends the creation of a RACI decision-rights matrix showing activities against roles with decision responsibilities described as Responsible, Accountable, Consulted or Informed. Activities can be split into governance domains such as service delivery, communication, sourcing strategy or contract management. ITIL identifies the key roles for the client for sourcing governance as Service Management Director, Contract Manager, Product Manager, Process Owner and Business Representative.

The trends in IT sourcing have gradually moved from total internal sourcing through single vendor outsourcing to today, where the majority of organisations are choosing to participate in some form of multi-vendor sourcing. Unfortunately the drive for more flexible outsourcing arrangements has not been matched by the additional sophistication in governance arrangements required. The ITIL recommendations for multi-vendor governance go part way to meeting the overall governance needs but do not adequately address the intangible elements of the relationship networks that make up a multisourcing arrangement. The identified client sourcing governance roles will need to be matched by similar roles with each vendor. The governance of the relationships and cooperation between vendors can become quite complex, especially if the major provider of domains of service vary between lines of business or geography. In these situations, mandating decision rights for activities to high levels of granularity is not only costly from a reporting and compliance perspective, but can suppress the motivation for vendors to offer innovative solutions for fear that their contributions may be conscripted by a fellow, but competing vendor. From a networks perspective, the ITIL governance recommendations provide the skeleton for a required multisourcing governance arrangement. What is additionally required is to flesh out the intangibles to establish the trust network needed to make complex multisourcing arrangement operate effectively.

The ITIL strategy module addresses the issue of intangibles and networks in its section on service strategy principles and service structures. In its discussion on the migration from value chains to value networks ITIL notes that:

Much of the value of service management, however, is intangible and complex. It includes knowledge and benefits such as technical expertise, strategic information, process knowledge and collaborative design. Often the value lies in how these intangibles are combined, packaged, and exchanged (ITIL, 2007 p.47)

This statement provided a natural lead into the introduction of a technique for analysing value networks called Value network analysis (VNA), which will now be addressed in more detail.

VALUE NETWORK ANALYSIS

A value network can be defined as:

...any web of relationships that generates tangible and intangible value through complex dynamic exchanges between two or more individuals, groups, or organizations   -Verna Allee

VNA is therefore the business modeling technique for capturing, visualising and then analysing the network of interactions for improvement opportunities, whether they result in an organisational structure change or the implementation of a new IT system. The technique inherits the attributes of a traditional business process mapping technique, with the addition of some unique features for identifying intangible flows (Allee, 2006a).

Figure 58. Basic VNA components

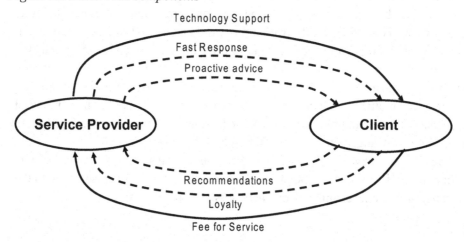

A VNA map consists of three basic elements. The ovals identify "participants". Participants can be at the individual or group level, but at all times represent human decision makers. The arrows identify a flow between participants. They are always uni-directional. Solid lines represent tangible flows, dotted lines are intangible flows. Labels on the arrows are "deliverables" that move from one participant to the next. They can be tangible or intangible. Boundaries are typically drawn to limit the scope of the analysis to a workable level of detail.

A methodology (Allee, 2006b) for conducting a typical VNA workshop exercise may follow the following steps:

1. Review Current Project Status

In the ITIL context, a business improvement project activity may be underway for say, installing a new change management and configuration facility. Prior to the workshop it would be expected that a clear purpose will have been defined and appropriate stakeholders identified and ready to participate.

2. Define the Boundaries of the Question You are Exploring

It is important to define the scope of the mapping exercise and the level of abstraction through posing a focusing question. For example, a question like "should we off-shore our data centre?" is likely to have a high market level scope. Alternatively, a question like "how should we organize the new change and configuration management function?" would dictate a more detailed internal focus.

3. Determine Who Needs to Participate

Once the scope has been determined, the participants for the mapping exercise should be representative of all the roles and activities that might participate in the scoped activity.

4. Facilitation, Materials and Room Setup

VNA mapping is quite visual. White "butchers paper" and felt pens are common instruments. A good workshop facilitator is essential. For larger groups it may be best to split into groups and synthesize the results at the end. The important factor is that everyone has the opportunity to participate in the conversation around the map building.

5. Create the Value Network Map

The basic elements were described earlier. A good staring point is to define the core participants or roles. These are real people or groups, not computers or systems. Example nodes could be individuals, groups, business units, organisations, regions etc. A good rule of thumb is to settle on five to eight roles. Arrows joining roles reflect a transaction or activity that results in a deliverable. Typically tangible deliverables can be thought of as "contracted activities". Intangibles are additional deliverables that are not formally contracted but are essential to achieving a smooth operation. For example, tips and hints passed on, informal references, market intelligence and the like.

6. Validate the Map by Sequencing Activities

A good validation step is to do some "walk throughs", sequencing the natural order of activities by numbering the flows between nodes. In this way you should be able to "tell the story" through the map.

7. Undertake Analysis Scenarios

Once a map has been constructed the critical analysis can start. A number of typical analysis scenarios can be conducted, for example:

1. **Exchange Analysis:** looks at the value dynamics in the network. How equitable are the value flows? Are the roles clear or confused? Any gaps or redundancies? Are there obvious winners or losers? For example, do tight "time per call" metrics limit the capacity of the desktop technician for providing those little coaching tips that clients value so much.
2. **Impact Analysis:** looks at each role and whether or not value is being realised from its inputs. Ask a participant currently in that role what value they really believe they receive. Can we determine a cost/benefit for each input to the role?
3. **Value Creation Analysis:** looks at how each role or participant is adding value to the system. It is complementary to the impact analysis as it looks at what value the role creates for others with its outputs.
4. **Developing Performance Indicators:** in theory a performance indicator could be generated for each identified flow on the map. If some of the intangible deliverables appear too hard to characterise into a metric, then they are probably framed incorrectly. For example, an intangible deliverable labeled "increased trust" might be better labeled "increased reliability" as it leads

more easily to a measurable indicator. A VNA map could therefore be used to populate a Balanced Scorecard for the network as a whole.

8. Take Action

This is the "act" part of the Plan-Do-Check-Act cycle. Having created the value network map and conducted the value analysis, it is time to convert the findings to action. This typically might take many forms, from re-defining roles, re-defining value flows or creating a performance scorecard. While ITIL may identify some typical service management roles, the context for these roles may differ for each organisation depending on the outsourcing, multi-sourcing or co-sourcing strategies that currently exist or are being considered.

HOW DOES VNA FIT WITH OTHER MODELING METHODS?

The most distinguishing feature of VNA, when compared to other modeling techniques adopted by the IT industry, is the incorporation of intangibles into the analysis (Allee, 2008). As business applications move beyond simple automation to more sophisticated decision support activities, the impact of intangibles is significant. The majority of modeling tools developed for the IT industry were developed with automation of processes in mind. Where people played a role it was usually cast as facilitating a process, rather than as an independent decision maker. Techniques like data flow diagrams and business process mapping effectively remove the individual from the analysis in favour of a process focus. This is fine when automation is the objective, but disastrous for decision support, where the end user is an independent agent.

Perhaps the closest modeling technique to VNA can be found in the object oriented (O-O) techniques and "Use Case" modeling. Use Case models do preserve the individual actor or role in the model. The use case interaction model could be cast as a VNA model by adding intangibles into the list of interaction deliverables (Lock Lee, 2007) as shown in the example in Figure 59 .

A VALUE NETWORK MAP EXAMPLE FOR THE IT MARKET

The following map (Figure 60) is an example of a VNA map created at the IT industry level. A typical focusing question that would have preceded the creation of a map like this might be "What value could we achieve my adopting a different IT sourcing model?" Participants could be drawn from internal sources plus

Figure 59. VNA and use case example

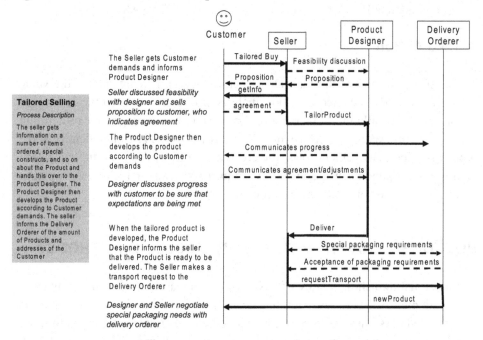

Figure 60. Value network map for the IT industry

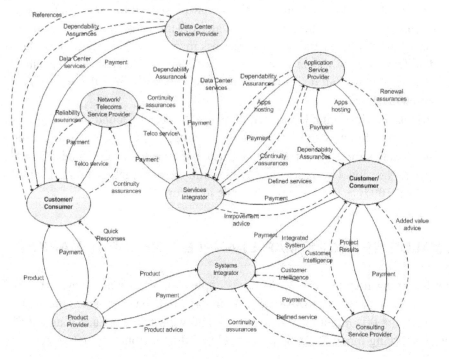

representatives from external providers representing the nodes identified, either currently contracted providers or prospective providers.

The solid lines show the "contracted" transactions that might typically be identified in a Use Case analysis. The dotted lines show the added intangible flows. It is the intangibles that will create the most discussion and debate. Note that in many cases the intangible contributions are balanced i.e. reciprocity is being demonstrated. Where there is an imbalance in value flows, for example, when intangibles only flow one way, one might question the longer term stability of that relationship. Where no intangible flows exist (e.g. the Systems Integrator and the Customer), either the transactions are purely for commodity services or alternatively an "arms length" relationship exists which again could be quite fragile. Other examples indicate where the systems or service integrators are "receivers" of intangible benefits that are not explicitly flowing on to the customer.

SO HOW DID ITIL MEET VALUE NETWORKS?

The evolution of ITIL from an "Infrastructure Library" to "Service Management Practices" could be described as a classic example of "Knowledge management maturation". Two fundamental concepts in Knowledge management (KM) are, that knowledge can be characterised as both explicit (information), and tacit (in the minds of individuals). Early KM initiatives took the view that if the majority of our tacit knowledge could be codified as explicit knowledge, then it could be effectively shared widely in electronic form, hence the ITIL infrastructure library. What KM practitioners quickly discovered was that there were natural limits within which this scheme could work. Tacit knowledge was proving particularly "sticky" and difficult to extract for sharing in library form. Hence a movement toward a greater emphasis on "connections" over "collections" began. In order to share critical tacit knowledge, a mechanisms for having people connect, either in person or virtually, became the most effective way of sharing important knowledge. Once we start connecting people in large numbers (think about LinkedIn), it is only a short step to appreciate networks.

The other significant change is a relaxation of our thinking around "process". ITIL is a best "practices" framework. Practices are not equivalent to processes. When one observes an expert practitioner at work, one sees far more than a slavish adherence to process. One observes the expert improvisations, subtle relationship management tactics and a plethora of other "hard to document" activities that collectively constitute "good practice". This is not to say that process is abandoned. What it does say is that an optimum balance of process and practice is required (Lock Lee, 2005). VNA attempts to surface these intangible value contributions, along with the more tangible process flows, to enable more holistic analyses of the value flows across the business. This is totally consistent with the objectives of ITIL V3, to integrate the business and IT services management into a single ecosystem. VNA is a tool to help study this ecosystem and instigate improvements to it.

VALUE NETWORKS AND IT GOVERNANCE FOR MULTISOURCING

So how can VNA be used to assist with the governance of a multisourcing arrangement? As has been indicated in this chapter, current IT Governance practice, whether promoted by ITIL or other frameworks like COBIT largely identify with the tangible value flows between roles within the governance arrangements. Contractual terms, service level targets, RACI charts for decision rights and even codes of conduct identifying appropriate behaviours are all examples of tangible relationship aspects. The important intangible value flows that, amongst other things, contribute to development of the trust network between stakeholders are largely left unsaid. VNA exposes these intangibles by making them explicit. Once explicit they are available for negotiation, exchange, clarification, adaptation, providing the transparency necessary to achieve an effective and trustful governance arrangement. Additionally, accountability can still be measured and monitored via scorecard techniques. However, in this case the scorecard is not simply a mechanism for a client to monitor vendor performance. The scorecard is monitoring the partnerships, and therefore all stakeholders are being equally monitored against the VNA generated scorecard, including the client.

To illustrate how VNA can be used for governing a multisourcing arrangement the following tutorial style scenario is presented.

VNA AND MULTISOURCING GOVERNANCE SCENARIO

FinCo is a mature major banking and financial services firm. FinCo was an early adopter of IT outsourcing and is just coming to the end of a 10 year sole vendor sourcing arrangement with a major vendor ABCTech. Consistent with the experiences of other organisations that had embarked on long term sole sourced IT outsourcing contracts, FinCo had initially struggled with the relationship with ABCTech. The original contract had undergone many changes and renegotiations as both FinCo and ABCTech had been unable to achieve a workable alignment of expectations that could be commonly understood in the terms of the contract. The relationship had reached its lowest point only a year into the contract, requiring changes in personnel on both sides before the organisations could move forward with renegotiating a workable contract. While the latter years of the contract had progressed in relative harmony, FinCo suspected that the concessions that they had made to achieve a workable arrangement with ABCTech had limited their ability to extract maximum value from their IT resources. Both organisations astutely avoided assessing performance against the original FinCo business case for outsourcing.

While they were now comfortable with the core infrastructure services, having successfully standardised their facilities and management processes across the organisation, their business clients had been critical of the lack of pro-activity and innovation from the IT function. While ABCTech had made several attempts to inject more innovation into the account, FinCo suspected that the ABCTech executive were not that serious in investing further in the FinCo account, given the angst it had been through in achieving profitability from the account over the term of the contract.

The FinCo executive had decided to follow many of their peers and move away from the sole sourcing arrangement with ABCTech and invite other vendors to participate in providing IT services to FinCo. FinCo wanted to take back some control of the IT services that ABCTech now controlled. Hence it decided against the option of using ABCTech as a prime contractor. It also decided against a consortia approach as it felt that such an arrangement would not provide FinCo with the control it desired. FinCo was therefore preparing to rebuild a program office to act as the integration point for multisourced vendor services. The decision was not taken lightly. FinCo acknowledged the risk of damaging the relationship with ABCTech. It was also mindful of the contractual experience they had with ABCTech and the potential for "multiplying the pain" with multiple contracts required. On the other hand FinCo had learnt a lot about IT outsourcing contracts through its experience with ABCTech. It felt confident that the contractual trials of the past could be avoided through learning from this experience. What they were less confident about were the softer or intangible aspects of the new relationships it would be forming. It had taken many years for the ABCTech relationship to stabilise. Even today FinCo felt that the relationship could easily deteriorate should a significant change in personnel or a major business change like a new merger or acquisition came in to upset the current equilibrium, despite the maturity that now existed in the contractual terms. The real wildcard for FinCo however was the relationships that FinCo would need to facilitate between the different suppliers. It was aware that the providers they had selected for their panel were also competitors in the market place. The danger for FinCo was that the additional value that could be generated through the use of "best of breed" providers could be diminished or removed completely through the additional requirements for governance and resolution of disputes between providers.

FinCo had read about Value Networks and VNA in the ITIL Service Strategy documentation. FinCo felt that VNA may provide the vehicle for developing the platform for their new multisourcing governance arrangement. FinCo had already put selected IT services to tender and announced the successful tenderers who would now be represented on their IT Governance board. The governance structure as informed by the ITIL sourcing governance recommendations was established as shown in Figure 61:

The FinCo CIO chairs the governance committee on behalf of the FinCo board of directors. The Director of service management is the CIO's deputy and is responsible for all IT service delivery on behalf of the FinCo business units. The Contracts Manager is responsible for contracts with each of the providers. The Product Manager is responsible for defining the lines of service to be provided by the vendors. The Process Owner is the keeper of the standard business processes for the major business units. The role is responsible for assessing the fit between the product offerings and the business. The business unit representatives have been drawn from the three major FinCo divisions. These representatives are responsible for identifying the business value being achieved from the current IT service

Figure 61. FinCo multisourcing governance structure

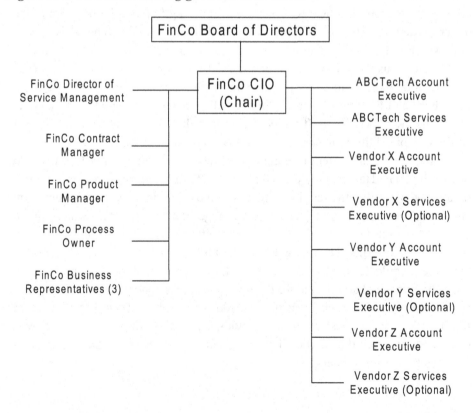

providers and to also propose new value creation opportunities. The vendors are represented by their FinCo Account Executive. Depending on the size or breadth of the services being provided by a vendor, the vendor account executive can optionally be accompanied by their senior services executive. This governance committee can be supported by various subcommittees monitoring particular developments like major ERP implementations or infrastructure refreshes. A FinCo Programme Office also reports through the Director of Service Management.

The CIO, having established the governance committee, has now invited ValueNets Inc to run a series of VNA workshops with the committee. The objective of the workshops is to establish a common understanding of how value will be generated for all parties in the multisourcing arrangement. FinCo had learnt from bitter experience that driving vendor prices to the point where the vendor could not profit was counter productive as vendors were forced to "cut corners" to reduce the cost of services, usually with detrimental results for FinCo. It was therefore an objective of the CIO to reach a situation where each of the stakeholders in the multisourcing arrangement could receive value commensurate with their relative contribution. Value in this sense was not always financial or tangible. The workshops would give the stakeholders the facility to negotiate and exchange value contributions in order to reach a workable equilibrium. An additional objective to help sustain the arrangement post workshops was a "Partners Scorecard". This scorecard would provide the ongoing data by which the governance committee could monitor IT services performance for FinCo.

ValueNets Inc began their task by reviewing the current status. The CIO had advised that the governance committee had just been established and constituted by the structure shown in Figure 61. The contracted services had been defined, determining which vendor was principally responsibility for each service product line. The following table identifies which vendors were responsible for given service product lines.

The initial workshop was to be conducted at the governance committee level. The identified roles to be used in the VNA were to be those identified in the Governance

Table 12. Service product line responsibilities

Responsible Service Provider	Service Product Line
ABCTech	Mainframe and Midrange Services
Vendor X	Desktop Management and Help Desk Services
Vendor Y	Networks, Telecommunications and Security
Vendor Z	Application Development
In-House	Applications maintenance other non-outsourced services

committee. It was anticipated that further workshops would be needed for lower level roles as a natural flow-on from this initial workshop. The deliverables expected from ValueNets Inc were a Value Network Map identifying the agreed value flows between the identified roles, and a draft partnership scorecard. The scope for the exercise was clearly limited to the governance roles identified by the committee. The key question to be resolved during the workshop was, what attributes would be managed and monitored across the multisourcing arrangement by the governance committee? The participants in the workshop were all to be members of the newly formed governance committee.

With 16 participants ValueNets Inc decided that there were too many to facilitate as a single group. It was decided that the workshop should be split into two groups of roughly balanced representation from each of the stakeholder groups. The first group was given the task of developing a value net map with all FinCo roles and a single vendor role. The second group was to look at the vendors and the FinCo inhouse service providers and the potential value network for the major supplier roles. Value Nets Inc knew from experience that the workshop participants would find it easier to identify the tangible or "contracted" deliverables between roles, so they suggested the participants identified these first before moving onto the intangible deliverables between roles. The first team moved quickly into identifying the tangible flows. Much of this information had already been identified through the

Figure 62. Team 1 tangible value flows

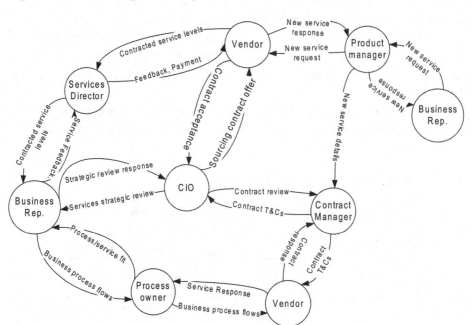

initial design of the FinCo governance structure. An early version of their efforts is shown in Figure 62.

Team 1 acknowledged that this initial value net diagram was similar to their existing business process mapping that had been produced to assist with the governance role identification. The difference, as some of the participants commented, was that the value network map encourages the identification of value "exchanges" with many reciprocal flows, whereas the business process mapping largely showed one way linear flows. This was seen as an early benefit of the value network representation. The next stage was to add the intangible or "non-contracted" value flows. The ValueNet Inc facilitators asked the participants to think back to any positive experiences that they had, and think about the "little extras" that had made the governance arrangement work well. Conversely, they were to recount any poor governance situations they had experienced to identify the intangibles that may have been missing. Several participants noted that they had seen situations with identical governance structures and roles, but vastly different performance, and therefore were looking forward to exploring the intangibles. The facilitators also reiterated that the flows must be "deliverables" that the roles could be held accountable for and not simply attributes of a role or individual, such as "competence" or "expertise".

Figure 63. Team 1 initial intangible value flows

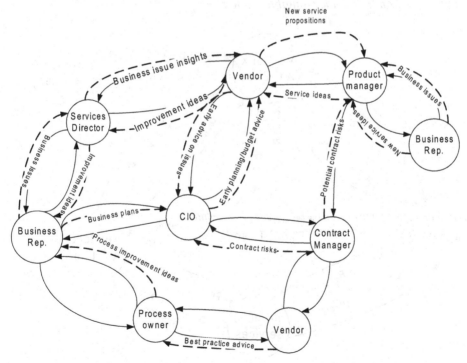

The team began their task enthusiastically. The discussion was lively, but the crafting of the labeling for the intangible flows did prove a challenge. However with the help of the facilitators the group came up with this initial value network for the intangibles.

The intangible flows were shown as additional dashed arrows. Taking a short break, the group reflected on what they had come up with so far. They noted that not all of the intangible flows were reciprocated. Was this going to be a problem? Also they noted that between some roles there appeared to be few intangible value flows. This prompted a discussion on whether this was appropriate or not. For example, if the role was a very process intensive activity using well accepted practices, then perhaps intangible value flows may not add any value overall? The second observation made was on the nature of the intangibles identified. The nature of the intangibles was largely either early advice on potential issues, proactive promotion of improvement ideas or fast response to potential issues. Several participants commented on their previous positive experiences where they spoke of the positive "energy" that existed. In contrast the negative experiences exhibited negative energy, with information only exchanged under duress or according to contracted terms. Most activity appeared to be reactive to complaints more than proactive around improvement opportunities. Overall, the group felt positively about

Figure 64. Team 2 provider tangible value flows

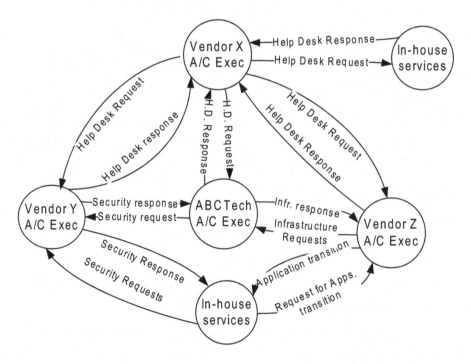

the identification of the intangible value flows as a means of making explicit what constituted the positive energy that they had previously experienced and hopefully could replicate for FinCo.

In the meantime the second team went about their task of looking at the value network for the provider side. As with the first team, the facilitators encouraged the team to identify the tangible flows first. Their initial attempt is shown in Figure 64.

Like the first team, the second team noticed that the value networks representation did encourage the identification of exchanges or two-way value flows. However, unlike the first team, they noticed that few of these so called "contracted" value flows existed in any of the current contracts. The formal contracts had been formed between the vendors and FinCo and only peripherally addressed the obligations between providers. The FinCo participants acknowledged the shortcomings of the current contractual arrangements in this area and felt that more time could be spent in formalising more of the contractible value flows. The ValueNet Inc facilitators however encouraged them to move on to identifying the intangible value flows that might exist between the vendors. The participants struggled initially. The external vendors were more use to competing than collaborating with their fellow providers. However, they did manage to come up with this initial attempt.

Figure 65. Team 2 intangible value flows for service providers

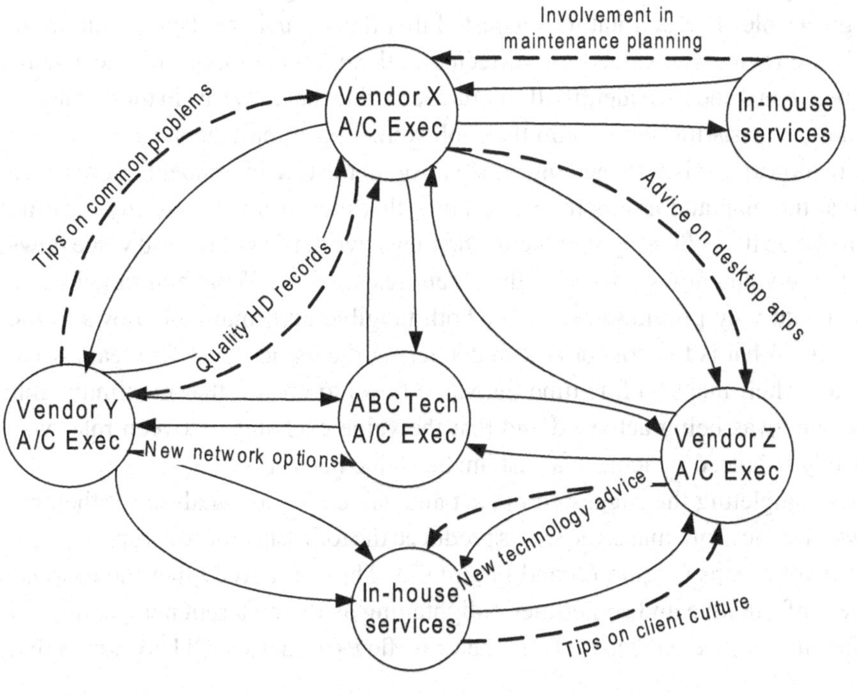

Team 2 participants acknowledged that it had been difficult to come up with potential intangible value flows as few of them had been in situations where this form of collaboration was required. They also noted that only a few of their identified intangible value flows were reciprocated. The question was raised as to what motivation was there to sustain a relationship if value flows were only in one direction. At this point the ValueNet Inc facilitators introduced the concept of "exchange analysis". They noted that it may not be necessary to balance the intangible value flows but to be effective, the combination of tangible and intangible value flows would need to be balanced if stable relations were to be achieved. With this in mind the team returned to the map to identify where potential value flow mismatches existed. They identified that Vendor X, being responsible for the help desk services, could meet their contractual commitments by the timely capture and escalation of help desk calls. However, this would not necessarily contribute to reducing the root cause of the calls themselves. With the help of ABCTech and Vendor Y, the Vendor X help desk could spend time educating the callers, rather than simply recording call details. In this way they could reduce the number of calls needing to be made. The group identified that a balance of performance measures would have to be designed to ensure that each vendor had performance targets that reflected this need i.e. a good candidate for inclusion in the Partnership Scorecard.

At this point the ValueNet Inc facilitators brought the teams together and reviewed some additional analytical practices that the teams could now apply to their maps. Impact analysis was introduced as a means for assessing the value flows directed into a given role. The facilitators suggested that those participants acting in these roles should review the value flows directed to them, and perhaps provide a value score (between 0 and 5) to identify the perceived value that they saw in the particular value flow, in assisting them to do their job well. The complementary practice of value creation analysis was then introduced. Again the role incumbents were asked to look at the map and assess the value flows that they were supposedly creating from the value flows flowing into them. Did they have sufficient inward value flows to create the value flows for which they were responsible? What additional value outputs could they provide in terms of both tangible and intangible flows to the other roles? What is the cost or risk in delivering the value flow? The teams then returned to their maps to fine tune the value flows to ensure that maximum collective value was being achieved and that the value exchange between roles was sufficiently balanced to achieve a sustainable value network.

After completing the suggested impact and value creation analyses of their respective value network maps, the teams produced the following more comprehensive value network maps (Figure 66 and Figure 67): They all agreed that the exercise had been informative and sometimes enlightening as the different perspectives of the different roles were discussed and the value flows adjusted. All had agreed that

Figure 66. Team 1 completed value network map for FinCo

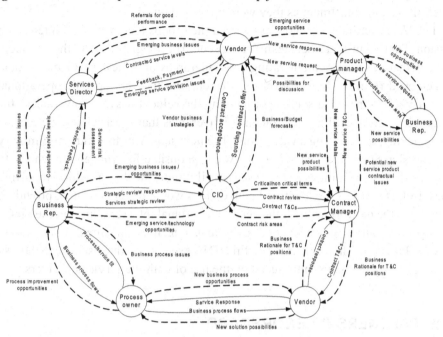

Figure 67. Team 2 completed value network map for service providers

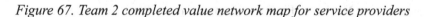
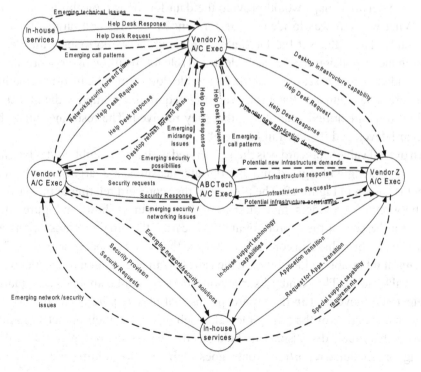

what they had produced was a good start but felt that the flows would need continual redefinition and adjustment as they were operationalised.

The ValueNet Inc facilitators assembled the groups together for an integration session. They identified where team 2's map could be integrated under the "Vendor" label of Team 1's map, demonstrating how a hierarchy of value network maps could be achieved from the higher level roles through to the very specific operational roles. By following the discipline of labeling the value flows as "deliverables" the group could now see that each role had deliverables that it was either responsible for achieving, or assessing a value from. The next stage was to build a preliminary "Partnership Scorecard", showing who was responsible for what and to whom. In this case the responsibilities were not necessarily aligned with hierarchical reporting lines. In fact many of the identified deliverables would be reciprocated, providing stability to the network without the need for continual intervention from the FinCo management. The achievement of a self managed team arrangement was precisely why the FinCo CIO had embarked on this VNA exercise, as the response to the risk of increasing governance introduced by the use of multiple service providers.

THE PARTNERSHIP SCORECARD

A deliverable for ValueNet Inc to FinCo was a preliminary Partnership Scorecard. The value network maps would provide the data for the responsibilities for each role. What was left was to identify performance measures and targets for each deliverable. The ValueNet Inc facilitators provided the workgroups with a chart showing the responsibilities for each identified role for inclusion in the scorecard. It was decided that the assessment of the intangible flows would be incorporated into a quarterly questionnaire. Each role would be required to complete the questions relating to the identified value flows that they received. The resulting intangible scorecard developed is shown in Figure 68.

An overall value scorecard was then generated with both tangible and intangible value flows along with agreed and appropriate measures and targets, of which an extract is shown in Figure 69. The portion of the scorecard relating to the partnership between the providers, including the in-house team is shown in Figure 70.

As can be see on these preliminary scorecards, the tangible transactions are often already formalised in contracts and those that aren't probably should be. The majority of intangible value flows are measured by the perception of the recipients of the value flows. The standard survey questions would be applied each quarter to detect any movement in these perceptions that may require corrective action. A key characteristic of the intangible value deliverables is their proactive nature. Ensuring that timely discussions are held on emerging issues or topics, rather than waiting for scheduled reporting events, goes a long way to building and enhancing

Figure 68. Intangible value flow assessment scorecard

Intangible Deliverables	Delivered by:	Survey Question	Assessment -2: strongly disagree -1: disagree 0: neutral +1: agree +2: strongly agree	Assessed by:
Service Risk Assessment	Services Director	I feel well informed about potential service delivery risks		Business Rep
Emerging Business Issues	Services Director	I feel well informed about emerging business issues that could demand on our services		Vendors
Referral for good service	Services Director	We receive referrals for services that we perform well		Vendors
Emerging Business Issues	Business Reps	I feel well informed about emerging business issues that could demand on our services		Services Director
Emerging Business Issues/Opportunities	Business Reps	I feel well informed about business issues and opportunities that IT could assist with		CIO
Business Process Issues	Business Reps	I feel that I have a good understanding of the current business processes used		Process Owner
New Business Opportunities	Business Reps	I am regularly engaged in discussions about new business opportunities for IT		Product Manager
New Solution Possibilities	Vendors	The vendors keep me well appraised of new solution possibilities that meet our process needs		Process Owner
Business rationale for T&C positions	Vendors	I appreciate and understand the vendors positions on formal T&C in the contract		Contract Manager
New Service Possibilities	Vendors	The vendors keep me well appraised of potential new service offerings		Product Manager
Emerging service provision issues	Vendors	The vendor keeps me well appraised of potential service delivery issues well ahead of time		Service Director
Vendor Business Strategies	Vendors	The vendors keep me well appraised of their strategic business directions and activities		CIO
Contract risk areas	Contract Manager	I am full appraised of the major risk areas in our contracts		CIO
Potential new product contract issues	Contract Manager	I am fully appraised on potential contractual issues with new service product prospects		Product Manager
New Service Possibilities	Product Manager	I am regularly appraised of new service possibilities by the product manager		Business Reps
Emerging New Service Ideas	Product Manager	I regularly discuss contract implications for new service ideas with the product manager		Contract Manager
Emerging Service Opportunities	Product Manager	The product manager keeps us well appraised on new service opportunities		Vendors
Business/Budget Forecasts	CIO	We are kept will informed on IT budget forecasts, both long and short term		Vendors
Critical/Non-critical T&Cs	CIO	I'm given a good assessment of the criticality of the contractual T&Cs from the business's perspective		Contract Manager
Emerging Service/Technology Opportunities	CIO	We are well appraised of the major technology trends and risks as well as the opportunities that they may provide		Business Reps
Emerging Call Patterns	Vendor X	Vendor X provides us with early warning on abnormal call patterns of issue to us		In-House Services
Desktop Refresh Forward Plans	Vendor X	Vendor X includes us in their desktop refresh planning		Vendor Y
Emerging Call Patterns	Vendor X	Vendor X provides us with early warning on abnormal call patterns of issue to us		ABCTech
Desktop Infrastructure Capability	Vendor X	Vendor X provides us with honest appraisals of the desktop capacity available for our applications plans		Vendor Z
Inhouse Support Technology Capabilities	In-House Services	We are honestly appraised of in-house technical capabilities		Vendor Z
Emerging Network/Security Issues	In-House Services	We are given early notice of emerging networking/security issues		Vendor Y
Emerging technical issues	In-House Services	We are given early notice of emerging technical issues that might impact on us		Vendor X
Emerging Network/Security Solutions	Vendor Y	We are well appraised on emerging networking/security solutions		In-House Services
Network/Security Forward Plans	Vendor Y	Vendor Y keeps us well appraised of their network/security forward plans		Vendor X
Emerging Security Possibilities	Vendor Y	Vendor Y regularly discusses emerging security possibilities with us		ABCTech
Special Support Capability Requirements	Vendor Z	Vendor Z gives us early notice of any special support requirements their planned application might have		In-House Services
Potential new infrastructure demands	Vendor Z	Vendor Z regularly discusses potential infrastructure demands with us		ABCTech
Potential New Application Demands	Vendor Z	We are adequately involved in new application roll outs undertaken by vendor Z		Vendor X

Figure 69. Extract from preliminary partnership scorecard FinCo/Vendors

Deliverables	From	To	Measure	Target
Contract service levels	Services Director	Business Rep	as per contract	as per contract
Service Risk Assessment	Services Director	Business Rep	As per Intangibles Survey	+1
Formal Services Feedback	Services Director	Vendors	as per contract	as per contract
Payment for services	Services Director	Vendors	as per contract	as per contract
Emerging Business Issues	Services Director	Vendors	As per Intangibles Survey	+1
Referral for good service	Services Director	Vendors	As per Intangibles Survey	0
Formal Services Feedback	Business Reps	Service Director	as per contract	as per contract
Emerging Business Issues	Business Reps	Service Director	As per Intangibles Survey	+1
Strategic service review response	Business Reps	CIO	Quarterly workshop	scheduled & held
Emerging Business Issues/Opportunities	Business Reps	CIO	As per Intangibles Survey	+1
Business Process Flows	Business Reps	Process Owner	BP documentation review	minimum 2/year
Business Process Issues	Business Reps	Process Owner	As per Intangibles Survey	+1
New Service Request	Business Reps	Product Manager	As required	N.A.
New Business Opportunities	Business Reps	Product Manager	As per Intangibles Survey	+1
Service Response to business processes	Vendors	Process Owner	As required	N.A.
New Solution Possibilities	Vendors	Process Owner	As per Intangibles Survey	+1
Contract Response	Vendors	Contract Manager	Quarterly review	scheduled & held
Business rationale for T&C positions	Vendors	Contract Manager	As per Intangibles Survey	+1
New Services Response	Vendors	Product Manager	As required	N.A.
New Service Possibilities	Vendors	Product Manager	As per Intangibles Survey	0
Contracted Service	Vendors	Service Director	as per contract	as per contract
Emerging service provision issues	Vendors	Service Director	As per Intangibles Survey	+1
Contract Acceptance	Vendors	CIO	Sign-off as required	2 week turnaround
Vendor Business Strategies	Vendors	CIO	As per Intangibles Survey	0
Contract T&Cs	Contract Manager	CIO	Quarterly review	scheduled & held
Contract risk areas	Contract Manager	CIO	As per Intangibles Survey	+1
New Service T&Cs	Contract Manager	Product Manager	Amended contract	1 week turnaround
Potential new product contract issues	Contract Manager	Product Manager	As per Intangibles Survey	+1
New Services responses	Product Manager	Business Reps	Timely formal response	1 week turnaround
New Service Possibilities	Product Manager	Business Reps	As per Intangibles Survey	+1
New Service Details	Product Manager	Contract Manager	Formal request	N.A.
Emerging New service Ideas	Product Manager	Contract Manager	As per Intangibles Survey	+1
New Service Request	Product Manager	Vendors	Formal request	N.A.
Emerging Service Opportunities	Product Manager	Vendors	As per Intangibles Survey	+1
Sourcing Contract Offer	CIO	Vendors	Formal offer	N.A.
Business/Budget Forecasts	CIO	Vendors	As per Intangibles Survey	+1
Formal Contract Review	CIO	Contract Manager	Quarterly review	scheduled & held
Critical/Non-critical T&Cs	CIO	Contract Manager	As per Intangibles Survey	+1
Services Strategic Review	CIO	Business Reps	Quarterly review	scheduled & held
Emerging Service/Technology Opportunities	CIO	Business Reps	As per Intangibles Survey	+1

Figure 70. Provider level partnership scorecard

Deliverables	From	To	Measure	Target
Help Desk Requests	Vendor X	In-House Services	as per contract	as per conract
Emerging Call Patterns	Vendor X	In-House Services	As per Intangibles Survey	+1
Help Desk Requests	Vendor X	Vendor Y	as per contract	as per conract
Desktop Refresh Forward Plans	Vendor X	Vendor Y	As per Intangibles Survey	+1
Help Desk Requests	Vendor X	ABCTech	as per contract	as per conract
Emerging Call Patterns	Vendor X	ABCTech	As per Intangibles Survey	+1
Help Desk Requests	Vendor X	Vendor Z	as per contract	as per conract
Desktop Infrastructure Capability	Vendor X	Vendor Z	As per Intangibles Survey	+1
Request for application transition	In-House Services	Vendor Z	Formal request	N.A.
Inhouse Support Technology Capabilities	In-House Services	Vendor Z	As per Intangibles Survey	+1
Security Requests	In-House Services	Vendor Y	Formal request	N.A.
Emerging Network/Security Issues	In-House Services	Vendor Y	As per Intangibles Survey	+1
Help Desk Responses	In-House Services	Vendor X	Formal response	as per contract
Emerging issues	In-House Services	Vendor X	As per Intangibles Survey	+1
Security Responses	Vendor Y	In-House Services	Formal response	as per contract
Emerging Network/Security Solutions	Vendor Y	In-House Services	As per Intangibles Survey	+1
Help Desk Responses	Vendor Y	Vendor X	Formal response	as per contract
Network/Security Forward Plans	Vendor Y	Vendor X	As per Intangibles Survey	+1
Security Responses	Vendor Y	ABCTech	Formal response	1 week turnaround
Emerging Security Possibilities	Vendor Y	ABCTech	As per Intangibles Survey	+1
Application Transition	Vendor Z	In-House Services	Formal request	N.A.
Special Support Capability Requirements	Vendor Z	In-House Services	As per Intangibles Survey	+1
Infrastructure Requests	Vendor Z	ABCTech	Formal request	N.A.
Potential new infrastructure demands	Vendor Z	ABCTech	As per Intangibles Survey	+1
Help Desk Responses	Vendor Z	Vendor X	as per contract	as per contract
Potential New Application Demands	Vendor Z	Vendor X	As per Intangibles Survey	+1

trust in the network. Unlike other balanced scorecards that are used to assess an organisation as a whole, the Partnership Scorecard is more granular. Each role will have particular value flows that they will be accountable for and at the same time have value flows of which they will be the sole assessor. In this way accountability and performance issues can be accurately targeted for timely attention.

Overall, the group agreed that the Partnership Scorecard would be a welcome addition to their performance measurement schemes. In particular, it was felt that an IT Governance "Balanced Scorecard" could be generated from the Partnership Scorecards. The ValueNet Inc facilitators reinforced this view, adding that a critical contribution of the Partnership Scorecard was that it focused on cooperation, with all stakeholders being both reviewers and subjects for scorecard methods, unlike traditional Balanced Scorecards which tended to be targeted at service provider performance only.

IMPLICATIONS FOR IT GOVERNANCE AND MULTISOURCING

In this chapter the emerging practices of VNA and the Partnership Scorecard have been directly applied to an IT Governance and multisourcing scenario. The unique value of the approaches described is in how the intangibles and relationships are explicitly treated. While experienced practitioners are acutely aware of the impact of intangibles and managing relationships on successful governance and multi-sourcing arrangements, by making them explicit, one can begin to more effectively manage them. By practicing these emerging techniques, it is possible to accelerate the creations of good working relationships between vendors, and between vendors and their clients. By managing the intangibles, differences in perceptions and ex-pectations can be identified early and resolutions negotiated to mutual satisfaction, before more harmful relationship fallouts can occur.

SUMMARY AND CONCLUSIONS

This chapter has reviewed how the IT industry develops and promulgates its best practice experiences. The ITIL best practice framework was chosen for review, in terms of its recommendations for IT Governance, based on its focus on business alignment as the purpose of IT Governance, more so than the compliance approach of other frameworks. ITIL itself started as a best practices library, from which its name was formed. Over its 20 year history the documented practices have been carefully promoted as guides more so than standards. In terms of governance, ITIL has taken the position that the objective of IT Governance is to maximize the business return on investment from IT resources and therefore governance starts with sourcing, whether internal or external. While some IT Governance commentators viewed that IT Governance should be a board level concern, data shown in this chapter indicated that this was far from being achieved and that IT Governance would at least for the time being, be conducted below that level.

Using the ITIL sourcing governance recommendations and the identified governance roles the Value network analysis (VNA) technique was introduced. VNA had been identified by ITIL as a best practice IT strategic planning practice. VNA had its genesis in the field of Knowledge management. The inventor of VNA had recognised that traditional business process analysis techniques avoided many of the intangible value contributions that were often the difference between a well performing or poor performing organisation (Allee, 2008). By making these intangible contributions explicit, along with the formal contracted transactions linking roles within a network diagram, it would be possible to examine the dynamics of value flows as they traverse the organisation. In this way, imbalances of value contributions and value creation shortcomings could be identified and corrected. The recognition of intangible value flows also explicitly recognises the importance of the trust network within sourcing arrangements, as it is the intangibles that contribute most to the development of such trust networks.

The final section in the chapter provided a case study scenario of how VNA and ITIL could be combined to establish an IT Governance for multisourcing arrangement. This comprehensive scenario walked through how value network maps could be created and analysed by the governance role players participating in value network workshops. A key deliverable from the workshop was the so called "Partnership Scorecard". The scorecard is distinctive in that the intent is to measure and monitor relationship interactions, both between and within the client and provider organisations. With sourcing relationships being seen as the greatest point of weakness in current outsourcing arrangements, the Partnership Scorecard offers unique value in centrally addressing the relationship issues.

This chapter has principally addressed the client/provider interface with value networks. In the next chapters the networking paradigm will be extended to the global IT marketplace. As identified in previous chapters it is no longer possible for clients to view vendors as independent entities. The growth in network alliances between IT market actors and the increasing specialisation found within the market can mean that selecting and integrating "best of breed" providers can be a hazardous task. The next chapter takes a network perspective of the global IT market place. The perspective is then expanded into an examination of the outsourcing relationship using case study examples.

REFERENCES

Allee, V. (2003). *The Future of Knowledge: Increasing Prosperity through Value Networks*. Butterworth-Heinemann.

Allee, V. (2006a). *Value Network Mapping Basics*. Retrieved 5/1/08, from http://www. value-networks.com/howToGuides/ValueNetworkMappingBasics.pdf

Allee, V. (2006b). *What is ValueNet Works Analysis?* Retrieved 5/1/08, from http:// www.valuenetworks.com/howToGuides/What_is_ValueNet_Works_Analysis.pdf

Allee, V. (2008). Value network analysis for Accelerating Conversion of Intangibles. *Journal of Intellectual capital, 9*(1), 5-24.

Broadbent, M. (2002). *CIO Futures—Lead with Effective Governance*. Paper presented at the ICA 36th Conference, Singapore.

Campbell, P. (2005). A COBIT Primer. Retrieved 4/1/08, from http://www.itgi. org/

Carr, N. G. (2004). *Does IT matter? information technology and the corrosion of competitive advantage*: Harvard Business School Press, Boston.

ITIL. (2007). *Service Strategy*. The Stationery Office (TSO), London.

ITIL.org. (2007). *Information technology Infrastructure Library*. Retrieved 9/12/07, from http://www.itil.org.uk/

Lock Lee, L. (2005). Balancing business process with business practice for organizational advantage. *Journal of Knowledge management, 9*(1), 29-41.

Lock Lee, L. (2007). What's Wrong With Current Systems Development Methods? *A Case for Value network analysis*. Retrieved 5/1/08, from http://www.value-networks.com/Articles/VNA%20&%20Systems%20Analysis.pdf

Nolan, R., & McFarlan, F. W. (2005). Information technology and the Board of Directors. *Harvard Business Review, October*.

PriceWaterhouseCoopers. (2007). *IT Governance in Practice: Insight from leading CIOs*. Retrieved 4/1/08, from http://www.pwc.com/extweb/pwcpublications. nsf/docid/790d48a25a3505008525726d00567783

Weill, P. (2004). Don't Just Lead, Govern: How Top-Performing Firms Govern IT. *MIS Quarterly Executive, 8*(1).

Williams, P. (2007). *IT Governance Roundtable*. Retrieved 4/1/08, from http://www. itgi.org/

Chapter X
The Global
IT Outsourcing Market:
A Network Perspective

The IT outsourcing market was launched in the early 1990s with a number of mega outsourcing deals between major organisations and global IT service providers. As indicated in the introductory chapter, while the growth in IT outsourcing has stabilised, the level of outsourcing has been sustained. The nature of outsourcing has evolved however, to a situation where multisourcing is now nearly "a given". Deal sizes have contracted along with average deal terms. This chapter will initially take a closer look at the extent of networking in the global IT markets. Novel market research techniques are used to discover relationship centric intelligence, typically missing from traditional market analyses. This will be followed by a section on networks spanning the client/provider interface, looking at how network structures can enhance the client provider relationship. The client provider interface is often governed through formal structures and roles. This analysis provides some insight into the potential negative impacts of relying solely on this style of governance. Finally, the topic of innovation, and innovation networks, will be addressed. Injecting innovation into the IT sourcing relationship has proven somewhat elusive given the twin objectives of cost reduction through implementing standard IT infrastructures and processes, while at the same time creating new business opportunities through the innovative use of IT. The network perspective provides new insight into this conundrum and some avenues for profitable change.

THE EVOLUTION OF THE GLOBAL IT INDUSTRY

When one reads the many accounts of the evolution of the IT industry, it is common to be following the fortunes of the major players of the time; IBM, Control Data, Hewlett Packard, Unisys, Digital Equipment, Data General, EDS, CSC, Oracle, Microsoft, SAP, Yahoo, Google, eBay and the list continues. In the early years of the industry, hardware manufacturers dominated the headlines. As hardware became more commoditised, it was the software and services firms that came to the fore, with many of the major equipment vendors disappearing or having to transform to software and service companies, as IBM so successfully did from the late 1980s. The current Internet Age has seen the emergence of the Internet Company, whose market valuations are now beginning to exceed those of their predecessor industry leading firms, as had happened in the past with the movement from hardware to software and services. Traditional market research on the IT industry is focused on revenues and market shares. While profitability is important in the fast paced IT industry, revenue growth is often seen as a leading indicator of future success.

Figure 71 provides an example of a revenue focused analysis of the global IT outsourcing industry. The charts show the value of existing outsourcing contracts as at the end of 2007, as identified from the Datamonitor IT contracts data base. As at this time there are nearly $US900 billion in outsourcing contracts in place globally. IBM Global Services was a clear market leader, followed by EDS and CSC. The distribution showing the number of contracts that each provider has for generating the revenue stated provides some insight into the strategies that they are adopting. One might infer that firms with higher average revenue/contracts, have a more targeted sales force than those with many contracts generating smaller levels of revenue.

What is missing from the traditional approaches to market research is that it provides only limited insight into how each firm is achieving its results. Industry trends toward more specialisation and higher levels of partnering, suggest that new ways of analysing markets centred on relationship networks, are required. Information on alliances and joint ventures are regularly reported, but the use of this information in understanding the dynamics of the industry is rarely forthcoming. Chapter V provided an in depth example of how the network of relationships between IT vendors could constitute a tangible resource in the form of Corporate Social Capital (SC), which in turn can have a tangible impact on their overall performance. The IT market place however, includes clients as well as vendors, which collectively constitute a network which is the IT market place. The increased interconnectedness in all markets was previously addressed in reviewing "theories of the firm" in Chapter III. By viewing a market from a networks or relationship perspective, new insight is available to those looking to thrive in an increasingly networked market place.

Figure 71. Traditional market analysis for the global IT outsourcing service market

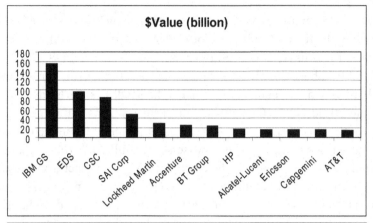

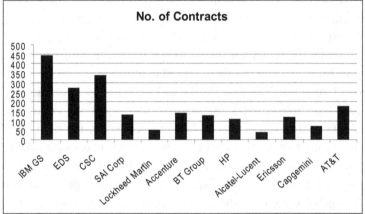

The next section provides a market analysis of the global IT outsourcing market from a network perspective. The new insights available from this form of analysis are highlighted.

THE GLOBAL IT OUTSOURCING MARKET FROM A NETWORK PERSPECTIVE

Relationships in the IT market place can take many forms, from the formal joint venture partnership, to very informal joint marketing initiatives. The research described in Chapter V identified joint venture relationships between vendors that were gleaned from the business press. These relationships were seen as serious enough to attract media attention, but also informal enough to enable them to be dismantled and new ones formed.

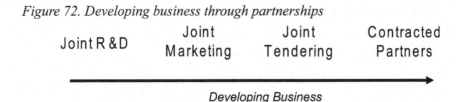

Figure 72. Developing business through partnerships

If one follows the typical progress of a partnership driven business development cycle, as illustrated in Figure 72, one can see that leverage can be gained at each point of the cycle. Pooling R&D resources can provide the complementary skill bases that are required to achieve breakthrough innovations. Joint sales and marketing means more resources and therefore further reach across disparate market sectors. Joint tendering can lower the cost for the individual firms, which is particularly important for major government contracts. Often partnering is the only means for smaller firms to be part of major contracts. Finally, as indicated by the trend to multisourcing, it is the case now that the majority of outsourcing contracts will have multiple suppliers.

To illustrate the extent to which the IT market place is becoming networked, data on "contracted relationships" identified from Datamonitor's IT contracts data base, will be used. It should be appreciated that the relationships identified here would only be a fraction of those that exist across the market, given that the data is limited to contracted relationships only i.e. a contractual relationship between vendors and a client and between the vendors themselves, where multisourcing is in place.

The following network maps have been established by identifying contractual links. A link is formed between the prime vendor nominated on the contract, and the client. Further links are established between the prime vendor and any subcontracted vendors. The network maps are presented cumulatively on a year by year basis to indicate evolutionary patterns.

Figure 73 identifies the early years of IT outsourcing. Only contracts valued at over $US1 million are included in the data. Up to and including 1996 only six IT vendors were identified from the data. Even at this early stage, United Health Care and the HM Revenue and Customs were practicing multisourcing, using two providers for their outsourced services. In 1997 many new clients for outsourcing have been identified with a few additional service providers. From this point, the subsequent years show an escalation in the density of the networks as illustrated in Figure 74, as new clients begin to outsource services and new providers enter the market.

The ensuing growth in IT outsourcing and multisourcing makes it challenging to keep track of who is partnering with whom. Therefore SNA techniques are the method of choice for analysing large and complex relationship networks. While originally designed for sociological applications and mapping personal relation-

Figure 73. Outsourcing networks: The early years

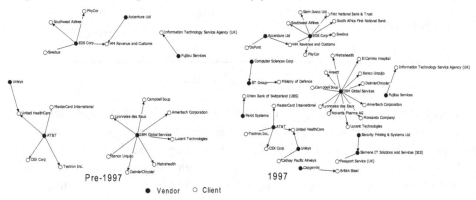

Pre-1997

1997

● Vendor   ○ Client

Figure 74. The increasingly networked IT market place

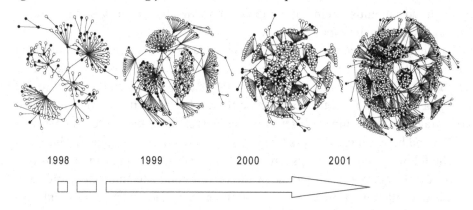

1998   1999   2000   2001

ships, SNA techniques scale well for analysing relationship networks in complex market places. The visualisation facilities offered by SNA can provide some powerful pictures as to what is happening across a network, though clearly there are limits when the data stores become large, as evidenced by the network plots of the IT market for 2002 and beyond, which are therefore not shown here. The existence of network measures for centrality, as described in Chapter VI, are however still applicable, even for very large networks. It is therefore possible to use such measures to identify those firms that are preferentially located in the network, in terms of being centrally connected or in brokerage positions. With the addition of other attribute data like financial soundness and human capital, one could create a Corporate SC measure for each firm in the network, and therefore begin to predict the likely success of these firms.

ISSUES WITH CRM AND BI SYSTEMS

Customer relationship management (CRM) and Business Intelligence (BI) systems have traditionally been held up as the technology solutions for managing relationships with customers and identifying internal business enhancement or improvement opportunities. Both solutions are data repository centric, meaning that the value from such CRM and BI solutions is meant to be derived from analysing large volumes of transactional data. The large IT infrastructures required to support such activities, and the sophistication of the software required to analyse and filter "intelligence" from such repositories has often resulted in these systems becoming expensive legacies with questionable ROIs. In fact the business literature is filled with stories of failed CRM and BI implementations, with much of the failure being attributed to implementation issues.

If one steps back to reflect on what the core purpose of a CRM system is, the "R" stands for Relationship, not Record, which most CRM systems appear to focus on. Recording customer transactions may be an important function for tracking buying patterns of customers on an individual or sector basis. But how much does it really tell you about the value and quality of the relationship you might have with a customer? Are they only staying with you because there are currently few alternatives? Are their buying patterns being fuelled by things other than their love for your products or services? Are they actually spending more with some of your competitors? In other words there is a plethora of customer intelligence that one might like to have that is only modestly supported by the CRM repository. Of course the repository is also only historical and its connection to future buying intentions could be fragile at best. Additionally, it tells you nothing about what your competitors or other organisations are doing that might impact on your customer relationships.

For BI systems the same issues are present. A firm's operational transactions have the potential for generating more data than can reasonably be analysed by even the most sophisticated software systems. Again if one steps back and reflects on the core purpose of a BI system it is about gaining new intelligence on business improvement opportunities. No doubt having data on internal operations can and does inform business improvement opportunities for the firm, but is there an over-reliance on such historical information to generate such business improvement intelligence? Repository based BI systems are best suited to the parts of the business that tend to be routine or process centric. The basis of popular business improvement frameworks like Six Sigma and Lean Manufacturing is in driving out process variation from business routines. But what about the less process oriented activities that a business participates in? Areas like new product design, business planning, marketing and research and development, are major activities that firms undertake that don't lend themselves to repository based BI solutions and statistical based improvement mechanisms.

For both CRM and BI solutions that rely on large data repositories the key issue is understanding the knowledge or intelligence that can be gained from them. From a knowledge perspective it is often the unique tacit knowledge that a firm formulates from its intelligence gathering activities that result in competitive advantage or unique improvement opportunities. Such intelligence is usually gathered through relationships or "connections" more so than inferred from "collections". Understanding relationships of this type therefore does not require the expense and complexity of a huge data base. From a technology perspective an investment in helping people meet and collaborate may in fact be far more effective in intelligence gathering, be it about customers or internal operations. These issues are addressed more comprehensively in the following chapter. The following sections provide examples of a different style of intelligence gathering, one that is focused directly on relationships.

MARKET RESEARCH USING NETWORK ANALYSIS TECHNIQUES

Network analysis techniques like Social Network Analysis (SNA), are now being increasingly used for business applications like market research. As an analytical technique, SNA shares many of the same attributes as other traditional data driven market research techniques (Green & Tull, 1978). Similar to other data centred analytical techniques, SNA relationship data can be filtered to enable more specific analyses to be conducted. For example, if one is interested in the major relationships in the industry, one could choose to select only those contractual relationships worth over a given dollar value threshold.

Figure 75 shows current outsourcing contracts worth over \$500million. The network shown is therefore indicative of the larger end of the scale and also enables some visual interpretation that would not be possible if a lower threshold had been chosen. This analysis identifies the clusters that form around the market leading IT outsource service providers IBM GS, EDS, CSC and SAI Corp. It also identifies BT Group and the US Army as the biggest multisourcers, by both the number of vendors used and the size of their contracts. There are multiple uses for an analysis like this. For a smaller vendor with a particular market sector target, they could look to see which combinations of firms are currently servicing their target firms' outsourcing needs in their sector and then devise an alliance strategy for positioning themselves favorably with these firms. For the buyer, one could look at vendors who naturally cluster together, who have successfully worked out how to work together. By sourc-

Figure 75. Global IT outsourcing relationship network (Contracts > $500mill.)

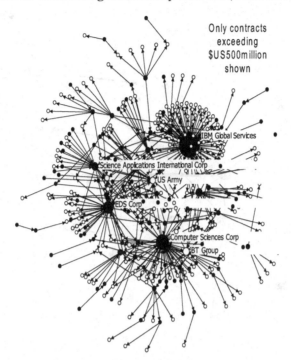

ing from pre-allianced clusters the buyer is therefore able to avoid the potential governance headaches that might arise from competition between "best of breed" selected providers. It is also useful to know which clients may have successfully used a combination of providers previously and are therefore able to provide references for the "partnership" as well as the individual providers.

An example of how SNA techniques can be used to identify common "buying patterns" amongst client firms is to use an affinity analysis. The affinity analysis infers a relationship between firms based on who they sell to or buy from.

Figure 76 shows the affinity network or vendors as drawn from the data set of contracts greater than $500million. The thickness of the links identifies the degree to which the vendors share common clients. An interesting observation from Figure 76 is the strong affinity between IBM and EDS, the two leading IT outsourcing providers, and one would think, fierce competitors. Further investigation would discover that IBM and EDS have many common clients who rely on IBM's IT infrastructure management services but also EDS's business process outsourcing services as a complement. Buying firms have clearly preferred to use IBM and EDS's services in a complementary arrangement than sole sourcing to either firm. IBM and EDS in true "co-opetition" style have also embraced the arrangements.

Figure 76. Affinity network of vendor firms

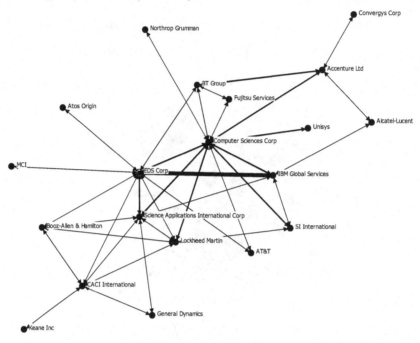

Figure 77. Affinity network of common buyers

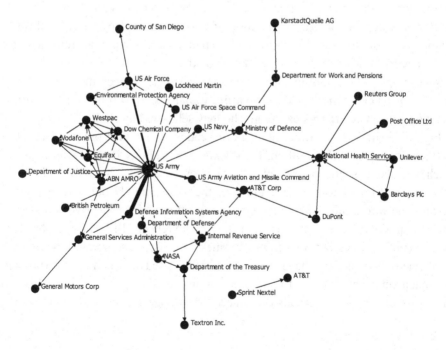

The affinity analysis can also be used to look for common buying patterns between firms, as illustrated in Figure 77. The map shows those firms who tend to go to the same firms for procuring their IT services.

The thickness of the links again reflects the degree of common vendor usage. As one would expect there are strong common vendors amongst the defence buyers, which is to be expected, given the specialisation of that market sector. For firms considering their multisourcing strategy, the network map provides the names of firms from which referrals could be sought. Is there a reason why particular firms buy from particular clusters of vendors? For example what common needs do Westpac, Vodafone, Dow Chemicals, Equifax and ABN AMRO have that would have them cluster together? Are your needs similar to theirs?

In summary, SNA techniques applied at a market level can open up a whole new level of enquiry for market intelligence. Complemented by traditional market research products, Network Analysis can start to address how firms are creating value, or otherwise, through their relationship networks. Understanding the interdependence between companies in the market place can inform a vendor's business development strategy or a buyer's procurement strategy. As firms move from situations of relative self sufficiency to a market place today, where no firm can hope to survive on such a strategy, the need to be able to effectively analyse relationship networks will become critical.

Having looked at the IT market at the industry level the next section will focus on an individual vendor-client relationship. In this section the relationship will be analysed from a networks perspective and will be conducted by way of a case study.

LOOKING INSIDE A VENDOR-CLIENT RELATIONSHIP: A CASE STUDY

The objective of this study was to analyse the dynamics of the relationships across the vendor, account team and client boundaries, looking for opportunities for maximising value through optimal relationship structures. The study made use of Organisational network analysis (ONA) techniques to achieve its objectives. The outsourcing relationship structure revolved around a vendor account team which acted as the single source of contact for the client, as shown in Figure 78. An objective of the analysis was to look beyond the formal structure of the relationship to the often hidden human relationships both between the vendor and the client and within the vendor account team itself.

Vendor staff were surveyed asking them to nominate those individuals they interacted with in doing their day to day job, and also the people who they believe would help them do a better job if they were able to have more of their time.

Figure 78. Outsourcing relationship structure

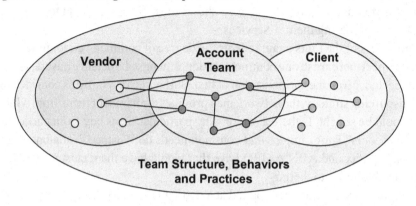

Figure 79. Vendor staff interactions

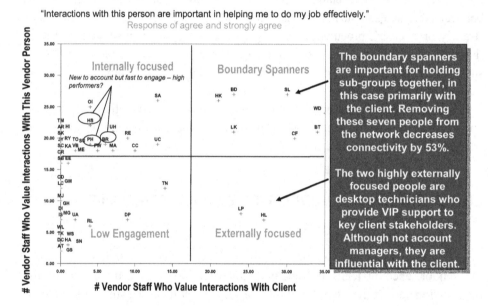

The results showed that the density of vendor account team and client interactions was relatively high. However, the client relationship was also critically dependent on a handful of "boundary spanners". These staff members were also the most sought after by both vendor staff and client staff. Interestingly enough the other staff members critical to the client relationship were two desktop technicians who provide a VIP service for the client executive. The personal networking elements of the survey showed that most of the staff did not reach out beyond their immediate work colleagues in developing work based relationships. This potentially could have the effect of limiting the introduction of new ideas or innovations available from other areas of the vendor or beyond.

The recommendation from the study indicated that additional coverage and succession planning would be needed for these critical staff. A "quick win" for the account team from the ONA was the organising of coverage for one of the critical boundary spanners who was about to go on extended leave. The analysis was able to identify the specific relationships that this officer maintained, and then to suggest which other officers were best placed to cover her relationships while she was on leave. The other recommendation was to more explicitly leverage the tight client relationship that the VIP desktop technicians had with the senior client staff. By encouraging these technicians to act as information brokers, the vendor could both gain some informal intelligence on senior client sentiment of some very senior client staff members, while at the same time informally communicate some of the key messages that the vendor wants to deliver to the client as a means of informal reinforcement.

VALUE NETWORKS AND THE OUTSOURCING RELATIONSHIP

The previous case study demonstrated the use of ONA techniques to look inside an outsourcing relationship at the individual level. This case study illustrates the use of Value network analysis (VNA) to look at the relationship at the "Role" level and the eventual creation of a Partnership Scorecard to manage and monitor the relationship over time. The methods for VNA and the Partnership Scorecard were described in detail in Chapter IX and will now be illustrated by an actual case study.

Mike is the CIO of a medium sized industrial firm. His firm had outsourced the provision of IT services to a major multi-national outsourcing firm. The outsourcing arrangement had now been in place for seven years and therefore his own internal IS team and the outsourced providers had had ample time to learn how to work with each other. To Mike, however, the relationship always appeared on a "knife edge". For 90% of the time the relationship was cordial, with each side of the partnership appearing to work well together. However it was the other 10%, when something had gone wrong, when the relationship deteriorated into finger pointing and accusations.

The providers were always somewhat puzzled by this as their performance to contracted service levels had always been reasonably good. They could not understand how unhappy their client could be when their contracted performance was always more than adequate.

Mike had been introduced to Value network analysis at a recent seminar. The added focus on intangibles really resonated with Mike and he was convinced that the source of his ills was in the intangible, rather than the tangible aspects of his relationship with the outsourcer. With the agreement of his outsourcing provider he invited consultants in to run a VNA workshop across the partnership with the intent of developing a better mechanism for measuring, monitoring and improving the partnership performance. The mechanism would incorporate the intangible aspects of the partnership. Participants were drawn from both sides of the partnership, representing the key roles. It quickly became apparent that little conflict existed on the tangible value flows. Both sides were able to easily identify the tangible contractual flows for the VNA map and were anxious to get on to identifying the important intangible value flows.

At this stage the facilitators felt it wise to break up the participants into organisational teams so they could separately identify the intangible value flows that they both generated and expected from the other roles. On bringing the groups back together again they were able to compare each others' perceptions as to what was important or not to each other. Interestingly enough there was not a lot of commonality in perceptions. As Mike had suspected, it was the intangible value flows that proved to be the area where the largest disconnection occurred between his team and the outsource providers.

Figure 80 provides an illustration of the Value Network map between the key roles in Mike's and the Vendor's teams, showing only the identified intangible delivery flows . When assessing the intangible value flows identified by the two groups, it was not surprising to find some significant perceptual difference, therefore exposing where the real issues were in the partnership.

By way of illustration a particular intangible flow that Mike's team had identified as critical was the "visibility of its desktop support staff in the field". Mike's team had set a requirement for the provider to keep them informed of the whereabouts of each field staff member on a day to day basis. The provider was puzzled by this as they felt that their help desk processes were such that if there was a problem they would be able to have staff on site as contracted. They felt that Mike wanted to meddle in their business and therefore they were resistant. For Mike however, the critical intangible was how he was perceived by his own business clients. The desktop support staff was the most visible "face" of the IT function to his client base. Even small glitches in service had the potential to have large reputational impacts on himself and his staff. The issue was not Mike wanting to know where all the field staffs were, but one of protecting his hard won reputation with his own business clients.

On the other side of the partnership, one outsourcing provider role identified an intangible flow related to "having confidence to let them get on with the job". This

Figure 80. Value network showing intangible value deliverables

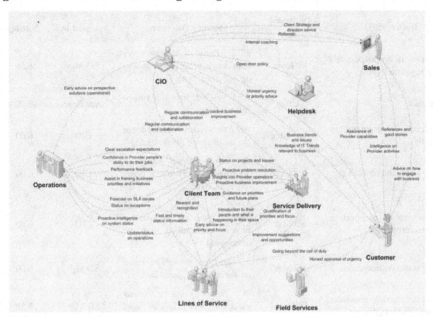

issue appeared to be that some members of Mike's team were micro-managing and not being consistent with their provision of business priorities. Like Mike's need to protect his reputation, the provider had a need also to have his reputation for professionalism respected. In both situations failures in process, be it a field service process or an IT request process exposed sensitivities around intangibles and often misguided remedies. However, by framing the intangible value flows in terms of the real intangibles like reputation protection/enhancement or confidence in doing the job, the right measures could be put in place and corrective actions for process issues more accurately focused.

After the workshop, the facilitators arranged a follow on survey of the participants. The value deliverables were framed as statements and the participants were asked to provide a rating on their current assessment of performance along with a rating of the relative criticality of the deliverable to them. The participants were also asked to provide a rating of cost and/or risk involved in providing the value deliverables for which they were accountable. A simple formula was designed to rank the high potential value deliverables based on perceived criticality, perceived cost/risk to deliver and the current performance gap. The results of the survey analysis showed that 18 of the top 20 high value opportunities were related to intangibles. The opportunities were equally balanced between Mike's team and the outsourcing

Table 13. Partnership scorecard assessment survey results

Deliverables	Delivered by:	Survey Question	Assessed by:	Rating
Confidence in Vendor people's ability to do their jobs	IS Team	IS Team demonstrates confidence in us to be able to do our work	SO Mgr	6.50
Referrals	CIO	CIO regularly provides valued referrals to us	Acc Exec	6.00
Confidence in accuracy in invoicing	Acc Exec	Acc Exec gives me confidence in the accuracy of the invoicing	CIO	6.00
Vendor goals and objectives	Acc Exec	Acc Exec keeps me well appraised on Vendor's goals and objectives	CIO	6.00
Early advice on prospective solutions (project)	SD Mgr	SD Mgr provides me with early advice on prospective project solutions as they are developing	CIO	6.00
Update/status on operations	SO Mgr	SO Mgr keeps me well informed on the status of operations	SD Mgr	6.00
Assist in framing business priorities and initiatives	IS Team	IS Team provides clear guidance on priorities and initiatives	SO Mgr	5.50
Performance feedback	IS Team	IS Team provides regular feedback on our performance	SO Mgr	5.50

partner, meaning that both sides of the partnership had quite specific and equally distributed accountabilities for improving the relationship. Table 13 lists the top 10 intangible value deliverable opportunities. The majority of the opportunities were identified as minimal cost/risk to deliver, but would provide high perceived value to the receptor when compared to current performance.

Mike was happy with the outcome and the new insights it provided about the partnership. A team review of the results endorsed the findings as consistent with the perceptions of the participants, providing a solid platform from which to move forward in the relationship. Mike moved quickly to bed down the progress made in the form of a new Partnership Scorecard for himself and his outsourcing partners.

The above case study identifies many of the intangible elements required to achieve an excellent outsourcing relationship. One of the themes identified in the value analysis was the perceived value of the pro-active contribution of service improvement ideas or innovation to the partnership. In Chapter VI the important role of the broker in the innovation and diffusion of good ideas was highlighted. The above case study identifies some of the critical roles that potentially could act as brokering roles into the partnership. In the case study presented previously on vendor—client relationships, one can see that individual brokers have been formally identified through the use of ONA. Some or all of these brokers are therefore well positioned to act as innovation catalysts in the relationship. The following section takes a closer look at how innovation can be best achieved through the use of innovation networks and a networking perspective of innovation.

MAKING INNOVATION NETWORKS WORK

Working on the premise that successful innovation is underpinned by social networks, it is useful to explore the topic of innovation from a network perspective. Innovation is defined here as "good ideas, implemented", meaning that unless an idea is formally implemented and contributing new value, it is still just an idea. The three E's of innovation: Exploration, Engagement and Exploitation is developed here both as a categorisation of the innovation process and to also provide some insight as to why success has proven to be so elusive to so many firms and organisations.

There is much more to the "small world" effect than the catchy Walt Disney tune "it's a small world after all". Naturally occurring social networks show distinctive characteristics that are loosely described as the "small world effect". Essentially the effect shows clusters or cliques of highly connected individuals, some of whom are more central than others. The connections or "ties" are described as either strong or weak, reflecting the differences between say, a strong friendship and a casual acquaintance. The clusters or cliques are then often connected through individuals who share membership of two or more cliques. These individuals are called brokers or bridges and become the main conduit for information or knowledge flows between the clusters.

The figure above shows a typical small world effect with four clusters with a combination of weak (dotted) and strong (hard) ties connecting them. There exist two competing, yet complementary theories describing the so called SC of networks.

Figure 81. Small world effect

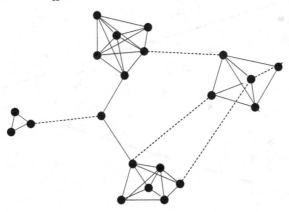

The theory of closure (Coleman, 1990) suggests that high SC exists inside the tight knit clusters where trustful relationships can be established through regular and frequent interaction. Conversely, the theory of structural holes (R. S. Burt, 1992) suggests that maximum benefit lies in bridging the gaps between the clusters, called "structural holes".

In support of the argument for bridging "structural holes", empirical research has shown that the probability of an individual having his or her idea accepted by management is inversely correlated with the density of ties that the individual has. That is, members of tight clusters have a very low probability of having an idea accepted by management and in fact have a low probability of even voicing a new idea. Conversely, less constrained individuals have a much higher probability of having their ideas positively reviewed by management (R. Burt, 2003).

On the surface the 3 E's looks like a straight forward linear process with stage gates and ultimately 100% success. In practice, reality is far messier than this. Social networks are neither linear nor mechanistic. Feedback loops between phases will occur as brokers travel to and fro between exploration, engagement and exploitation. However, networks can be assessed and orchestrated to an extent, to maximize your chances of innovation success. The schematic below describes the innovation process in terms of networks. The exploration process is seen as the environmental scan for new ideas, with the points of intersection between clusters or cliques representing separate disciplines or cultures, seen as the most fertile areas for exploration. The role of the broker or bridge between clusters is seen as critical to the exploration process. The engagement process is where the informality of the exploration process meets the formality of the management hierarchy, required to fund the progres-

Figure 82. The three E's of innovation

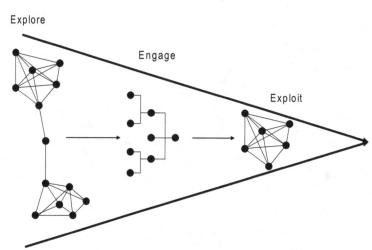

sion of prospective ideas. The success or otherwise of the engagement process will rely critically on the influencing skills of the brokers/bridges. Having survived the management filter prospective ideas now need to be developed and implemented in practice. This exploitation process relies on close collaboration and cooperation of exploitation teams as ideas are implemented, adapted and fine tuned to meet the demands of a real world environment.

In terms of the IT function, there is a key role that the IT Governance Committee can play in the "Engagement" process. It is often the case that IT providers and clients have good access to new ideas either through their own resources or the commercial IT market research firms and consulting groups. It is also often the case that through the use of service management frameworks like ITIL or COBIT that formal exploitation processes are well tuned and capable of implementing a new idea or invention should the organisation commit to it. The missing link in the innovation process is more often than not the engagement process, where the worlds of explore and exploit need to be fused together. This is a role and an opportunity for the IT Governance team. It would however require a focus of IT Governance on value creation and over compliance if this is to be achieved.

IMPLICATIONS FOR IT GOVERNANCE AND MULTISOURCING

The preceding sections have been very much about relationships and relationship networks at both the market and firm level. Good governance and effective multisourcing is predicated on good relationships. Historically much of the intelligence gathering required for good governance and multisourcing has relied on repository based technologies exemplified by current CRM and BI offerings. It has been argued in this chapter that large data repository based technologies are not the most efficient or effective means for forming intelligence about relationships. In fact by relying largely on informational resources only to inform intelligence on relationships, one may be committing the organisations to the expensive development and upkeep of these resources for very little gain.

The techniques identified in this chapter focus directly on the relationship aspects. They can provide a richness of intelligence on relationships far beyond what can be gleaned from CRM or BI systems at modest investment. A shift in emphasis from repository technology and "collections" approaches to collaboration technology and "connections" is likely to have benefits all round for achieving effective governance and multisourcing arrangements.

SUMMARY AND CONCLUSIONS

This chapter began by taking a network view of the global IT outsourcing market. Through the use of SNA tools, the growing interconnectedness of actors in the sector became clearly evident. Looking at contractual relationships alone, SNA was able to visually illustrate how complex the sector has become in terms of relationships between vendors and clients and vendors with other vendors. Clients were also shown to be interconnected through common vendors. Once one adds non-contractual relationships to the mix, one can only imagine the complexity of the interconnections and relationships that exist within the market place. Given the rapidity with which the interconnectedness of the market has developed, it is little wonder that traditional market research techniques that are centred on individual actors, have limited utility in the networked market place. The use of SNA as a novel market research tool focuses on not only the individual actors, but also the relationships between them. It therefore has the promise to open up new fields of view for market exploration and analysis activities.

Having established the power of the network perspective, when viewing the IT market place, the next section looked at a specific case study of what the character of a vendor's social networks might be within an IT outsourcing relationship. Through the use of SNA/ONA it was shown that there existed only a small number of key brokers for the relationship with the client. Some of these brokers were in account management roles, where these roles have been institutionalised as brokering roles. That staffs in particular, were identified as overloaded and therefore potentially acting more as gatekeepers than true brokers. The VIP desktop technicians who were designated to service senior client staff were also identified as key brokers and powerfully positioned from a network's perspective. Like many outsourcing relationships, the vendor was struggling to deliver on the innovation expectations of the client. The networking elements however were in place. The final section provided a schema for how innovation could best be achieved. The "Explore, Engage, Exploit" or 3 E's framework was described as a guiding platform for achieving innovation across networks and specifically the client/vendor divide.

The Information technology Services sector has often been described as being at the forefront of business innovation, mostly driven by the technical products of its membership. The most recent "trend" which the sector has facilitated the introduction of is Web 2.0. Web 2.0 is differentiated from its predecessors by its increased focus on facilitating collaboration over simply publishing content. This move is most evidenced by the growth in Social Networking software like Linked-in, Myspace and Facebook. The next chapter explores the impact of technology trends on IT Governance, moving on to focus on the most recent developments in this field and the impact that Web 2.0 might have on IT Governance and Corporate SC in multisourced environments.

REFERENCES

Burt, R. (2003). Structural holes and good ideas. *American Journal of Sociology?*

Burt, R. S. (1992). *Structural holes*: Cambridge: Harvard University Press.

Coleman, J. (1990). *Foundations of social theory.* Boston, MA: Harvard Business.

Green, P., & Tull, D. (1978). *Research for marketing decisions.* Englewood Cliffs, NJ: Prentice-Hall.

Chapter XI
Technology, Web 2.0 and Beyond

Thomas Friedman's best selling book entitled *The World is Flat* (Friedman, 2005) brought into focus the impact that technology was having not only in the world of work, but increasingly in our personal lives. The division between our world of work and home is becoming increasingly blurred. Much of this transition can be attributed to technology advances, particularly those emanating from the Information technology sector (ITS). The ITS can claim to have a significant impact on the way we work and increasingly, the way we live, despite its relatively short history. Up until the 1980s the impact of IT had been mostly felt in the business world. Routine and often tedious manually executed business processes lent themselves well to automation with the help of IT. With the widespread introduction of the personal computer in the 1980s, computers were brought into our homes and hence into our personal lives for the first time. Up until the 1980s corporate IT managers were only concerned with the technology that existed within the confines of their own firms. The development of computer programs was a specialist task. The available range of hardware and software suppliers was far less than it is today. The task of IT Governance was largely limited to selecting a vendor and dealing with the complexity of the technology. Business applications were custom built and therefore the need still existed to understand the business requirements and translate those into IT solutions. However, the processes to be automated were usually quite transparent and the business clients were happy to have their manual processes sped up through automation without significant changes to the process itself.

The major challenges for IT Governance and the sourcing of IT came once the technology had moved into our homes. The technical world of the IT worker was opened up to those without the specialist training needed to work in the field. Admittedly the early adopters of home computing were usually the IT workers themselves, and therefore still notionally under the umbrella of the IT Governance regime. However, as the technology became more within reach of even modestly educated people, workers who had not grown up within the IT function could start to understand the mechanics of IT. The ubiquitous electronic spreadsheet became the systems development tool for the masses. IT Governance regimes now had a challenge on their hands. For the first time, IT executives were being questioned about why technologies freely available in the home market at commodity prices were either not available or exorbitantly expensive in the workplace.

The commoditisation of IT reached a peak with the advent of the Internet and the World Wide Web, leading up to the so called dotcom boom and consequent bust at the turn of the century. This technology alone is credited with facilitating the major changes that have occurred across the world's economies, as articulated in Friedman's book. What the World Wide Web enabled was for the average citizen to publish their own content to the world. Together with Internet connectivity, the business world was also transformed, enabling businesses large and small to transact business globally without the sophistication previously required to conduct global trade. The web facilities spoken of here are now referred to as Web 1.0 or the first generation of the World Wide Web. For the large part Web 1.0 is a publishing facility. Web 2.0 is the so called second generation of web applications. Web 2.0 is not an official release of a set of enhanced software, but a notional signpost that web technology was now delivering on some significantly new and powerful functionality. That functionality is largely related to people to people collaboration. Tim Berners-Lee is a critic of the terminology of Web 2.0, reminding people of his original intent for the World Wide Web:

The Web is more a social creation than a technical one. I designed it for a social effect—to help people work together." (Berners-Lee, 1999, p.123)

That said, despite the initial aspirations of Berners-Lee in the early 1990s, it is only now that many of these aspirations are being realised. The most important of these is the facilities the Web now provides for people to not only work together, but socialise in a way that had previously not been possible. Web 2.0 is forcing individuals to think seriously about their work/life mix. From an IT Governance and sourcing perspective, the ability to control what staff do with IT and what IT they choose to use is continuously diminishing. In this chapter the impact of the technology trends implied by web 2.0 and beyond, on IT Governance and sourcing will be addressed.

The remainder of this chapter will provide a description of the evolution of IT developments through to the introduction of Web 2.0 technology, as it relates to IT Governance and sourcing strategies. Automating business processes has been the "bread and butter" IT application. Business process management technologies are still being actively developed to push the limits of business process automation. Today however, tacit knowledge intensive business practices do not lend themselves to automation. The role of technology therefore becomes a symbiotic sharing of responsibilities between the human worker and IT technology. The changing technology needs required to support knowledge based business practices will be addressed here. The final part of the chapter identifies new measurement technologies appropriate for managing in a networked business environment. These emerging "Net Mining" techniques can be used to provide the necessary business monitoring and intelligence capabilities with networks, that data warehousing techniques provide for conventional business processes.

EVOLUTION TO WEB 2.0 AND BEYOND AND ITS IMPACT ON IT GOVERNANCE AND SOURCING

The evolution to Web 2.0 and beyond is characterised by a movement from a more structured business environment to one which is less structured, less routine and therefore less predictable. IT developments have now removed many of the manual tasks that workers in a more industrial age had to endure, leaving the more knowledge based tasks to today's workforce. While the focus on business processes has not diminished, these so called processes are now much more ill-defined, making automation success elusive. Arguably such processes should not be called processes at all, but more accurately labeled "business practices", to reflect the large knowledge based content found within them (Lock Lee, 2005). The next section addresses the process/practice divide and the technical and governance issues that it promotes.

BUSINESS PROCESS VS. BUSINESS PRACTICE

The concepts of codification, explicit knowledge, tacit knowledge, routine work, processes and practices are not new, but still engender a degree of confusion through their different interpretations. It is important to delineate "process" from "practice" if one is to attempt to operationalise them. "Process" is strongly associated with concepts like "explicit knowledge", "routine" and "codification" while "practice" has similarly strong associations with "tacit knowledge", "heuristics" and "non-codification". Three themes can be traced back to Simon's theory of "bounded rationality" (Simon, 1979).

This theory identifies the limitations within which managers can employ rational decision-making techniques. Rational decision-making implies an ability to make explicit the "process" of decision-making. Outside the bounds of rationality, managers will rely on intuition and emotion to guide their decision-making (Simon, 1987).

The first theme traces Simon's work through to the field of artificial intelligence and knowledge based systems. Within this field the CYC project, in development since 1984, is aimed at developing a system for storing commonsense knowledge and stands out as the most ambitious attempt to codify knowledge (Lenat, 1995). Identifying standard means for codifying knowledge evolved during the late 1980's supported by the European ESPRIT collaborative research program (Hickman *et al.*, 1989), though these efforts have stagnated in favour of addressing knowledge from a more holistic perspective i.e. Knowledge management (KM). The KM pioneers viewed knowledge from an organisational perspective, in many cases making the argument for sharing tacit knowledge through socialisation techniques e.g. Communities of Practice, rather than blindly attempting to codify tacit knowledge within large knowledge bases for sharing (Allee, 1997; Lesser & Prusak, 1999; K. E. Sveiby, 1997).

The second theme could be called the business process theme. Nelson and Winter (1982), in their work on the evolutionary theory of economic change, refer to Simon's work in speaking of routine as the distinctive package of economic capabilities and coordinating functions that a firm possesses and can deploy in a repeatable fashion. For Nelson and Winter this includes the heuristic problem solving patterns of say a firm's R&D department. The linkage between Nelson and Winter's "routine" and the business process reengineering (BPR) phenomenon is more implied than explicit, with BPR promoting a focus on processes or routines that are core to businesses, removing all others that are deemed to be non value adding (Hammer & Champy, 1993). This position evolved to a finer articulation of classes of business processes e.g. identity or core processes, priority, mandatory or background processes (Keen, 1997). The terms "business process" and now "business process management" (BPM), have been loosely used to identify with just about every activity in which a firm participates. Zairi's (1997) examination of the literature has found that BPM is far from pervasive and is no more than structural changes, the use of systems such as EN ISO 9000 and the management of individual projects. Key features identified with a process were its predictable and definable inputs; a linear, logical sequence; a clearly definable set of activities; and a predictable and desired outcome.

The concept of process infers something that is definable, describable and repeatable. In the context of BPM, one must tighten the specification to the extent that the process must be describable in a standardised business process language and computationally executed to provide the expected outputs in a repeatable fashion. This tighter specification of process will similarly require a tightening of the associated terms of explicit knowledge, codification and routine. An important contribution of the recent BPM initiatives is the creation of standard languages to describe a business process in computer executable form e.g. BPML, BPEL. Languages like BPML provide a link between the typical process designer's flow charts and process maps and executable computer code (H. Smith & Fingar, 2002).

The third theme encompasses the dialogue around tacit, explicit and codified knowledge, which could arguably be seen as a pre-curser to the KM theme, but has been identified for individual treatment here. Cowan, David and Foray (2000) put forward an economist's skeptical argument that very little knowledge is inherently tacit and that its codification is simply an argument of a cost/benefit analysis. In proposing this argument, the authors engage in a discussion around articulation and codification, which converges on a view that what can be articulated, can be codified for economic benefit. Johnson, Lorenz, & Lundvall (2002) counter Cowan et al. specifically on the impracticality of the proposition on a number of fronts. The art of bicycling is used as an example of how attempts at both articulation and codification of the practice of bicycle riding would rarely be useful to the novice rider, even if it were economically viable (Johnson et al., 2002). Of course these economic arguments ignore the very real sociological issues present. Polanyi considered human knowledge from the premise that "we know more than we can tell" (Polanyi, 1967,p.4) with the natural extension that "we tell more than we can write down" (Snowden, 2002). Snowden adds the further heuristics that "knowledge can only be volunteered; it cannot be conscripted" and "we only know what we know when we need to know it" for managing knowledge, in contrast to the pure economic argument. Looking back to the BPM context, we could extend the analogy further to "we can write down more than we can write in BPML". Put succinctly, "we know far more than we can effectively automate", the gap arguably being attributable to business practice.

Some license has been taken in defining a business practice as the gap between what a human might know and use, and what knowledge can be effectively converted for execution within a BPM system. A conventional use of the term "business practice" might refer to a medical or legal practice that would encompass both the tacit understandings and experiences of the staff within the practice as well as the business processes that the firm conducts. The more limited usage of the term here is justified by the emphasis the term connotes around a distinctive expertise developed around extensive work experiences.

To summarise the above discussion the differences between process and practice can be characterised as shown in Table 14. It is accepted that both good process and good practice are essential for organisations to succeed. Seely Brown and Duguid (2000; Seely Brown & Duguid, 2001) have written extensively about the delicate balance that must be achieved between practice and process, between effectiveness and efficiency, between doing the right thing and doing it right. There are many commentators in the business process management field that would claim that everything

Table 14. Process vs. practice (Seely Brown & Duguid, 2000)

Process	Practice
The way tasks are organised	The way tasks are done
Routine	Spontaneous
Orchestrated	Improvised
Assumes Predictable Environment	Responds to a changing unpredictable environment
Relies on explicit knowledge	Relies on tacit knowledge
Linear	Network or web like

can be defined as a process, and as such accurately measured and managed. An underlying thesis of this review is that process will never totally replace practice. That is, there will always be critical business knowledge that will never be able to be made explicit and therefore we must invent ways to facilitate its use in its current tacit form. This is particularly the case in fast changing industries like biotechnology and information technology.

Process thinking has been present since the days of Frederick Taylor, the founder of scientific management principles. There is little argument that increasing the amount of knowledge that can successfully be articulated in the form of an explicit process will be beneficial. The important point in trying to achieve an appropriate balance between process and practice is to know which areas of tacit knowledge are the best candidates to try to make explicit, and which areas should not even be tried. Significant guidance can be taken from the Artificial Intelligence / Expert Systems discipline in this regard. What was learnt is that knowledge acquisition and representation can be particularly difficult. Some attempts have been made to develop a standardised method for knowledge acquisition and representation. Perhaps the best known of these is the KADS (Knowledge Acquisition Documentation and Structuring) methodology for developing knowledge based systems (Hickman et al., 1989), initially launched as a European Cooperative Research project. KADS could be viewed as the knowledge equivalent of BPM. Eventually the complexity of the different models required for KADS to be effective, worked against its larger scale adoption, and little is seen of it now.

Expert systems are currently the most sophisticated means for capturing tacit knowledge and making it explicit. Yet the majority of successful expert systems that have been deployed over the past 20 years have been in well defined and constrained areas like fault diagnosis, credit assessments, schedule checking and process control. They have largely failed in areas requiring some creative thinking like business planning, schedule creation, new product development etc. In summary, there are definitely limits to which one can practically make tacit knowledge explicit. These limits are both in terms of the ability to accurately represent the knowledge in explicit form and practical limits on the "knowledge engineering" time it would take to achieve it, if indeed it were possible.

Most business processes found within organisations are simply documented in "rules and procedures" manuals that are distributed with an expectation that they will be consistently understood and applied. For anything other than simple routine tasks this is a dangerous assumption. Firstly, for complex processes the business process designer has the challenge of accurately representing his or her tacit understanding of the business process intent in explicit written form. Secondly, those expected to perform the process will internalise their understanding of the written process, with significant scope for this understanding to be quite different to the intent of the designer. This is where KM processes can assist in developing a common understanding of the business process intent by connecting designers and performers of the business process. This socialisation process will eventually evolve into a common business practice around the business process.

Figure 83 shows two cycles of process / practice interaction. The inner cycle is the "shared understanding" cycle. Its starts with the process designer documenting the business process (tacit to explicit knowledge conversion). For a complex process one could argue that the document might represent less than 30% of what the designer actually understands about the process. The process performer is then expected to

Figure 83. Process / practice interaction

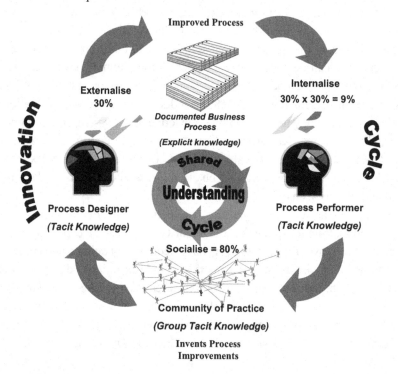

internalise this knowledge from the document (explicit to tacit conversion) that likewise for a complex process, might be 30% efficient. Therefore the degree of common understanding between process designer and process performer could be less than 10%. To improve the level of common understanding, socialisation (tacit to tacit knowledge transfer) processes are required. Common vehicles for these socialisation processes within organisations are Communities of Practice i.e. cross-organisational groups which form naturally around a common interest or cause.

The outer cycle is the innovation cycle. The improvement cycle for business processes is triggered by a gap between current and desired performance. Ideas for improvements need to be solicited, tested and agreed on for implementation. Again the Community of Practice is an excellent vehicle for socialising improvement ideas and innovations.

In terms of IT Governance the key lessons relate to the limits by which IT management processes can be articulated and interpreted in a consistent way. For example, one can easily document the steps by which an IT help desk agent should process a call. The processes for problem identification, classification, recording and action can be provided formally, and staff trained for compliance against these standards. Help scripts can even be written to assist help desk agents to respond to particular situations. Anyone who has acted as a help desk agent or listened in to a help desk call will know that many calls do not always follow the script. Simply identifying the problem could require sophisticated conversational and personal skills on the part of the agent to tease out the essence of some problems. Many of these people related or softer skills do not lend themselves to documented procedures. How these skills are transferred from the experienced staff to the novice is likely to require mentoring style practices rather than formal process adherence. As we move up into the more management oriented IT decisions, the softer skill requirements only increase and the reliance on good "practice" rather than good "process" becomes more critical.

In summary, in terms of process vs. practice, the IT Governance regime is more likely to be dealing with practices more so than processes. As such, the compliance approach to governance will be difficult to implement as the standards of measurement are less than crisp. Governance in an environment where the work practices being governed rely mostly on the tacit understanding of the staff, implies that the socialisation of the IT management and staff will be an important aspect of IT Governance. In this case, socialisation is not taken to mean "after work" activities, but making time for the necessary conversations to be had between IT Management, Business Management and IT staff to ensure that IT Governance intent is well understood and that staff fully appreciate the value to the organisations of operating an effective governance regime.

In terms of sourcing decisions the same rules apply. While processes for service provider selection can be documented in terms of selection criteria, provider history etc., this must be complemented by activities allowing time for conversations to occur. This is particularly so for non-commodity products and services. Time and space needs to be allowed to assess the trust potential between the firm and its providers. As indicated in Figure 83, the quality of the trust network between the firm and its providers will be critical to the level of innovation and business improvement that can be achieved.

The issues of "process" vs. "practice" and "explicit knowledge" vs. "tacit knowledge" described here can be compared to the differing approaches to IT Governance and Sourcing. As identified in Chapter II, approaches to IT Governance can vary from a compliance driven approach through to a broader business value focus or points in between. In the next section the challenges facing the different governance approaches, as they relate to major technology developments, are addressed.

TECHNOLOGY TRENDS, IT GOVERNANCE AND SOURCING

IT Governance as a practice has had to be continuously adapted with changes in information technologies. In the early years of IT, the choice of providers and the hardware and software solutions were limited, with the governance decisions often technically based and therefore could be made with minimal input from the business at large. While the need for technical knowledge is sustained there are now other factors that executives need to be aware of. Issues of provider relationships, intellectual property, end-user application development, information management, business continuity are just a few of the additional dimensions for IT Governance.

Figure 84 identifies some major technical signposts arising over the past four decades along with the typical governance and sourcing issues faced. In the 1960s and 1970s the focus was on in-house computing capabilities and the beginning of the trend toward distributing computing away from the central data centre. Software was largely custom written by in-house staff. The 1980s saw a continual distribution of computing machinery to the point where personal desktop machines had became available with the first commodity level packaged software. The packaged software replacement of custom developed software continued and was scaled to larger enterprise applications as Enterprise Resource Planning (ERP) software gained in popularity. The wider availability of enterprise level packaged software in the early 1990s forced executives to consider what part software applications played in a firm's competitiveness. The common wisdom of the time was that it was appropriate to standardise on packaged software when the business processes that such software supported, were not considered a competitive advantage for the firm. Therefore, implementing quicker and cheaper packaged solutions for such processes was seen as a way of preserving the firm's internal IT resources for building custom software for the firm's competitive or distinctive business processes.

Figure 84. Technical signposts and IT governance

Era	Signpost	Decisions	Issue
2000s	Web 2.0/social software	Corporate/Personal	*Social software? Is this business or personal?*
	SaaS/Cloud	Buy/Use	*Can I trust it? Will I lose control?*
	E-business	Private/Public Protocols	*Private markets, private protocols or consumer market protocols?*
1990s	Internet/WWW	Intranet/Extranet/Internet	*Where should our web technologies focus be?*
	Distributed computing	Insourcing/Outsouricng	*Should we outsource? Infrastructure/Applications?*
1980s	ERP Packages	Package/Custom Software	*Should we use standard packaged software in place of custom developed software?*
	PC Applications		
	Personal Computers	Centralised / Distributed	*Should individuals be able to have their own computers? Who should have them? How will we maintain control?*
1970s	Minicomputers	Mainframe / minicomputer	*Should department be able to have their own computers? How will we maintain control?*
1960s	Firm owned mainframes	In-house Mainframe / Bureau	*Should we own our own computer or use bureau services?*

Around the same time, telecommunications technology had evolved to the extent that it was no longer necessary to have data centres located close to the point of use. Data centre consolidation provided the opportunity for the emergence of large scale infrastructure firms to provide outsourced IT infrastructure services to multiple clients. Outsourced service providers argued that scale advantages inherent in their operations could provide lower cost IT infrastructures on a global scale. On the applications front, the growth in the use of packaged ERP software, externally sourced, could also be externally managed. Hence from the early 1990s, large scale long term full outsourcing contracts emerged with the promise of large scale IT cost reductions. To what degree the firm would consider outsourcing to external vendors was a key governance and sourcing decision at the time.

The late 1990s saw the emergence of global IT connectivity as Internet technology became available to the commercial world. Internet platforms like the World Wide Web and low cost e-business applications together with the Year 2000 date change fear combined to create the greatest acceleration of IT investment seen in the industry to date. Compliance style governance was put under its greatest pressure during this period as business executives raced to be part of the dotcom boom.

The market adopted WWW standards and the web browser as the user interface of choice. IT executives were challenged to lead the way in leveraging the exciting prospects promised by the WWW while at the same time ensuring the firms' information assets were secured against unauthorised access. Interestingly the market enthusiasm for e-business applications resulted in quick cooperation of vendors to agree on protocols for electronic exchange. This cooperation had previously defied the efforts of standards committees looking to achieve an agreed electronic data interchange (EDI) protocol. That is, the market place was starting to push the standards agenda to achieve the required cooperation.

Post 2000 saw a dotcom bust and an IT investment winter. The largesse of pre-2000 IT investment had led to many failed investments and IT Governance controls came back into favour. In the early years of the new millennium, IT executives had the opportunity to "take stock" and refocus on IT/Business alignment without the distraction of a dotcom boom. The post 2000 "shakeout" in the IT vendor market also resulted in a much needed "cleaning out" of vendors with unsustainable products, services or business models. The outsourcing market was still being sustained but a growth plateau had been reached (as illustrated in the introductory chapter, Figure 1). The major change in the nature of IT outsourcing has been the increased uptake of multisourcing as a sourcing strategy, largely at the expense of sole source arrangements.

In recent times the abundance of global bandwidth is resulting in a "back to the future" look at the IT bureau services common in the 1960s. However this time the labels have changed to Software as a Service (SaaS) delivered via the ubiquitous facility of "cloud" computing. Cloud computing is essentially IT infrastructure delivered over the Internet. Underneath there is the same large scale data centres regularly operated by the major outsourcing firms, but for use by public rather than private clients. Like the bureaus of the 1960s, you only paid for what you used. Unlike the 1960s the bureaus are now global and can offer low cost services from a virtual central facility. Attractive as it appears the governance and sourcing issues of adequate flexibility, control and security are still front of mind. Only time will tell if these concerns can be adequately addressed by the SaaS providers.

The most significant technology trend from around 2005 has been the emergence of social software and its related Web 2.0 technologies. While debates continue on what are and are not Web 2.0 technologies, the following table identifies those technologies that are mostly identified with the Web 2.0 generation.

As can be seen from Table 15, the early targets for Web 2.0 technologies are individuals on typically "away from work" activities. The popularity of these technologies however, particularly with the younger generations, has attracted the attention of mainstream businesses, either to limit their use in business hours or to explore how they could be used for business advantage. From a governance

Table 15. Common Web 2.0 technologies

Web 2.0 Technology	Description
Blogs	An online diary or journal, usually identified with an individual.
Wikis	Collaborative publishing tool which allows multiple people to edit the same document online. The most famous example of a wiki is the Wikipedia encyclopedia.
Social Networking Tools	Online tools that allow individuals to, upon invitation, share personal details, with other individuals. The most common examples are Facebook, MySpace and LinkedIn
Peer-to-Peer (P2P) Networks	A file sharing mechanism which does not rely on a central facility, but cooperative sites agreeing to share at a peer to peer level. Most commonly used for sharing music and video.
RSS (Really Simple Syndication)	A facility which enables people to subscribe to particular information resources, like news lists, blogs, pod casts
Podcasts	Audio or video recordings typically designed for downloading to a mobile device like an Ipod.
Mash-ups	Aggregated content from independent online sites. An example would be showing restaurant listings from different web sites on a street map from say Google Maps

perspective, the dilemma is "what is for business and what is for personal use?" At this time there is no clear resolution. Many organisations have taken the easy option of simply blocking their use from within the firm's firewall. However, a quick search through the "groups" listing for Facebook will find that a number of social network groups have been established for many of the major corporations like GM, GE, IBM, Wal-Mart, Boeing, often under the company logo. Many of these have been established by employees of the firm, but some may have been established by key client groups for the firm. Company firewalls are merely "speed bumps" against the freedom of speech afforded by the Internet and social networking tools. Whether a company has a social software use policy or not, it will not prevent discussions being had on the company's activities on social networking sites. In fact, the terminology of "Enterprise 2.0" has been coined to cater for workplace applications of Web 2.0 technologies (McFee, 2006).

Many firms have now accepted that social networking tools and other Web 2.0 technologies are part and parcel of their employees' work and home life and therefore more is to be gained by "trusting" their staff to manage their own work/home life balance and allowing access to social network sites. David Stewart, the CEO of John Holland, a major Australian building and construction firm wrote in the company newsletter about Facebook:

While many organisations have banned access to such sites, we have no intention of regulating what people do in the workplace to that degree, or to rule by policy just for the sake of policy. In my view, using Facebook at work is no different from any other communications platform. It is no different from taking personal calls or doing your banking online. With the majority of our employees in the Gen X and Y demographic, it's a fundamental communication tool for probably half of our people

—John Holland, Employee Newspaper, Issue 3, December 2007.

It is anticipated that many firms will start to follow John Holland's insightful lead. For those with long enough memories, the same governance dilemmas were faced on the introduction e-mail and the Internet, two technologies that have become critical mainstream communications tools today, though many firms did ban their use initially.

A recent McKinsey survey (Bughin & Manyika, 2007) had indeed indicated that firms were learning lessons from the past. The majority of surveyed firms were treating Web 2.0 as a potential strategic investment. More importantly however, they were also accepting that its introduction would happen at the grass roots level and involve a degree of experimentation, rather than through the use of top-down and large scale corporate roll outs. In terms of IT Governance, this is a significant departure from the traditional compliance driven approach, where corporate groups would have been tasked with designing "standards for use" and then attempted to have staff comply with these standards. Looking back to the Cynefin Framework from Chapter II (Snowden & Boone, 2007), one can see that the approach fits comfortably within the "complex" regime, where the true business value of Web 2.0 has yet to emerge and therefore a degree of probing, sensing and then responding is the appropriate governance approach to take.

Reviewing the major trends as identified in Figure 84, from an IT Governance and sourcing perspective, the early years were mostly about technology selection, with most of the technology and management conducted internally. Over the years the distribution of both hardware and software, from a centralised to a more distributed model was the major concern. With the increased distribution of IT resources, emerged the question of who should own or have principal responsibility for these resources. Indeed should some or all of these resources not be owned by the firm at all, but be outsourced to external providers? Finally the increased commoditisation of IT resources used by company staff today could be privately owned or subscribed to by the staff themselves. Taken to its extreme, one could see a situation where IT Governance moves into the hands of the staff themselves. Sourcing is left in the hands of the staff, with the central governance regime being converted into a central advisory group of consultants, made available to assist staff make the most appropriate sourcing and IT management decisions. The following table illustrates the potential scenarios that IT governors could be faced with as one moves from company owned IT resources to staff or publicly owned infrastructure:

Figure 85. Technology trends and governance implications

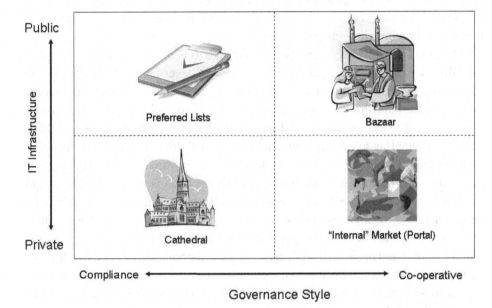

One can see that when operating with a compliance style of IT Governance, firms will need to adopt a "preferred list", approach to advise staff and external providers of the technologies deemed to be "acceptable". For major acquisitions that are financed by the firm, enforcement is easier than if the resources are funded by the employees themselves. In this situation, firms may choose to influence the procurement decision by selectively providing support for the preferred options or even subsidising their purchase.

For those firms preferring a cooperative style of governance, where the majority of the IT resources are owned by the firm, the facility exists to establish "internal market places" using Web 2.0 technologies. Labeled "Enterprise 2.0" as Web 2.0 tools applied inside the organisation (McFee, 2006), these tools are typically used to facilitate knowledge sharing and exchange. They therefore could be used to facilitate a sharing and internal sourcing of IT resources and capabilities, and a signaling to the IT function when new resources need to be procured. The knowledge sharing portal could also be used to seek feedback on the performance of the firm owned IT resources to assist the IT function to ensure that the resources are appropriately aligned with the needs of the business. In terms of the movement to the use of non-company owned IT resources, the cooperative governance approach will be challenged to avoid a "free for all" situation where individuals would be free to negotiate and procure IT resources reflecting local, rather than firm wide needs. This will be particularly evident with enterprise software. How much choice should be allowed say in selecting a SaaS CRM application? In this situation the IT function will need to engage with the communities and network leaders to expose the potential issues with this style of IT resource management, as described in Chapter VII on intra-organisational networks.

The evolution of web technology from Web 1.0 to Web 2.0 and beyond will also have differential impacts, depending on the style of governance a firm adopts. The use of Web 1.0 technologies under a compliance governance regime could be compared with the publishing of a newspaper. A level of control is exercised as to who can contribute as well as an editorial review of what is contributed. In the world of Web 2.0, attempting to exercise too much control will drive activities underground to the externally available social networking sites, over which the firm has virtually no control. The best form of governance in this situation is to set boundaries that the firm is comfortable with. An example could be that something like the firm not being financially responsible for any commitments made via social software sites, or that making it understood that personal contributions to these sites are personal opinions and do not necessarily reflect the views of the business overall. Inside these boundaries, staff should be able to conduct their business in any way they see fit.

For those preferring a cooperative style of governance, Web 1.0 technologies provided the facility for staff to communicate up and down and across the organisational hierarchy using bulletin board style tools. Governance could be limited to moderation of extreme contributions in a way akin to the moderation of public

Figure 86. IT Governance and the Web evolution

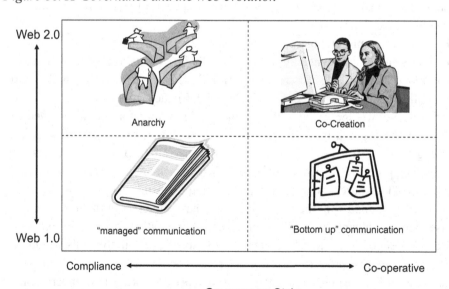

bulletin board style sites. The key opportunity for this style of governance and Web 2.0 technologies is the opportunity it provides for value co-creation from contributors across and beyond the firm. By facilitating brokering techniques described in chapter VI on personal networks, the use of Web 2.0 under a cooperative governance regime could result in new innovations and the creation of distinctive business value for the firm.

Chapter VII introduced the concept of knowledge sharing networks and Communities of Practice. Earlier in this chapter the concepts of process and practice were contrasted, with the inference that practices were often not made explicit and could therefore be best shared through human contact or collaboration. Sharing tacit knowledge was largely about establishing a social and technical environment which supports such contact. The next section addresses collaboration across business processes. Business Process Management Systems (BPMS) are designed to assist the business to execute these processes in the most efficient way possible, which usually means some form of electronic workflow support. However, experience with workflow systems has shown that implementing BPMS are far from straight forward, especially when the workflow involves people. More often than not, whether a person will accept a task from another person and achieve that task in the shortest possible time often requires a negotiation. People are largely responsible for their own "to do" lists and therefore achieving optimal workflow performance is heavily reliant on negotiated commitments, follow up and transparency in terms of where the task is at, at any given time (Howard Smith & Fingar, 2004).

A FRAMEWORK FOR BUSINESS PROCESS COLLABORATION WITH WEB 2.0 AND BEYOND

The previous sections have identified the pitfalls and opportunities for organisations adopting Enterprise 2.0/Web2.0 technologies. This section provides a framework for managing the use of collaboration tools within the organisation. Business process collaboration can be thought of as people to people business process management, and is something all executives are looking for. It will therefore always be high on the list of IT resource requirements. In supporting the collaboration activities of the organisation, the choice of the technical tools to use is only one factor to be considered by the IT Governance committees. The initial challenge is to determine what the specific IT requirements for collaboration support are. The framework below captures the key activities required to identify such requirements.

Figure 87. Framework for collaboration support

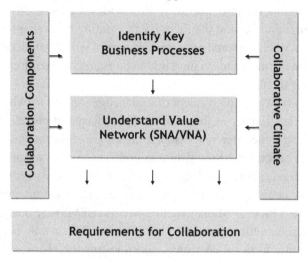

Identify Key Business Processes

In chapter III supply chains and the evolution toward supply networks was discussed. For organisations with a distinct supply chain it can be relatively straight forward to identify the processing paths that constitute the key business processes. Manufacturing companies are perhaps the clearest examples of key business processes representing the core supply chain for the business. However, not all businesses can be simply described in terms of supply chains. Other forms of business configurations like value shops and value networks have been identified for which the business process significantly differs from a traditional supply chain model (Stabell & Fjeldstad, 1998). An example of a value shop is a consultancy practice or medical centre. Rather than describing the key processes that a value shop conducts in terms of a supply chain, it is more appropriate to describe them in terms of problem identification, information search, solution choice and evaluation. Value network businesses are configured to mediate connections between clients. Examples are telephone, retail banks, insurance and postal companies. For a network business, the benefit comes from the number of members in the network. A mobile phone company may offer free calls between members to build their customer base. Therefore the marketing related business processes for building membership to a critical mass becomes important. Billing for network use is also a critical process, at times made more complex by the array of interlinked and at times, overlapping services and pricing schemes. Finally, maintaining and operating the technical facility to support the network of clients will also contain some critical business processes. In term of collaboration requirements it is therefore important to identify the type

Table 16. Key business processes identification

Value Configuration	Business Process Characteristics	Collaboration Characteristics
Chain	Interlinked material and processing flows e.g. manufacturer	Workflow management
Shop	Expert consultation e.g. solicitor, doctor	Problem solving
Network	Mediated network connecting clients e.g. telecommunication, retail bank	Mediation

of value configuration your business has and then to identify the critical business processes accordingly. Once identified the characteristics of the required collaboration can then be determined. Table 16 summarises the different characteristics for value chain, value shop and value network style businesses.

Understand the Value Network

Chapter IX introduced the concept of Value network analysis (VNA) and Chapter VI described social/organisational network analysis (SNA/ONA). VNA builds on the formal business process mapping by including the intangible flows, which often identify the value generated through role to role interactions. SNA identifies the trust network within the organisation at a more granular individual level. Both techniques are people centred. Either technique will expose the people to people interactions that are critical to "how things work" and are often missing from business process descriptions alone. In terms of critical collaboration requirements, what is important is that whatever collaboration solution is chosen, it does not hinder, but enhances the critical relationships identified by the network analysis techniques.

Collaboration Components

These components describe the core activities for collaboration. The emphasis here is mainly on virtual collaboration situations:

- **Finding the appropriate people to collaborate with:** What form of directory services does the organisation have available to it? Web 2.0 examples might include LinkedIn and Facebook which both have facilities to identify people.
- **Making contact:** social software tools differ from a conventional directory in that they force you to make contact through a shared contact. The advantages over the "cold calling" approach is that the intermediator can provide both qualification and an introduction, making the relationship development process much smoother.

- **Scheduling meetings:** this may seem trivial, but if we consider that collaboration can be virtual as well as physical and we need to deal with time zones and technology to facilitate the contact, it is usually the case that global meetings with multiple attendees can be a scheduler's nightmare. It is likely that technical solutions will be required to smooth this process.
- **Discussion:** again, the complexity of this component surfaces mostly during virtual meetings with multiple attendees. As with scheduling, the choice of technology may be dictated by the purpose of the collaboration e.g. informational, analytical/problem solving, joint planning etc. Low cost tools like Skype and Webex are examples of toolsets that can facilitate low cost discussion.
- **Actions:** being the output of any collaboration, be it the joint production of a document or plan. Sharing the results of the action will require some form of shared repositories. Again, the Web 2.0 tools provide enhanced facilities for sharing multiple forms of media to enrich the collaboration experience.

Collaborative Climate

Identifying the process areas ripe for enhancing collaboration and then identifying the particular technical requirements is still not a guarantee of success. There will be no collaboration unless the participants are willing.

Sveiby and Simons (2002) have undertaken empirical studies on what they call the "collaborative climate", finding that the appreciation of collaborative climate depends on the vantage point of the person. In their study they analysed 8,200 responses from people working in both private (63%) and public sectors (37%). The survey looked at 4 elements making up the collaborative climate:

- Organisational Culture
- Immediate Supervisor
- Employee Attitude
- Work Group Support

For each element the respondents were asked to rate the degree to which they agreed with a number of statements. For instance, under Organisational Culture one of the statements was "Open communication is characteristic of the Department as a whole", and respondents could rate the degree to which this statement was true for their own organisation.

A number of interesting conclusions were drawn based on the responses.

Collaboration Improves with Age

It is a myth that older employees are not interested in collaborating. The survey data supported the hypothesis that with age comes more experience in sharing knowledge via access to larger networks and easier access to knowledgeable colleagues. So the older respondents actually regarded the collaborative climate more favourably than other groups.

Employees with 3-5 Years in the Job are More Cynical About Collaboration

The new employee thinks highly of the collaborative climate, but it doesn't last for long. 3-5 years into the job the new employee becomes more cynical. It is suggested that it takes a lot longer for new employees to become truly effective than previously thought, and that organisations need to put more effort into helping new employees get past the cynical period.

More Experience Leads to a Higher Appreciation of Collaboration

The study found that employee attitude peaks after 15 years. Reaching this plateau appears to be quite normal and is probably something organisations should expect to happen.

Educated People Appreciate Collaboration—Managers Don't

The better educated people are, the more favourably they regard the collaborative climate. But the data did not verify the hypothesis that progressing into managerial positions equals higher regard for the collaborative environment.

Large Organisations Have a Better Collaborative Climate

The larger the organisation is the better the collaborative climate is. It is a myth to think that smaller organisations have a better collaborative climate. This is an interesting finding as many would have thought that employees in smaller organisations are more likely to know each other and therefore should be more willing to collaborate.

Distance is Bad

As one would imagine, the more geographically distributed the workforce is, the less favourably they rate the collaborative climate. This is of a particular concern as one of the key trends today is to move work to employees, which will create an even more disparate workforce.

Private Sector is Better

Currently the private sector rates the collaborative climate more favourably than the public sector. Sveiby and Simmons argue that there is no reason why this should be the case as the public sector employees represent a high number of knowledge workers, suggesting that there is a great potential for improving effectiveness through better collaboration in the public sector.

Understanding what drives the Collaborate Climate is very important input to any project aimed at improving collaboration. Does your workforce consist of primarily highly educated employees? How geographically distributed are they? How long have they been with the organisation? These questions must be answered for the employees that are involved in the process areas identified for improving collaboration.

The Sveiby and Simmons research was conducted pre—Web 2.0. While it is not anticipated that the existence of Web 2.0 would invalidate the results, with some elements like the "distance" effect, Web 2.0 is likely to moderate the negative effects experienced. That said, the main tenet of the research is the willingness to collaborate and no amount of technology is likely to influence an unwilling collaboration target. The requirement is therefore to work to understand the collaborative climate within the organisation and try to work with it, rather than against it.

In summary, the collaboration framework presented in this section highlights the need to focus the attention initially on the critical business processes, acknowledging that different types of businesses will have different business process characteristics. A further analysis is required to identify the critical relationship aspects across these processes that may not be explicit in the business process descriptions. Having identified the critical value flows one can then look at these flows in terms of the mechanics for conducting the collaboration. The collaboration components provide a means for evaluating and selecting appropriate support technology. In this space the Web 2.0 tools add substantial functionality, especially relating to the social aspects of collaboration. Finally, once the mechanics for effective collaboration in the highest leverage areas have been identified, one must address the issue of willingness to collaborate. Research on collaborative climates has identified some common characteristics found across organisations. The contribution that

Web 2.0 can make to impact the collaborative climate is to extend the socialisation opportunity to geographically distributed staff and therefore moderate the negative effects distance can have on collaboration.

The emergence of the richer social software based collaboration tools should be good news for IT governors. The IT function looks to engage with its business clients at a deeper level, not just as an "arms length" service provider. At the same time traditional means for measuring performance in terms of cycle times and minimum cost process performance is not appropriate in the networked business environment. New measurement tools are required to assess ongoing performance and the facilitation of business improvement activities. The next section identifies some emerging tools that can be applied for measuring and monitoring performance in the networked business world.

MEASURING PERFORMANCE IN THE NETWORKED BUSINESS WORLD

"If you can't measure it you can't manage it", is a common catch cry for proponents of business performance measurement systems. While the traditional double ledger accounting reports have been with us since first described by Italian mathematician Luca Pacioli over 500 years ago, modern managers are now fully aware that one needs to do more than measure transactions, but also to measure processes that generate the transactional outcomes. Popularised initially by the Total Quality Control movement and quickly followed by Six Sigma, in-process measures attempt to identify variations in the process that would eventually lead to poor product or service outcomes and consequently poor financial performance. At the strategic management level we have seen the adoption of Balanced Scorecard methods (R. S. Kaplan & Norton, 1992), which acknowledges the need to report on and manage non financial aspects of the business along with the financial results. Other reporting mechanisms for intangible or Intellectual capital assets have also been developed over the past decade or more (R. Kaplan & Norton, 2004; Roos & Roos, 1997; K. E. Sveiby, 1997).

This section introduces prospective measurement methods that provide a degree of performance measurement and monitoring of network or relationship activities, as opposed to only process activities. Like process monitoring methods, network measurement methods rely on data from the activities being conducted. In the case of networks this means making use of data from collaborative activities and using this data to infer performance issues and opportunities for improvement.

Table 17 contrasts network measures with traditional performance measures.

The Balanced Scorecard (BSC) is today the preferred method for measuring

Table 17. Traditional vs. network measures

	Traditional Measures	**Potential Network Measures**
Strategic	Balanced Scorecard	Partnership Scorecard (see chapter IX.)
Operational/ Organisational	Service level metrics Key Performance Indicators Financial Measures	Organisational network analysis Metrics
Transactional/ personal	Accounting reports	Personal Network Analysis

performance and strategy alignment. The Partnership Scorecard as introduced in chapter IX is a variant of the Balanced Scorecard with a number of important differences. The Partnership Scorecard measures value flows, rather than output levels commonly found in a BSC. By using flows rather than levels, one is able to identify who is accountable for a particular deliverable and who will ultimately judge the performance (the receiver of the value flow). The Partnership Scorecard also does not rely on predetermined measurement categories, but is custom developed to reflect the important value flows identified in a Value network analysis exercise. Unlike the BSC, the accountability for each measure is identified to the personal or role level, at whatever level of granularity that the organisation sees fit.

At the operational level it is common for organisations to make use of output measures like service level measures or production targets. It is also common to identify a number of key performance indicators that could be used to predict potential performance issues, like resource utilisation, cycle times, output per employee etc. Such measures are predicated on the ability to extract data from a process, for example, how much of a resource is being utilised, how long the process took, how many people it required for completion. For networks, the principal activity is collaboration. One way of measuring collaboration might be to measure the efficiency with which it occurs, for example, the time to make contacts, jointly develop a product or action and implement a solution. Time based measures however do not reflect the quality of the collaboration and only indirectly indicate the willingness to collaborate. SNA, as described in chapter VI, is a means of measuring both the efficiency and effectiveness of networks. Data for SNA can be secured through traditional survey means, but with the increasing use of collaborative tools, the usage logs associated with these tools, including the Web 2.0 tools are now providing a rich suite of data from which to draw SNA measures. SNA measures can also be applied at the personal or collaborative transaction level. The next section will address these measurement techniques in more detail.

SNA PERFORMANCE MEASUREMENT

SNA are regularly performed inside organisations to help understand the personal relationships that drive productive action. It is common to overlay the identified trust networks over the formal organisation chart to identify potential bottlenecks or missing linkages. An abundance of network measures have been designed by sociologists in interpreting the social network dynamics exposed by an SNA (Scott, 2000; Wasserman & Faust, 1994). The core measures however relate to centrality and are:

- **Degree Centrality:** the number of nodes that are linked to a given node in the network. This can be divided into "in-degrees" to reflect the number of nodes seeking a connection to the given node and "out-degree", reflecting the number of nodes sought for connection by the given node.
- **Betweenness Centrality:** identifies the degree to which a particular node is at the intersection between paths in the network. Betweenness, in essence, measures the intermediation potential of a given node.
- **Closeness Centrality:** measures the distance of a given node from every other node in the network i.e. how centrally located a node is in terms of reaching every other node in the network.

Figure 88. Demand matrix

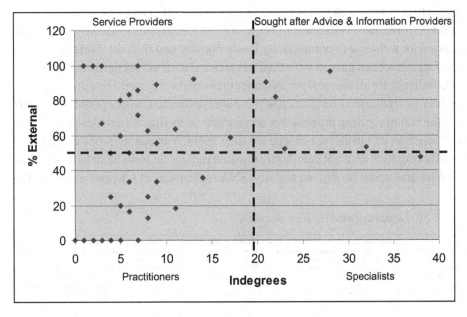

An example of how degree centrality could be used across departments is to identify the individuals who are most sought after from outside their own departments.

The distribution above shows the individuals who are in most demand and whether the demand is coming from inside or outside their own departments. The above matrix identifies a number of staff who are most sought after by others outside their own departments. This may be because of some specialised knowledge they may have. Alternatively they could be acting as gatekeepers, organisationally positioned such that they must be "gone through" to reach others. The example above also shows a potential lack of internal specialists who are highly sought after from within their own departments.

The other SNA measures relate to the network as a whole. The most common of these is network density. Density is measured as the number of links that exist in the network as a proportion of the total number of possible linkages. The common use of the density measure is to look at the density of connections within and between internal departments. A simple density table can identify how well departments are connected within themselves and also with other departments.

As can be seen in Figure 89, the diagonals show the connectivity inside the given department. The other cells identify the connection into and out of the different departments to other departments. There is no real "benchmark" density measure for connectivity as it very much depends on the type of activities that the department is conducting. A 10% connectivity might be appropriate for say a department like sales, where most of the individuals could be out with prospective clients, rather than with their fellow sales staff. Conversely, 10% might be considered poor for a project team where close cooperation and high connectivity is related to good project performance. The appropriate use of these measures is to identify a preferred direction for a change in connectivity levels initially and then set levels once some experience has been gained with their association with actual performance.

A challenge for all business performance measurement systems is sourcing quality raw data. For manufacturers, much of this data is extracted, where possible, directly from the manufacturing process. For service providers time based measures are the most common as businesses charge for time spent. Various methods can be used for gathering such data but commonly it would require an individual to time record or report time spent on a given activity. SNA measurement schemes are no differ-

Figure 89. Departmental density measures

	Business Support	Sales	Major Projects	CEO Office	Printing	Operations Analysis	Operations
Business Support	2%	3%	12%	15%	1%	1%	13%
Sales	1%	13%	11%	3%	0%	0%	9%
Major Projects	7%	6%	33%	8%	0%	3%	8%
CEO Office	3%	3%	8%	12%	0%	0%	16%
Printing	0%	1%	11%	2%	42%	0%	14%
Operations Analysis	5%	2%	33%	9%	0%	50%	13%
Operations	4%	2%	25%	3%	3%	0%	17%

ent. A common method for data collection is via personal surveys. Unfortunately unlike say time recording, individuals are less likely to agree to accurately report on their collaborative activities on a regular basis. SNA measurement schemes are therefore becoming increasingly reliant on the mining of collaborative tool logs to extract collaboration patterns and network performance measures. It is still early days in terms of the maturity of such methods, but some examples are reported here as an indicator of what the future might hold in terms of network performance measures.

NET MINING FOR PERFORMANCE MEASURES

E-mail and the telephone are the most pervasive electronic collaboration tools in current use. While both facilities capture logs of connections between senders and receivers, e-mails also regularly captures the content, which could potentially be used for classifying the type of collaboration (allowing for privacy issues). Research into patterns of collaboration identified through email logs have been conducted for some time now (Bontis *et al.*, 2003; Bulkley & Alstyne, 2006; Tyler *et al.*, 2002), resulting in a number of commercially available tools[1]. How patterns extracted from e-mail logs relate to the effectiveness of a given community social structure is still contentious given the breadth of activities that e-mail is used for (Grippa *et al.*, 2006).

Beyond email, the other collaborative tools like discussion lists, wikis, blogs and other social software tool logs are now being used to infer network performance (Gloor & Zhao, 2006; Lock Lee, 2003; Muller *et al.*, 2008). The advantage of these tools over e-mail is that the interactions are more likely to be voluntary in nature and therefore likely to be associated with collaborative, more so than administrative process activities.

The following example contrasts an organisational network for a global petroleum technical community. This experiment related to the network's use of a custom developed Community of Practice (CoP) tool, compared against a traditional survey based ONA assessment of the Network. This Global Network was divided into several topic specific CoPs, that each made use of the space provided by the electronic CoP tool. Network members were free to volunteer to join the "electronic CoPs", but clearly not all CoP members joined. It is estimated that about 60% of Network members had joined the CoP electronic space. Some were members of multiple CoPs.

The traditional ONA analysis was conducted across the Network to assess inter-office interactions and connections within particular professional disciplines. Around 40 Network members were surveyed, being asked to nominate their key "trusted

Figure 90. Traditional SNA characterisation of the network

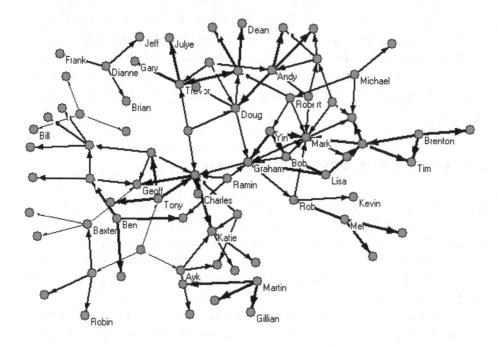

advisors" within their specialty domain. The resulting sociograms described the connections amongst some 70 members, approximately half of the total Network membership. The directional links in Figure 90 indicate nominated "advisers", with the thickness of the arrow indicating the level of perceived value.

The digitally derived sociograms were developed by looking for Network members who tended to join the same electronic CoPs; hence inferring a relationship of common interests. Of the 125 online members and 77 members in the traditional (offline) study, there were 33 common members. The analysis was therefore restricted to this sub-community.

Table 18 compares the top 10 (out of 33) rankings for both the offline and online networks. For the traditional SNA the rankings were determined based on degree centrality i.e. the number of input links from colleagues. For the online community the relationships were inferred by the number of different colleagues a member shares more than one CoP membership with. e.g. Mark is a member of two CoPs that both Charles and Gary are also members of.

The results show that 70% of the top 10 are common between the online and offline communities, which would suggest that those well networked members who choose to join the online world are happy to participate in multiple CoPs together. Rank orders within this grouping do not correlate that well, suggesting that there

Figure 91. Online community

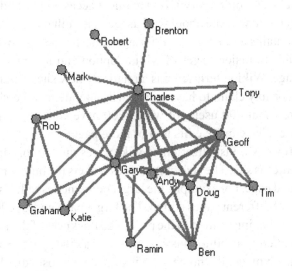

Table 18. Offline vs. online comparison

Top 10 "Online" participants (in rank order)	Top 10 "Offline" participants (in rank order)
Charles	**Mark**
Gary	**Graham**
Geoff	**Geoff**
Doug	**Andy**
Andy	Trevor
Graham	**Katie**
Katie	**Doug**
Rob	Tim
Ben	**Rob**
Mark	Bob

is a limit to how well networking behaviour might map from the offline to online world. The top two ranking members for the online community do not figure in the top ten of the offline community. Charles is the Network's leader and clearly plays a facilitative and oversight role in the online world, but is perhaps regarded more as a "manager or information broker", than discipline specialist in the offline world.

A more recent example is one of using wiki logs to identify relationships between individuals undertaking collaborative editing of wiki pages. Using SNA tools the wiki transaction logs are used to visualize the relationship between wiki pages and editors, looking for who is editing what; who are the most active editors, both in page edits and breadth of pages edited; which pages are being edited the most, and by whom.

For this study, the Wikipatterns.com wiki site[2] was chosen as a subject, mainly because of its subject, community size, technical accessibility and public nature. Wikipatterns.com is a wiki site about wiki usage. It is built with Atlassian's Conflu- ence wiki and contains a toolbox of wiki usage patterns and anti-patterns. The site aims to be a guide to major stages of wiki adoption and it explores patterns that apply at each stage. Wikipatterns.com is a relatively new site, it started in January 2007, and can probably claim to have a very wiki literate membership. As of June 2007, there were about 400 users, of which 200 have edited a page and of these 200, about 40 users have made edits to 5 or more page.

Figure 92 provides a visualization of wiki pages and editors from an extract from the Wikipatterns site: The size of the nodes reflects the number of connections between editor and page. For example, the larger editor nodes reflect relative editing activity in terms of different pages edited. The larger page nodes reflect the number of different editors having written to the page. The thickness of the links reflects the relative number of edits an editor has conducted on a given page. Some interesting observations can be made: the home page is one of the most edited pages, but the edits appear to be mostly done by infrequent editors, many for whom the home page is their only edit. The broad based editors appear to be seeding many new pages. There is a pattern of many lightly edited pages and many one page only editors

Figure 92. Wikipatterns editor/page relationships

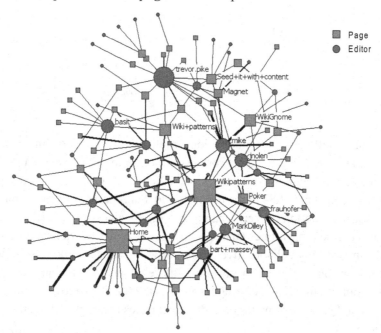

Figure 93. Wiki mapping

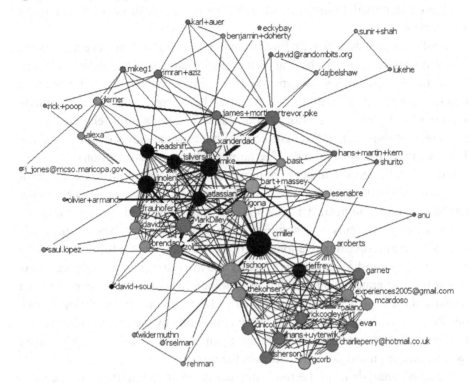

compared to multi-edited pages or multi-page editors. This is in fact common in the world of social networks and is called the "small world" effect.

Another interesting use of the data is to look at which editors are affiliated through editing common pages. That is, a relationship between editors could be inferred based on their co-editing of a page. Figure 93 illustrates these affiliations: The nodes are all editors. The link thickness represents the relative strength of affiliation through common page edits. The size of the nodes reflects the relative number of affiliations with other editors. The colours show an attribute gleaned from the e-mail addresses i.e. whether they were free e-mail accounts like hotmail or gmail; dot gov or edu; Atlassian (the company who created the wiki space) or a corporate e-mail account.

What one can see is that the Atlassian editors are pretty much central to the network of editors and all are active. There appears to be two clusters emerging, one of which is around five of the Atlassian editors. Cmiler and fschop are playing "broker" roles between the two clusters.

A survey based SNA conducted on the community showed similar results to the Petroleum community for central brokers (see Table 18: offline vs. online comparison). In the case of Wikipaterns.com editors, 4 of the top 5 most central actors were common and there was a 77% correlation between the centrality of editors, as determined through the networking mining, and those identified by the direct survey.

One of the more interesting findings from the study was the impact participation in the Wikipatterns.com was having on the generation of new and valued relationships. In the survey respondents were asked to nominate contacts and their perceived value of the relationship with these contacts. They were also asked to nominate the type of relationship as: a prior relationship > 2 years; a prior relationship < 2 year; a relationship created through the wiki but now extending beyond it; and a relationship through the wiki only. The number after the classifications in the key in Figure 94 indicate the number of nominated relationships in this class e.g. 16 of the nominated relationships had pre-existed for more than 2 years. Each bar in the chart reports the results against the relationship value nominated by the respondents e.g. for those respondents who nominated the relationships as "very important", some 35% were pre-existing relationships of more than 2 years, a further 25% were pre-existing relationships of less than 2 years and interestingly some 35% were new relationships generated from meeting in Wikipatterns.com. As one can see from the chart, of the 22 new relationships developed through meeting in Wikipatterns. com, the majority have been rated as "very important" by the respondents. This is an extremely positive result for the community in its ability to broker highly valued new relationships through participation in the wiki.

The above analysis is a little too immature to begin extracting network measures from. However, other more comprehensive wiki log analyses have been able to look at network density measures and average path lengths over time, which

Figure 94. Brokering valued relationships via the wiki

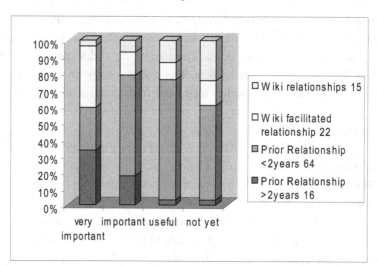

can provide, along with the volume of edits made, an indicator of the degree of collaboration activity within the community of editors. At an individual level, the degree centrality of key actors in the network can also be monitored over time (Muller et al., 2008).

Like discussion lists and wikis, blogs also provide the potential for analysing and measuring network activities. Blogs are largely personal diaries that either publish links to other blogs and web sites, but also attract links from other blogs. It is these linkages that would be used to build a social network representation from the blog activity (Stutzman *et al.*, 2003). Of course the commercial hosting sites for social software applications would have access to the complete relationships data, which is proprietary, and therefore not freely available for individual organisational use. However, publicly available friendship links are now being made available to application developers through application programming interfaces[3].

PERSONAL NETWORK MEASURES

At the personal, or collaboration transaction level, log information could be used by individuals to assess their own network behaviour. Privacy considerations would prevent such analyses being conducted at an organisational level. Technical tools however exist to enable one to use SNA tools and measures to investigate one's own networking patterns. For example, by looking at e-mail patterns over time, one can decide whether the patterns are reflective of what you are looking to achieve personally. If you are looking to build competency through close associations with a few known experts, then you would anticipate a fairly closed network around these mentors. However, if you are looking to explore new fields you would hope to see a diverse range of contacts and an open, exploratory network.

Figure 95 was generated using a tool called Condorview[4]. Condorview takes as input your mailbox and plots the interactions as network maps and as a series of snapshots over time. Email links can be filtered according to attributes like frequency of contact or relationship to a chosen subject matter. One can "play a movie" of the network mapping patterns over time to enable you to observe the dynamics of your own email patterns over time. Condorview also provides network metrics for centrality of selected actors in your network that can be plotted over time. Textual analysis of the e-mail message content can enable the filtering of the displayed messages to only show particular topics of interest. Condorview is a powerful network analysis tool that can take input from a wide variety of collaborative tool logs like wikis, blogs, discussion lists and web page links. Tools like Condorview have the potential to become the network metrics platform equivalent of ERP and Business Intelligence platforms used for business process metrics.

Figure 95. Personal e-mail tracking

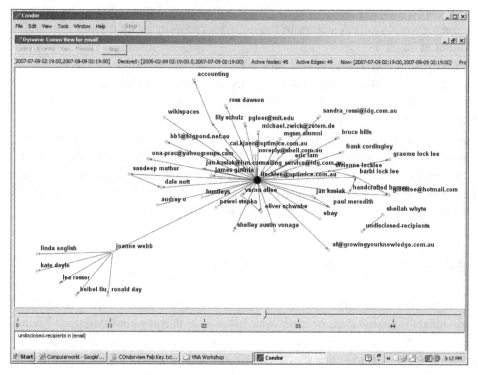

The network metric examples shown here are preliminary and somewhat exploratory, but do give some insight as to what is possible. Network maps are to networks what Six Sigma process charts are to processes. Network metrics are the equivalent of business process measures like cycle time and resource utilisation. Network measures used in conjunction with business process measures will provide a holistic business measurement scheme which better represents actual performance than the traditional process centric measures alone.

SUMMARY AND CONCLUSIONS

This chapter has addressed the major technical trends that will impact on IT Governance and sourcing over the coming years. The emergence of Web 2.0 and social software has signaled a new phase in the use of collaborative software to enhance relationships. Together with the increased commoditisation of these technologies, the challenge for IT Governors will be as much to do with influencing networks of individuals as it is to compliance to predetermined processes. The emergence of knowledge based "practices" as a distinguishing factor for many organisations was contrasted with traditional business processes to emphasise that the means for developing and sharing practices goes beyond simple documentation processes. Knowledge sharing was shown to be more related to effective socialisation than documentation i.e. connections are more effective than collections.

Web 2.0 technologies were then identified with the potential impact that they might have on IT Governance. The impacts were shown to be differentiated according to the preferred governance style that one adopts, be it a compliance or cooperative centred style. The complexity of the collaboration technology offerings, calls for some assistance in identifying requirements for collaboration upon which to make the sourcing decision. In this section a framework was presented to guide the requirement gathering processes. Critical to identifying the right requirements was the understanding of the hard business process requirements with the softer collaborative environment issues.

The final section addressed business performance measures for the non-process elements of the business. These elements were mostly seen as relationship network related. As such, the measurement tools centred on the use of network analysis tools and metrics. As with business process measurement, network measures are supported by visualisation, analysis and standard metric reporting. Together they represent a truly holistic business measurement scheme, covering business process and practices for both tangible and intangible value flows. From an IT Governance perspective, the support for business network measures will be an important factor as the business environment becomes more networked and market participants more interconnected.

The material provided in this book to this point has been free ranging and at times quite exploratory. Much of the material will be foreign to the typical IT management reader, and no doubt, somewhat confronting. The next section is aimed at convergence. The essence of the messages delivered in this book will be distilled in a way that the reader can gain some specific guidance on what can be done to succeed in IT Governance and sourcing in the emerging networked business environment.

REFERENCES

Allee, V. (1997). *The Knowledge Evolution: Expanding Organizational Intelligence*. Oxford: Butterworth-Heinman.

Berners-Lee, T. (1999). *Weaving the Web*. HarperCollins, San Francisco.

Bontis, N., Fearon, M., & Hishon, M. (2003). The e-flow audit: an evaluation of knowledge flow within and outside a high-tech firm. *Journal of Knowledge management, 7*(1), 6-19.

Bughin, J., & Manyika, J. (2007). How Business are using Web 2.0: A McKinsey Global Survey. *The McKinsey Quarterly*(March).

Bulkley, N., & Alstyne, M. V. (2006). *An Empirical Analysis of Strategies and Efficiencies in Social Networks*. Paper presented at the SUNBELT 2006, Vancouver.

Cowan, R., David, P., & Foray, D. (2000). The Explicit Economics of Knowledge Codification and Tacitness. *Industrial and Corporate Change, 9*(2).

Friedman, T. (2005). *The World is Flat*: Penguin Books.

Gloor, P., & Zhao, Y. (2006, 5-7 July 2006). *Analyzing Actors and Their Discussion Topics by Semantic Social Network Analysis*. Paper presented at the Proceedings of 10th IEEE International Conference on Information Visualisation IV06, London.

Grippa, F., Zilli, A., Laubacher, R., & Gloor, P. (2006, June 22—23, 2006). *E-mail May Not Reflect The Social Network*. Paper presented at the North American Association for Computational Social and Organizational Science, Conference, Notre Dame IN.

Hammer, M., & Champy, J. (1993). *Reengineering the Corporation: A Manifesto for Business Revolution*. New York: HarperCollins.

Hickman, F., Killin, J., Land, L., Mulhall, T., Porter, D., & Taylor, R. (1989). *Analysis for Knowledge-Based Systems: A Practical Introduction to the KADS Methodology*. Chichester: Ellis Horwood.

Johnson, B., Lorenz, E., & Lundvall, B.-A. (2002). Why all the fuss about codified and tacit knowledge? *Industrial and Corporate Change, 11*(2).

Kaplan, R., & Norton, D. (2004). Measuring the Strategic Readiness of Intangible Assets. *Harvard Business Review, 82*(2), 53-63.

Kaplan, R. S., & Norton, D. P. (1992). The Balanced Scorecard—measures that drive performance. *Harvard Business Review, 70*(1), 71-79.

Keen, P. (1997). *The Process Edge: Creating Value When it Counts*. Boston: Harvard Business School Press.

Lenat, D. (1995). CYC: A Large-Scale Investment in Knowledge Infrastructure. *Communications of the ACM, 38*(11).

Lesser, E., & Prusak, L. (1999). *Communities of Practice, Social Capital and Organisational Knowledge*: IBM Institute of Knowledge management.

Lock Lee, L. (2003, April 2003). *Does your community leave a digital footprint? Measures and metrics for communities of practice*. Paper presented at the KM Challenge 2003, Melbourne.

Lock Lee, L. (2005). Balancing business process with business practice for organizational advantage. *Journal of Knowledge management, 9*(1), 29-41.

McFee, A. (2006). Enterprise 2.0: The Dawn of Emergent Collaboration. *MIT Sloan Management Review, 47*(3), 21-28.

Muller, C., Meuthrath, B., & Baumgraß, A. (2008). Analyzing wiki-based networks to improve knowledge processes in organisations. *Journal of Universal Computer Science, Forthcoming.*

Nelson, R., & Winter, S. (1982). *An Evolutionary Theory of Economic Change.* Cambridge, MA: Harvard University Press.

Polanyi, M. (1967). *The Tacit Dimension.* New York: Doubleday.

Roos, G., & Roos, J. (1997). Measuring your Company's Intellectual Performance. *Long Range Planning, 30*(3), 413-426.

Scott, J. (2000). *Social Network Analysis* (2nd ed.): Thousand Oaks, CA: Sage.

Seely Brown, J., & Duguid, P. (2000). Balancing Act: How to Capture Knowledge Without Killing It. *Harvard Business Review, May-June.*

Seely Brown, J., & Duguid, P. (2001). Creativity Vs. Structure: A Useful Tension. *Mit Sloan Management Review*(Summer).

Simon, H. A. (1979). Rational Decision Making in Business Organizations. *The American Economic Review, 69*(4), 493-513.

Simon, H. A. (1987). Making Management Decisions: the role of intuition and emotion. *The Academy of Management Executive, 1,* 57-64.

Smith, H., & Fingar, P. (2002). *Business Process Management: The Third Wave.* Tampa, FL: Meghan-Kiffer Press.

Smith, H., & Fingar, P. (2004). The Process of Working with People: Person-to-Person Business Process Management. *BPTrends*(Sept.).

Snowden, D. (2002). Complex Acts of Knowing: Paradox and Descriptive Self Awareness. *Journal of Knowledge management, 6*(2).

Snowden, D., & Boone, M. (2007). A Leader's Framework for Decision Making. *Harvard Business Review, November.*

Stabell, C., & Fjeldstad, O. (1998). Configuring Value for Competitive Advantage: on Chains, Shops, and Networks. *Strategic Management Journal, 19,* 413-437.

Stutzman, F., Lazorchak, B., & Wilbur, J. (2003). *Metric Aggregation for Social Network Analysis in Blogspheres*: School of Information and Library Science, University of North Carolina.

Sveiby, K.-E., & Simons, R. (2002). Collaborative Climate and Effectiveness of Knowledge Work: An Empirical Study. *Journal of Knowledge management.*

Sveiby, K. E. (1997). *The New Organizational Wealth: Managing & Measuring Knowledge-Based Assets*: Berret-Koehler Publishers, Inc.

Tyler, J., Wilkinson, D., & Huberman, B. (2002). *Email as Spectroscopy: Automated Discovery of Community Structure within Organisations*: HP Labs.

Wasserman, S., & Faust, K. (1994). *Social Network Analysis: Methods and Applications*: UK: Cambridge University Press.

Zairi, M. (1997). Business process management: a boundaryless approach to modern competiveness. *Business Process Management Journal, 3*(1).

ENDNOTES

[1]   http://www.etelemetry.com/ (accessed 23/1/08); https://www.visiblepath.com/ (accessed 23/1/08)

[2]   http://www.wikipatterns.com/display/wikipatterns/Wikipatterns (accessed 23/1/08; analysis conducted in June 2007)

[3]   http://code.google.com/apis/socialgraph/ (accessed 6/2/08)

[4]   http://galaxyadvisors.com (accessed 23/1/08)

Section IV
Leveraging Emerging Practice

Chapter XII
Guidelines for
IT Governance and
Multisourcing in the
Networked Economy

This book set out to present an alternate, but complementary view to traditional ways of thinking about IT Governance and governance activities in general. Fuelled by the obvious changes in the world's economies toward higher levels of collaborative activity, it has been argued that the time has come "to get serious" about the sociology of IT Governance. The "governance" term itself creates images of rules, regulations and bureaucracy. It has not been the intent of this book to suggest that such compliance driven approaches are no longer relevant. These are tangible artifacts that form the foundation for virtually all governance schemes. The concepts of Corporate Social Capital (SC), incorporating the less tangible concepts of SC, Intellectual capital and Corporate Reputation are promoted as representing the important intangible elements that, if used astutely, can mean the difference between an effective and an ineffective governance arrangement. It is argued that the intangible elements are growing in importance as the world's economies become increasingly interdependent. Therefore the time is right to extend IT Governance practices to incorporate the management of the intangible aspects of your business or organisation.

The extensive reviews of the foundation literature provided in Chapters III, IV & V were designed to demonstrate that the ideas presented in this book do have a solid theoretical foundation in the academic literature. The subsequent chapters on personal networking competencies, intra-organisational networks and value networks, converted theory into practice by providing frameworks, supported by case study research. It was argued that the formal organisational hierarchy was becoming less effective in achieving IT Governance objectives, as the organisations themselves became more internally networked beyond the formal organisation chart. The ability to engage, influence, excite, conscript are becoming critical IT management competencies, complementary to the ability to plan, organise and direct. The changes in the business and working environment were used to illustrate the increasing relevance of incorporating these more sociologically based techniques into the IT Governance and multisourcing "kit bag".

Section I: Chapters I to IV provided foundation material for considering IT Governance in a networked world. A mixture of theory and practice was used to position the governance and multisourcing function within the context of a changing business landscape oriented toward networks. **Section II:** Chapters V, VI and VII provided the view of IT Governance from a sociological perspective. Starting with comprehensive reviews of the academic literature on Corporate SC and Intellectual capital, the reader was exposed to emerging issues relating to personal competencies for operating effectively in a networked world, and then to new forms of intra-organisational networks. Having provided a sociological view of IT Governance, **Section III:** Chapters VIII to XI highlighted applications for emergent practice. This section began by describing a substantial research project undertaken by the author, demonstrating the linkages between Corporate SC and firm performance. Empirical research studies are a critical link between management theory and practice. It is therefore hoped that management scholars may build on some of the techniques reported here to extend this research. For the non-academic reader, it is hoped that one might appreciate the rigor with which the research has been conducted and accept the results as evidence supporting many of the arguments in this book. Part III moves on to address the emerging network focused practices for identifying and enhancing value in networks, and reporting on how such techniques are now being adopted within the ITIL best practice framework. This evolution is important as it flags a new maturity in IT management practices in acknowledging the changes in our business environments. It also offers a further legitimisation of the practice of Value network analysis. The following chapter addressed the global outsourcing market by introducing new networked base tools for generating new market intelligence for both vendors and clients. The intent of this chapter was to move from the more academic research to more market level research. The chapter provided a number of new and novel ways of visualising a market place through the use of Social Network Analysis (SNA) tools. Uncovering the "relationships" dimension of the IT market place has been difficult to achieve with traditional market research techniques focusing on firm specific and industry sector attributes alone. SNA not only provided a means for visualising market place relationships, but also indicated that some of the sociological network centrality metrics could also be equally applicable to business and markets.

The network perspective was able to provide new insight into the client vendor interface. It was demonstrated that some relationship governance structures, designed for management and control, could in fact be hindering business value generation. This has been most evident in the area of innovation. By viewing governance arrangements from a network perspective, it was shown that through the use of the 3E's framework for innovation, the contrasting objectives of compliance and innovation could be effectively managed.

The penultimate chapter on the impacts of technology on IT Governance and multisourcing could have occupied a whole book in itself. The Internet, the World Wide Web, Web 2.0, and now Enterprise 2.0 and beyond, have launched a publishing frenzy in recent years. The intent of this chapter however, was not to inform on the details of each technology, but to step back and look at the overall technology trends and the potential impact those trends will have on the IT Governance and multisourcing task. The chapter identified that technology movements were putting more power into the hands of the individuals and that IT governors should look to leverage, rather than fight against this trend. Consistent with this view, a simple requirements assessment framework was presented for soliciting collaboration systems requirements. The remainder of this chapter was devoted to introducing new methods for performance measurement in a networked business environment. Where IT has been profitably used for measuring process performance found across supply chains, new measurement techniques would be required for measuring collaborative behaviour. Data collected from the activities of collaboration, facilitated by the increasingly sophisticated collaborative technologies, would provide the next generation of "data warehouses" and business intelligence reporting.

The remainder of this chapter is devoted to firstly looking at the basis of governance decision making from a complexity perspective. This will be followed by the synthesis of specific guidelines from the preceding chapters and presenting them in a way that the IT Governance practitioner can more easily leverage them in their day to day work.

IT GOVERNANCE DECISION MAKING

In chapter II, the Cynefin framework (see Figure 6) for decision making was introduced and discussed in the context of IT Governance. At this point it is worth reflecting on where IT Governance decision making is at with respect to the trends identified in the preceding chapters. Part of the governance task is to be able to identify the business and technology trends that provide both threats and oppor-

Figure 96. Business and technology trend impacts on IT governance

Business Trend	Hierarchical Control	Matrix Management	Business Network
Technology Trend	In-house data centres	Distributed Computing	Pervasive Computing
Governance Trend	**Simple**	**Complicated**	**Complex**

tunities for the business. Early identification and action in response to such trends is therefore part and parcel of an effective governance regime. In chapter II, it was agued that current governance regimes would occupy the "Complicated" domain of the Cynefin framework. However, the trends identified in the previous chapters might indicate that the IT Governance task is rapidly moving into the "Complex" domain, as indicated in Figure 96.

Recall that the advice for operating in the "Complex" domain is one of probe, sense and then respond within agreed boundaries. The impact of these trends will be different, depending on the individual context of the readers. Not all organisations will be currently embedded in business networks, or have staff demanding to use their own IT resources, or at least have more say over what they are asked to use. That said, it will be difficult for any organisation to avoid the environment in which one exists. Even for organisations with successful compliance processes and highly standardised and well managed IT infrastructures, the question will always arise as to whether the organisation is really getting the best out of its IT resources. Are opportunities being missed? Will one look back and say we managed our costs effectively but missed a major opportunity to change the nature of our organisation's value proposition? Whatever your individual situation, the business environment is becoming more complex, and governance practices need to adapt accordingly. The following guidelines should therefore be identified with "emergent practice", rather than "best practice". You are encouraged to probe and experiment with them. Their impact will differ, depending on your context. However, after the experimentation, take what has worked for you and turn it into good practice for you.

PERSONAL NETWORK COMPETENCIES

This section is equally relevant for IT executives, managers or individual contributors. An overview of the changing competency requirements, as one moves from an internal or sole source arrangement to a multisourced, networked arrangement was provided in Chapter VI, and summarised in Figure 97.

Figure 97. IT competency requirements

	Closed Source	Open Source
Leadership / Management	• Project / Commercial Management skills • Team Management • Client management	• Influencing / motivational skills • Large scale design skills • Technical skills • Community building skills • Altruistic
Individual Contributors	• Technical skills • Team participation skills • Developer methodology process skills • Ability to focus and sustain attention	• Technical skills • Community participation skills • Exploratory / inquisitive • Altruistic
	Private Infrastructure Use	**Public Infrastructure Use**
Leadership / Management	• Commercial Management skills • Cost Management • Client Management	• Business alliance skills • Employee negotiation skills • Public affairs skills • Auditing skills
IT staff Contributors	• Customer service skills • Team participation skills • Process adherence • Ability to focus and sustain attention	• Coach • Community participation skills • Exploratory / inquisitive
	Core Single Sourcing	**Core Multisourcing**
Leadership / Management	• Commercial Management skills • Cost Management • Client Management	• Facilitation skills • Complex Negotiation Skills • Political skills • Community development skills
IT staff Contributors	• Customer service skills • Team participation skills • Process adherence • Ability to focus and sustain attention	• Relationship skills • Community participation skills • Exploratory / inquisitive

One can see that for the leader/manager the development of competencies listed on the right hand side of the table are not inconsistent with what one might expect of senior business executives in virtually any field, whether it be in the private or public sector. Effective senior executives need to be in touch with their environment, and their stakeholders, whether they be clients, suppliers, partners, regulators or the public. They therefore need to build competencies in working effectively with disparate stakeholders. What the above table suggests is that the IT executive with IT Governance responsibilities will now have to exhibit similar competencies to his or her senior business executives. This is of course a positive development, providing the opportunity for senior IT executives to move more smoothly into the mainstream executive ranks than had been the case in the past, when the IT executive roles were more technically oriented.

The specific guidance for the IT executive is to embrace opportunities to build your influencing skills. Put yourself in positions where you have little or no formal authority, perhaps as a member of purpose formed task forces. In particular, look for opportunities to engage in alliance networks, even volunteering for roles in a local professional society. These usually voluntary roles require one to use influencing skills for building and sustaining membership and relevance that is consistent with the networked business environment. John Schubert is the Chairman of Commonwealth Bank of Australia, Australia's largest bank, as well as being a director of global giants BHP Billiton and Qantas, so very much a corporate executive leader. He also happens to be the chair of the Great Barrier Reef Foundation, a not-for-profit community looking to coordinate the efforts of many stakeholders in protecting Australia's Great Barrier Reef. His reflection on leadership challenges as reported in Gerencser, Van Lee et al (2008) is indicative of the leadership challenges identified in this book:

We've all seen the sort of hard-driving, take-no-prisoners, suffer-fools-not-at-all use of position power. That can be quite effective within a business organisation. But within a megacommunity, that would be totally ineffective. You don't have a direct control over so many parts of it, so you need to be much more subtle. You just can't go and tell somebody to do something. Even in large organisations, that doesn't work all the time, as executives find out pretty quickly. You go and decide something and then three months later you find out—nothing's happened.

From an IT Governance perspective for a large organisation one could envisage the board of directors signing off on a governance arrangement and then instructing the governance committee to make it happen. But large organisations involved in a multitude of alliances are starting to behave like megacommunities and hence new leadership approaches along the lines of influence and cooperation will be required.

For the individual contributor, the expansion of competency requirements from purely technical and team orientation could also be seen as positive. Of course the facility to remain technically focused will still be available for many. However, the trend suggests that client interaction and coaching skills will be in greater demand. Unless one is working for specialist technology vendors, it may be increasingly difficult to "hide" within large technical teams. As well as a strong appreciation of the technology, IT staff will be increasingly called on to be engaged with the business users of the technology, both as the implementer, and also trusted advisor and coach. Even for the product development firms, staff will be increasingly asked to engage with their end user community to ensure that products are effectively aligned with need. And as product development becomes increasingly globalised, the ability to work in geographically distributed virtual teams will become a necessary competency.

Those individuals who are active in the Open Source development communities have perhaps gained a running start. Such individuals have already learnt what it is like to work in a team of "volunteers". They will understand the negotiation and cooperation skills required to be productive in this environment. They will also understand the level of individual "passion for the task" that is required to sustain the required effort, and the incredible things that can be achieved when passions are aligned.

The specific guidance for the individual contributor is therefore to learn to work in community environments. If appropriate, join an open source community and be an active contributor. Otherwise join one the many public technical forums/communities that have emerged on the Internet. After an appropriate time spent observing, aim to be an active contributor, even if those contributions are only modest to start with. The important learning from working in a "community" environment is the flexibility that one learns to achieve, through participation. At times you will need to lead an initiative to achieve anything. At other times it is also important to be a "good follower", supporting other initiatives that someone else has taken the lead on. Throughout your participation, the value of reciprocity in building and sustaining an activity, will become evident and a strong lesson can be carried into the traditional workplace. The rewards from active participation may not be obvious at first. As with Open source software, the principles and lessons learned through participation will have positive impacts, even in the traditional work environment.

In summary, for both the executive and individual contributor, the new core competency requirement is the ability to work within a community without the benefit of hierarchical power afforded by a formal organisation structure. Being able to effectively work with ambiguities in lines of authority and relying on your own passion for the task at hand to influence or align with others of a similar passion, is a core competency requirement in the networked business environment.

"Learn to be an effective member of a community"

INTRA-ORGANISATIONAL NETWORKS

Chapter VII spoke of the "hidden organisation", being the informal networks that exist in all organisations. The general guidance was that it is easier to work with these networks by influencing them in ways most aligned with the needs of the business. The specialty of the IT discipline is such that technically aligned communities will form naturally along particular "religious lines", be it Java vs. .NET; Unix vs. Windows; Facebook vs. MySpace and the list would go on. For the IT executive, many professional societies exist as forums for knowledge sharing and IT management practice development.

For many larger organisations that have embraced the Knowledge management (KM) initiatives of the past decade or so, formal Community of Practice (CoP) programs would have been established. The KM team would act as facilitator for those wanting to establish a Community of Practice and advising them on "best practice" processes for establishing and sustaining a community. CoP programs had proven the most effective means for sharing knowledge across large and disparate organisations. Substantial resources now exist to advise on the establishment and successful operation of CoPs. For the IT function, a CoP's familiarity with the various means of collaborative systems support should be a benefit in helping to sustain itself. IT staff are naturally inquisitive about new IT technologies. It is therefore not likely to be necessary to encourage such experimentation. However for the IT executive, the guidance is to take advantage of the natural inquisitiveness of IT staff by legitimising these experimental activities by sharing the results with business stakeholders. Show leadership with new technologies by having your staff be the seen as leading adopters, and best positioned to consult on its effective application.

For the IT governors, developing IT CoPs is not enough. As identified in the vendor/client case study in Chapter X, engaging with the business is more than simply establishing formal client engagement structures and assigning responsibility to a few select individuals. Informal contact needs to exist at all levels. It is easy for IT functions to be seen as "closed shops" hiding behind the mystique of the technology. However, as indicated in Chapter VII, the IT function needs to move beyond being simply the interface to increasingly commoditised IT services. IT executives need to create opportunities for staff to engage with the lines of business, at multiple levels. For example, opening up IT CoPs to non-IT staff to attend selected meetings, where technologies can be showcased, can be effective. Allowing staff to spend time coaching business staff on particular aspects of a technology or service could be valuable. Institute a "day in the life" program where IT staff are able to spend time working in other departments, doing whatever they are able to assist with the normal operations of the department. In this way, informal relationships can be built and sustained, enabling the subtleties of the business to be communicated over time, rather than as a "big bang" requirements gathering exercise.

In summary, the core guidance from this chapter was to work with the informal organisation, rather than working against it. Use community structures to gain a deeper engagement with your business stakeholders,

"Aim to become a trusted member of your organisation's business networks"

VALUE NETWORKS

Chapter IX introduced value networks and Value network analysis. The critical contribution that this chapter adds to IT Governance is the guidance it provides to conversations about "value". What "value" is IT adding to the business, is precisely what IT Governance is responsible for. Of course if one's concept of value is thought of in purely economic terms, then the simplified cost/benefit analyses might determine that IT is not adding much value to the business at all. For example, it is hard to put an economic value to the company's e-mail system. Yet today it would probably rank as the most critical IT resource that an organisation can have. In chapter V, substantial attention was given to a review of intangible business assets, or Intellectual capital (IC). Traditional accounting based performance measures are "lagging" indicators. However, today's stock markets are "valuing" firms based on attributes other than past performance. In fact, up to 80% of stock market values can no longer be explained by the tangible assets of the firm. Therefore in a very tangible way, intangibles are having an impact on a firm's value.

The Value network analysis technique helps identify intangibles, in conjunction with the tangible value flows across an organisation. Like tangible assets, once identified, they are able to be negotiated and exchanged. Therefore for the IT function looking to introduce a new facility or application, it is not just the tangible value flows that one needs to be concerned with, but also the intangible flows. In fact there will be new IT systems that may provide some very tangible results, but at the same time destroy other intangible value flows to the detriment of the business overall. A graphic example of this would be the implementation of automated voice response systems. The tangible benefits are obvious, with a reduction in call centre staff. However, if implemented in a business context, where the relationship with the call centre staff is a value cherished by the client, the system could in fact lose clients for the firm at a tangible cost far exceeding the cost savings achieved.

The major challenges with multisourcing are the effective management of the multiple relationships, not just with the additional providers, but also between these providers. While a good legal contracting framework provides a foundation, it falls far short of ensuring that all parties will work together in a cohesive and productive way. In these circumstances a cooperative approach to governance is likely to be more effective than a compliance approach. The multisourcing Value Networks Analysis example provided in Chapter IX identified how one can begin to engage all parties in a cooperative arrangement based on reciprocity and negotiated value exchanges. Once all the tangible and intangible elements of the multiple relationships that need to be managed are made visible, one can start to manage the complexity of the arrangement for maximum benefit to all.

In terms of the IT function's interactions and relationships with the core lines of business, understanding the intangible value flows is also critical. Often a tense relationship, the IT/business interface can be improved and adapted by understanding the intangible flows, as well as the tangible flows. As shown in Chapter IX, it can be used to negotiate value flows in multisourcing arrangements with multiple stakeholders. In terms of specific guidance for the IT Governance function, the following organisational level elements have been adapted from material available from the open source support site for value networks[1]:

Phase 1: Briefings, Assessments and Pilots

- Look for initiatives that appear to have obvious business appeal, yet are struggling to articulate a traditional business case.
- Undertake briefings with stakeholders on intangible business assets and the tangible value that they can bring. The share values of companies like Google, Microsoft and Cisco, which have few physical assets, is a good case to highlight.
- Look for the use of other complementary analyses that are being conducted. Areas involved in business process mapping are potentially ripe for value network extensions.
- Make good use of the Open Source Value Networks site resources to do some pilot runs in "friendly" environments, while you learn the technique.

Phase 2: Development

- Begin to expose the lines of business to value networks in their interactions with the IT function.
- Build a value networks representation for the IT Governance function using the material in chapter IX and on the Open Source Value Networks web site for guidance.
- Complete an analysis of the above network to the satisfaction of all stakeholders.
- Use the value network representation to communicate how the IT Governance function is delivering value to the business.
- Aim to have a number of internal consultants trained in the Value network analysis technique.

Phase 3: Integration and Support

- From the governance level value network, look to take the analysis to the subsidiary roles until the majority of the IT functional roles and their interactions have been assessed for value contribution.
- Review the IT function as a whole in terms of how value is created and exchanged with the other lines of business.
- Look to acquire/develop electronic tools to support the maintenance of the value maps, having them ready for re-assessment as new issues arise.
- Consider the implementation of Partnership Scorecards, as illustrated in Chapter IX, as a means of reporting on performance of the IT function.

As indicated in Chapter IX, Value network analysis has achieved a level of legitimisation through its incorporation with the ITIL services best practice framework. The adoption of Value network analysis is therefore consistent with what is considered best practice services management for the industry.

"Remember that value is not only financial. Use Value network analysis to identify and maximise the effectiveness of multisourcing arrangements and consequently the IT function's value contributions to the business"

BUILDING CORPORATE SOCIAL CAPITAL

The research project linking Corporate SC to firm performance resulted in some specific guidance on the particular elements of Corporate SC investigated. The context for the study would make such guidance particularly relevant to IT vendors operating in the global IT market place. Generalising the results to other industry sectors would be done with caution as no claims can be made to its validity without performing additional studies. That said, several of the results obtained were confirming of prior theory or other empirical research results, and therefore it is reasonable to expect that the results could be relevant to other sectors, in particular those that exhibit similar alliance patterns to the IT sector, like biotechnology, building and construction, pharmaceuticals and health.

Table 19 provides a commentary on the impacts of the elements of Corporate SC on firm performance. For vendors operating in the global IT market place, Table 19 provides some specific guidance for improving performance. The lessons of the dotcom bust are well learnt and were apparent in the data used for this research. Having a perception of financial soundness is definitely a situation to aspire to and rightly should take precedence in any executive's considerations. Of course

Table 19. Corporate social capital impacts on firm performance

Corporate SC Element	Commentary on impact on performance
Financial Soundness	The most predictive element for influence on firm performance. An exception was its impact on Total shareholder return with large or non-software firms, where no positive impact was determined.
Human capital	Investments in human capital were found to be a positive influence on firm performance in the majority of scenarios. Importantly for small, or loss making firms, human capital was the most common investment that would positively impact performance.
Centrality	High centrality was found to have a positive effect on a firm's market to book ratio, which is related to its longer term performance. This is especially so for firms in the software sector. Increasing centrality was also seen to have a positive impact on market to book ratios for loss making firms. Interestingly, high centrality was found to have a negative impact on TSR for large firms and/or non-software firms.
Internal capital	Investments in internal capital were found to have a negative impact on performance, in particular, market to book and TSR for firms that were not financially sound, and therefore perceived to not be able to afford such investments.
Research Intensity	Like Internal capital, investments in R&D could have a negative effect, especially on ROI, if the firms are not financially sound.

the IT industry is characterised by a majority of small firms, many just starting out, and many would find it difficult to achieve a financially sound position in the short term. For these firms the guidance is that investments in human capital are important. In other words, if you have good people, good finances will follow. Additionally, actively building your market centrality through alliances can also have a positive impact. Alliance partners with large, financially sound firms could result in "reflected reputation" benefits for the smaller firm. For the larger, established firms, especially those in the hardware or non-software areas, the guidance differs a little. For these firms, being seen as financially sound has less of an impact on overall performance, perhaps because this is an expectation, or a given for such firms. Also for these firms, high centrality can actually be a liability. The inference is that an over-connected firm could be distracted by having to manage many non-value adding alliances.

Overall however, investments in Corporate SC were seen to have a positive impact on firm performance. In fact the research showed that the impact of the non-financial related elements of Corporate SC had the biggest impact on total shareholder return, the performance metric by which the majority of firms in the global IT sector are measured.

"Aim to be financially sound and hire good people. Pay attention to how you are allianced in the market place".

IT MARKET RESEARCH

The global IT market is one of the fastest moving and most dynamic of all of industry sectors on the world's stock markets. The complexity of the industry and the demand for market intelligence is evidenced by the healthy market research industry that has grown up supporting it. For the large part, these firms will dissect the market in different ways; for example, by product lines, service lines, regions, new technologies and the like. Vendor firms are interested in market shares, revenue and profit growth opportunities and growth rates for emerging new product or service lines. Client firms are interested in the activities of the vendor firms as well as which vendor firms other client firms are buying from. They are interested in the dynamics of the market place, who are the likely "winners", the ones who will be around for a while? Who may acquire whom? Which emerging standards are likely to win out? What major geographic movements are occurring? Market research in the industry is therefore supportive of both vendors and clients.

There exists a plethora of market information available on the global IT market. Online resources are becoming increasingly popular. IT news level research can generally be accessed free of charge. More detailed analyses will usually incur a membership or subscription fee. Despite the depth in the IT market research market, there are yet to emerge firms providing the market research techniques identified in Chapter X. The ability to view holistically the relationship networks at a market sector level, is still an emerging capability and not generally available. That said, there are some simple activities that one can perform inexpensively, that can provide some intelligence on market place relationships:

- For the client looking at multisourced vendor candidates, use a search engine to uncover recent and existing alliance relationships. Often major alliance activity will attract some media attention. Failing that, search the firm's web site for alliance announcements.
- Once you have identified alliances of interest, you can plot them out by hand. For the more adventurous there are available a number of Social Network Analysis tools[2] that can inexpensively allow you to visualise these alliance networks.
- Ask your staff or industry colleagues to comment on your map. They may be able to qualify some of the linkages in terms of the quality of the relationships or alliances.
- Use the map to try and identify potential clusters of providers that could meet your IT requirements as a pre-allianced entity, hence minimising your governance risks.

- For the vendor, the above approach can also be applied to competitor analysis or product/service positioning. Use the same techniques mentioned above to build the network map.
- Having identified key competitors or alliance prospects/targets, look for gaps in the network where your product or service can provide complementary value to the prospective partners. If your niche proves to be quite crowded and likely to be too competitive, think about how small adaptations to the product or service could place you in a better position to leverage performance. Recall that the brokerage or bridge positions can be a powerful place in a network. Can your product or services provide some unique integration or bridging opportunity?

For those willing to invest a little more in data acquisition or analytical tools, there are a growing number of tools becoming available for market relationship analysis. Proprietary data sources are available, like the Datamonitor IT contracts data base and the Factiva news services used for the research reported on in Chapters V. Proprietary tools like Visible Path[3], enable firms to uncover the market intelligence held within the social networks of its own staff. In fact competitive intelligence commentators[4] suggest that a majority of sought after intelligence will be available through the firm's own staff. Visible path software can mine the firm's collaborative tool logs to identify existing social networks, while still protecting the privacy of the individuals. As identified in Chapter VII, the "hidden network" discovered can then be leveraged for profitable activities like market research.

Another emerging relationship mapping tool is Condorview[5] , which uses the Internet as its data source and mines for nominated relationships. Condorview was developed by Peter Gloor, the co-author of *"Coolhunting"*, a book on searching out the latest trends from the Internet (Gloor & Cooper, 2007).

Figure 98 provides an example output from Condorview. The overall plot gives one a sense of the amount of material around IT outsourcing and IT multisourcing. The individual nodes are web sites that reflect the major information points on the topic and can be accessed directly from the map.

In summary, the use of relationship mapping as a means for searching relationship networks in the global IT market place is still somewhat immature. However new tools are emerging at a rapid rate. But even without sophisticated tools, a start can be made with a simple web browser and a hand drawn map.

"Start mapping market place relationships and then look for the unique opportunities for your organisation"

Figure 98. "Coolhunting" for information on outsourcing and multisourcing re-lationships

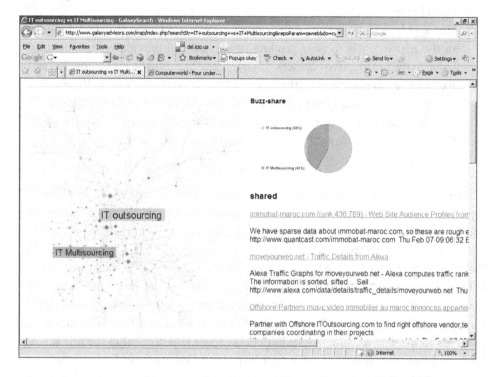

BUILDING THE COLLABORATIVE ENVIRONMENT TECHNICALLY

The previous chapter identified the growing importance of collaborative systems applications. A framework was provided to assist with the capturing of collaborative tool requirements. The choice of collaborative systems is a politically charged activity that will challenge the IT Governance regime. The personal nature of such tools means that virtually everyone has an opinion and is willing to voice it. It is not intended to provide specific guidance on particular tools here as they are far too numerous and constantly changing. However, there are some key learnings that are available from the author's experiences with collaborative technologies used to support global communities of practice (Lock Lee & Neff, 2004), and adapted for inclusion here:

- Technology can at best sustain communities between face to face events and perhaps reduce the number of face to face events required.
- The technology choice needs to respect the "lowest common denominator" members, such that no member is excluded from participation for technical reasons.

- Technology alone will not launch and/or sustain an effective community, without the complement of an active leadership group. Expect to have a large "electronic community graveyard", with those started with good intentions, but eventually not sustained.
- Technologies must be robust and well supported. The slower adoption of newer technologies is more related to supportability than acceptance. The drop off in video conferencing use and the continued reliance on teleconferencing is reflective of this.
- Measuring the financial value of collaboration is problematic given its less formal mode of operation. Activity levels and relationship maps can provide useful proxy measures for business value. Specific "stories and anecdotes" appear to be the most useful mechanism for communicating business value from technology facilitated collaboration.

"For successful collaboration: People first, technology second"

THE FINAL WORD

This book was written on the premise that much of the literature published on IT management and governance had highlighted the criticality of relationships in achieving successful outcomes, yet provided only a limited or shallow treatment of the topic. For the major part, this book has therefore taken a "deep dive" into the relationship aspects of IT Governance and multisourcing. The sociological aspects of the relationships were developed in the form of Corporate SC, to sit along side the economic elements of a business relationship. The academic literature was reviewed in search of theories underpinning the sourcing relationship. This was accompanied by some comprehensive research demonstrating the important role that Corporate SC plays in the global IT market. The constant evolution in technology and the resultant power that new IT developments have placed in the hands of the end users has ensured that the IT Governance task has migrated from a complicated task to now a truly complex one, with little hope of the situation simplifying in the foreseeable future.

With such attention placed on the softer, intangible aspects of the business relationship, it would be easy to believe that what has been presented here is a governance arrangement that will replace the traditional compliance driven modes of IT Governance that the majority of firms operate with today. The truth is that there needs to be elements of both approaches to be successful. Beyond the IT world, the corporate collapses of Enron and Worldcom have shown what an overzealous concentration on "business value", at the expense of responsible

Figure 99. Co-existing IT Governance arrangements

compliance with accepted governance standards, can result in. On the other hand, blind concentration on compliance to pre-determined standards can place a critical barrier on business innovation and growth, as well as leaving employees frustrated and disgruntled.

For the IT executive and the IT Governance team, it is therefore critical to achieve an appropriate balance between IT compliance and cooperation in order to achieve superior business value. The business value in compliance is not always easily observed, compared to activities that are more closely aligned with business activities. However, if such compliance activities are positioned as enabling more effective collaboration across and beyond the firm, then its acceptance is more easily accommodated. By adopting "enhancing the relationship" as a core principle for IT Governance and sourcing, governance decisions can be positioned effectively to enhance supply chain cooperation, improve internal project collaborations, enhance knowledge sharing across formal organisational boundaries, improve client relationships and ultimately build your Corporate SC in the market place.

REFERENCES

Gerencser, M., Lee, R. V., Napolitano, F., & Kelly, C. (2008). *Megacommunities: How leaders of government, business and non-profits can tackle today's global challenges together.* Palgrave Macmillan.

Gloor, P., & Cooper, S. (2007). *Coolhunting.* New York: AMACOM.

Lock Lee, L., & Neff, M. (2004). How information technologies can help build and sustain an organisation's cop: Spanning the socio-technical divide? In P. Hildreth & C. Kimble (Eds.), *Knowledge networks: Innovation through communities of practice*: Idea Group Inc.

ENDNOTES

[1]   http://www.value-networks.com/index.htm

[2]   See http://www.insna.org/INSNA/soft_inf.html (accessed 8/2/08)

[3]   See https://www.visiblepath.com/ (accessed 8/2/08)

[4]   Private discussions with Babette Bensousson (www.mindshifts.com.au) (accessed 8/2/08)

[5]   See http://www.galaxyadvisors.com/condorview.html (accessed 8/2/08)

Appendix
Corporation Social Capital Links to Firm Performance:
Research Methods Used

Appendix
Research Methodology

This appendix provides a detailed description of the methods, analytical techniques and data sources used to address the two research questions, and provide tests for the five hypotheses reported on in Chapter VIII. Hypotheses and/or propositions have been formulated for identifying the impact of Corporate Social Capital (SC) and its component parts on firm performance. Many of the constructs used in defining Corporate SC are qualitative in nature. This called for some innovative methods for operationalising these concepts into quantitative terms. For instance, archival data is used as the primary means for operationalising the Corporate SC concepts for analysis. The justification for this approach over a traditional survey approach was the desire to develop a methodology that could be applied across all market sectors, without needing to be concerned with how representative a survey group may be, and indeed how regularly the analysis could be repeated or updated.

The remaining sub sections can be summarised as presenting details of the methodology employed, addressing sampling procedures, time period of study, data sources used and test methods employed. For completeness the results of the data screening and transformations are also described.

OVERVIEW OF METHODOLOGICAL APPROACH

As noted in the introductory chapter, in order to operationalise the concepts identified in the research path model in Figure 47, a mix of methods was required. A
summary overview of the methodological approach is shown here:

At the top of the figure are the three key archival data sources (Computer Wire,
Factiva and Compustat) used in this research. The triangles show the analytical
technique used to quantify or operationalise the core concepts identified in Figure
47. The four codes within the triangles stand for:

- **CA:** content analysis, which provided quantitative measures from the analysis
  of textual sources;
- **SNA:** social network analysis, which produced quantified measures for describing the positioning of an "actor" in a "network of actors". In this case, the
  actors were at the "firm" level and the network was a networked representation
  of the IT market;
- **FA:** financial analysis which, for this research, was mostly related to selecting
  or developing measures based on financial and market metrics available in the
  Compustat database; and

Figure 100. Methodological overview

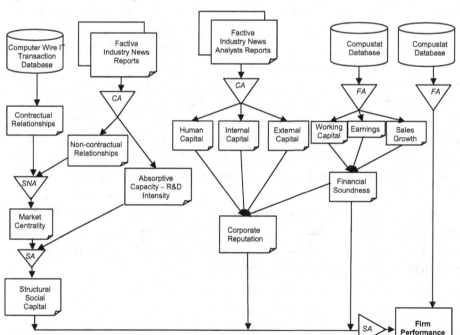

- **SA:** statistical analysis, which refers to the multivariate statistical analyses applied to confirming or otherwise, the hypotheses proposed.

A more detailed description of the above methods is provided in a later section on methods for constructing the variables for analysis.

SAMPLING

This research has been limited to a single market sector, the global IT software and services sector of firms listed on the US stock exchange. The rationale for the selection was for reasons of scope management, but also for the high intangible characteristics of this sector. Given that Corporate SC incorporates largely financially intangible elements, the selection of a sector high in intangibles was more likely to provide a richer source of data from which to conduct the research. The period for sampling was from 1st January 2001 to 31st December 2004. The sampling period was purposely chosen to avoid the extreme and abnormal firm valuation movements during the dotcom boom and bust, preceding this period.

The sampling method for this research was centred on selecting a sub-set of the global IT market where the firms are connected through some form of alliance or joint venture arrangement. It was this networked representation of the marketplace which was used to derive the market centrality variable. The firms represented in this sample were consequently used to derive all other variables used in the analysis.

A snowball sampling procedure for network data was used for this research (Frank, 1979). For large networks, where the identification of all network actors is impractical, a sampling method is required. For large networks there exists no systematic theory of network sampling (Granovetter, 1976; Rothenberg, 1995). Snowball sampling enlarges an initial node selection by adding adjacent nodes through a number of stages (Rothenberg, 1995, p105). Frank (1979) builds a mathematical theory to demonstrate a connection to probability theory. Theory aside, snowball sampling has proven to be the most pragmatic method for sampling large networks. Rothenberg (1995) argues that empirically driven sampling, as identified above, provides a more representative sample for network data than methods that try to satisfy probabilistic criteria.

For the IT Services (ITS) marketplace, the systems integration firms, identified as those firms with the most service contracts, were selected as the initial sample, with the knowledge that these firms were likely to be central to the network of firms operating in the market. The next sample stage selected those firms that were connected, i.e. adjacent to the selected ten systems integrators. Pilot studies indicated that just one additional sampling stage selected some 160 firms, or around

20% of all software and services firms listed on the US stock exchange. Additional snowball sampling stages would provide diminishing additional information from a structural SC perspective and the two-stage sample was deemed sufficient for the purposes of the statistics conducted.

The four-step process of analysis highlighted in Figure 101 was used to construct the network market structure for developing market centrality measures. The data sources, which will be described in more detail in the next section, were the Factiva news service, the Computer Wire industry transaction database and the Compustat financial database. The Computer Wire transaction database records the day of the transaction. The Factiva news sources were updated on a daily basis during this period. The Compustat financial database contains data of differing periodicity depending on the factor selected. The financial data drawn to calculate attributes for financial soundness, Tobins Q (TOBQ), earnings and Total Shareholder Return (TSR) were calculated on a calendar year basis. Step 1 created an initial sample of the top ten systems integrator firms which were identified as those with the most IT contracts in the 2001-2004 period. The second step looked at the firms with which the top ten have contractual relationships. The third step, according to the snowball sampling method, looked for those firms connected to the systems integrators via alliance relationships. These second-stage firms were identified as having business development-type relationships as identified from the Factiva news database (the Computer Wire and Factiva databases are described in more detail in the next section).

The final step was to constitute the resulting sample as a network of firms connected by either contractual or alliance relationships, that is the "vendor side"

Figure 101. Process for generating ITS market network

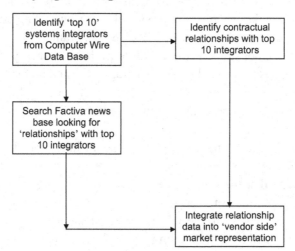

representation of a marketplace (i.e. excludes clients). The rationale for building the networked marketplace around the major ITS systems integration companies was that these firms are the major channel through which ITS are delivered to end clients. The market relationships were identified as either contractual, from the Computer Wire contracts database, or market-based, from Factiva. The process of identifying relationships from Factiva-sourced data was achieved through entering a firm's name and then the Factiva "joint venture" intelligent taxonomy term. It should be noted that the Factiva intelligent taxonomy terms are able to identify multiple synonyms of the "joint venture" term and therefore do not rely on the exact term being present to identify a relevant document. Factiva treats company names intelligently by matching against all different spellings or abbreviations of the company name, even to the extent of previous names that may have changed during a takeover or merger. The identified documents from the Factiva search were then reviewed to extract the firm names described in the selected articles. Firms mentioned more than once in unrelated articles were recorded as an additional "strength" to the relationship. The additional count was not made where multiple articles were clearly reporting on the same piece of news. Special treatment was required for firms that span both the IT hardware and software sectors of interest. Firms like Hewlett Packard, IBM and Fujitsu fall into these categories. For Hewlett Packard and Fujitsu, the selected firms were those that were clearly partnering on software or services. For IBM, the IBM Global Services company name was used, which represents only IBM's services business.

The above process took a selective sample of the ITS market. Relationships between firms that were not connected to the top ten systems integrators were not identified in the final market network representation. This is justified by the fact that these firms' market relationships were not likely to be significant in terms of SC. It is also likely that these firms would be small and unlikely to be listed on the US stock exchange, and therefore would have been excluded from this research anyway.

DATA SOURCES USED

Three key data sources have been selected for this research. First, the ComputerWire contracts database[1] provides more than ten years of data on major contracts signed in the IT sector worldwide. ComputerWire is a major source of data for market tracking in the IT industry. The second data source, Factiva[2], is a Dow Jones and Reuters company which provides global news and business information through online sources. The increasing power of text searching is now finding application in the research community (De Ruig, 2006; Scott, 2006). The third data source is the

Compustat financial database[3], which is considered a primary source of financial data for publicly listed US companies. It is a popular financial source for accounting-related empirical research, especially for studies relating principally to North American firms.

These data sources and how they were used are described in more detail in the following sub-sections.

Information Technology News and Business Information (Factiva)

The largest accessible source of business information is the Internet. While it might be appealing to use the Internet as the source of research data, it is largely an unqualified information source. That said, the search and analysis facilities available for the Internet are impressive and therefore similar search and analysis capabilities applied to qualified information sources is an attractive proposition. For this research, the textual repositories provided the bulk of the content for establishing the measures for Corporate SC. The Factiva subscription news and business intelligence service was chosen as the core source of textual data for this research.

The sources of information that Factiva makes available to its client base is qualified to the extent that the sources are considered by Factiva to be reputable. It is in the business interests of Factiva to ensure that its sources remain reputable, in order to sustain its subscription business.

The target IT sector is well covered by Factiva sources. Factiva provides the capability to search for content by date range. For this research, the period 2001-2004 was chosen for analysis. An additional function provided by Factiva that is important for this research is the provision of a regularly maintained intelligent taxonomy. Factiva has developed the taxonomy to provide key terms describing the content they are providing. These terms provide "concept" matching capabilities whereby relevant articles can be identified that do not necessarily contain exact textual matches. How this taxonomy was used in this research is described in more detail in a later section describing independent variables.

Information Technology Services Contracts Database

IT-sector research company Computer Wire has maintained a database of major transactions (valued in excess of $US1mill.) conducted worldwide since 1996. For this research, the important attributes were the primary and subsidiary vendors. The client name, value of contract and the date of signing were also used as added context when building the initial network maps. This information principally provided information on who the leading systems integration firms were and the contractual relationships they had with other vendors in delivering contracted solutions or services. This data was used to help build the network representation of the ITS marketplace, which is addressed in more detail in the section on independent variables. It was complemented by other relationship data developed from the Content Analysis (CA) of the news and business information sources.

Compustat Database: Information Technology Software and Services Sector

Data for financial analysis was sourced from the Standards and Poors Compustat database for USA-listed companies. The database provides comprehensive financial data on firms listed on the US stock exchange. It is made available to researchers and analysts on a subscription basis. The majority of publicly listed IT software and services are listed on the US stock exchange. The Compustat database is also a popular data source for research studies in the IT software and services sector. The IT software and services sector, GICS code 4510, has 817 listed firms (as at June 2005).

In summary, archival data sources have been used for the provision of the base data for this research. The next section looks at how the key variables used in the path model in Figure 47 are constructed from these data sources.

METHODS FOR CONSTRUCTING THE VARIABLES FOR ANALYSIS AND HYPOTHESIS TESTING

The following sections describe the methods used for sourcing or generating the variables used for the analysis. The methods for constructing the dependent variables for analysis are described in the next section, and the Corporate SC independent variables in following section. Justifications for the methods used are also provided.

Dependent Variables: Firm Performance

The dependent variable is firm performance which is measured through three alternative variables for TSR, TOBQ and ROI. TSR, a common and straightforward measure for wealth creation, measures the wealth creation achieved by a firm. Investors in listed companies are compensated through a combination of dividends, if they are paid, and/or appreciation in the share value. TOBQ is a measure of the market-to-book ratio and has a number of interpretations. One interpretation is as a measure of over- or under-valuation by the share market. Another is the value of the firm's Intangible Assets (IA). Both interpretations suggest using TOBQ as a leading indicator for investment strategy decisions. TOBQ uses replacement values, rather than historical values, for determining book valuations. As replacement values are not readily available for the industry sector under study, a popular approximation for TOBQ is used (Chung & Pruitt, 1994). ROI is included as a commonly used measure of firm performance employed by market analysts. A sensitivity analysis on the dependent variables showed that ROI, ROE and ROA were highly correlated for the data set used, and therefore ROI was selected as representative of all three.

The dependent variable measures were sourced directly from the Compustat database as follows:

TSR = Total Return Factor (TRFM)
TOBQ = (Market Value [MKVAL] + Preferred Stock Liquidation Value [PSTKL]
       + Total Debt [DT]) / Total Assets (AT)
ROI = Return on Investment (ROI)

Financial analyses of firm performance can take many forms. Selecting three separate but complementary measures of firm performance addressed the limitations of single measures not sufficiently representing important aspects of firm performance.

Independent Variables

The independent variables were constructed through the use of SNA, CA, or derived from data taken from the Compustat database. SNA is used to generate a market centrality (CENT) measure. CA is used to generate the variables for AC (operationalised as R&D intensity (RES)), Internal Capital (INC), External Capital (EC) and Human Capital (HC). Finally, financial soundness is derived using an index generated from Compustat data. These three methods are described below:

Social Network Analysis Method

The Social Network Method used in this research has been described previously in Chapter VI. For this research, the actors were at the firm level and the ties represented some form of inter-firm relationship. A CENT measure was used to represent the network centrality of a firm. Two complementary data sources were used to develop the network representation of the IT software and services market: the Computer Wire IT contracts database; and the Factiva news and business information repository.

The Computer Wire database provides some 6000+ transactions. Linkages between vendors and clients are denoted by a signed contract. Sub-contractors also denote contractual links between vendors. The Factiva service provided complementary information on alliances and joint ventures that may not have resulted in a contract with an end client. For example, marketing or R&D joint ventures would not be captured in the contracts database.

In developing the network representation, no differentiation was made between prime contractor, sub-contractor relationships and joint venture relationships identified via the two data sources. The relationships identified were simply combined to come up with an overall IT software and services sector network representation.

Selecting an appropriate centrality measure for assessing a firm's structural SC in the IT software and services market was needed. The question asked was: "What centrality measure best represents structural SC in the IT software and services market?" To help with this assessment a pilot network map was built through initially surveying a selected group of major systems integration firms, identified as market leaders in the business press, for their connections using publicly available information sourced from the Internet. The results of the pilot test are shown in Figure 102.

In Figure 102, the dark circles are the selected systems integration firms that were surveyed in the literature. The size of the nodes is scaled according to the

Figure 102. Pilot IT market network map

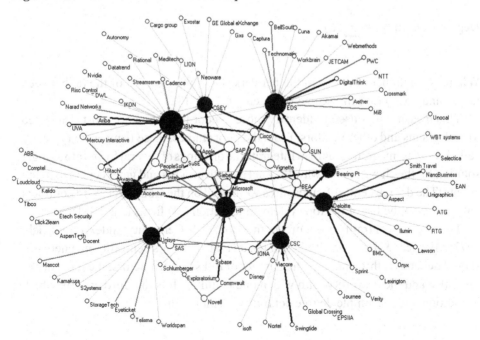

number of connections they have. The lines represent identified alliance relationships. The thickness of the lines represents the strength of the relationship based on the number of documents identified mentioning the connection. What is evident from this pilot map is that those firms in the centre of the map appear to have an advantageous position by having multiple relationships with the systems integrators, who often act as gatekeepers to the end clients. For example, one can see that IBM is a centrally connected node where the size of its node is dictated by the large number of connections IBM has. The larger white circle firms toward the centre of the map usually have connections to one or more of the surveyed firms. These vendors could be seen as being advantageously connected because of the multiple paths they have available to customers via the systems integration firms. The firms on the outside of the map appear to have less powerful positions through having more limited access to the end clients through the systems integrators. Therefore, two centrality measures appear appropriate:

1.   A "degree" centrality measure which identifies the firms that are most connected in the marketplace; and
2.   A centrality measure which identifies those firms which have multiple connections to firms that are highly connected (i.e. the centrally placed firms).

The first construct, degree centrality, is calculated by the number of connections a firm has (Wasserman & Faust, 1994).

$$\text{Degree Centrality}_i = \sum_{\substack{j=1 \\ j \neq i}}^{N} Rij$$

Where N = number of nodes in the network; Rij = the strength of the tie between node i and node j (usually scaled between "0" and "1").

This measure was used to identify those vendor firms that are most connected to both clients and other vendors. From the pilot studies, these firms were typically called systems integrators, as they integrate the offerings of several firms into a single solution for the client. In this way, they act as both brokers and gatekeepers to many clients. The degree centrality measures were used on the Computer Wire contracts data to derive the list of the top systems integration (SI) firms (e.g. IBM).

The second centrality measure is the Bonacich Centrality Index (Bonacich, 1972; Mizruchi & Bunting, 1981) that posits that an actor's centrality in a network should depend on three factors: the number of links to other actors; the intensity of the links; and the centrality with which one is linked. It is the third criteria which is additional to the simple degree centrality formulation.

$$\text{Bonacich Centrality } Ci = \sum_{\substack{j=1 \\ j \neq i}}^{N} Rij * Cj$$

Where Cj = Centrality of organisations linked to *i*.

Bonacich centrality is also often called "eigenvector centrality", which relates to the method Bonacich used for solving for C*i* using eigenvalues of the matrix representation of the network (Bonacich, 1972). For this research, the Bonacich centrality measure was selected as appropriate for this application. The choice is consistent with similar empirical studies making use of SN centrality measures (Podolny, 1993; Podolny *et al.*, 1996). From this point forward in this appendix, the term "centrality" will refer to the eigenvector centrality measure, unless explicitly stated otherwise. The UCINET SNA software[4] was used to calculate the eigenvector centrality for each firm in the network.

In summary, the four-step SNA process used in this research is illustrated in Figure 103. As can be seen in Figure 103, in the second step CA is used to select unique joint venture events to create a tie between firms, with the number of events reflecting the strength of the relationship (i.e. the larger the number of unique events, the stronger the inferred relationship). The UCINET software is then used to develop the centrality scores for each firm in the sample. The CA method is described in the next sub-section.

Figure 103. SNA process overview

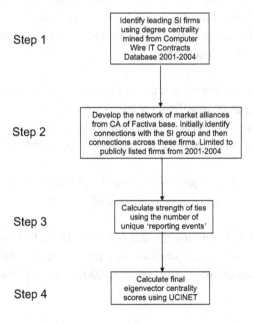

The Content Analysis Method

Content Analysis (CA) is a technique used to systematically analyse information sources for communication themes or patterns. Typically, the technique calls for human coding of concepts of interest that can be found in textual reports or publications. Once coded, the concepts can be weighted for relevance and combined to come up with a quantitative measure for the concept. Historically, the technique has been popularly used to track topics and trends in the public literature. The power of the approach is that it provides one of the few techniques available for analysing textual repositories, which make up the vast majority of business communications.

Krippendorf (2004) identifies stability, reproducibility and accuracy as key reliability measures. On the negative side, the objectivity of the technique can be questioned given that the human coder is susceptible to personal bias when performing the coding process. This susceptibility can be mediated to some extent by using multiple coders and performing inter-coder analyses to assess the consistency with which the task is being performed (Neuendorf, 2001). Another potential weakness is the possible substitution of quantity for quality, where frequency counts do not discriminate the quality of the classified unit. Again, the introduction of weighting schemes could mediate this weakness to some extent; though at the same time it could also introduce other classification challenges with respect to how weights are assigned.

In recent times, CA has been used to assess the degree of disclosure of IC components that companies are making in their annual reports (J. Guthrie *et al.*, 2004). The method has been replicated by several authors to assess the level of IC reporting in different countries around the world (Bozzolan *et al.*, 2003; Goh & Lim, 2004; J. Guthrie *et al.*, 2007). The authors provide a number of important points for performing CA. These include:

- Categories of classification need to be clearly and operationally defined to minimise ambiguous classification opportunities;
- The information needs to able to be quantified;
- The coding process needs to be objective and repeatable by different coders; and
- A unit of analysis is required, e.g. words, phrases, sentences, paragraphs, portions of a page, inclusive or exclusive of pictures.

In the area of social and environmental reporting (J. Guthrie & Parker, 1989), it has been shown that the quantity of disclosure has not always been representative of actual performance (Frost & Wilmshurst, 2000). For disclosure applications, being able to capture the quality of disclosure is required if disclosure is to be effectively related to performance.

Traditionally, CA was seen as a labour-intensive endeavour as large quantities of textual information needed to be manually coded and checked for accuracy and consistency. The manual nature of the technique effectively limits the scope of CA that can currently be conducted. Recent developments in computerised support for CA therefore offer an attractive proposition. Computer-assisted CA is also the topic of substantial technological development (Krippendorf, 2004; Neuendorf, 2001), as electronic search engines look to improve their "classification" of electronic content to provide more accurate and reliable search results from unstructured textual repositories.

Krippendorf (2004) discussed how computerised CA tools can be divided into a number of categories:

- Dictionary key word-based tools largely classify text pieces according to the presence of matching text to the concept of interests.
- Concept-based tools are a sophistication of the key word-based tools in that they develop their own dictionary of "concepts" that can be represented by multiple phrases or words such that accurate concepts can be identified even though they do not contain the specific words in the search terms.
- Classification assistants include tools like Nvivo[5] which are popular with researchers using qualitative research methods and who have a need to manage the collection and capture of large number of interview scripts.
- Electronic taxonomies are similar to concept-based tools in that they are developed from an analysis of existing content, looking for the best "descriptors" that can be applied to a given body of text. Taxonomies are hierarchical structures with the more abstract terms being closer to the top of the hierarchy and more specialised or descriptive terms being found lower down in the hierarchy. Taxonomies provide a navigation aid for those wanting to explore a body of text. By navigating the taxonomy, users can "drill down" from quite abstract concepts through to quite specific topics.

According to Krippendorff (2004), for CA criteria of stability, reproducibility and accuracy, computer-based CA tools could be seen as strong in terms of stability and reproducibility. With a given body of text, computer-based CA tools will provide the same repeatable result without fault. Of course, it is in the area of accuracy that computer-based tools are seen to be deficient. Artificial intelligence technologies have yet to deliver the capacity for the textual understanding levels that humans are capable of. Currently, little IC-based research has relied on computer-based CA. One exception was a study by (Bontis, 2003), who used electronic CA to identify

Intellectual Capital disclosure (ICD) levels for Canadian corporations. However, the low levels of disclosure found may be attributed to the inability of the electronic search used to identify disclosures, which did not contain an exact textual match with the terms being searched (Beattie & Thomson, 2005). Beattie & Thomson (2005) also raised concerns about the non-standard categorisations used to measure IC disclosure levels and went on to demonstrate how the level of disclosure is related to the number of textual concepts provided for each category of interest.

Using the IC disclosure activity as an example, if the absolute level of IC disclosure is desired for say, comparing changes in disclosure patterns over time, CA requires a standardised and consistent categorisation of IC that all researchers can use. Coding methods would also need to be standardised. On the other hand, if IC disclosure CA is being used for comparison between firms, market sectors or countries, accuracy becomes less of a concern (within limits), while consistency of categorisation and coding becomes important. In other words, even if the CA method under-represents IC, it does so in a systematic way, which will not impact the validity of comparisons between different entities. Of course, the CA technique needs to do a reasonable job of identifying IC elements, or at least the researcher would need to be able to quickly identify and remove false hits.

For similar studies that are looking to assess firms for qualitative attributes, research firms have tended to prefer a Delphi research technique, whereby subject matter experts or company executives are regularly surveyed for their opinions[6]. The weakness in these techniques is that there is little guarantee that the survey respondents are equally and adequately informed on the different firms in the marketplace. It also means that survey respondents are limited to those firms that they are familiar with and this in turn limits the coverage that firms in the marketplace might receive. However, systematic CA of news and business information sources at least provides a larger pool of reporters, many of whom provide the required commentary as a professional occupation. The trade-off is that the sought after data has to be "mined" from pre-existing publications, as against targeted information gained from a survey.

The scope of this research being a whole market sector containing hundreds of companies, made the use of manual CA techniques unfeasible. CA techniques in the Intellectual Capital disclosure areas have largely been limited to analysing annual reports. Where this research differs from the research focused on voluntary disclosures is the nature of the information being analysed. For this research, an independent source of information was used. While no news or business information source could be considered entirely objective, given the range and number of articles available in the Factiva information base, it was anticipated that bias from individual reporters would be minimised. It was also anticipated that both "good" and "bad" news items would be contained in the information base, giving a more balanced perspective. The advantages over voluntary corporate disclosures are that disclosures are selective and only favourable to firms providing the disclosure (i.e. they only tell the "good" stories).

The standardised approach for conducting CA in IC areas has been to define a set of descriptor terms for the elements of HC, INC and EC. The human coder would use these terms to identify concepts within the source documents, usually an annual report. It has been argued that the use of electronic classification of source documents is vastly inferior to the human coder in being able to identify appropriate concepts in the text (Beattie & Thomson, 2005). However, this critique was targeted at simple text matching searches. It has already been argued that it is the relative "between firm" measure that is important, as opposed to accurately identifying absolute values of concept identification. However, to at least improve the accuracy of the classification search, Factiva's intelligent taxonomy terms were used. This enabled more consistent identification of the IC concepts.

CA, both manual and computerised, has several identified limitations (J. Guthrie & Abeysekera, 2006; Hussey & Hussey, 1997; Krippendorf, 2004; Silverman, 1993). For instance, in regard to manual CA, the following limitations have been identified:

- The risk of human coders introducing personal bias in assessing content;
- The risk of inconsistent applications of coding methods used;
- Sensitive to the nature and number of key terms selected to represent the concept being analysed in the text;
- Sensitive to the sources used for the CA;
- Limited by the volume of text that can be effectively analysed manually; and
- Difficulty in assuring the ability to replicate studies.

Computer-assisted CA can guarantee a degree of consistency of processing but introduces limitations in its ability to assess text with the same degree of accuracy as the human coder. While the above limitations are acknowledged, for studies looking to draw from large, distributed and largely qualitative data sources, there appears to be few alternative approaches available (Krippendorf, 2004).

The following sections describe the CA process used to develop the quantification of IC components, HC, INC and EC, as well as firm RES. First, the IC elements of EC, INC and HC are described, followed by RES.

Intellectual Capital Variables
The IC variables were generated using the Factiva computer-assisted CA method. The use of the Factiva intelligent taxonomy terms was important in maximising

the accuracy of the classification in the electronic search. Factiva generate and manage a fixed set of taxonomy terms that are used to classify all documents in their database. Automated methods are used to assist in the classification. It is anticipated that some human supervision of the automated methods would occur. But for the larger part, the automation would assist in the consistency achieved, while the human supervision would correct gross errors. The exact details of the Factiva intelligent taxonomy are proprietary and not in the public domain.

A mapping was therefore required between accepted IC terms and the Factiva intelligent taxonomy terms. The IC classifications developed by Guthrie & Petty (2000) were mapped to terms contained within the Factiva intelligent taxonomy terms set. The mapping of terms is shown in Table 20:

As one can see from the above table, the Factiva taxonomy terms were more expansive than the IC terms. For example, Factiva terms like "Management Moves" and "Executive Pay" are HC terms that would only loosely map to the Guthrie and Petty (2000) terms. In addition, the Factiva terms would also identify articles that contained synonyms to the stated terms. It was therefore anticipated that the Factiva electronic search results would not suffer the shortcomings of basic keyword searches. It was also anticipated that the Factiva electronic search would approxi-

Table 20 Mapping of intellectual capital terms to Factiva intelligent taxonomy terms

IC Classification Equivalence (Guthrie & Petty, 2000)	Factiva Intelligent Taxonomy Terms
Human capital: Employee, education, training, work-related knowledge, entrepreneurial spirit	Employee Training/Development Workers' Pay Labour Disputes Lay-offs Recruitment Directors' Dealings Executive Pay Management Moves
Internal capital: Intellectual property, management philosophy, corporate culture, management processes, information/networking systems, financial relations	Intellectual Property Best Practice Competitive Intelligence Corporate Governance/Investor Relations Corporate Process Redesign Knowledge Management Supply Chain Information Technology Debt/Bond Markets
External capital: Brands, customers, customer satisfaction, company names, distribution channels, business collaborations, licensing agreements	Marketing Joint Ventures Contracts/Orders Profiles of Companies Society/Community/Work

mate the IC discovery levels of a human coder, but with the consistency afforded by computer-based searches.

The method for developing an index measure for HC, INC, EC and RES components followed a four-step process, as highlighted in Figure 104. The first step is to identify each firm with a Factiva company record. The second step takes the Factiva taxonomy terms for HC, INC, EC and RES, and searches for articles involving the selected firm. The third step is to classify each story as "positive" or "neutral" or "negative". The final step is to calculate the index for HC, INC, EC and RES, for each firm, using a method described later in this section.

One can see that, unlike IC disclosure analyses, the IC measures did not rely on counting concepts within a single document, like an annual report. Because of the large number of documents available, the level of IC content was only used to select a document for inclusion in a "document count" as representative of the attribute of interest (e.g. HC). Single documents may occur in more than one IC element (e.g. if the document contains information about both HC and EC). By raising the level of the CA to the document level, the sensitivity to the IC classification mode was lowered as the IC measure was spread across several, rather than a single document.

Figure 104. IC and absorptive capacity measurement process

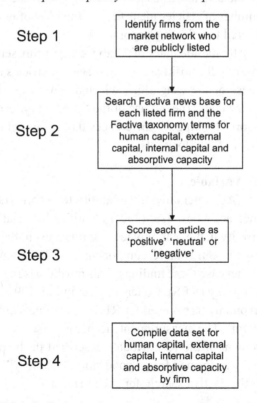

The challenge still existed for developing an algorithmic scheme for developing the measures from document counting. It was observed that most news and information articles were generally of a positive nature, though significant negative news existed and was likely to have a greater impact on firm perception than the more regular positive news (Kopalle & Lehmann, 1995; Novaes, 2002). This effect is also shown through the impact of good and bad news on stock price movements (Dean & Faff, 2004; Goeij & Marquering, 2004). The scoring algorithm therefore weights negative stories at twice the impact of positive news. The scoring algorithm is as follows:

$$Xi = \sum_{i}(Pi-2 * Ni)$$

Where X = the IC attribute measure for firm *i*
P_i = Positive (or neutral) articles for firm *i*
N_i = Negative articles for firm *i*

The general tenet used was that the existence of a news or business information report was considered a positive contributor unless its main purpose was to highlight negative news. For articles which contained both positive and negative news, the dominant tenet of the article was used. No attempt was made to normalise the score based on the number of articles identified, as the level of news coverage was seen to be directly related to a firm's Corporate SC.

As an additional test for the adequacy of the above algorithm, sensitivity analyses were conducted separately for positive articles, negative articles and total articles to assess the robustness of the weightings selected. This was achieved through correlating the raw story count (i.e. no use of the "good story, bad story" calculation) and the index scores looking for differences that could not be justified from a qualitative assessment of the story sets.

Absorptive Capacity Variable
"Absorptive capacity" (AC) refers to a firm's ability to absorb knowledge and capabilities from alliance activities. Tsai (2001) identifies the relationship between AC and network centrality in the marketplace. For this reason, the elements of AC, which would normally be seen as an IC component, have been separated out in the model to confirm or otherwise these findings. This attribute is regularly operationalised through a R&D proxy (RES) (Cohen and Levinthal, 1990; Tsai, 2001). The Factiva intelligent taxonomy terms used for RES were "Science/Technology" and "Research/Development". The measurement mechanism used was the same as that used for the measurement of the IC attributes described in the previous section, meaning that an index was formed from "good story, bad story" classifications of stories returned with the Factiva search, for each firm.

Financial Soundness Variable

Financial soundness is a measure of a firm's financial robustness (i.e. its ability to sustain an adequate financial performance) in the face of potentially unanticipated events like a sudden market downturn or natural disasters. Financial soundness was operationalised through the use of Altman's Z score (Zscore) (Eidleman, 1995), a proven method for prediction of business failure. Zscore is calculated as:

$$Z = 1.2* X1 + 1.4*X2 + 3.3*X3 + 0.6*X4 + 1.0*X5$$

Where:

X1 = Working Capital/Total Assets
X2 = Retained Earnings/Total Assets
X3 = EBIT/Total Assets
X4 = Market Value of Equity/Book Value of Debt
X5 = Sales/Total Assets

This measure was initially designed to assess the potential for a firm to become insolvent or bankrupt in the short to medium term. The measure was chosen for the simplicity of calculation from readily available data and its popularity as a financial soundness measure.

Financial soundness is an attribute identified from *Fortune*'s "Most Admired Companies" formulation of corporate reputation. There are many ways in which financial soundness could be operationalised. For example, profitability, revenue growth, volatility of share price are examples of proxies that could have been used. The selection of Zscore was justified as a tried and tested combination of financial measures used to achieve an overall financial soundness measure.

The financial soundness measure's use of Zscore could also be seen as a limited interpretation biased toward firm failure susceptibility. However, one could also argue that for most investors, financial soundness would be more reflective of survivability than growth-orientation.

Hypothesis Testing Method

The hypotheses relate to the influence of Corporate SC elements on firm performance. The proposed model is made up of several latent variables supported by observed or measured indicator variables as shown in Figure 47. Latent variables (the ovals) are theoretical constructs that have been either established in the literature or, in the case of Corporate SC, by this research. Latent variables have no direct operational method for their measurement. The observed variables provide measurable indicators of the latent variables. Only the measured variables participate in the hypothesis test. HC, INC, EC, network CENT, RES and financial soundness are the independent variables, while ROI, TSR and TOBQ are the firm performance dependent variables.

One can see that the IC concept is shown to illustrate the heritage of the measured variables of EC, INC and HC, but is totally encapsulated by the corporate reputation construct. The EC measure can be seen to be related to both the structural SC and IC concepts. The following statistical methods of factor analysis and multiple linear regression were used to operationalise the proposed analytical model. Table 21. Identifies the data elements available for statistical analyses. The annualised data for each of the four years was included in the sample set.

Factor Analysis

Factor analysis analyses the structure of the interrelationships between (usually) large numbers of variables. Factor analysis results in the identification of a smaller number of underlying factors describing the interrelationships (Hair *et al.*, 1998).

Table 21. Data elements

Data Element (variable name)	Derivation	Units
Dependent Variables		
Return on Investment (ROI)	Directly from Compustat	%
Tobins Q (TOBQ)	Calculated from Compustat	Ratio
Total Shareholder Return (TSR)	Directly from Compustat	%
Independent Variables		
Eigenvector Centrality[7] (CENT)	SNA	Calculated, numeric
Absorptive Capacity (RES)	Content analysis	CA score
Internal Capital (INC)	Content analysis	CA score
Human Capital (HC)	Content analysis	CA score
External Capital (EC)	Content analysis	CA score
Financial Soundness (Zscore)	Directly from Compustat	Calculated, numeric
Control Variables[8]		
Firm Size (SIZE)	Net sales (SALE) used as a proxy for firm size; sourced directly from Compustat	$
Profitability (P_L)	Earning per share (EPS); sourced directly from Compustat Positive = 1 Negative = 0	Dummy
Sub-Industry Sector (IND)	GICS divided into software (=1) and non-software firms (=0)	Dummy

Confirmatory factor analysis, as used in this research, was used to confirm a proposed analytical model, as opposed to creating one through exploration of data. Multiple linear regression analysis was used to explore the predictive power of structural SC and corporate reputation (collectively, Corporate SC) on the individual firm performance measures of TSR, ROI and TOBQ ratio.

In this research, confirmatory factor analysis was used to confirm or otherwise the analytical model proposed in Figure 105. The observable indicator variables were entered into the factor analysis. The resulting factors generated indicated the distinctive factors that underpin one or more of the measured variables. The factors generated were then compared with the latent variables in the proposed model, looking to confirm or otherwise, the viability of the proposed model. The process is summarised in Figure 105.

The confirmatory factor analysis was used to provide credibility for the proposed analytical model. To test the specific hypotheses, the multiple regression techniques used are described in the following section. The results are provided in the later section on confirmatory factor analysis.

Figure 105. Confirmatory factor analysis

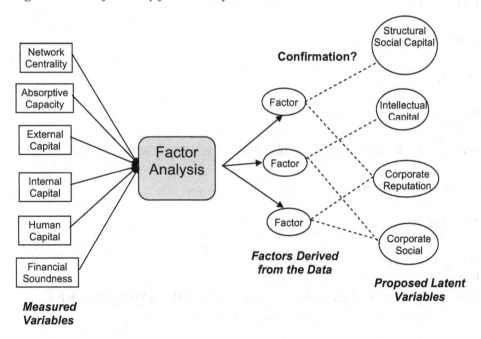

MULTIVARIATE REGRESSION MODELS

Multiple regression analysis was used to identify the explanatory power of the sub-components of Corporate SC for the selected firm performance measures, at each level of the Corporate SC formulation. This stepwise analysis is aimed at identifying the expected improvement in explanatory power with each additional Corporate SC layer. The model follows the building block representation of Corporate SC shown in Figure 46.

The regression models are:

Model 1:

$Perf_{ROI}$;
$Perf_{TOBQ}$;
$Perf_{TSR} = b_0 + b_1 CENT + b_2 SIZE + b_3 IND + b_4 P\_L + e$

Absorptive capacity level

Model 2:

$Perf_{ROI}$;
$Perf_{TOBQ}$;
$Perf_{TSR} = b_0 + b_1 CENT + b_2 RES + b_3 SIZE + b_4 IND + b_5 P\_L + e$

Intellectual capital level

Model 3:

$Perf_{ROI}$;
$Perf_{TOBQ}$;
$Perf_{TSR} = b_0 + b_1 CENT + b_2 RES + b_3 HC + b_4 INC + b_5 SIZE + b_6 IND + b_7 P\_L + e$

Corporate reputation level

Model 4:

$Perf_{ROI}$;
$Perf_{TOBQ}$;
$Perf_{TSR} = b_0 + b_1 CENT + b_2 RES + b_3 HC + b_4 INC + b_5 ZSCORE + b_6 SIZE + b_7 IND + b_8 P\_L + e$

Model 4 is used to test the five hypotheses relating the individual elements of Corporate SC with firm performance.

Based on prior research studies in related fields (Hand & Lev, 2003; Lev & Sougiannis, 1999; Stuart, 2000), firm size and industry sub-sector were used as control variables. The additional control variable of profitability was introduced owing to the relatively large proportion of loss-making firms (nearly 50%) in the sample. The proposition that the role of book values on share values differs for firms in loss-making, rather than profit-making situations (Collins *et al.*, 1999) further supports its selection as a control variable.

The choice of multivariate statistical analysis approaches has been based on the nature of the model constructs developed in support of the proposed theory of Corporate SC and its potential impact on firm performance as a dependent variable. The key Corporate SC constructs of structural SC, IC and corporate reputation are not directly measurable or observable, being derived from a series of indicators drawn from the literature. The dependent variable, firm performance, is also not a single measure, but a collective of the three measures of TSR, ROI and TOBQ.

The sample comprised pooled cross-sectional time series data from 2001 to 2004, resulting in 624 observations. For the CENT measure, which only had a single measure across the four-year period, the results were replicated for each year. The pooled cross-sectional time series data runs the risk of violating the independence of observations assumptions, through the presence of serial correlations within the time series. Lagrange multiplier (LM) tests were conducted to determine whether the panel data should be tested using a random effects model (Greene, 2000), rather than the classical regression model. It was anticipated that this would be the case for the longitudinal data contained within the panel data and therefore the random effects model was adopted for the multiple regression analyses. Heteroscedacity would also be controlled for with White's adjusted t-statistic (White, 1980).

DATA SCREENING AND TRANSFORMATIONS

Data Treatments

As indicated in the data descriptive analysis, none of the selected variables were able to meet the test for normality and therefore would need to be transformed if used for multivariate analysis. Both log and/or inverse transformations were trialled for each of the variables (Tabachnick & Fiddell, 2001). Largely, these traditional transformations were not successful in normalising the data. Given the nature of the distributions and the presence of several extreme outliers with many of the variables, rank transformations were used. While there is some loss in statistical power with rank regressions, monotonically increasing/decreasing distributions with the presence of outliers lend themselves to the use of rank transformations (Iman & Conover, 1979). The transformation to ranks avoids the need to exclude extreme outliers shown in the above distributions. All variables participating in the hypotheses tests were therefore transformed to ranked variables.

Missing data was treated by excluding cases where they exist for the model under consideration. For the four models used, the worst case reduced the sample from 156 firms to 137 firms or approximately 12% of the available data. For the full sample of 624 observations, the worst case (once missing data was catered for) resulted in 525 observations being available. Missing data analysis indicated that the slightly smaller sample size, along with the pattern of data missing, did not have a material effect on the validity of the results achieved.

Bi-variate correlations of the major variables are shown below. Both parametric (Pearsons) and non-parametric (Spearman's Rho) correlations are included. The table shows several statistically significant ($p < 0.5$; 2-tailed) correlations, but not to the level that might cause multicollinearity or singularity issues. This was confirmed by tests undertaken during the regression tests.

It is informative to look at the nature of the content that is included in the index. While the Factiva taxonomy was used to select articles for analysis, the search results tended to be polarised around a few particular classes of article. For example, with the HC index, the predominant "negative" story related to lay-offs, retrenchments or key executive movements. Articles could belong to more than one taxonomy classification, so the overall number of "hits" in the table below is not unique.

Figure 106 shows a table and plot that illustrates a typical distribution for HC searches of the Factiva news database according to the intelligent taxonomy mapping identified in Table 20. The sub-elements of HC relate to the specific Factiva intelligent taxonomy terms selected to represent HC in the analysis and show that management moves (around 1500 news articles) and lay-offs (around 850 news articles) are the most newsworthy elements of HC reported on.

INC: Internal Capital Index

The INC represents intangibles that exist internal to the firm, but are externalised through their reporting in the public press. Figure 107 shows the nature of the INC news: As expected, one can see the predominance of "information technology" stories, given the industry sector of focus for this research. Apart from IT, "Knowledge Management", "Intellectual Capital" and "supply chain" were the next most visible elements of INC.

Table 22. Bi-variate correlations

Test variables Pearson correlation coefficients above the diagonal and Spearman correlation coefficients below the diagonal.

	ROI	TOBQ	TSR	CENT	RES	HC	INC	EC	Zscore	Size	P_L	IND
ROI	1	0.310**	0.420**	0.312**	-0.140**	0.371**	0.349**	0.283**	0.597**	0.500**	0.850**	-0.110**
TOBQ	0.314**	1	0.330**	0.005	0.145**	0.093*	-0.098*	0.092*	0.476**	-0.162**	0.167**	0.214**
TSR	0.414**	0.330**	1	0.063	-0.080	0.235**	0.054	0.047	0.333**	0.120**	0.391**	-0.060
CENT	0.312**	0.002	0.061	1	0.086*	0.505**	0.728**	0.614**	0.204**	0.702**	0.269**	-0.376**
RES	-0.139**	0.148**	-0.080	0.085*	1	0.106**	0.181**	0.154**	0.025	-0.176**	-0.128**	0.009
HC	0.373**	0.086*	0.230**	0.505**	0.107**	1	0.556**	0.358**	0.237**	0.436**	0.354**	-0.229**
INC	0.350**	-0.098*	0.053	0.728**	0.178**	0.556**	1	0.544**	0.140**	0.682**	0.352**	-0.361**
EC	0.289**	0.088*	0.047	0.614**	0.153**	0.358**	0.544**	1	0.232**	0.473**	0.256**	-0.316**
Zscore	0.596**	0.482**	0.334**	0.203**	0.025	0.237**	0.139**	0.233**	1	0.255**	0.452**	-0.020
Size	0.499**	-0.165**	0.119**	0.703**	-0.180**	0.441**	0.683**	0.480**	0.259**	1	0.484**	-0.572**
P_L	0.851**	0.167**	0.390**	0.267**	-0.134**	0.358**	0.351**	0.262**	0.451**	0.483**	1	-0.145**
IND	-0.110**	0.214**	-0.060	-0.376**	0.009	-0.229**	-0.361**	-0.316**	-0.020	-0.572**	-0.145**	1

** Correlation is significant at the p< 0.01 level (2-tailed)
* Correlation is significant at the p< 0.05 level (2-tailed)

Figure 106. Human capital stories breakdown

Human Capital	News "Flavour"	"Hits"
Employee Training/Development		0
Workers' Pay	Mostly negative	132
Labour Disputes	Mostly negative	42
Lay-offs	Mostly negative	839
Recruitment	Positive to neutral	109
Directors' Dealings	Neutral	28
Executive Pay	Positive to neutral	116
Management Moves	Positive, negative and neutral	1499

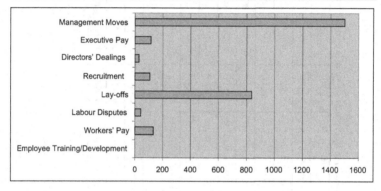

EC: External Capital Index

EC is related to those activities that are designed to engage stakeholders outside the firm, i.e. suppliers, customers, partners. The nature of the EC news is shown in Figure 108.

The data shows the dominance of "joint ventures", which is consistent with the conjecture that there exists an overlap between EC and CENT. Other important aspects of EC were "corporate crime" and "corporate credit rating".

ZScore: Financial Soundness

The Zscore is available directly form the Compustat database. The distribution was not normal, showing a majority of firms just above the "0" mark with a long tail of negative Zscores. The relatively large proportion of negative Zscores appears to reflect the nature of the IT sector. Loss-making firms make up nearly 50% of the firms sampled during the 2001-2004 period.

Figure 107. Internal capital stories breakdown

Internal Capital	News "Flavour"	"Hits"
Intellectual Property	Positive, negative and neutral	466
Best Practice	Mostly positive	45
Competitive Intelligence	Mostly positive	56
Corporate Governance/Investor Relations	Positive, negative and neutral	81
Corporate Process Redesign	Mostly positive	18
Knowledge Management	Positive	470
Supply Chain	Mostly positive	399
Information Technology	Mostly positive	1991
Debt/Bond Markets	Positive, negative and neutral	168

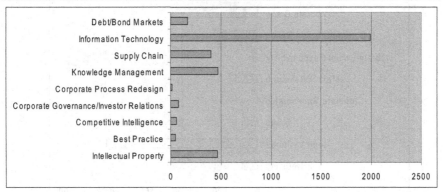

SIZE: Control Variable for Firm Size

Sales volume is a common proxy for firm size. For this research the cut-off between small and large firms was arbitrarily set at the median point.

P_L: Profitability Proxy (Dummy Variable)

The P_L identifies those firms that are profitable as determined by earnings per share performance. For profitable firms P_L = 1 and for loss-making firms P_L = 0.

IND: Industry Proxy (Dummy Variable)

The IND identifies those firms that are in the software industry sub-sector (GICS 4510) where IND = 1. For non-software industry firms, IND = 0.

The next section describes mechanisms used for the treatment of the raw data, described above, in order to achieve the required statistical validity for the hypotheses tests.

Figure 108. External capital stories breakdown

External Capital	News "Flavour"	"Hits"
Advertising	Positive	203
Joint Ventures	Mostly positive	1991
Brand	Mostly positive	210
Corporate Sponsorship	Positive	14
Market Research	Mostly positive	292
Corporate Social Responsibility	Positive, negative and neutral	58
Corporate Credit Rating	Positive and negative	460
Corporate Crime	Mainly negative	1122

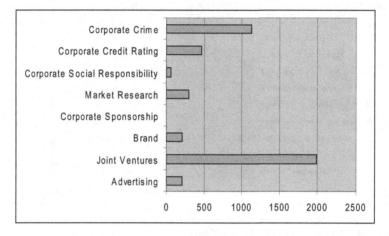

The major representation came from the software and services sector, which is considered a "high intangibles" sector (i.e. minimal tangible or physical assets). The 103 firms in this sector represent approximately 12% of the software and services firms listed on the US stock exchange (as at June 2005). The remainder of the sectors represented could be considered more physical asset intensive than the software and services sector. In total, the 156 firms represent just over 9% of listed IT companies (Table 23).

Confirmatory Factor Analysis

The path model shown in Figure 109 identifies a number of latent variables: structural SC, IC, corporate reputation and Corporate SC that are manifested in the identified measured variables.

The path model is a theoretical model derived from the literature reviewed previously. This section reports on how well the data aligns with the theory when

Table 23. Industry sector break-up

GICS		N	
2010	Capital Goods	9	5.77%
2510	Automobiles & Components	1	0.64%
2520	Consumer Durables	2	1.28%
2550	Retailing	1	0.64%
3030	Household Products	1	0.64%
4510	Software & Services	103	66.03%
4520	Technology Hardware & Equipment	34	21.79%
4530	Semiconductor Equipment	3	1.92%
5010	Telecommunication Services	2	1.28%

statistical classification methods are used to determine discriminating "clusters". Factor analysis was used to determine how well each of the measured variables clustered.

Factor analysis was conducted on the independent variables. Principal factors extraction with varimax rotation was set for the six independent variables. Using the default eigenvalue > 1 as the threshold, all variables were clustered into two factors. This supports the view that Corporate SC is a cohesive concept as represented by all of the clustered independent variables.

Figure 109. Path model

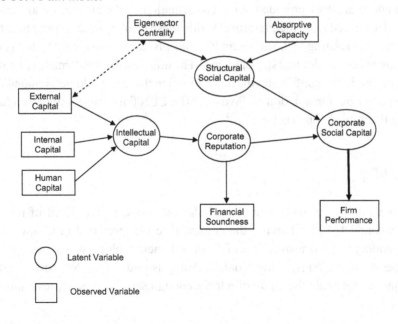

Table 24. Factor analysis forcing a selection of two factors

	Component	
	1	2
CENT	.861	-.057
RES	.227	.869
HC	.712	-.105
INC	.849	.092
EC	.753	.024
Zscore	.368	-.463

Extraction Method: Principal Component Analysis 2 components extracted

The above result suggests that the IC (HC, INC and EC) and eigenvector CENT could be represented by a single factor. The theoretical model suggests redundancy between CENT (eigenvector) and EC. The result demonstrates that EC could be substituted for by eigenvector CENT. A new IC formulation could therefore be constructed from CENT, HC and INC. However, based on the above results, research intensity could not be considered a sub-component of the new IC construct. The corporate reputation concept is formulated as a composite of two different factors (i.e. IC and financial soundness [Zscore]). An integrated Corporate SC construct was then made up of CENT, RES (R&D intensity), HC, INC and financial soundness.

The above analysis provided some confirmation of the conjecture around the path model derived from the literature. While these results could be used to inform future research relating to the different IC concepts, for this research the focus is on Corporate SC and its defined sub-elements. The utility of this confirmatory analysis for this research was confirming the determination that EC could be excluded from the Corporate SC formulation in favour of the CENT measure without violating existing theoretical constructs.

SUMMARY

This appendix was provided for the scholar interested in the detail of research methods conducted in achieving the empirical results provided in Chapter VIII. The appendix provided an overview of the overall methodology, which incorporated a number of innovations, using Content Analysis and Social Network Analysis techniques to facilitate the study of a large enough sample to be representative of a whole market sector. The sampling methods, data sources used and methods for constructing variables and hypotheses were detailed along with the hypothesis testing methods. The results of the data screening and transformation processes were also included for completeness.

REFERENCES

Beattie, V., & Thomson, J. (2005, October 18-20). *Lifting the lid on the use of Content Analysis to Investigate Intellectual Capital Disclosures in Corporate Annual Reports.* Paper presented at the 1st Workshop on Visualising, Measuring and Managing Intangible and Intellectual Capital, Ferrara University, Italy.

Bonacich, P. (1972). Technique for analyzing overlapping memberships. In H. Costner (Ed.), *Sociological Methodology*: San Francisco: Jossey-Bass.

Bontis, N. (2003). Intellectual Capital Disclosure in Canadian Corporations. *Journal of Human Resource Costing and Accounting, 7*(1-2), pp.9-20.

Bozzolan, S., Favotto, F., & Ricceri, F. (2003). Italian annual intellectual capital disclosure: an empirical analysis. *Journal of Intellectual Capital, 4*(4), pp.543-558.

Chung, K., & Pruitt, S. (1994). A Simple Approximation of Tobin's q. *Financial Management, 23*(3 Autumn), pp.70-74.

Collins, D., Pincus, M., & Xie, H. (1999). Equity Valuation and Negative Earnings: The Role of Book Value of Equity. *The Accounting Review, 74*(1), pp.29-61.

De Ruig, R. (2006). Tracking Politically Exposed Persons: A difficult (and now enforceable) procedure. *RMA Journal, 89*(1), pp.36-39.

Dean, W., & Faff, W. (2004). Asymmetric Covariance, Volatility, and the Effect of News. *The Journal of Financial Research, 27*(3), pp.393-413.

Eidleman, G. (1995). Z-Scores—a guide to failure prediction, *The CPA Journal Online http://www.nysscpa.org/cpajournal/old/16641866.htm (accessed 8/11/05).*

Frank, O. (1979). Estimation of population totals by use of snowball samples. In P. Holland & S. Leinhardt (Eds.), *Perspectives on Social Network Research* (pp. pp.319-347). New York: Academic Press.

Frost, G., & Wilmshurst, T. (2000). The adoption of environment related management accounting: an analysis of corporate environment sensitivity. *Accounting Forum, 24*(4), pp.344-365.

Goeij, P. D., & Marquering, W. (2004). Modelling the Conditional Covariance Between Stock and Bond Returns: A Multivariate GARCH Approach. *Journal of Financial Econometrics, 2*(4), pp.531-564.

Goh, P. C., & Lim, K. P. (2004). Disclosing intellectual capital in company annual reports. *Journal of Intellectual Capital, 5*(3), pp.500-510.

Granovetter, M. (1976). Network Sampling: Some First Steps. *The American Journal of Sociology, 81*(6), pp.1287-1303.

Greene, W. (2000). *Econometric Analysis*. Upper Saddle River, NJ: Prentice-Hall.

Guthrie, J., & Abeysekera, I. (2006). Using Content Analysis as a Research Method to Inquire into Social and Environmental Disclosure: What is New? *Journal of Human Resource Costing and Accounting, 10*(2), pp.114-126.

Guthrie, J., & Parker, L. (1989). Corporate Social Reporting: A Rebuttal of Legitimacy Theory. *Accounting and Business Research, 19*(76), pp.343-352.

Guthrie, J., Petty, R., & Ricceri, F. (2007). *Intellectual Capital Reporting: Lessons from Hong Kong and Australia*.Unpublished manuscript.

Guthrie, J., Petty, R., Yongvanich, K., & Ricceri, F. (2004). Using content analysis as a research method to inquire into intellectual capital reporting. *Journal of Intellectual Capital, 5*(2), pp.282-293.

Hair, J., Anderson, R., Tatham, R., & Black, W. (1998). *Multivariate Data Analysis* (Fifth ed.). Upper Saddle River, NJ: Prentice Hall.

Hand, J., & Lev, B. (2003). *Intangible Assets: Values, Measures and Risks*. Oxford: Oxford University Press.

Hussey, J., & Hussey, R. (1997). *Business Research: A Practical Guide for Undergraduate and Postgraduate Students*. London: Macmillan.

Kopalle, P., & Lehmann, D. (1995). The Effects of Advertised and Observed Quality on Expectations About New Product Quality. *Journal of Marketing Research, 32*(3), pp.280-290.

Krippendorf, K. (2004). *Content Analysis: 2nd Edition*. Thousand Oaks, CA: Sage Publications.

Lev, B., & Sougiannis, T. (1999). Penetrating the book-to-market black box: The R&D effect. *Journal of Business and Finance Accounting, 26*, pp.419-449.

Mizruchi, M., & Bunting, D. (1981). Influence in Corporate Networks: An Examination of Four Measures. *Administrative Science Quarterly, 26*, pp: 475-489.

Neuendorf, K. (2001). *The Content Analysis Guidebook*: Sage Publications.

Novaes, W. (2002). Managerial Turnover and leverage under a Takeover Threat. *The Journal of Finance, 57*(6), pp.2619-2649.

Podolny, J. (1993). A Status-based Model of Market Competition. *American Journal of Sociology, 98*(4), pp.829-872.

Podolny, J., Stuart, T., & Hannan, M. (1996). Networks, Knowledge, and Niches: Competition in the Worldwide Semiconductor Industry, 1984-1991. *American Journal of Sociology, 102*(3), pp.659-689.

Rothenberg, R. B. (1995). Commentary: Sampling in Social Networks. *Connections, 18*(1), pp.104-110.

Scott, A. (2006). Factiva reshapes marketing for better lead generation. *Journal of Organizational Excellence, 25*(2), pp.39-46.

Silverman, D. (1993). *Interpreting Qualitative Data: Methods for Analysing Talk, Text and Interaction*: London:Sage.

Stuart, T. (2000). Interorganizational Alliances and the Performance of Firms: A Study of Growth and Innovation Rates in a High Technology Industry. *Strategic Management Journal, 21*, pp.791-811.

Wasserman, S., & Faust, K. (1994). *Social Network Analysis: Methods and Applications*: UK: Cambridge University Press.

White, H. (1980). A Heteroscedacity-consistent covariance matrix estimator and a direct test for heteroscedacity. *Econometrica, 48*, pp. 817-838.

ENDNOTES

[1] http://www.computerwire.com/services/info/?file=itsercondb (accessed 14/5/07).

[2] http://www.factiva.com/ (accessed 14/5/07).

[3] http://www2.standardandpoors.com/portal/site/sp/en/us/page.product/dataservices_compustat/2,9,2,0,0,0,0,0,0,0,0,0,0,0,0,0,0.html (accessed 14/5/07).

[4] UCINET Version 6.

5   Nvivo is designed for qualitative researchers who need to combine subtle coding with qualitative linking, shaping, searching and modelling. http://www.qsrinternational.com/products/productoverview/NVivo_7.htm (accessed 8/4/07).

6   For instance, http://www.fortune.com/fortune/globaladmired/subs/2005/full-list/0,23176,,00.html (accessed 13/11/05) provides a list of global 'most admired companies' as determined through a Delphi research technique.

7   CENT was measured across the whole period, rather than on a year-to-year basis, given the cumulative nature of the measure. The panel data for CENT is just a replication for each year.

8   Net sales (SALE) and earnings per share (EPSPI) were sourced directly from the Compustat Database.

About the Author

Laurence Lock Lee is the co-founder of Optimice Pty Ltd, a firm dedicated to helping organisations optimise their business relationships. He is an acknowledged expert in knowledge management and applied social and value network analysis techniques. He has over 35 years of working experience in roles ranging from research, management and consulting for major global corporations. Prior to co-founding Optimice he was a principal consultant at Computer Sciences Corporation, where he led the knowledge and information management consulting practice and was a research member of the global leading edge forum. Prior to that he worked for many years with BHP Billiton within their corporate research laboratories, leading their research programs on knowledge based systems and artificial intelligence, and later as the knowledge management practice lead in the information technology division. He has consulted widely with major corporate and government clients. He has presented at academic and industry forums in Australia, Europe, Asia and the USA. He has also taught at master and doctoral levels in Australia and Asia. Laurence has a PhD from the University of Sydney, with his dissertation being on corporate social capital links to organisational performance.

Index